D1178171

Wolfsmund

Mitsuhisa Kuji

VERTICAL.

Wolfsmund ③
Inhaltsverzeichnis

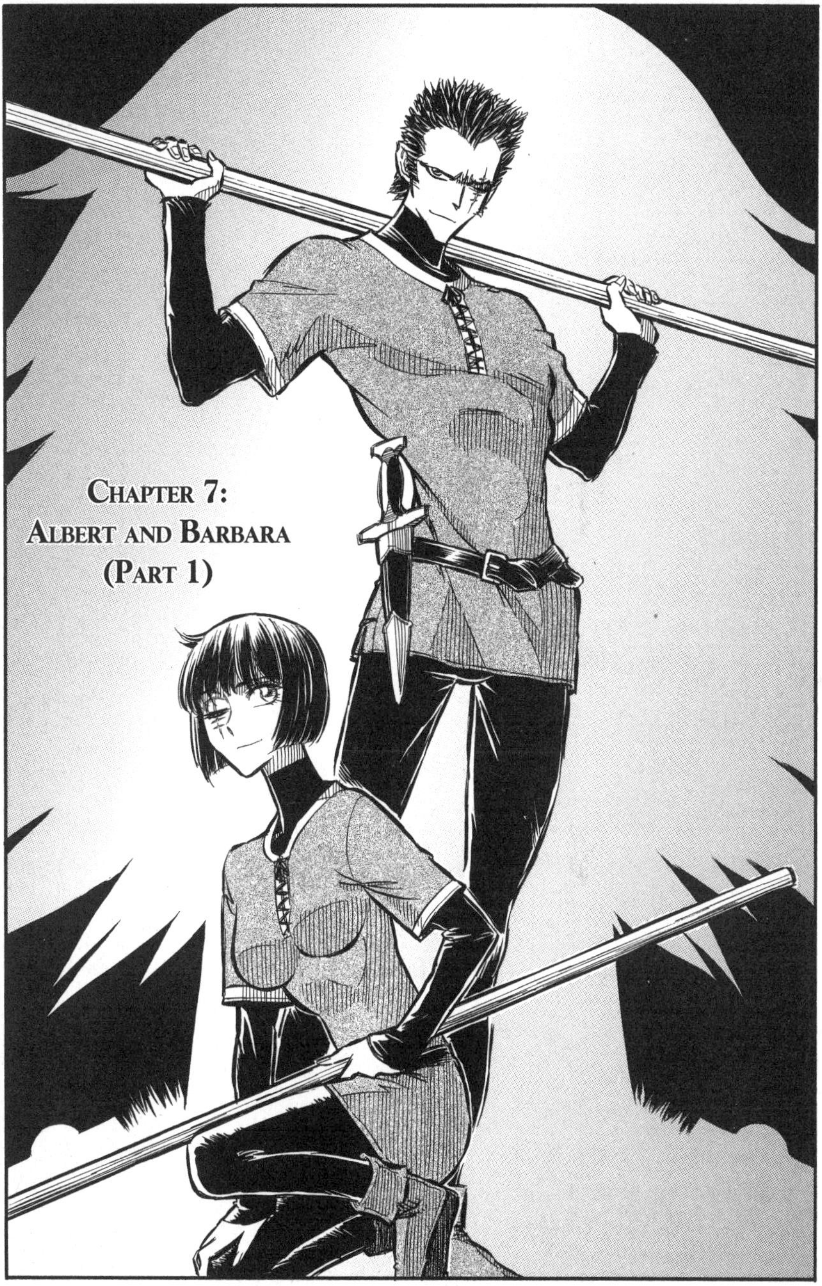
Chapter 7:
Albert and Barbara
(Part 1)

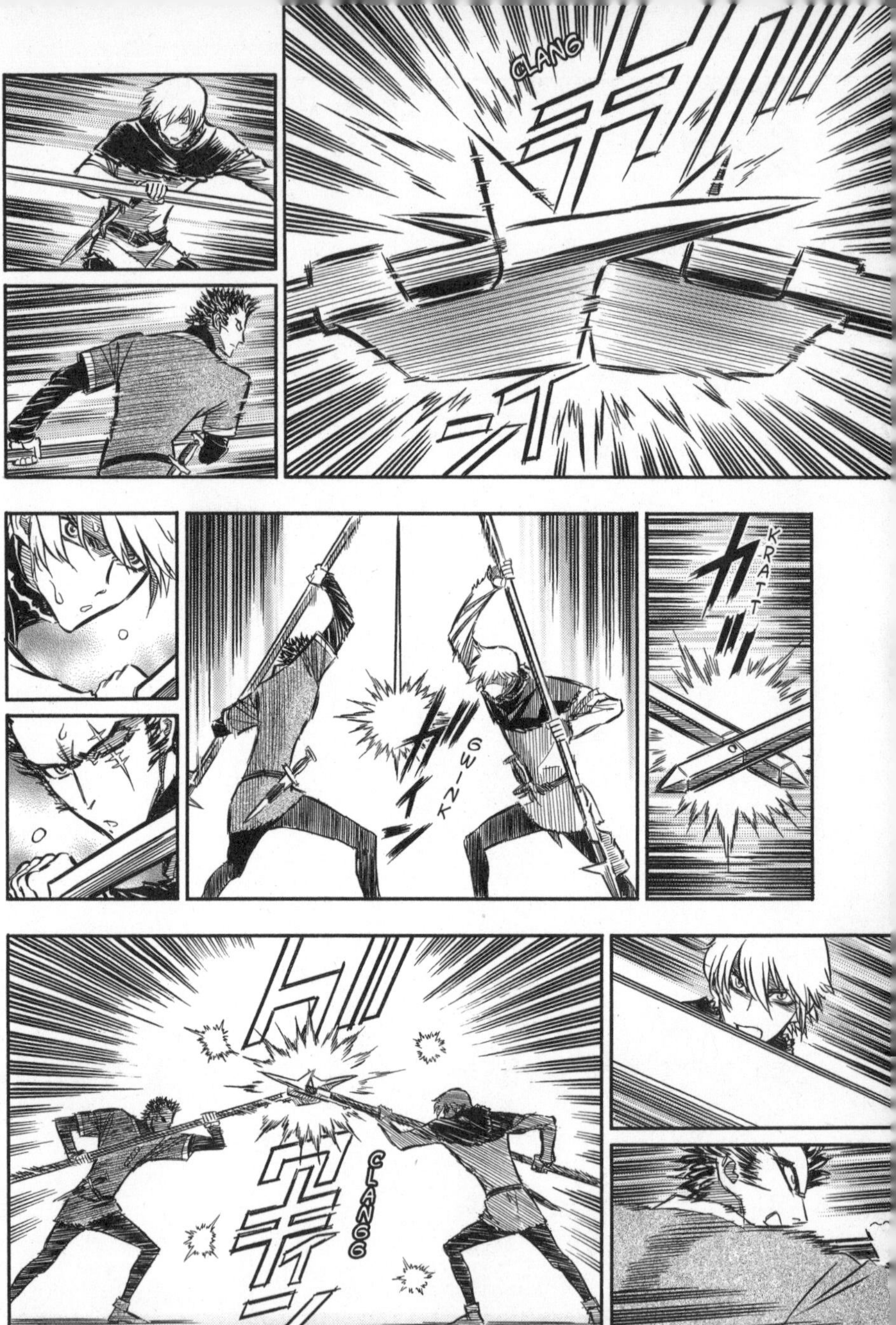
CLANG
KRATT
GWINK
CLANGG

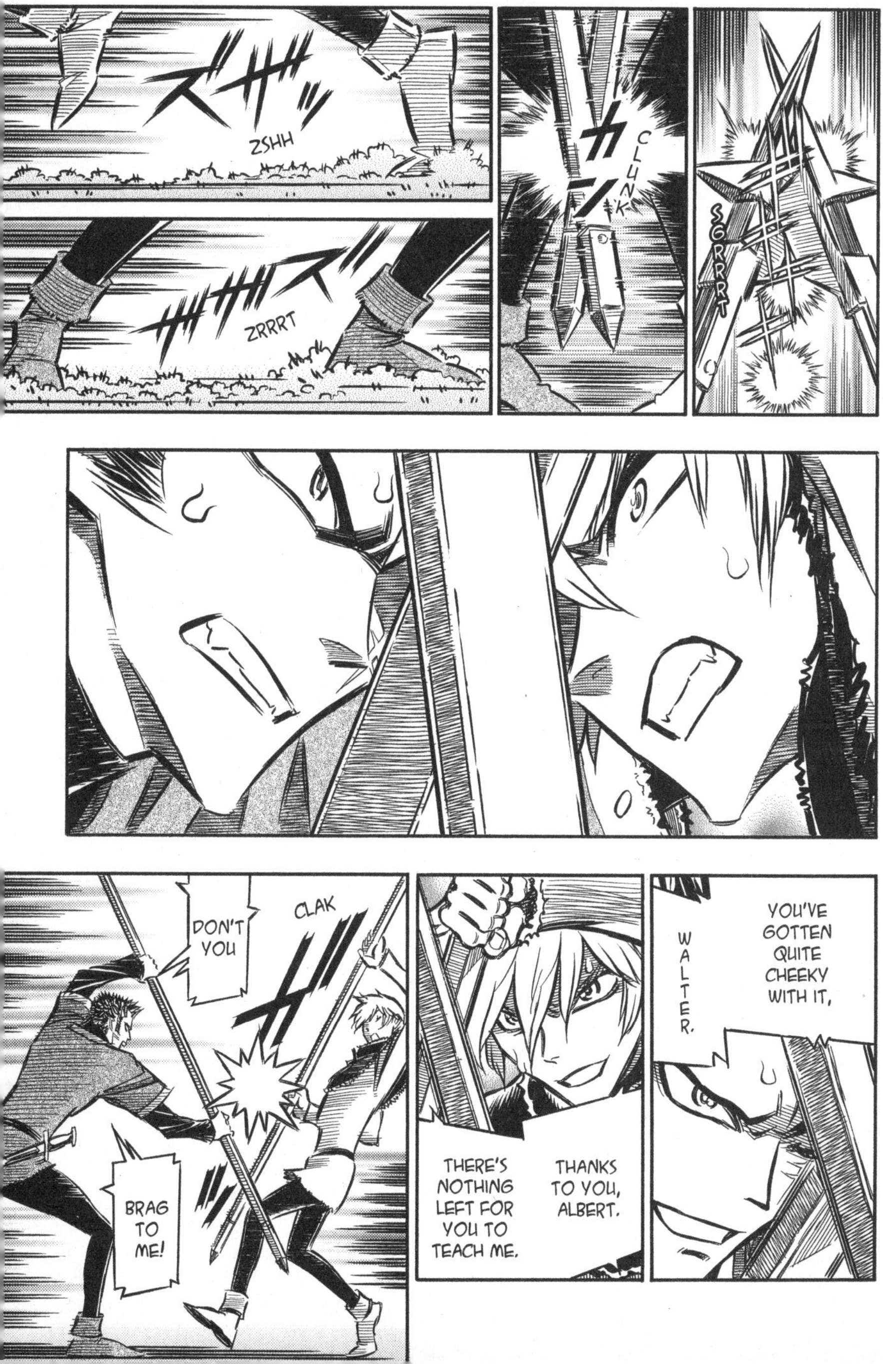
SGRRRT
CLUNK
ZSHH
ZRRRT
WALTER.
YOU'VE GOTTEN QUITE CHEEKY WITH IT,
THANKS TO YOU, ALBERT.
THERE'S NOTHING LEFT FOR YOU TO TEACH ME.
DON'T YOU
CLAK
BRAG TO ME!

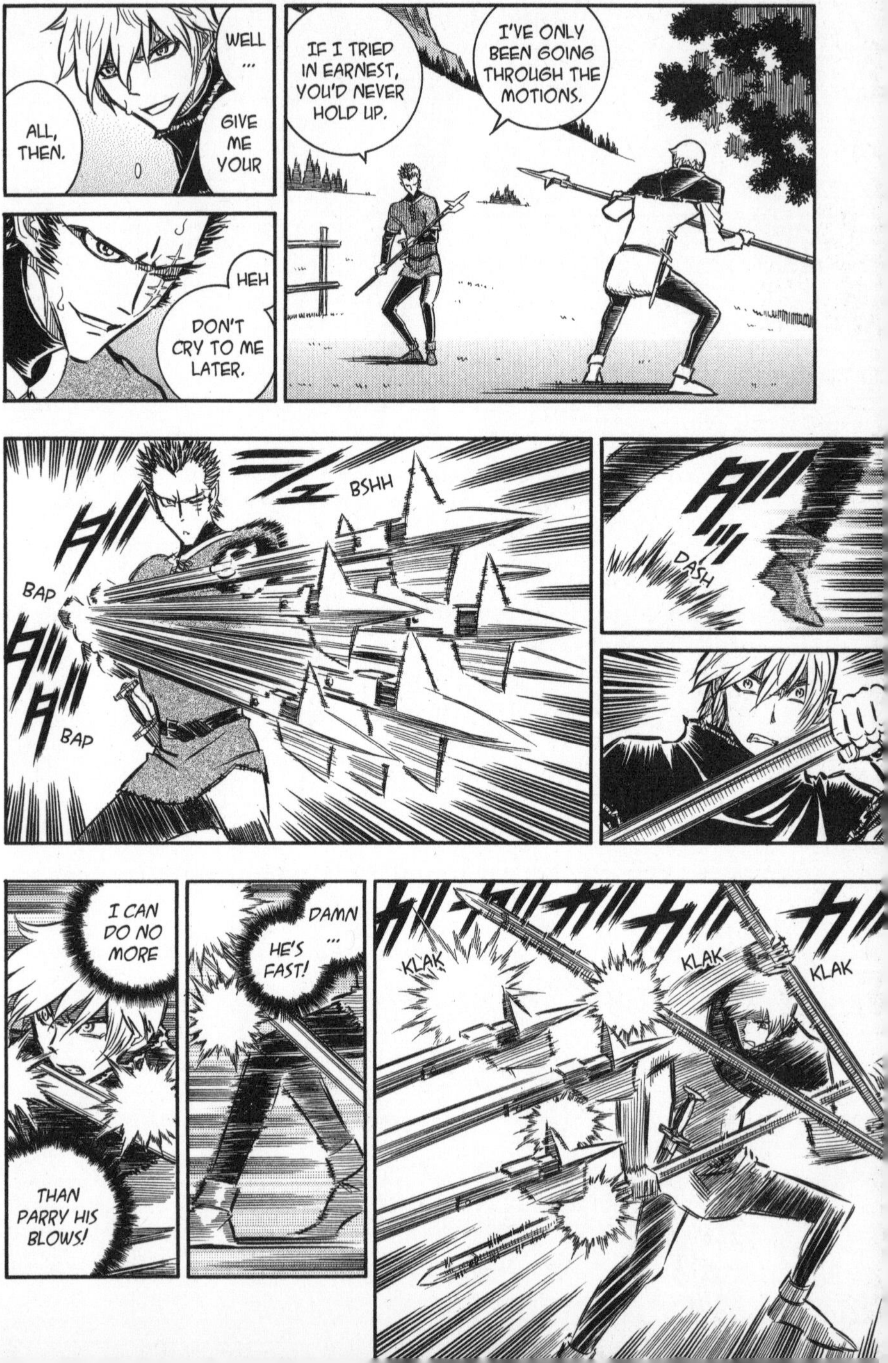
I'VE ONLY BEEN GOING THROUGH THE MOTIONS.
IF I TRIED IN EARNEST, YOU'D NEVER HOLD UP.
WELL ...
GIVE ME YOUR
ALL, THEN.
HEH
DON'T CRY TO ME LATER.
DASH
BSHH
BAP
BAP
KLAK
KLAK
KLAK
DAMN ...
HE'S FAST!
I CAN DO NO MORE
THAN PARRY HIS BLOWS!

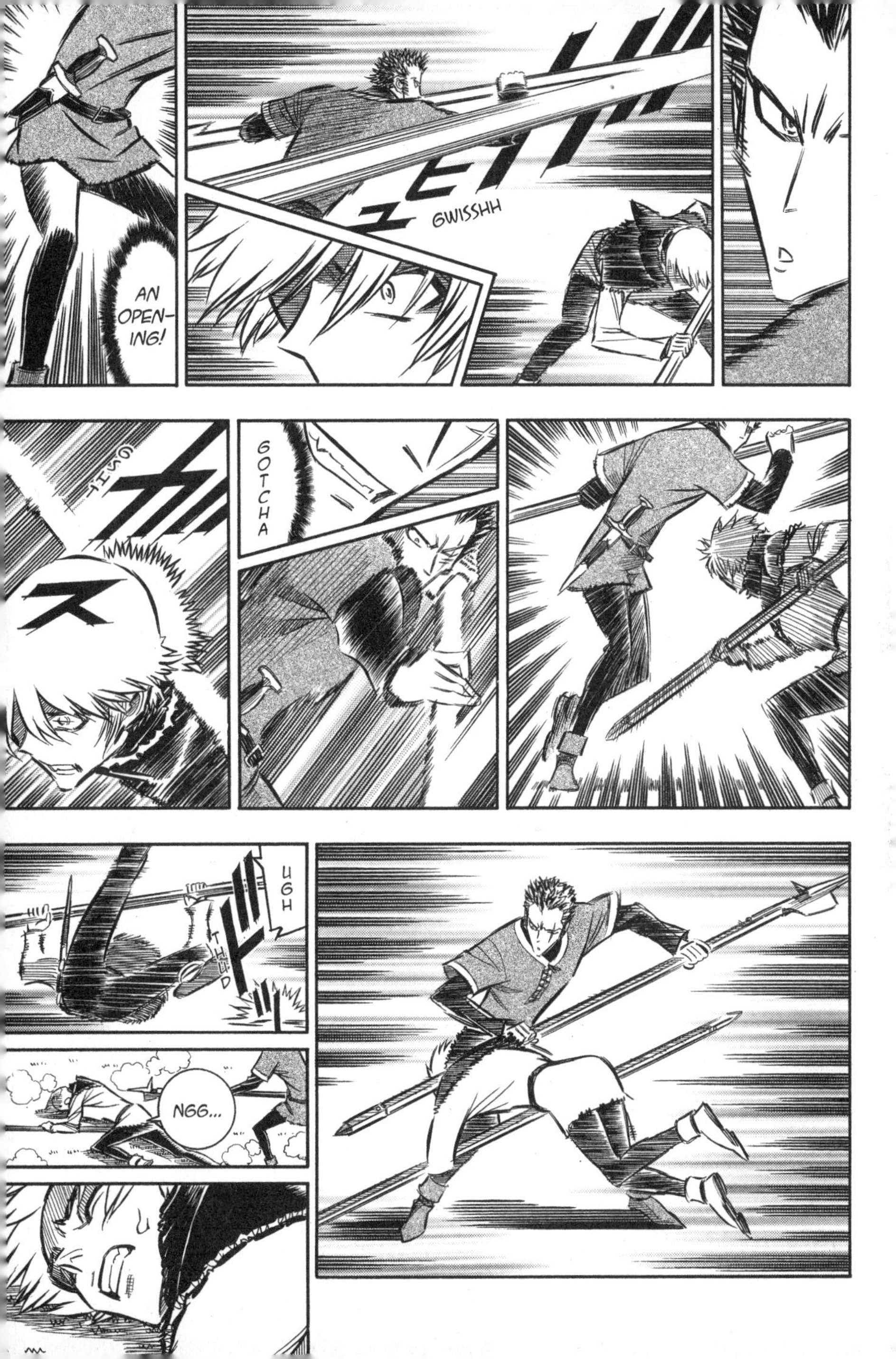
GWISSHH
AN OPEN-ING!
GOTCHA
GSIT
UGH
THUD
NGG...

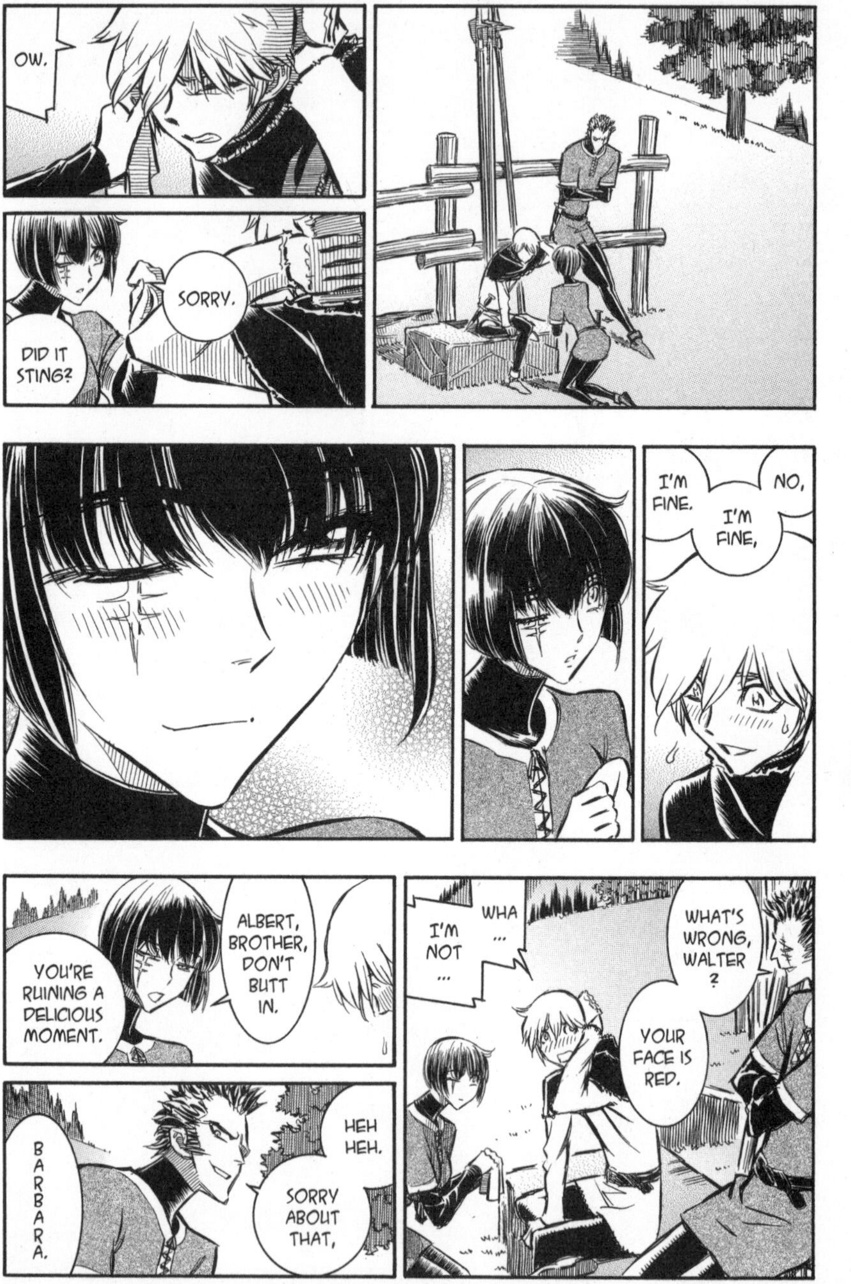
OW.
SORRY.
DID IT STING?
NO,
I'M FINE,
I'M FINE.
WHAT'S WRONG, WALTER?
YOUR FACE IS RED.
WHA...
I'M NOT...
ALBERT, BROTHER, DON'T BUTT IN.
YOU'RE RUINING A DELICIOUS MOMENT.
HEH HEH.
SORRY ABOUT THAT,
BARBARA.

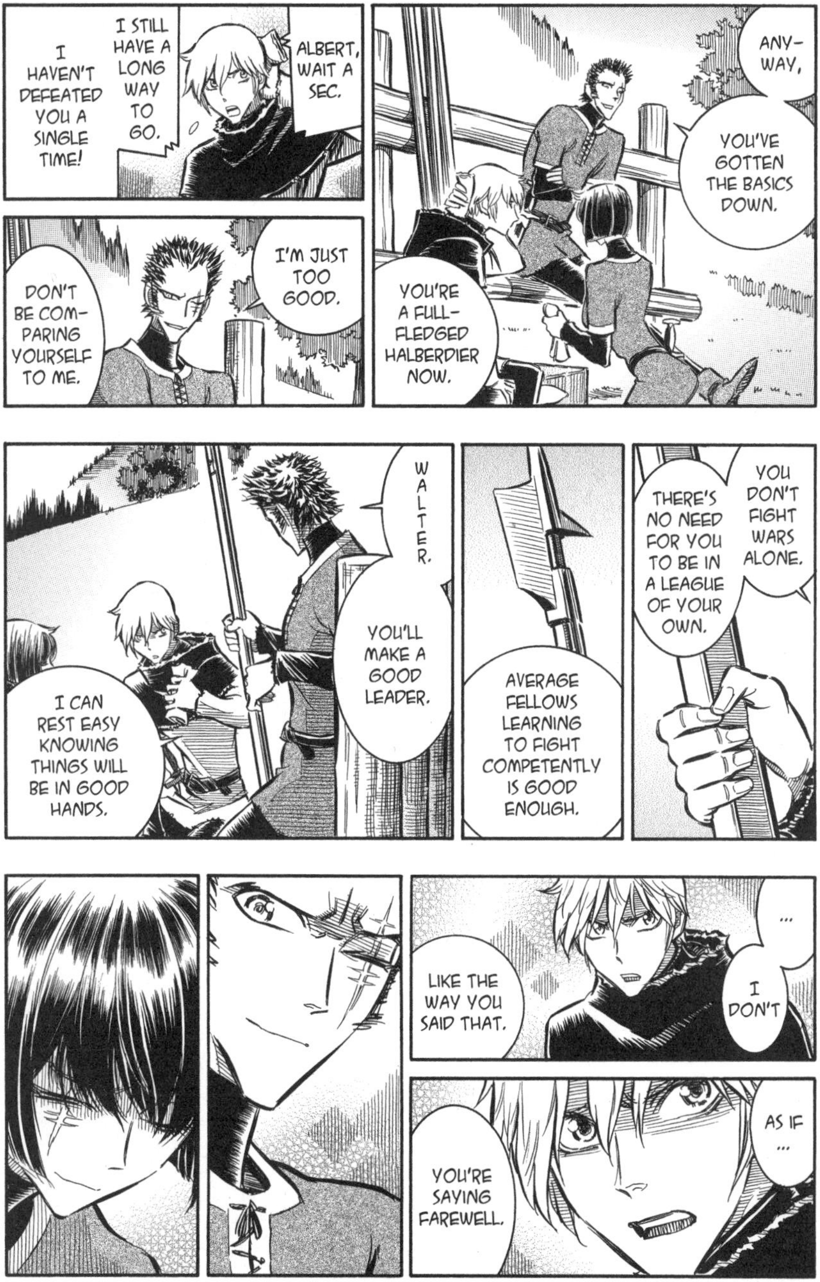
ANY-WAY,
YOU'VE GOTTEN THE BASICS DOWN.
YOU'RE A FULL-FLEDGED HALBERDIER NOW.
ALBERT, WAIT A SEC.
I STILL HAVE A LONG WAY TO GO.
I HAVEN'T DEFEATED YOU A SINGLE TIME!
I'M JUST TOO GOOD.
DON'T BE COM-PARING YOURSELF TO ME.
YOU DON'T FIGHT WARS ALONE.
THERE'S NO NEED FOR YOU TO BE IN A LEAGUE OF YOUR OWN.
AVERAGE FELLOWS LEARNING TO FIGHT COMPETENTLY IS GOOD ENOUGH.
WALTER.
YOU'LL MAKE A GOOD LEADER.
I CAN REST EASY KNOWING THINGS WILL BE IN GOOD HANDS.
...
I DON'T
LIKE THE WAY YOU SAID THAT.
AS IF ...
YOU'RE SAYING FAREWELL.

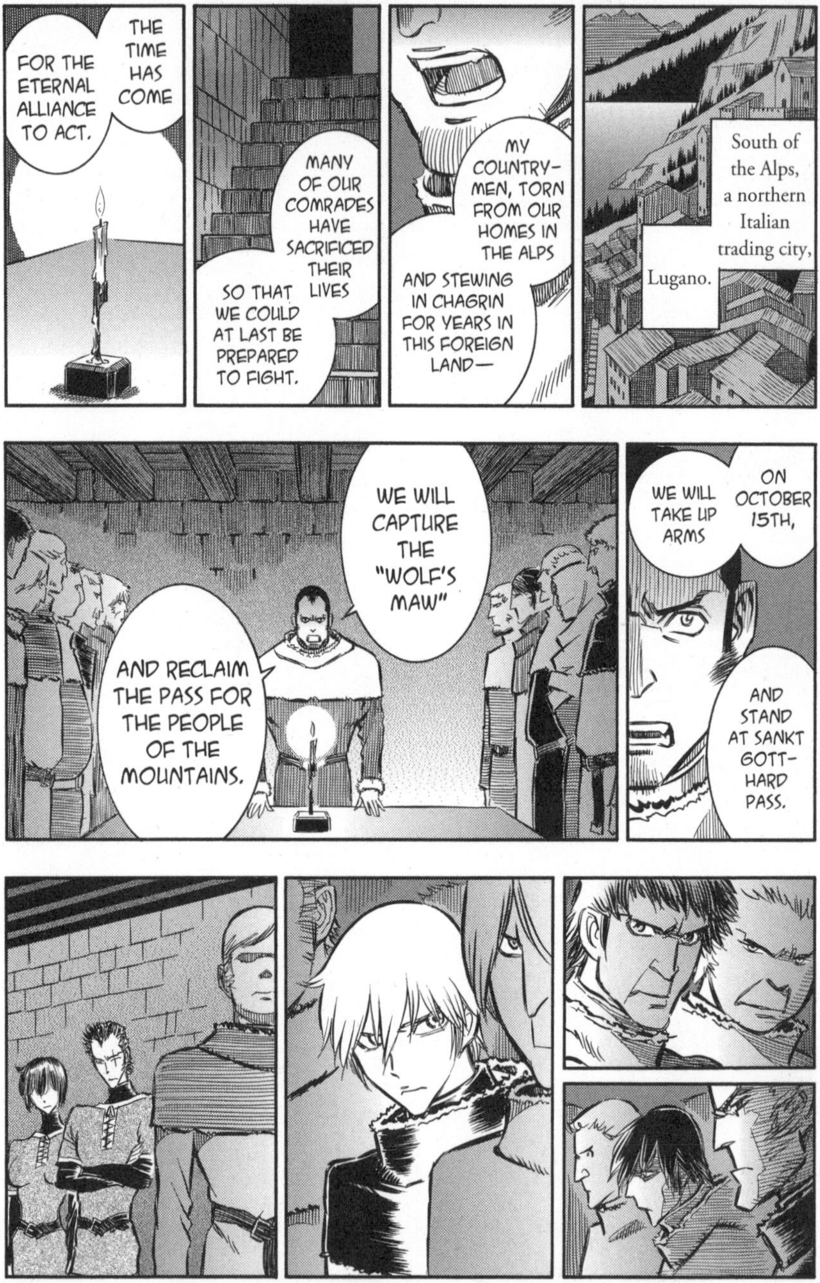
South of the Alps, a northern Italian trading city,
Lugano.
MY COUNTRYMEN, TORN FROM OUR HOMES IN THE ALPS
AND STEWING IN CHAGRIN FOR YEARS IN THIS FOREIGN LAND—
MANY OF OUR COMRADES HAVE SACRIFICED THEIR LIVES
SO THAT WE COULD AT LAST BE PREPARED TO FIGHT.
THE TIME HAS COME
FOR THE ETERNAL ALLIANCE TO ACT.
ON OCTOBER 15TH,
WE WILL TAKE UP ARMS
AND STAND AT SANKT GOTTHARD PASS.
WE WILL CAPTURE THE "WOLF'S MAW"
AND RECLAIM THE PASS FOR THE PEOPLE OF THE MOUNTAINS.

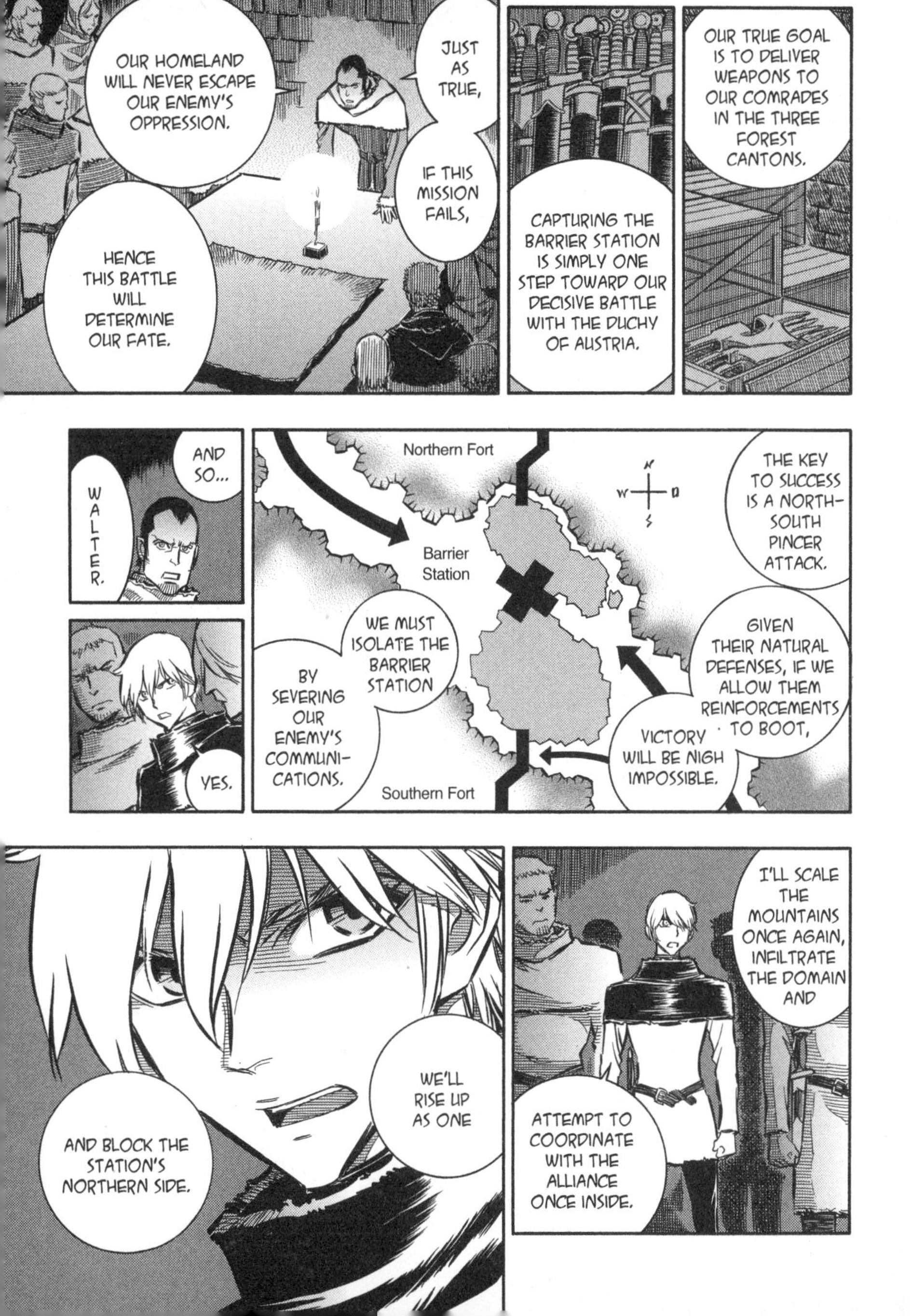
OUR TRUE GOAL IS TO DELIVER WEAPONS TO OUR COMRADES IN THE THREE FOREST CANTONS.
CAPTURING THE BARRIER STATION IS SIMPLY ONE STEP TOWARD OUR DECISIVE BATTLE WITH THE DUCHY OF AUSTRIA.
JUST AS TRUE,
IF THIS MISSION FAILS,
OUR HOMELAND WILL NEVER ESCAPE OUR ENEMY'S OPPRESSION.
HENCE THIS BATTLE WILL DETERMINE OUR FATE.
Northern Fort
Barrier Station
Southern Fort
THE KEY TO SUCCESS IS A NORTH-SOUTH PINCER ATTACK.
GIVEN THEIR NATURAL DEFENSES, IF WE ALLOW THEM REINFORCEMENTS TO BOOT,
VICTORY WILL BE NIGH IMPOSSIBLE.
WE MUST ISOLATE THE BARRIER STATION
BY SEVERING OUR ENEMY'S COMMUNICATIONS.
AND SO...
WALTER.
YES.
I'LL SCALE THE MOUNTAINS ONCE AGAIN, INFILTRATE THE DOMAIN AND
ATTEMPT TO COORDINATE WITH THE ALLIANCE ONCE INSIDE.
WE'LL RISE UP AS ONE
AND BLOCK THE STATION'S NORTHERN SIDE.

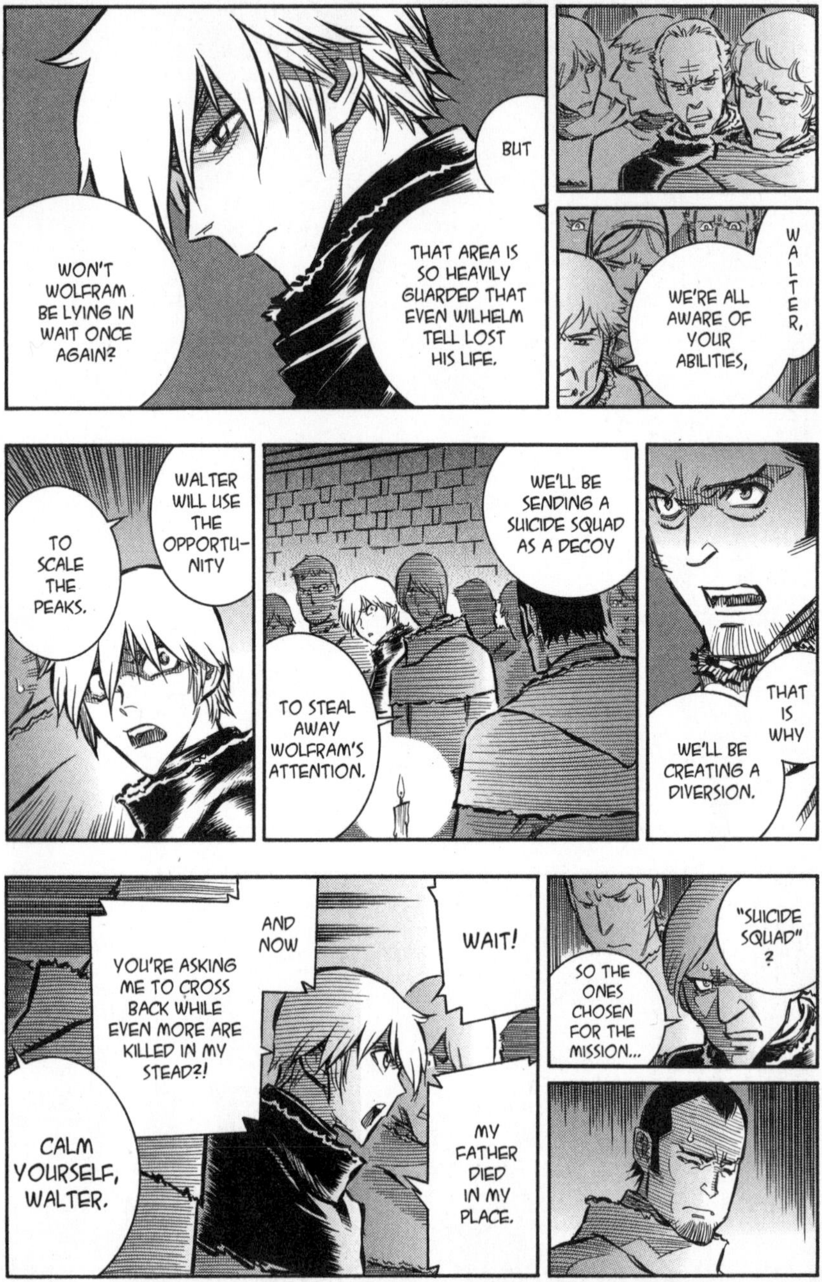
WALTER,
WE'RE ALL AWARE OF YOUR ABILITIES,
BUT
THAT AREA IS SO HEAVILY GUARDED THAT EVEN WILHELM TELL LOST HIS LIFE.
WON'T WOLFRAM BE LYING IN WAIT ONCE AGAIN?
THAT IS WHY
WE'LL BE CREATING A DIVERSION.
WE'LL BE SENDING A SUICIDE SQUAD AS A DECOY
TO STEAL AWAY WOLFRAM'S ATTENTION.
WALTER WILL USE THE OPPORTU-NITY
TO SCALE THE PEAKS.
"SUICIDE SQUAD"?
SO THE ONES CHOSEN FOR THE MISSION...
WAIT!
MY FATHER DIED IN MY PLACE.
AND NOW
YOU'RE ASKING ME TO CROSS BACK WHILE EVEN MORE ARE KILLED IN MY STEAD?!
CALM YOURSELF, WALTER.

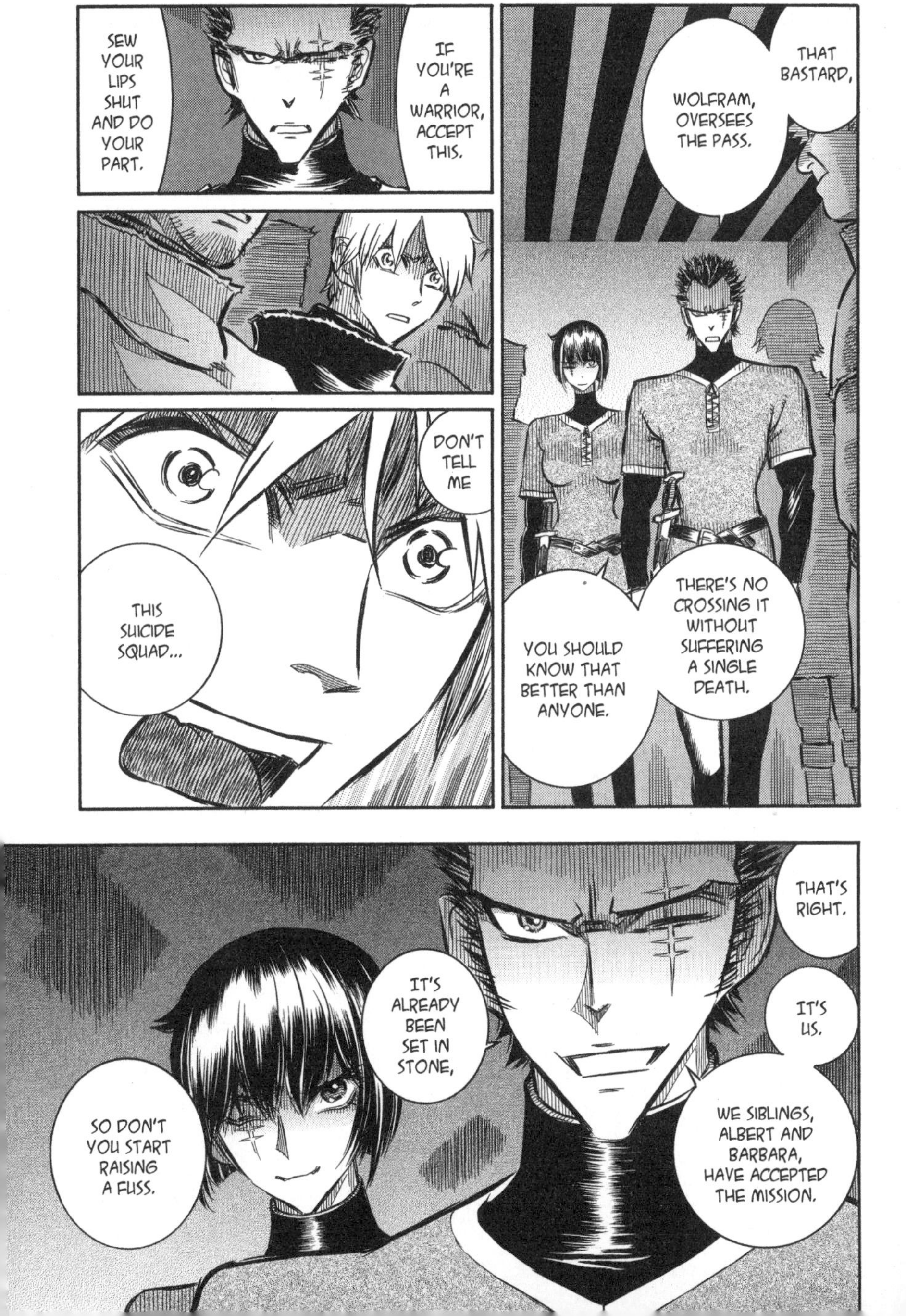
THAT BASTARD,
WOLFRAM, OVERSEES THE PASS.
THERE'S NO CROSSING IT WITHOUT SUFFERING A SINGLE DEATH.
YOU SHOULD KNOW THAT BETTER THAN ANYONE.
IF YOU'RE A WARRIOR, ACCEPT THIS.
SEW YOUR LIPS SHUT AND DO YOUR PART.
DON'T TELL ME
THIS SUICIDE SQUAD...
THAT'S RIGHT.
IT'S US.
WE SIBLINGS, ALBERT AND BARBARA, HAVE ACCEPTED THE MISSION.
IT'S ALREADY BEEN SET IN STONE,
SO DON'T YOU START RAISING A FUSS.

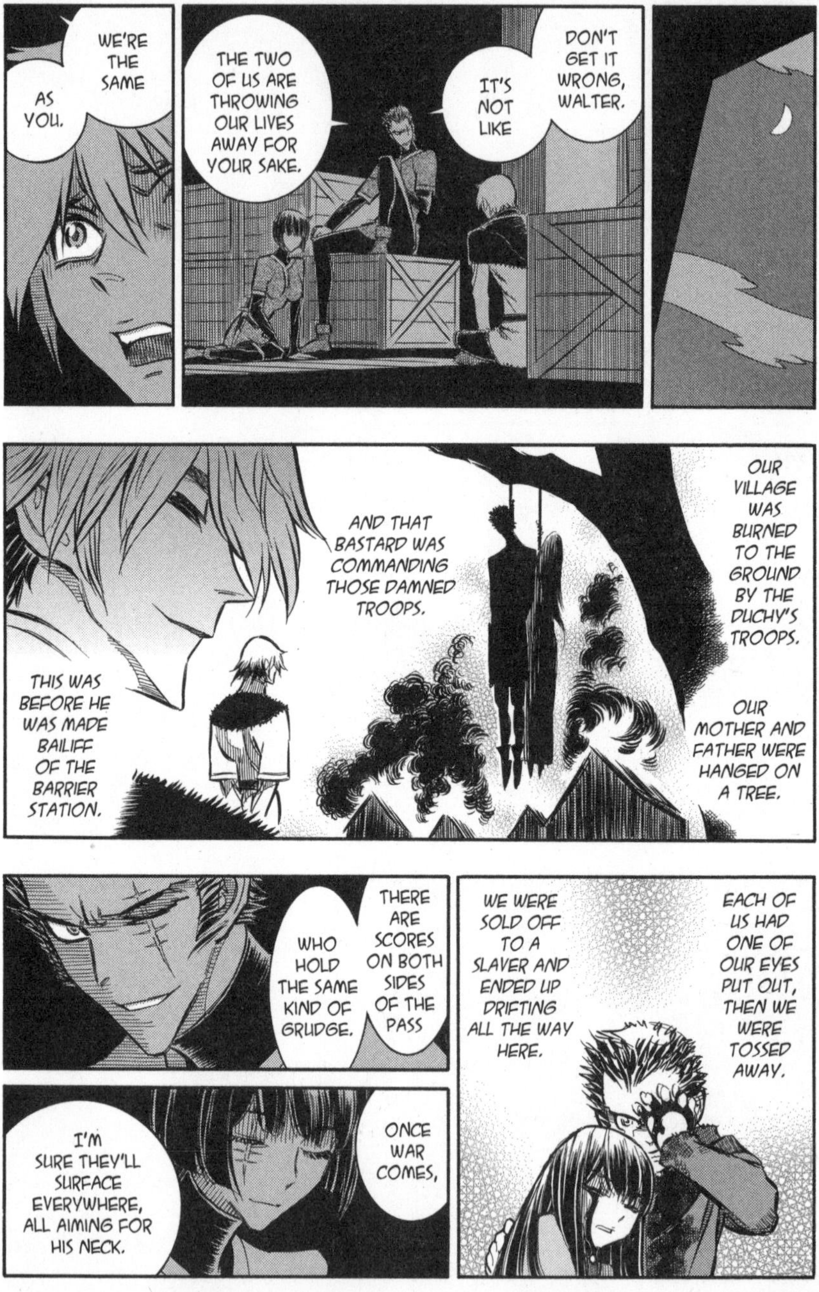
DON'T GET IT WRONG, WALTER.
IT'S NOT LIKE
THE TWO OF US ARE THROWING OUR LIVES AWAY FOR YOUR SAKE.
WE'RE THE SAME AS YOU.
OUR VILLAGE WAS BURNED TO THE GROUND BY THE DUCHY'S TROOPS.
OUR MOTHER AND FATHER WERE HANGED ON A TREE.
AND THAT BASTARD WAS COMMANDING THOSE DAMNED TROOPS.
THIS WAS BEFORE HE WAS MADE BAILIFF OF THE BARRIER STATION.
EACH OF US HAD ONE OF OUR EYES PUT OUT, THEN WE WERE TOSSED AWAY.
WE WERE SOLD OFF TO A SLAVER AND ENDED UP DRIFTING ALL THE WAY HERE.
THERE ARE SCORES ON BOTH SIDES OF THE PASS
WHO HOLD THE SAME KIND OF GRUDGE.
ONCE WAR COMES,
I'M SURE THEY'LL SURFACE EVERYWHERE, ALL AIMING FOR HIS NECK.

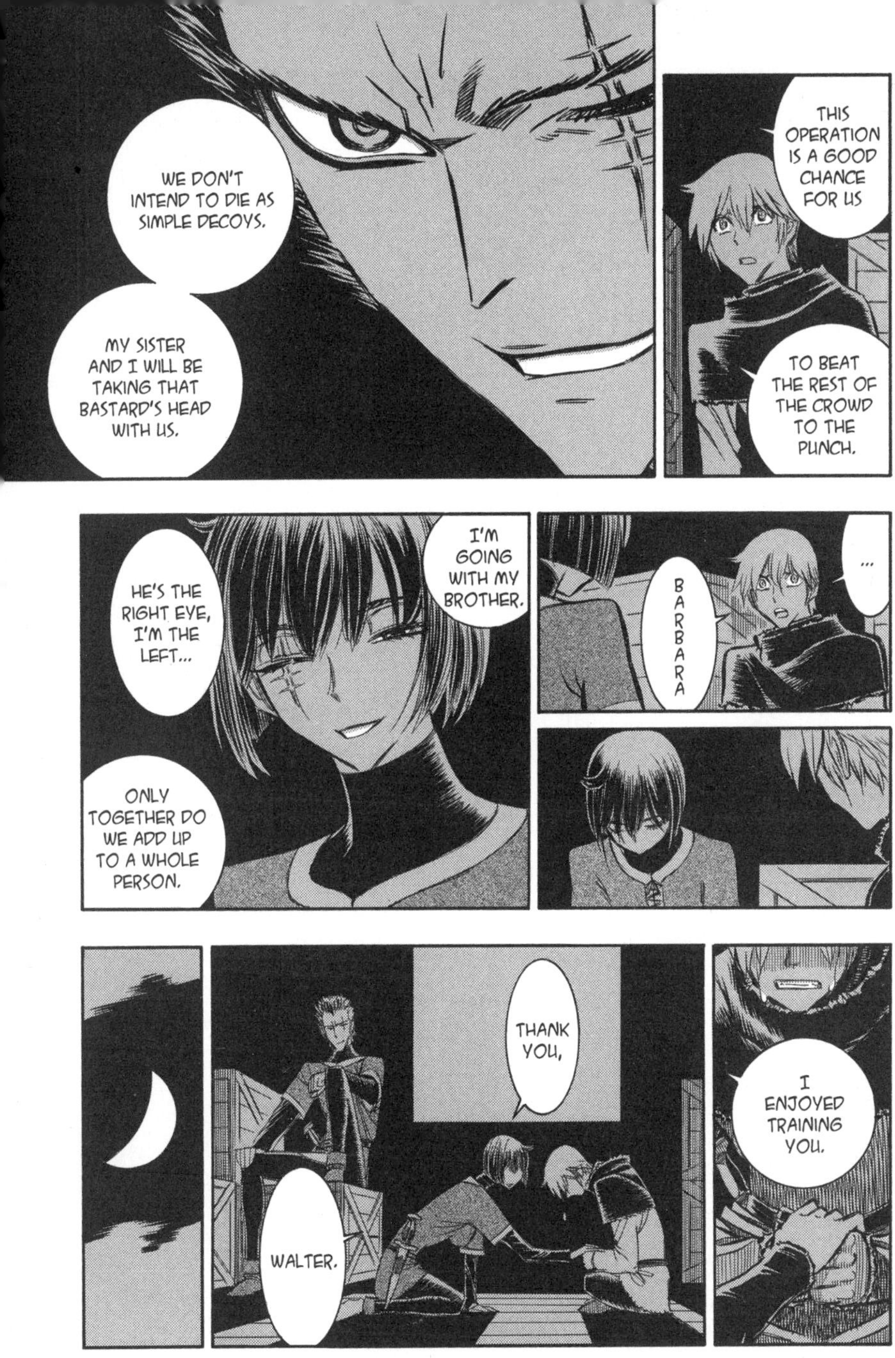
THIS OPERATION IS A GOOD CHANCE FOR US
TO BEAT THE REST OF THE CROWD TO THE PUNCH.
WE DON'T INTEND TO DIE AS SIMPLE DECOYS.
MY SISTER AND I WILL BE TAKING THAT BASTARD'S HEAD WITH US.
...
BARBARA
I'M GOING WITH MY BROTHER.
HE'S THE RIGHT EYE, I'M THE LEFT...
ONLY TOGETHER DO WE ADD UP TO A WHOLE PERSON.
I ENJOYED TRAINING YOU.
THANK YOU,
WALTER.

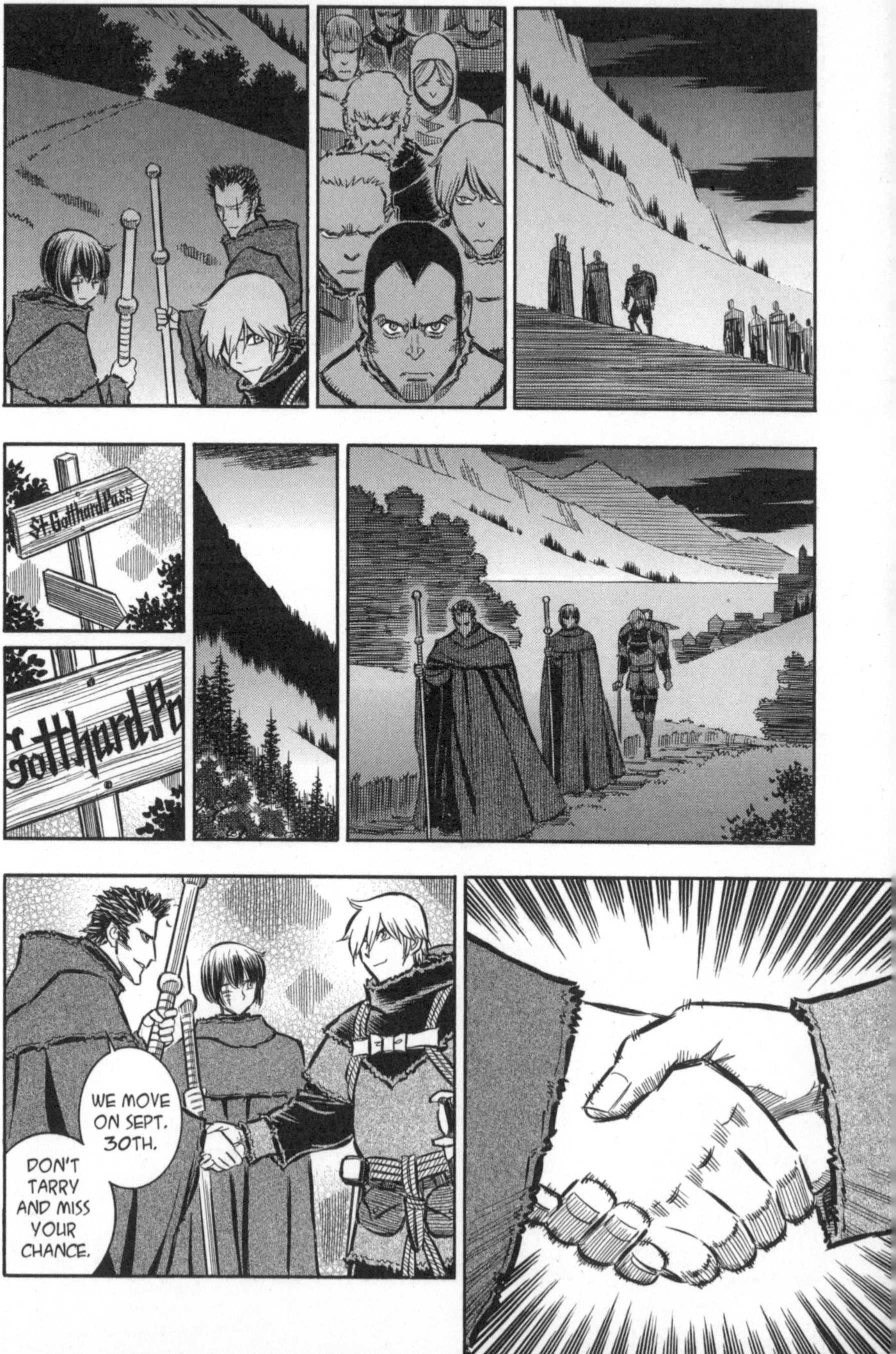
St. Gotthard Pass
Gotthard
WE MOVE ON SEPT. 30TH.
DON'T TARRY AND MISS YOUR CHANCE.

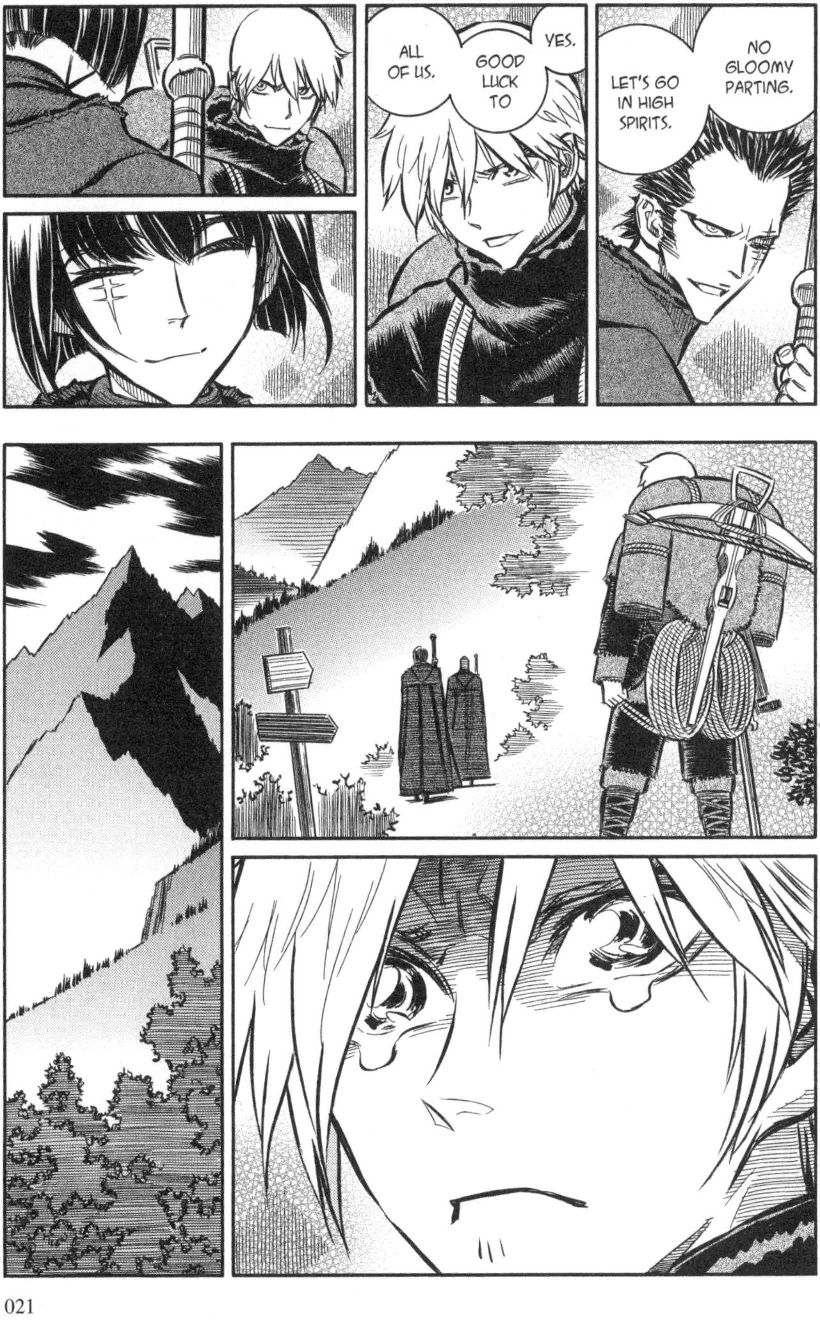
NO GLOOMY PARTING.
LET'S GO IN HIGH SPIRITS.
YES.
GOOD LUCK TO
ALL OF US.

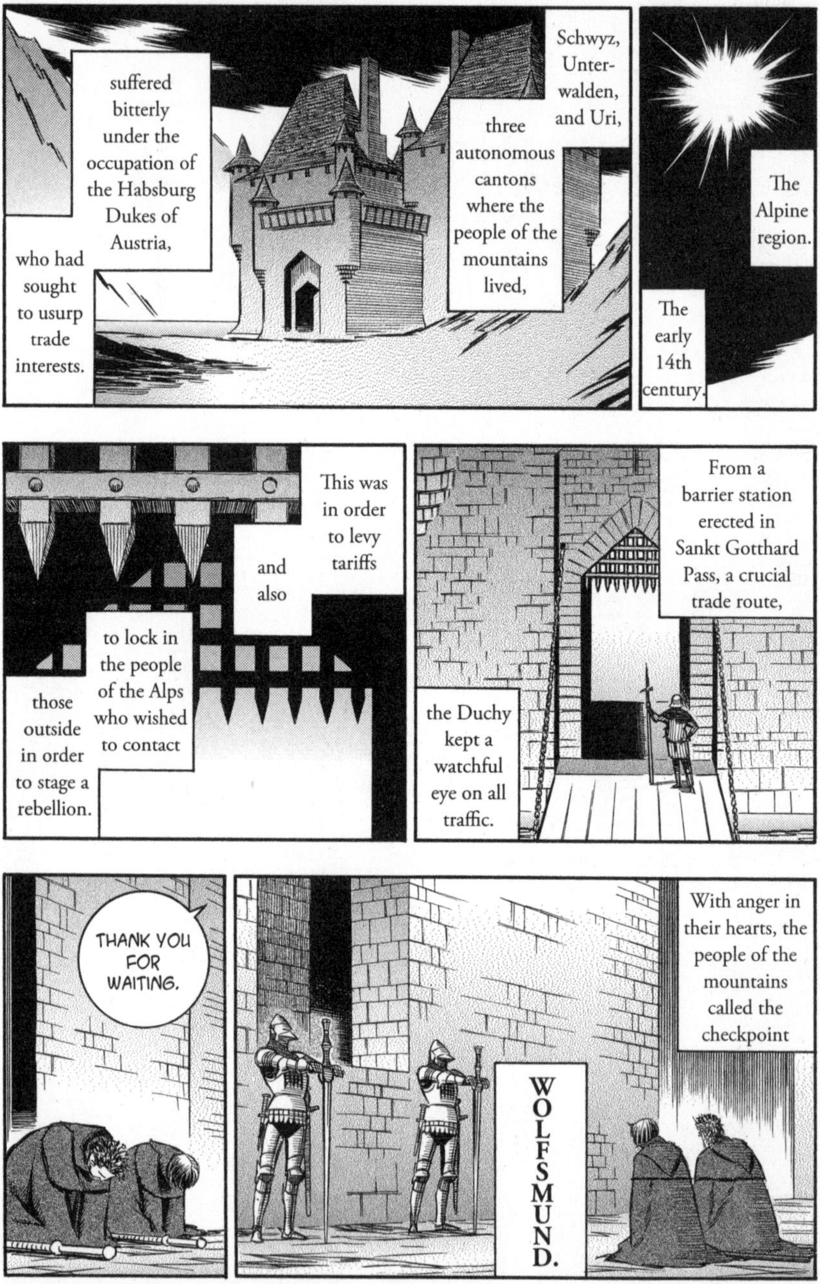
The Alpine region.
The early 14th century.
Schwyz, Unterwalden, and Uri,
three autonomous cantons where the people of the mountains lived,
suffered bitterly under the occupation of the Habsburg Dukes of Austria,
who had sought to usurp trade interests.
From a barrier station erected in Sankt Gotthard Pass, a crucial trade route,
the Duchy kept a watchful eye on all traffic.
This was in order to levy tariffs
and also
to lock in the people of the Alps who wished to contact
those outside in order to stage a rebellion.
With anger in their hearts, the people of the mountains called the checkpoint
WOLFSMUND.
THANK YOU FOR WAITING.

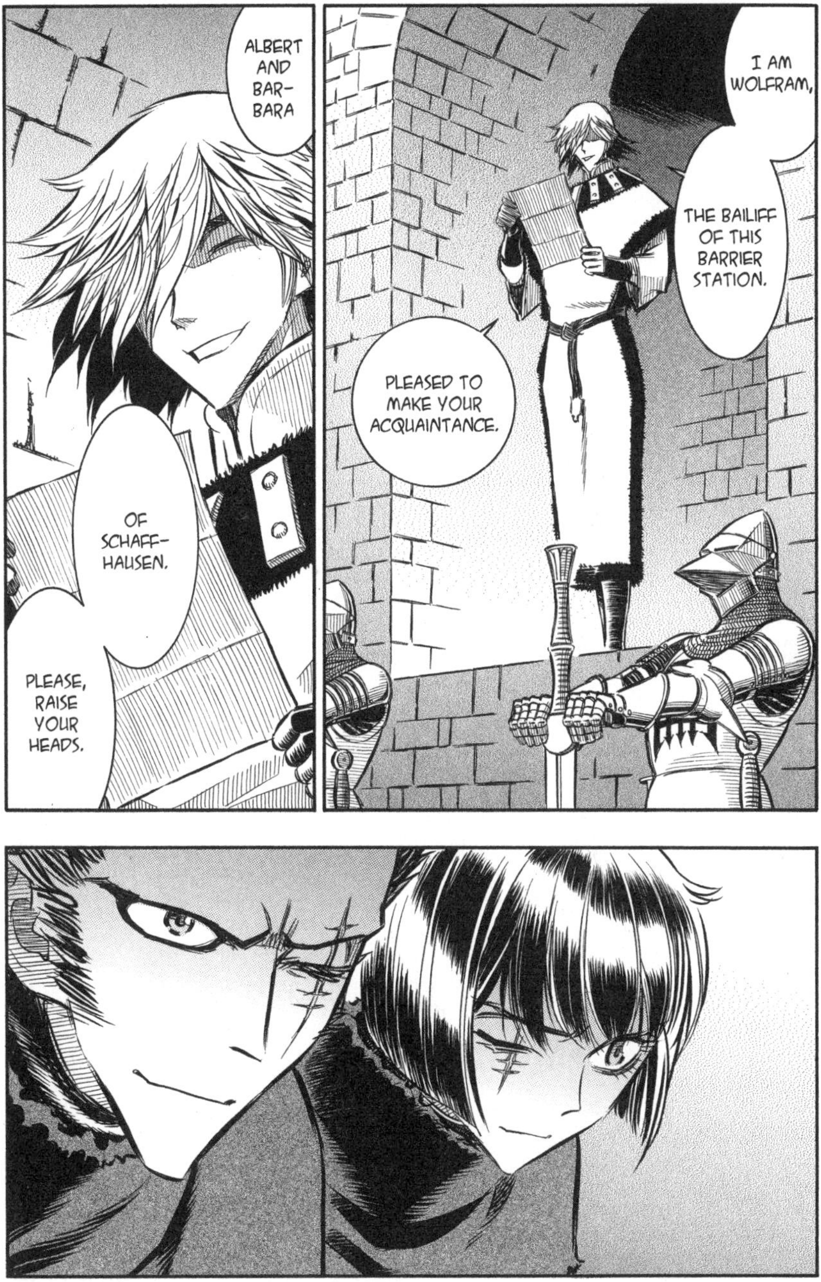
I AM WOLFRAM,
THE BAILIFF OF THIS BARRIER STATION.
PLEASED TO MAKE YOUR ACQUAINTANCE.
ALBERT AND BAR-BARA
OF SCHAFF-HAUSEN.
PLEASE, RAISE YOUR HEADS.

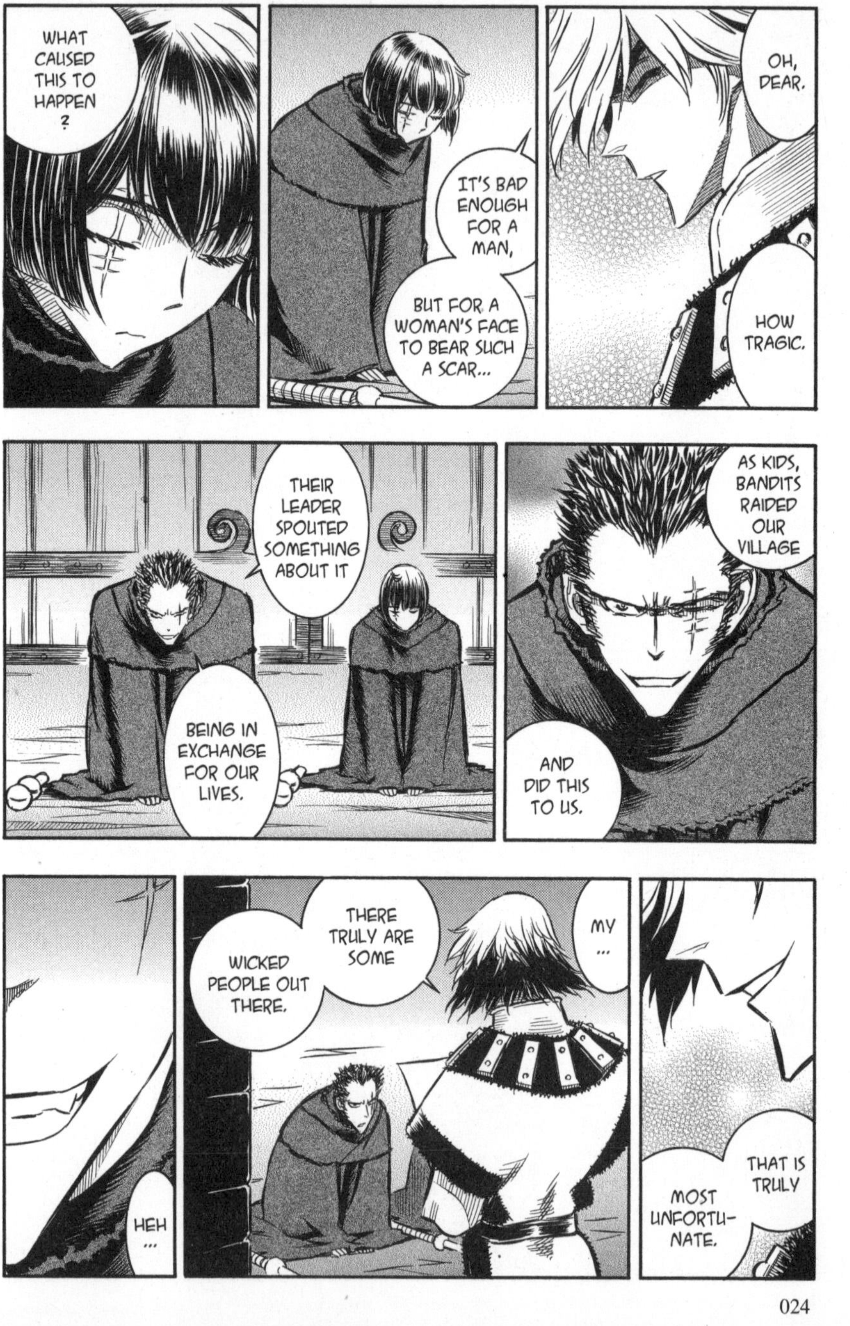
OH, DEAR.
HOW TRAGIC.
IT'S BAD ENOUGH FOR A MAN,
BUT FOR A WOMAN'S FACE TO BEAR SUCH A SCAR...
WHAT CAUSED THIS TO HAPPEN?
AS KIDS, BANDITS RAIDED OUR VILLAGE
AND DID THIS TO US.
THEIR LEADER SPOUTED SOMETHING ABOUT IT
BEING IN EXCHANGE FOR OUR LIVES.
THAT IS TRULY
MOST UNFORTU-NATE.
MY ...
THERE TRULY ARE SOME
WICKED PEOPLE OUT THERE.
HEH ...

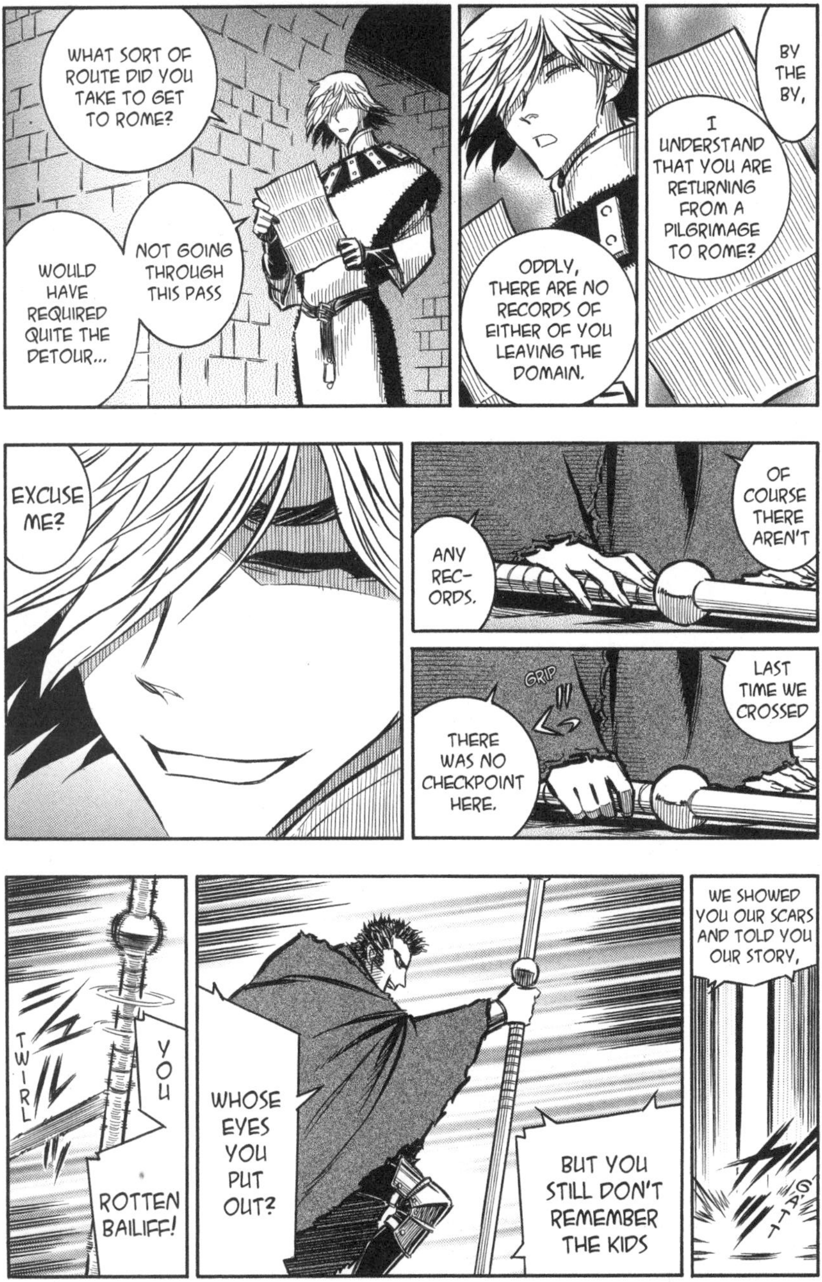

BY THE BY,
I UNDERSTAND THAT YOU ARE RETURNING FROM A PILGRIMAGE TO ROME?
ODDLY, THERE ARE NO RECORDS OF EITHER OF YOU LEAVING THE DOMAIN.
WHAT SORT OF ROUTE DID YOU TAKE TO GET TO ROME?
NOT GOING THROUGH THIS PASS
WOULD HAVE REQUIRED QUITE THE DETOUR...
OF COURSE THERE AREN'T
ANY REC-ORDS.
LAST TIME WE CROSSED
GRIP
THERE WAS NO CHECKPOINT HERE.
EXCUSE ME?
WE SHOWED YOU OUR SCARS AND TOLD YOU OUR STORY,
GATT
BUT YOU STILL DON'T REMEMBER THE KIDS
WHOSE EYES YOU PUT OUT?
YOU
ROTTEN BAILIFF!
TWIRL

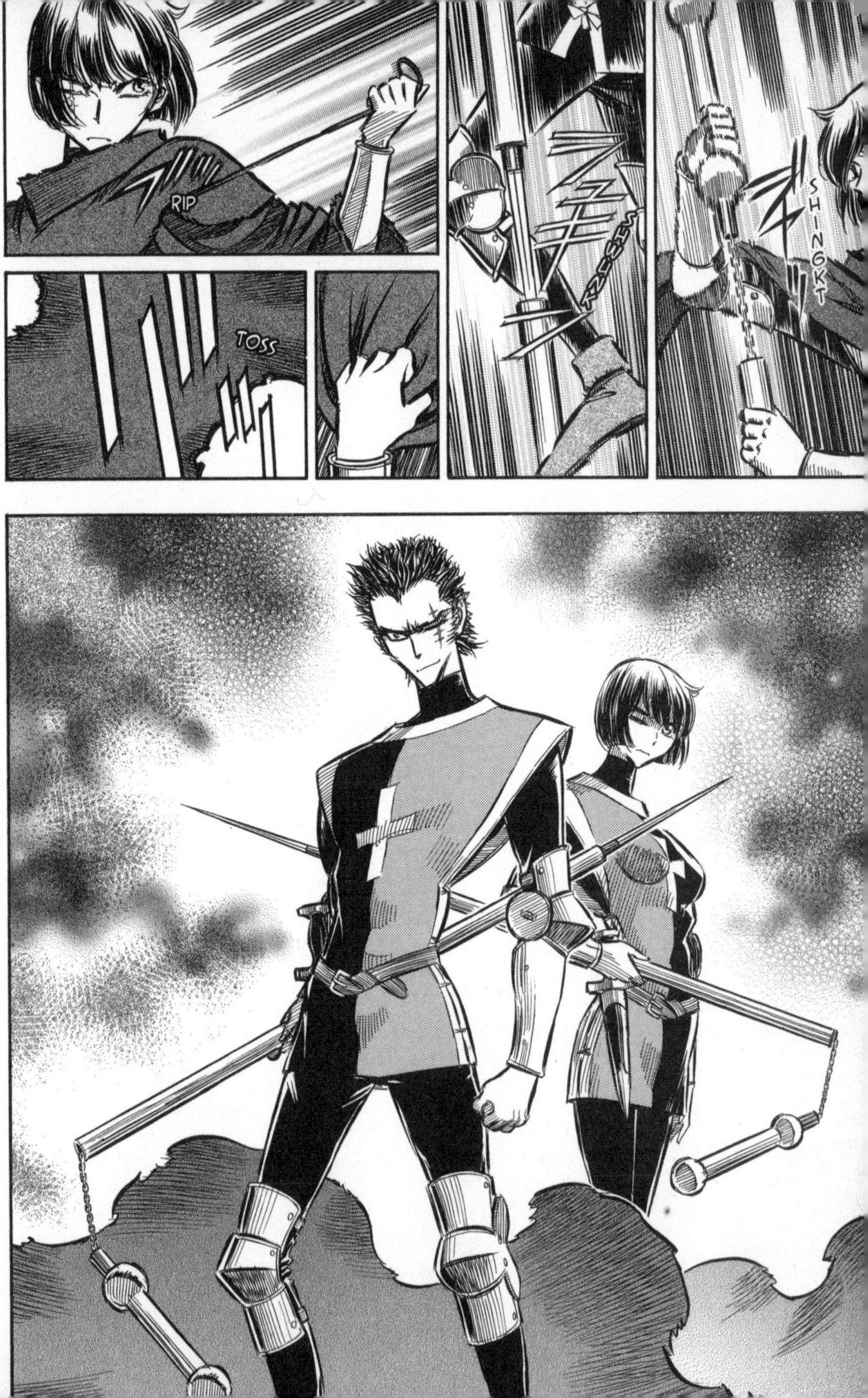
SHINGKT
RIP
TOSS

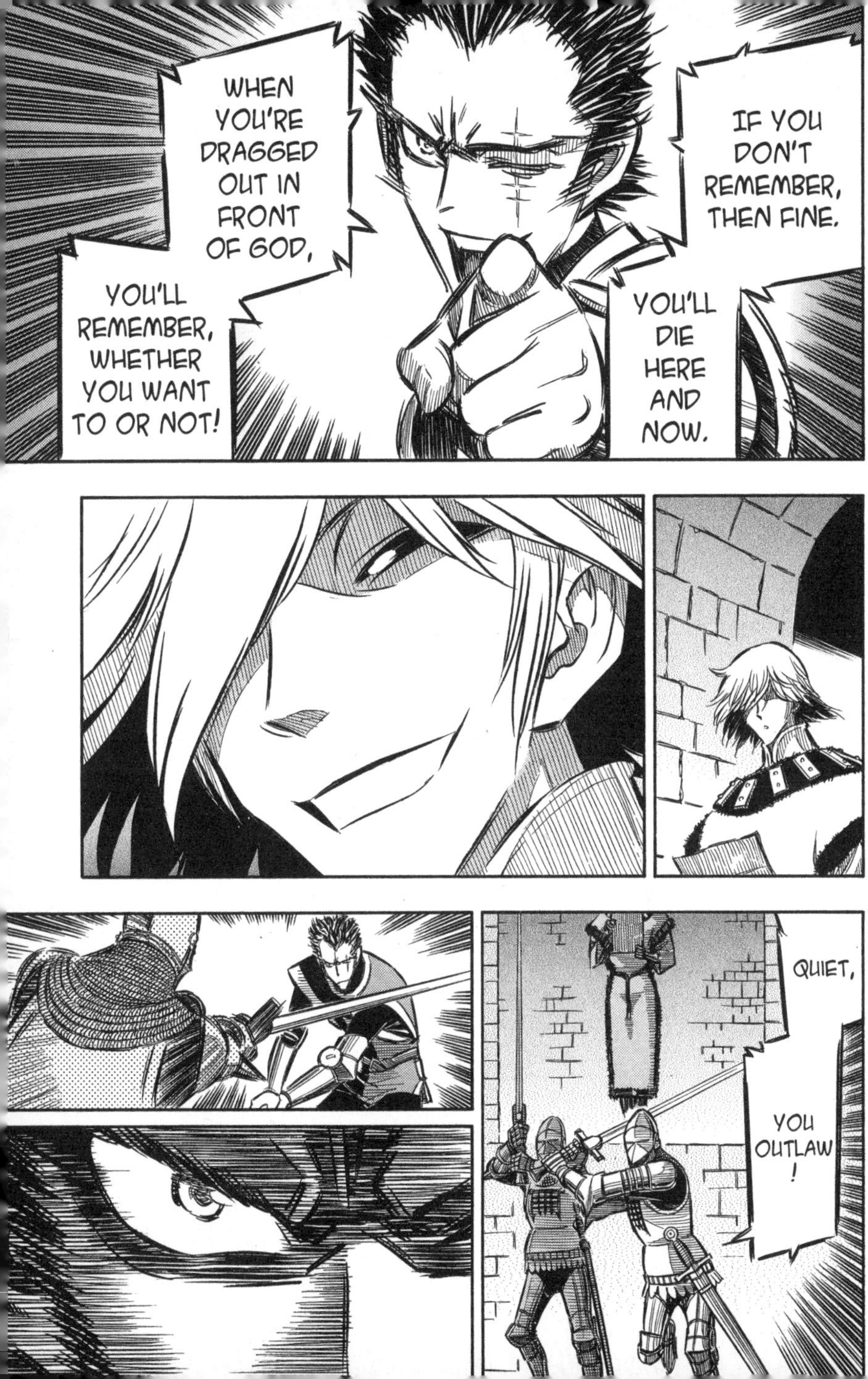
IF YOU DON'T REMEMBER, THEN FINE.
YOU'LL DIE HERE AND NOW.
WHEN YOU'RE DRAGGED OUT IN FRONT OF GOD,
YOU'LL REMEMBER, WHETHER YOU WANT TO OR NOT!
QUIET,
YOU OUTLAW!

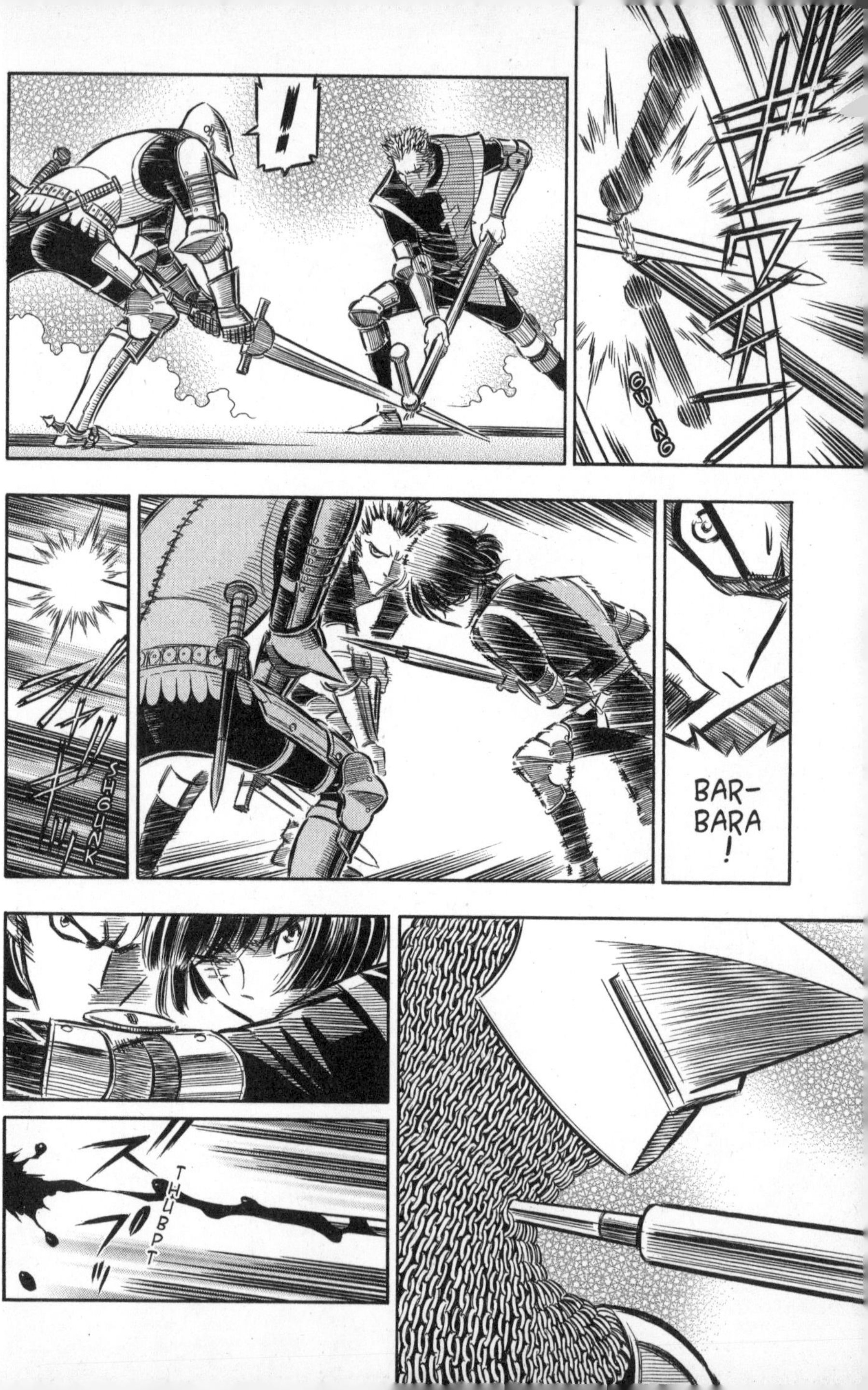
GWING
!
BAR-BARA!
SHGUNK
THUBPT

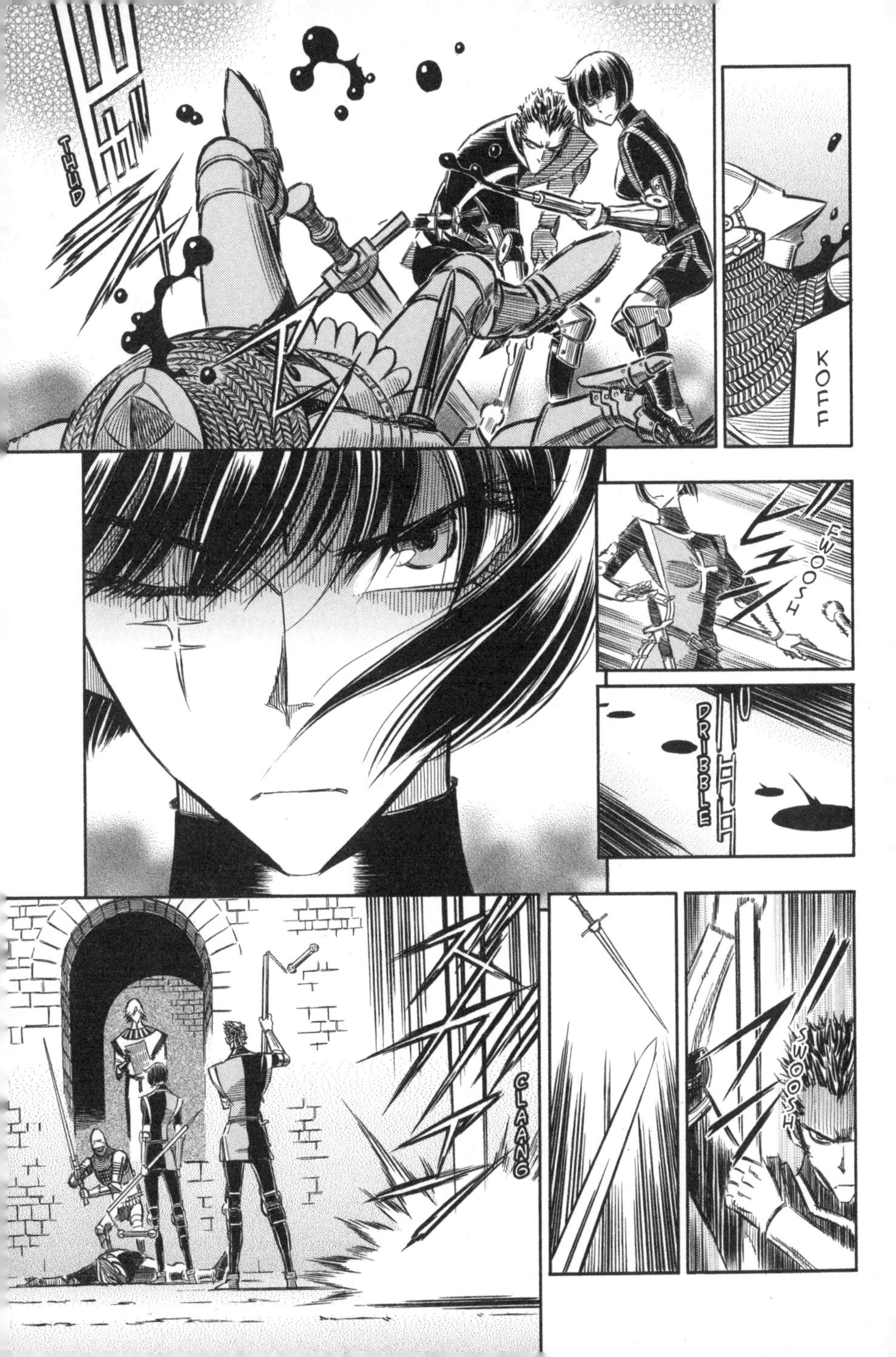
KOFF
THUD
FWOOSH
DRIBBLE
SWOOSH
CLAANG

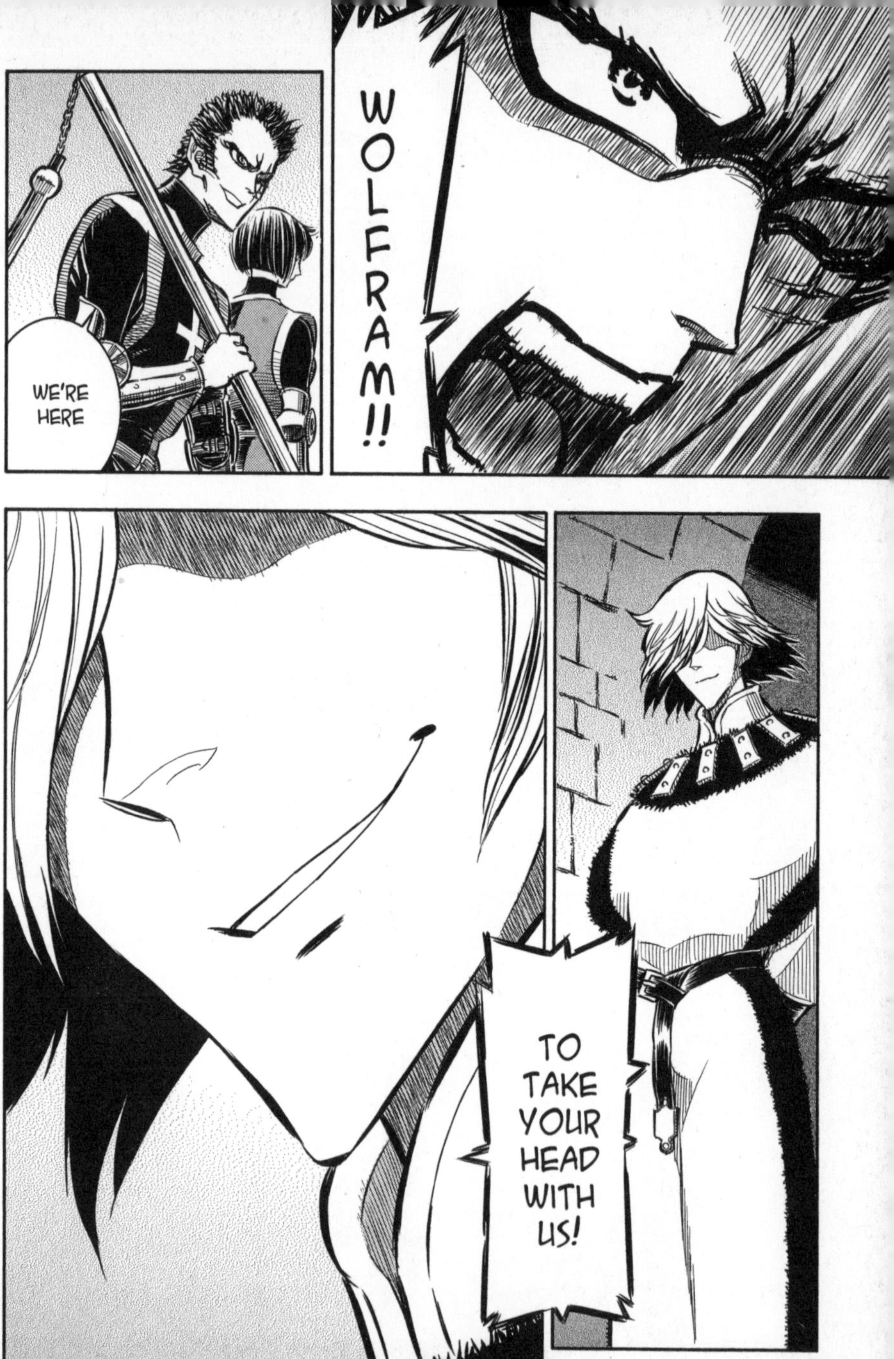
WOLFRAM!!
WE'RE HERE
TO TAKE YOUR HEAD WITH US!

Chapter Seven END

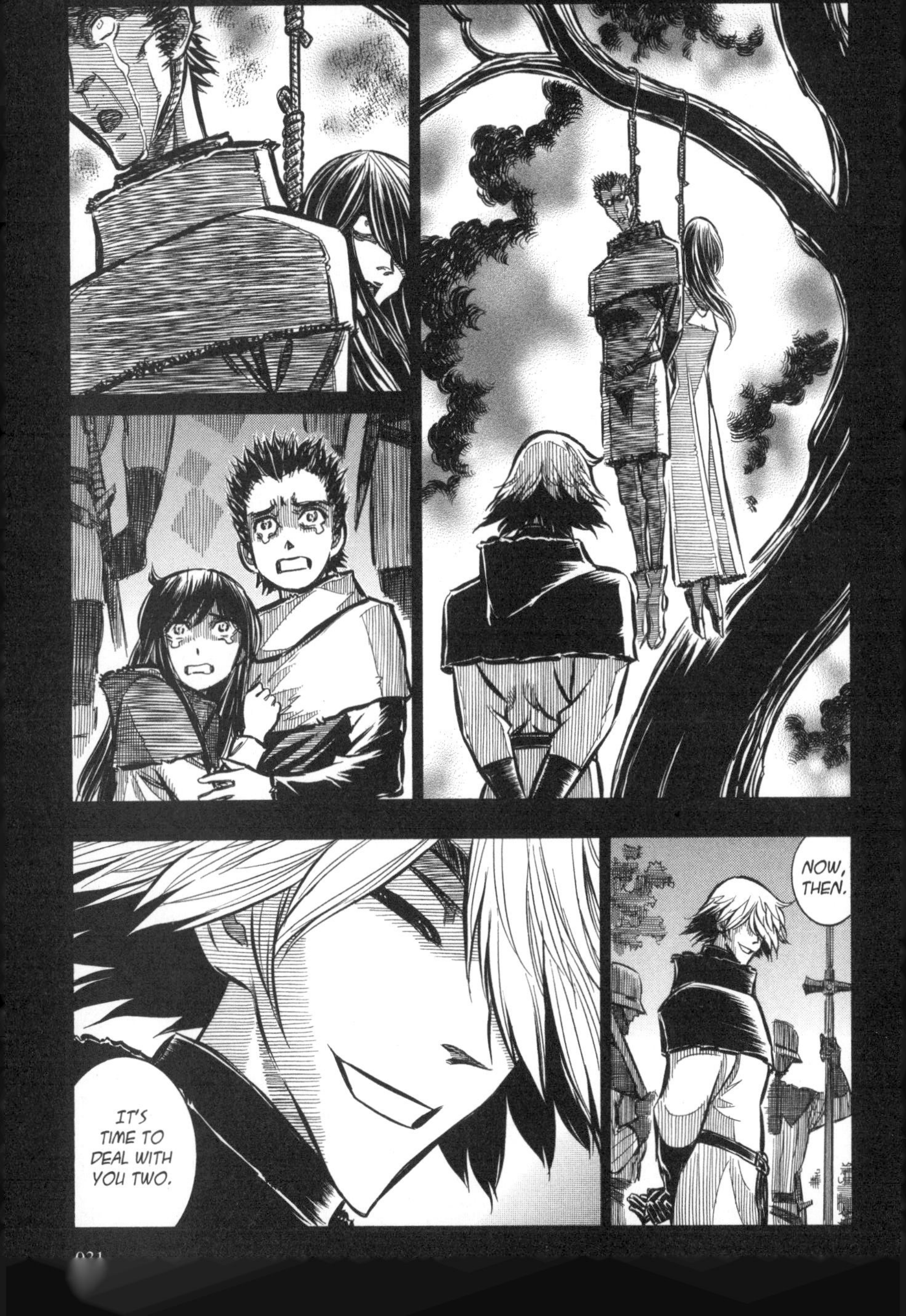
NOW, THEN.
IT'S TIME TO DEAL WITH YOU TWO.

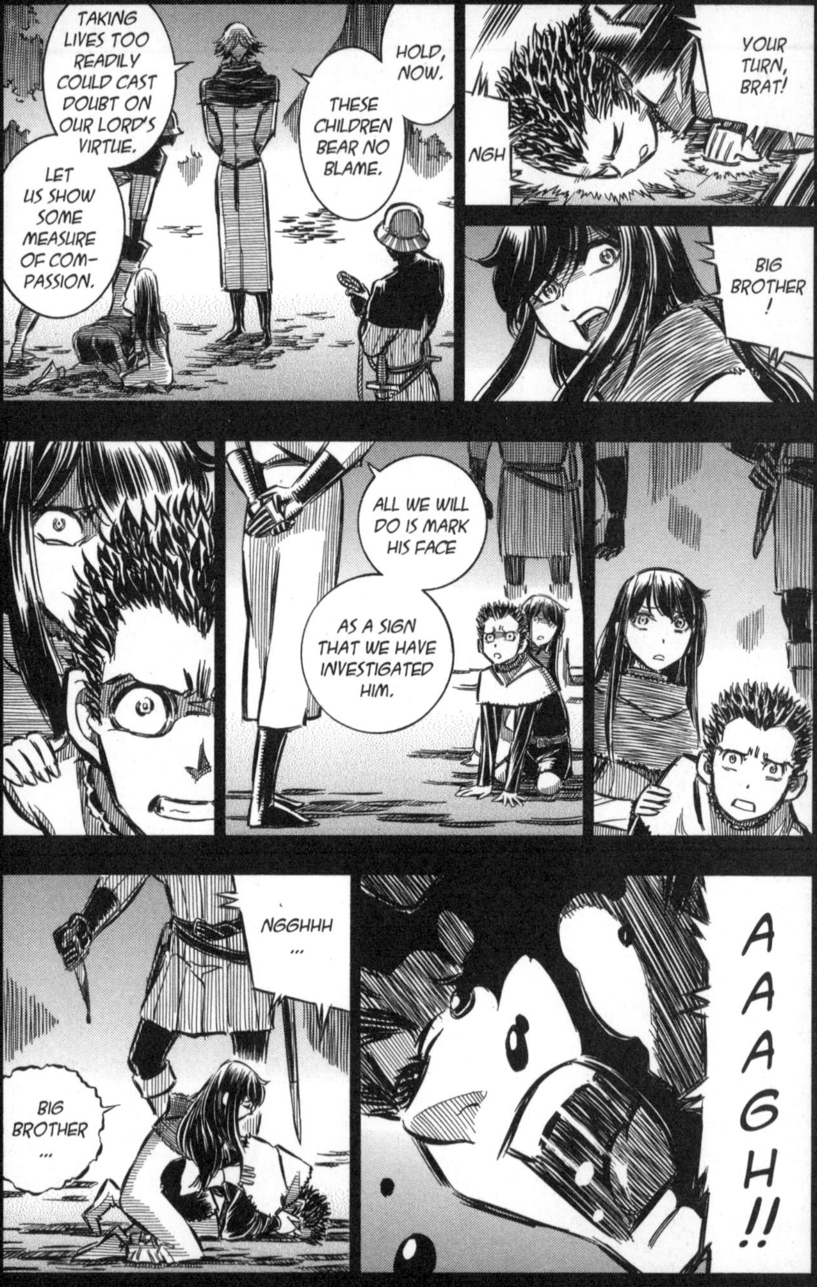
YOUR TURN, BRAT!
NGH
BIG BROTHER!
HOLD, NOW.
THESE CHILDREN BEAR NO BLAME.
TAKING LIVES TOO READILY COULD CAST DOUBT ON OUR LORD'S VIRTUE.
LET US SHOW SOME MEASURE OF COM-PASSION.
ALL WE WILL DO IS MARK HIS FACE
AS A SIGN THAT WE HAVE INVESTIGATED HIM.
AAAAGH!!
NGGHHH ...
BIG BROTHER ...

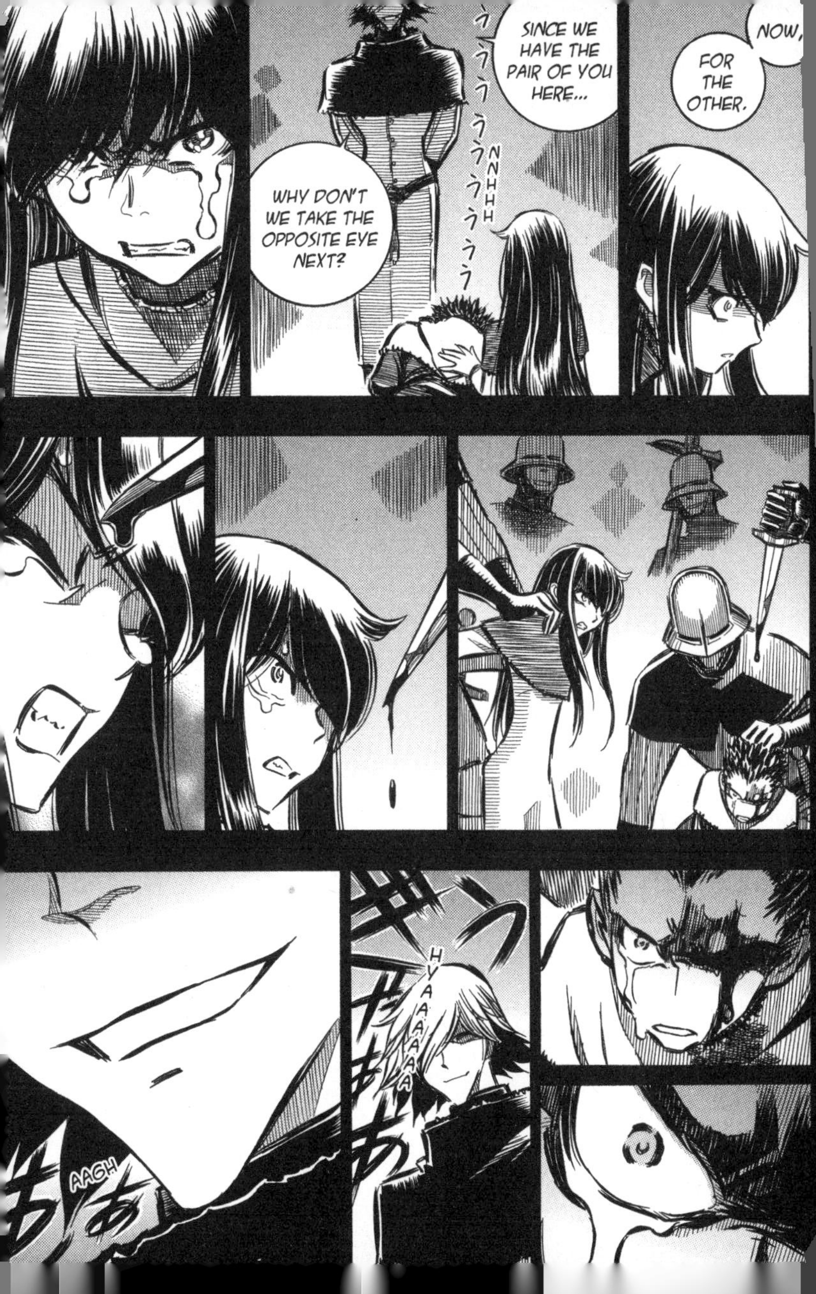
NOW, FOR THE OTHER.
SINCE WE HAVE THE PAIR OF YOU HERE...
WHY DON'T WE TAKE THE OPPOSITE EYE NEXT?
NNHHH
HYAAAAAA
AAGH

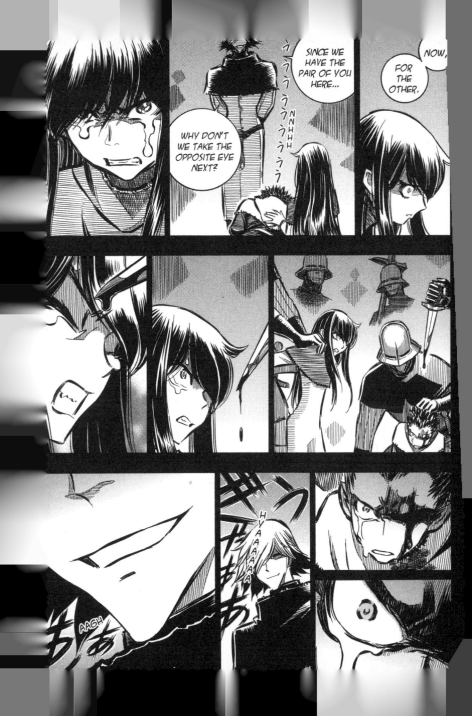

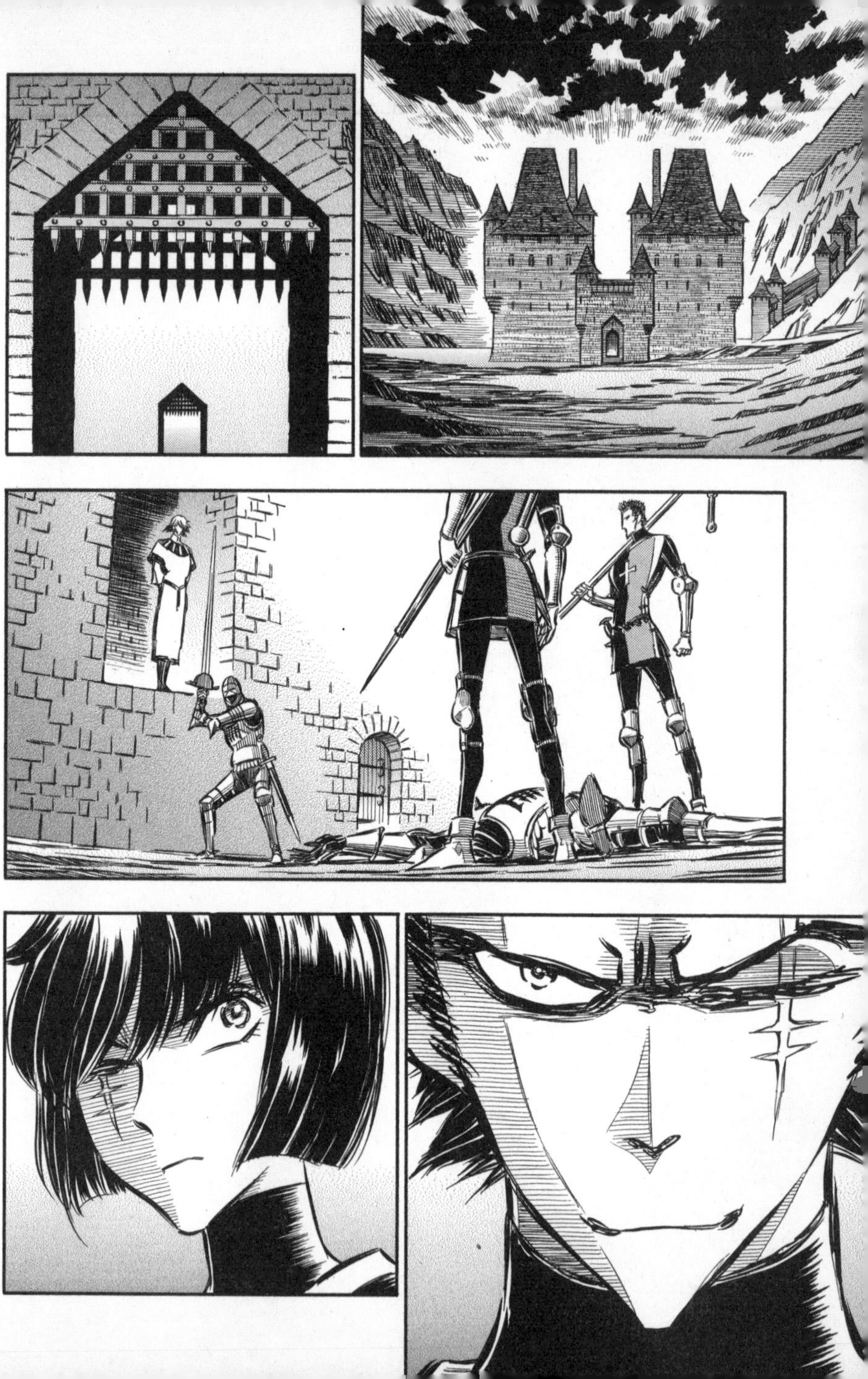

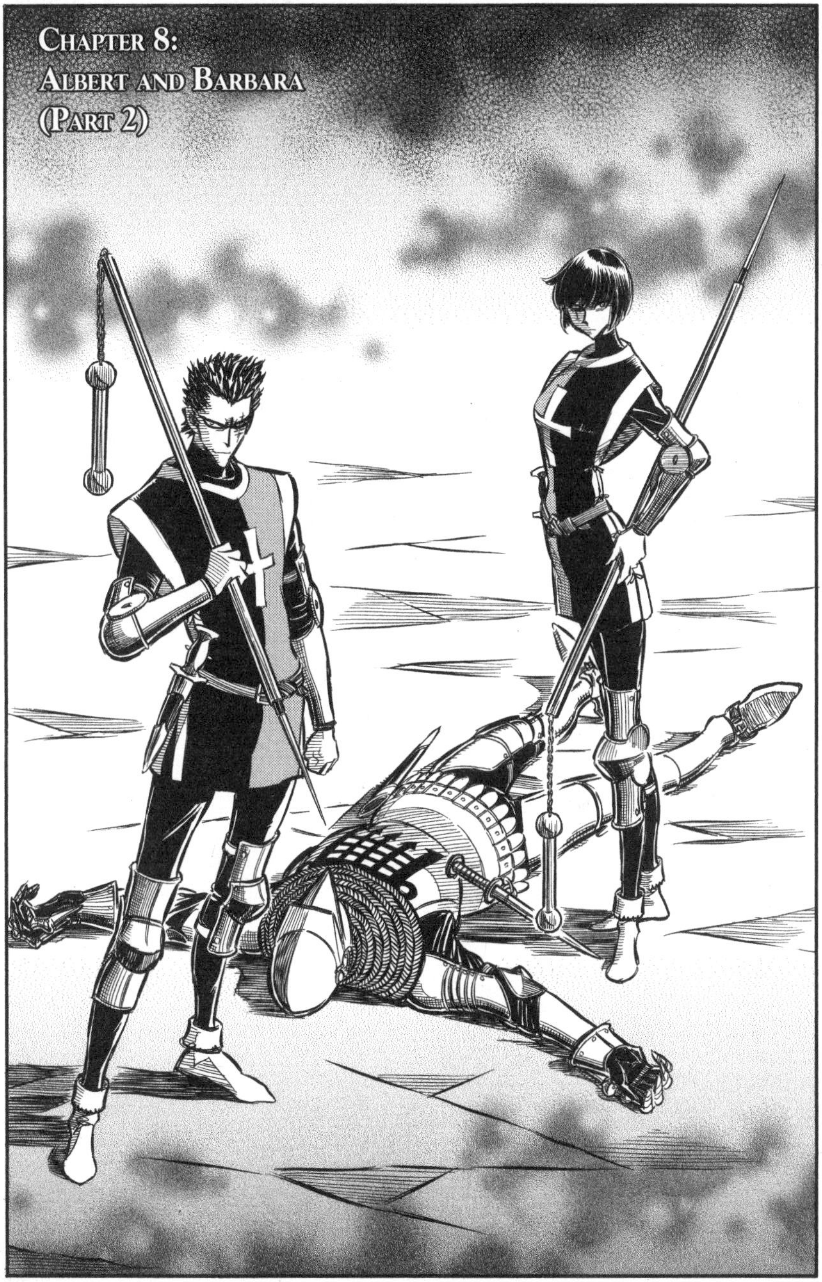
Chapter 8:
Albert and Barbara
(Part 2)

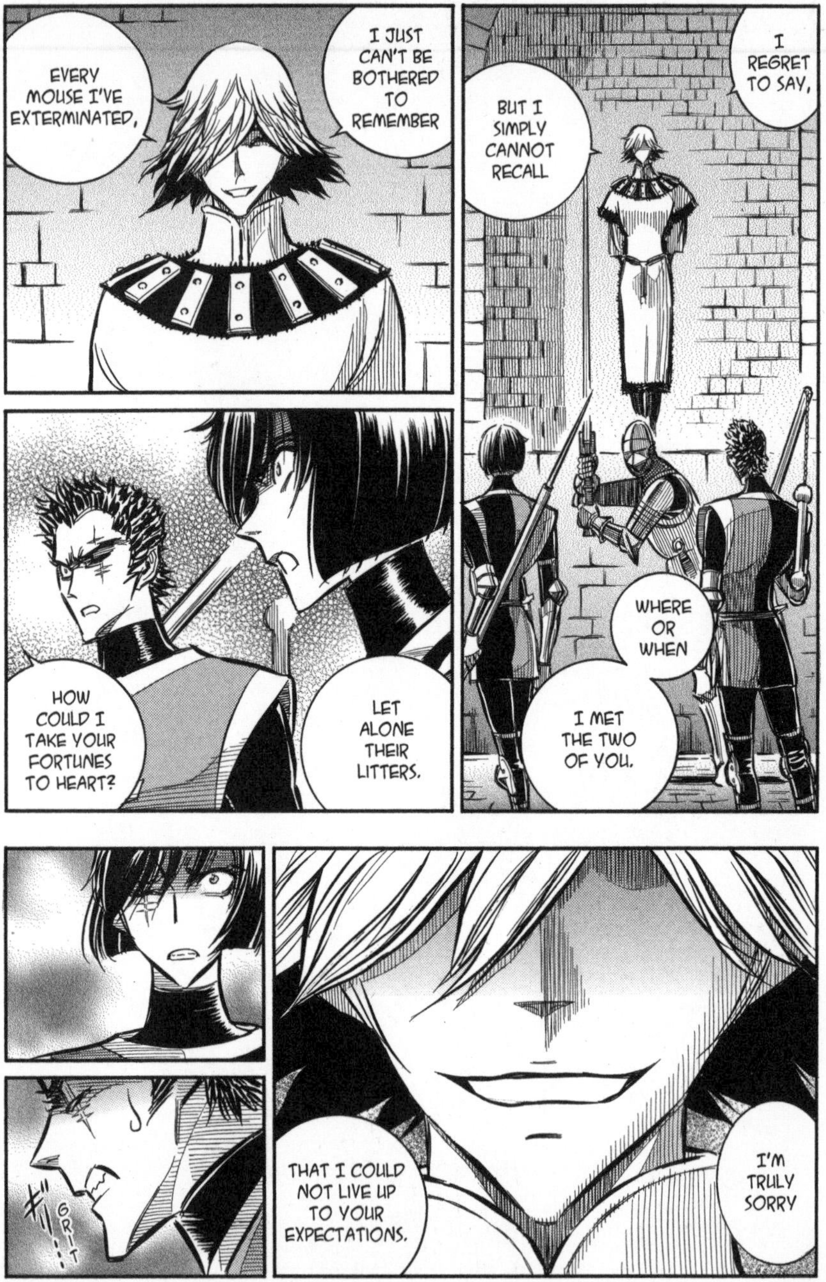
I REGRET TO SAY,
BUT I SIMPLY CANNOT RECALL
WHERE OR WHEN
I MET THE TWO OF YOU.
I JUST CAN'T BE BOTHERED TO REMEMBER
EVERY MOUSE I'VE EXTERMINATED,
LET ALONE THEIR LITTERS.
HOW COULD I TAKE YOUR FORTUNES TO HEART?
I'M TRULY SORRY
THAT I COULD NOT LIVE UP TO YOUR EXPECTATIONS.
GRIT

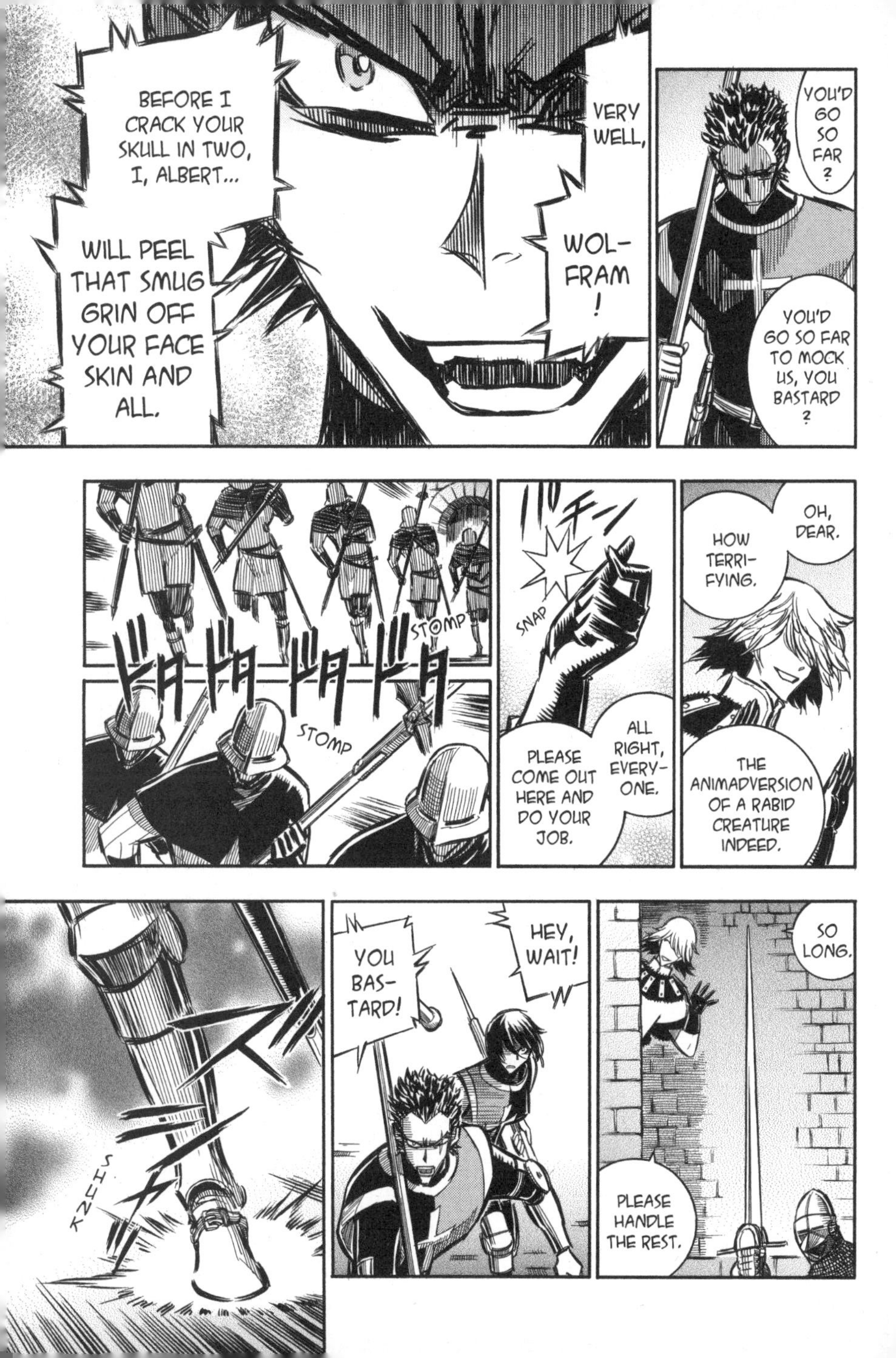
YOU'D GO SO FAR?
YOU'D GO SO FAR TO MOCK US, YOU BASTARD?
VERY WELL,
WOL-FRAM!
BEFORE I CRACK YOUR SKULL IN TWO, I, ALBERT...
WILL PEEL THAT SMUG GRIN OFF YOUR FACE SKIN AND ALL.
OH, DEAR.
HOW TERRI-FYING.
THE ANIMADVERSION OF A RABID CREATURE INDEED.
パチン
SNAP
ALL RIGHT, EVERY-ONE.
PLEASE COME OUT HERE AND DO YOUR JOB.
ドタドタドタドタ
STOMP
STOMP
SO LONG.
PLEASE HANDLE THE REST.
HEY, WAIT!
YOU BAS-TARD!
SHUNK

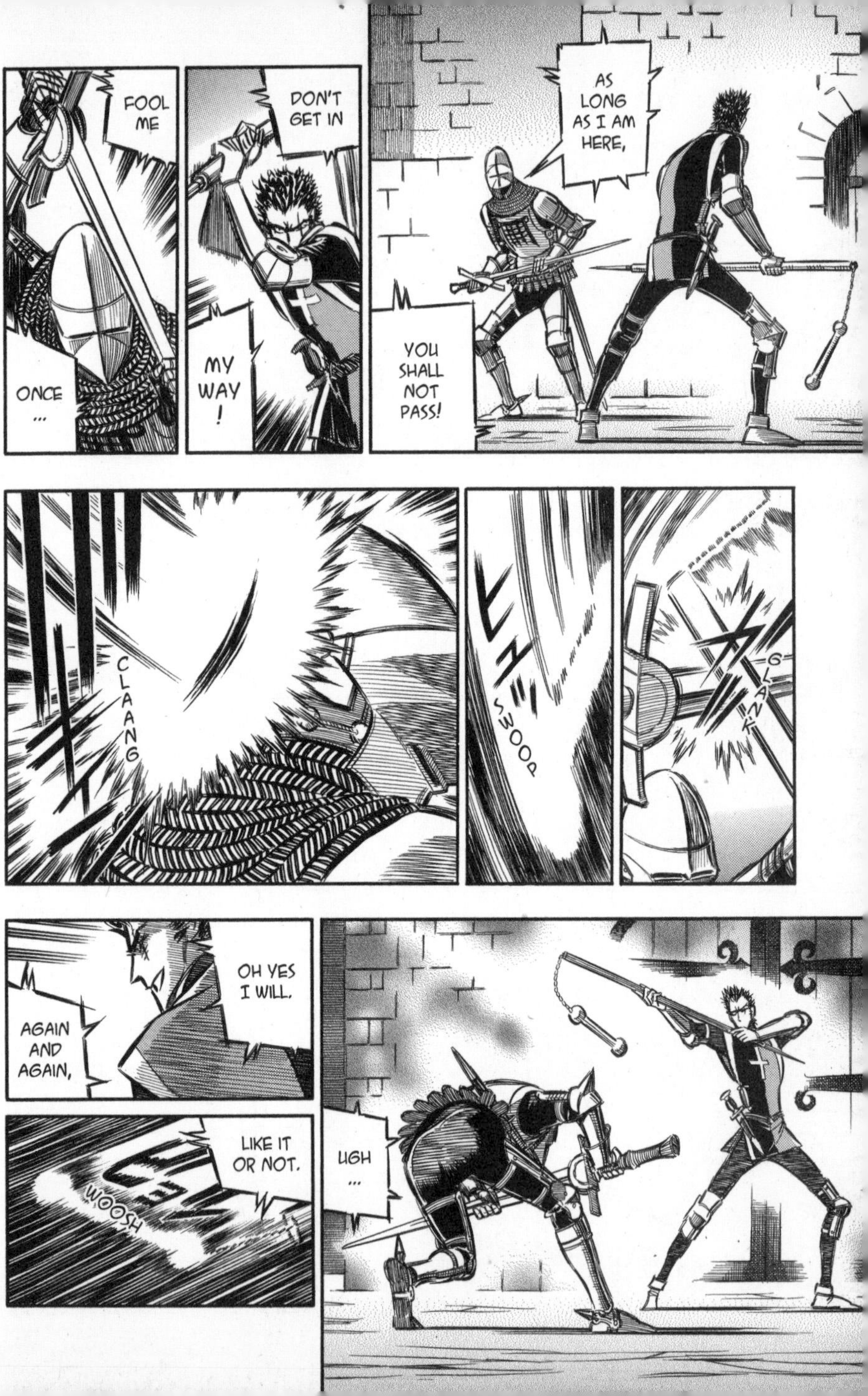
AS LONG AS I AM HERE,
YOU SHALL NOT PASS!
DON'T GET IN
MY WAY!
FOOL ME
ONCE ...
GLANK
SWOOP
CLAANG
UGH ...
OH YES I WILL.
AGAIN AND AGAIN,
LIKE IT OR NOT.
WOOSH

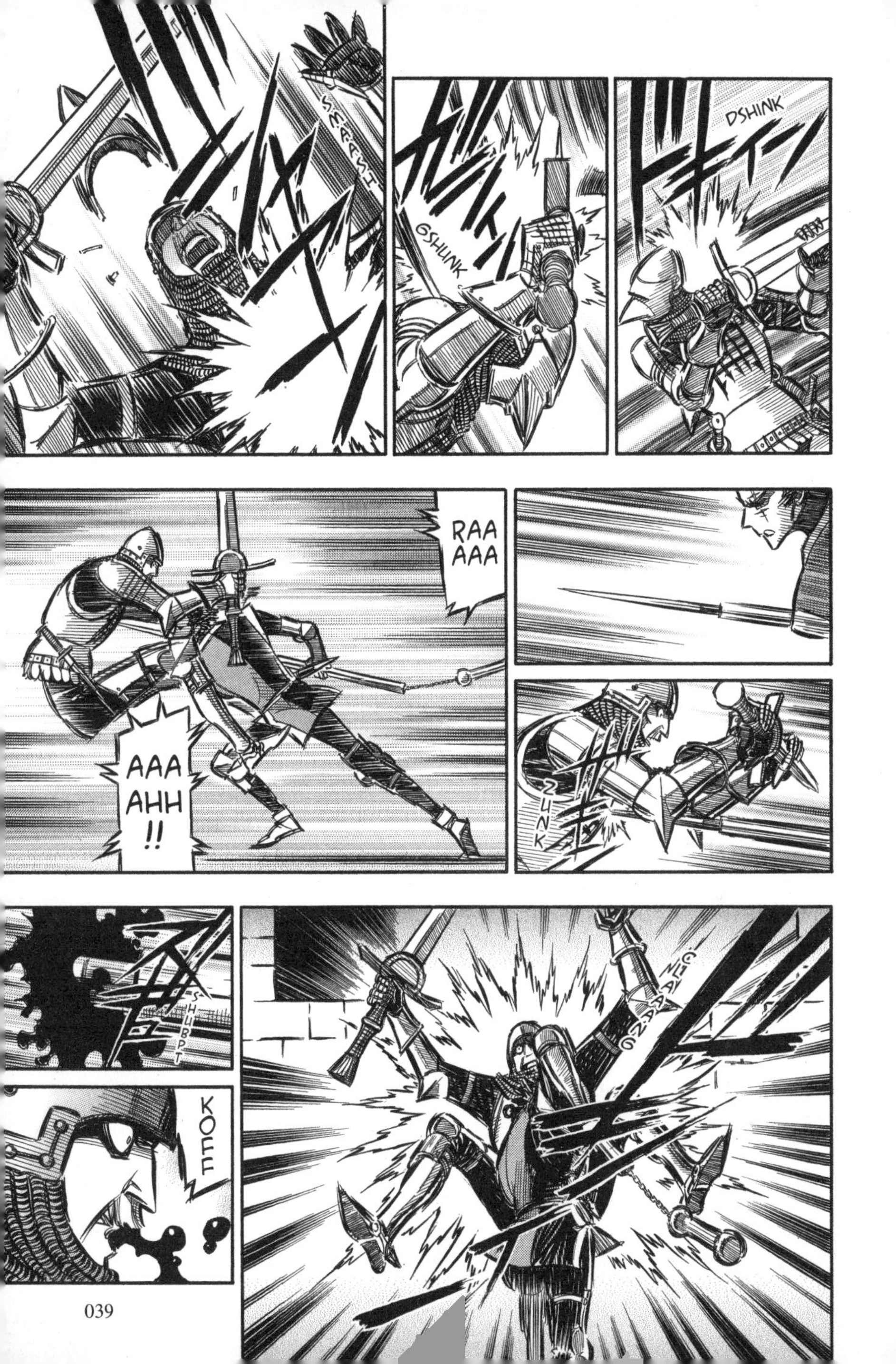
DSHINK
GSHUNK
SMAASH
ZUNK
RAAAAA
AAAAHH!!
CLAAANG
SHUBPT
KOFF

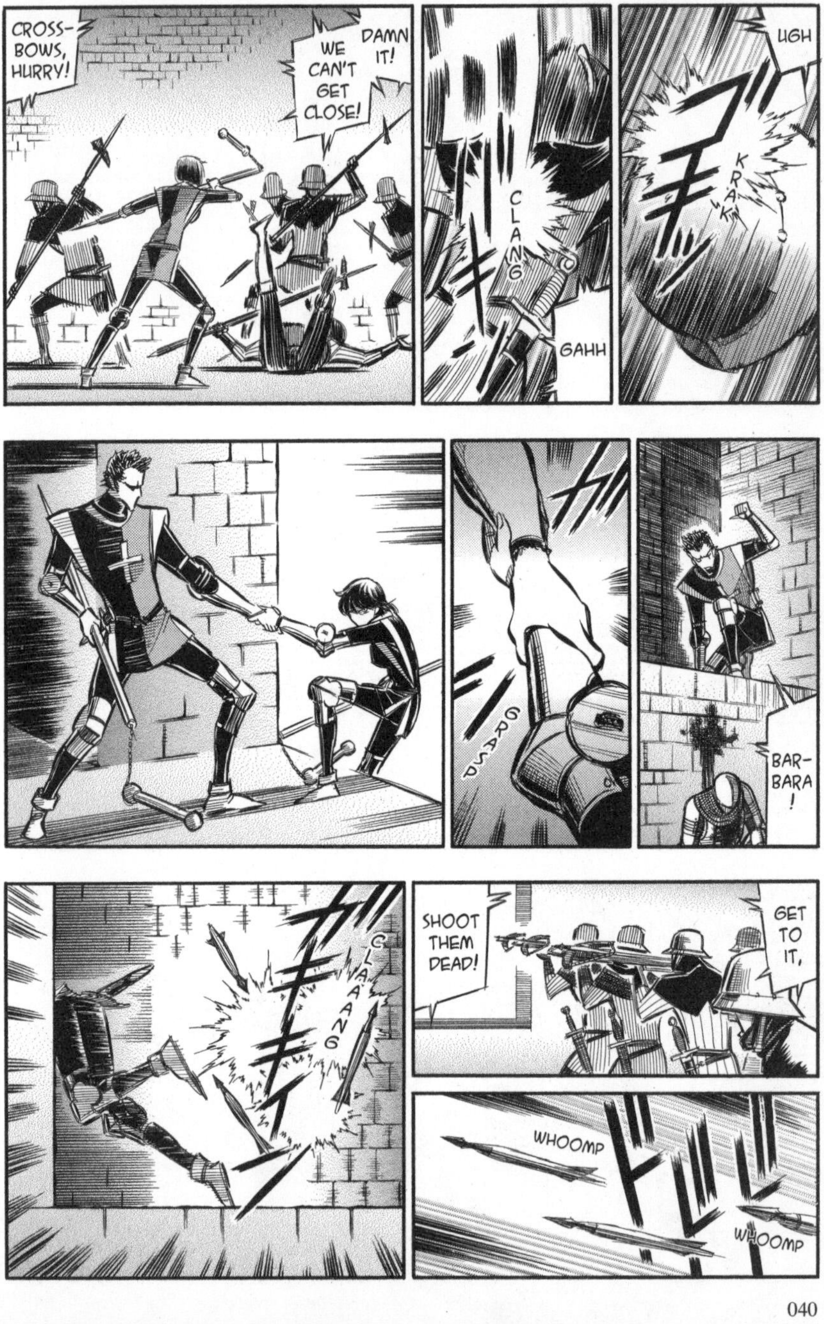
UGH
KRAK
CLANG
GAHH
DAMN IT!
WE CAN'T GET CLOSE!
CROSS-BOWS, HURRY!
BAR-BARA!
GRASP
GET TO IT,
SHOOT THEM DEAD!
WHOOMP
WHOOMP
CLAAANG

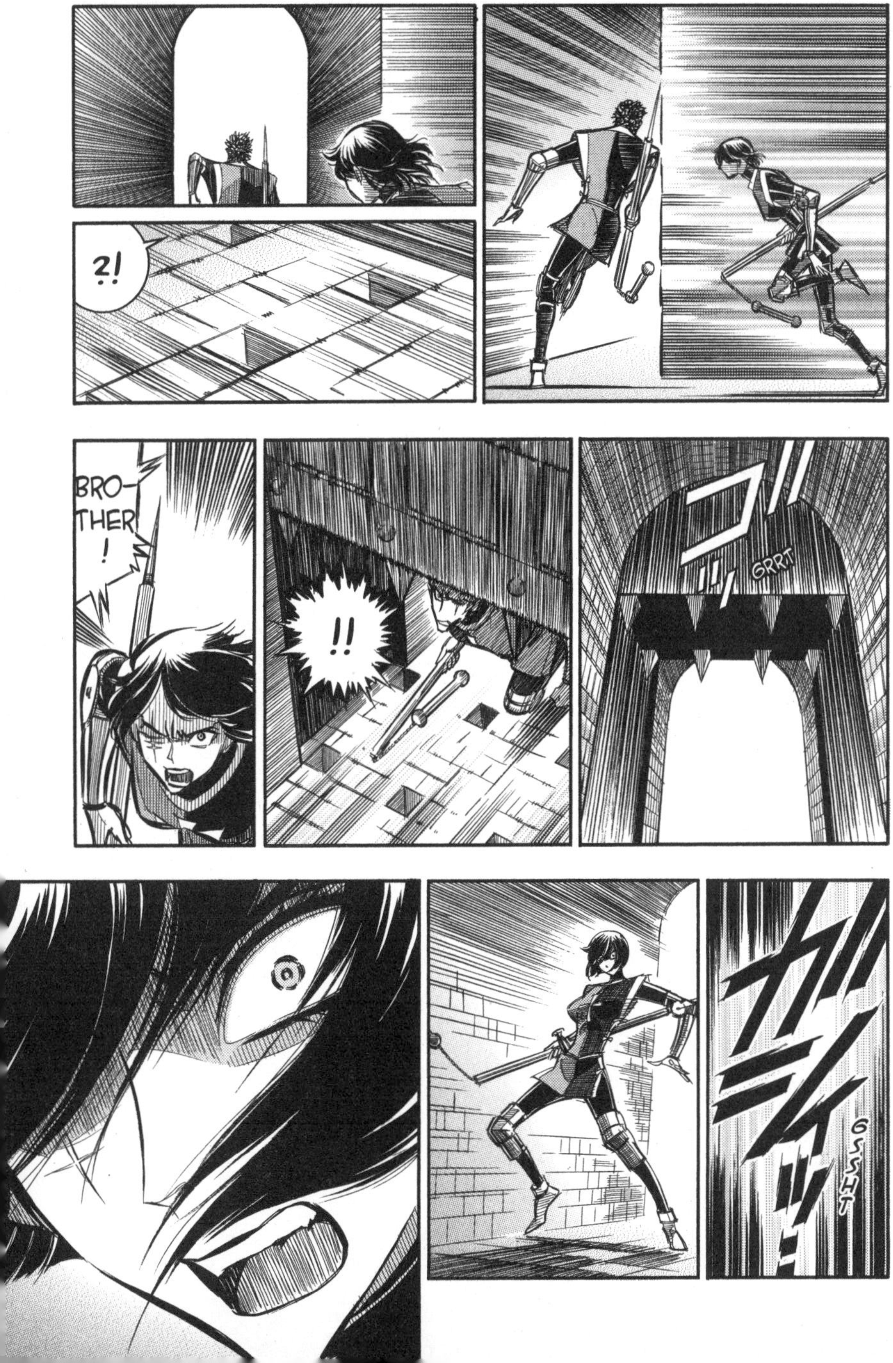
?!
GRRT
!!
BRO-THER!
GSSHT

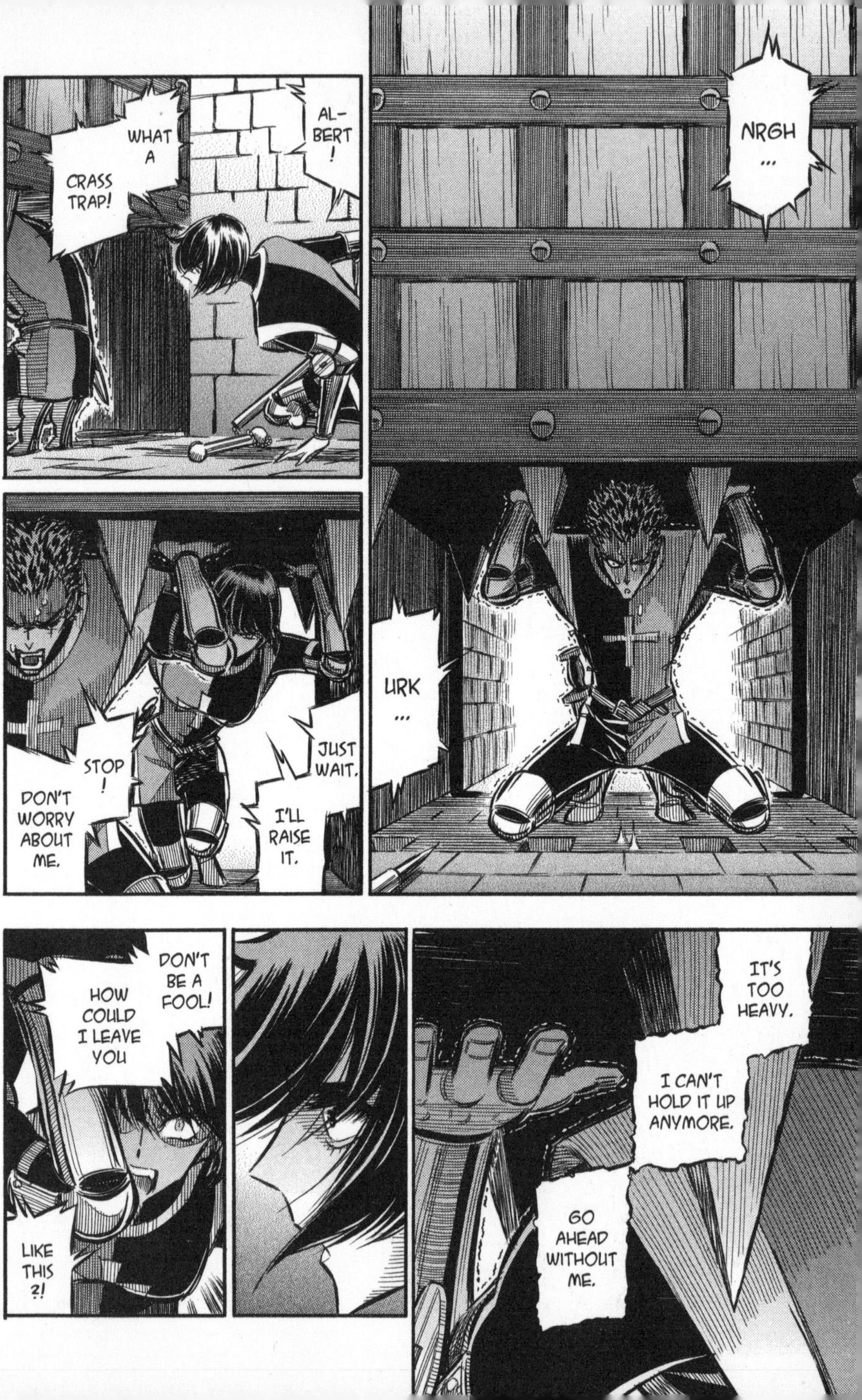
NRGH...
AL-BERT!
WHAT A CRASS TRAP!
URK...
JUST WAIT.
I'LL RAISE IT.
STOP!
DON'T WORRY ABOUT ME.
IT'S TOO HEAVY.
I CAN'T HOLD IT UP ANYMORE.
GO AHEAD WITHOUT ME.
DON'T BE A FOOL!
HOW COULD I LEAVE YOU
LIKE THIS?!

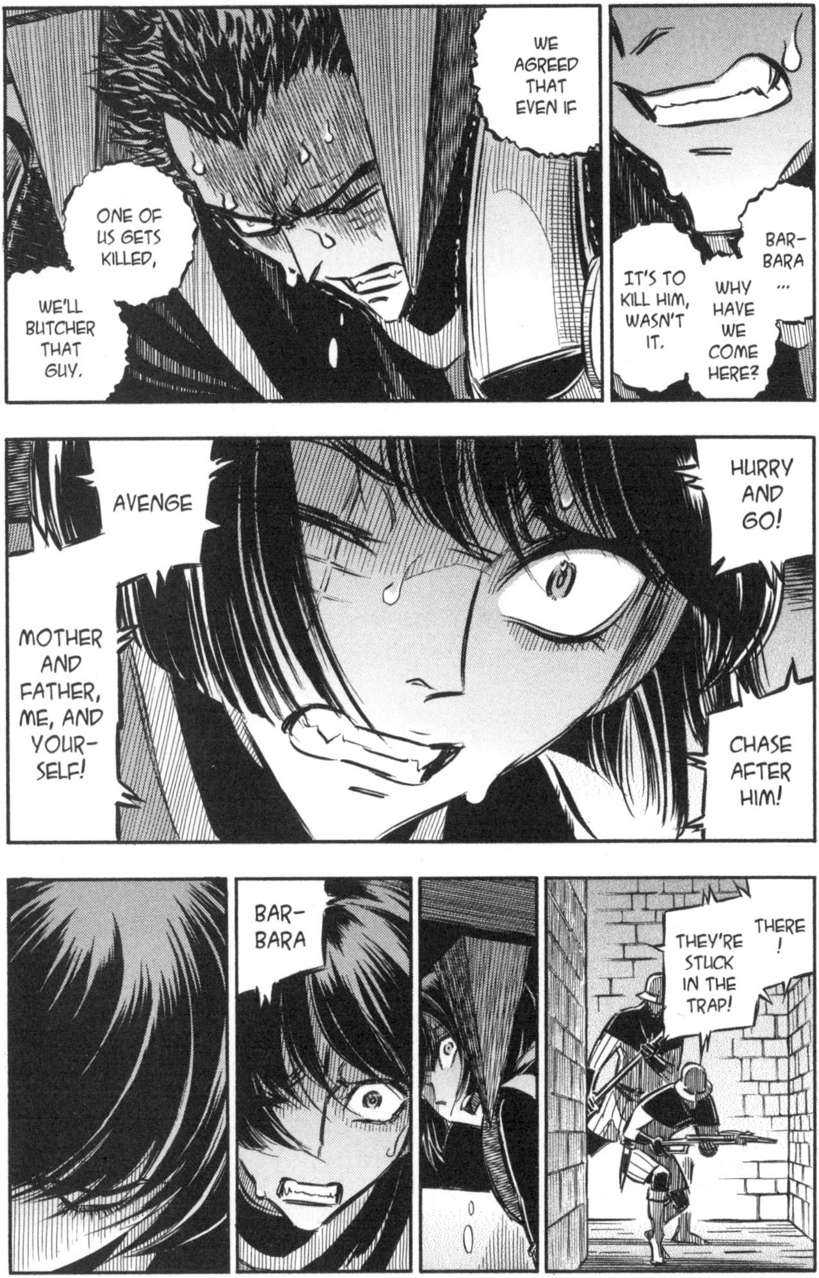
BAR-BARA ...
WHY HAVE WE COME HERE?
IT'S TO KILL HIM, WASN'T IT.
WE AGREED THAT EVEN IF
ONE OF US GETS KILLED,
WE'LL BUTCHER THAT GUY.
HURRY AND GO!
CHASE AFTER HIM!
AVENGE
MOTHER AND FATHER, ME, AND YOUR-SELF!
THERE!
THEY'RE STUCK IN THE TRAP!
BAR-BARA

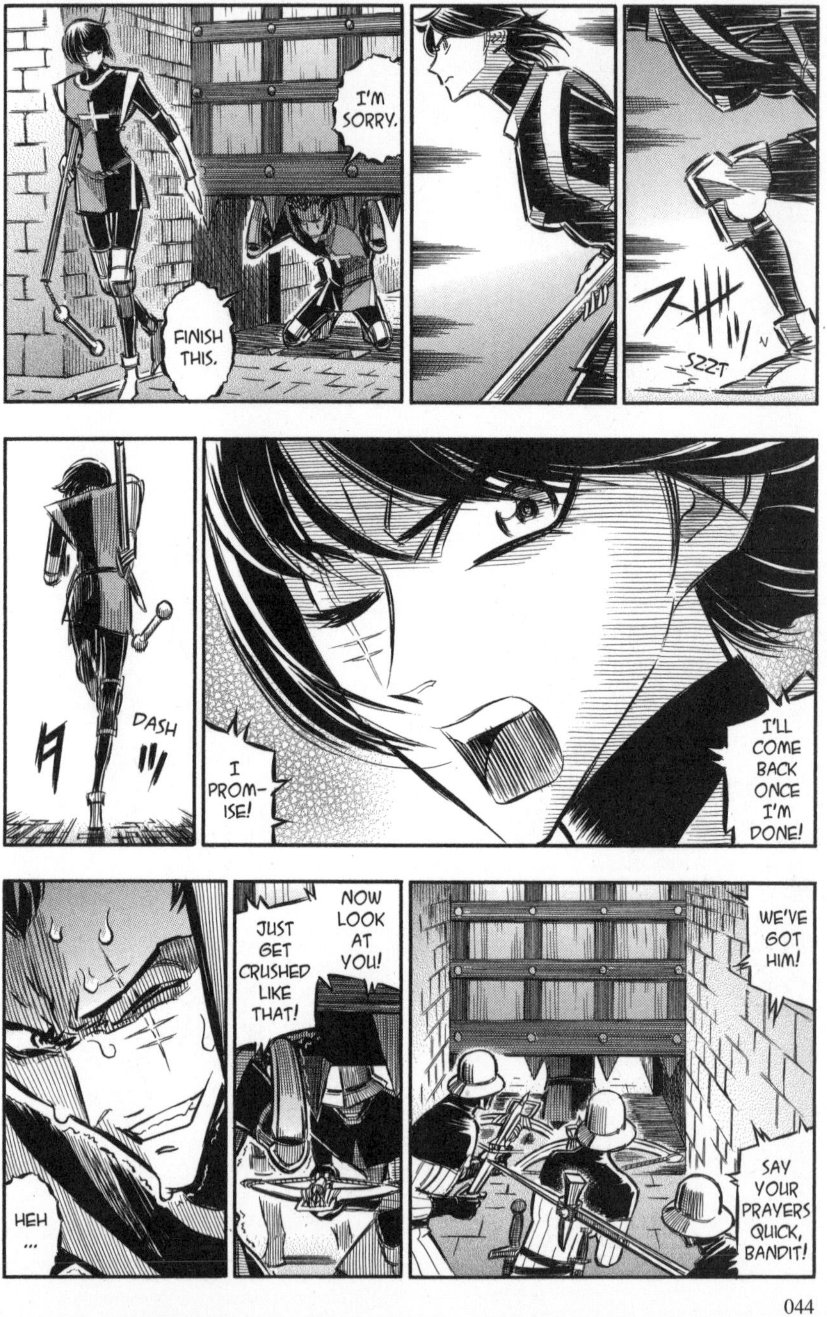
SZZ-T
I'M SORRY.
FINISH THIS.
I'LL COME BACK ONCE I'M DONE!
I PROMISE!
DASH
WE'VE GOT HIM!
SAY YOUR PRAYERS QUICK, BANDIT!
NOW LOOK AT YOU!
JUST GET CRUSHED LIKE THAT!
HEH ...

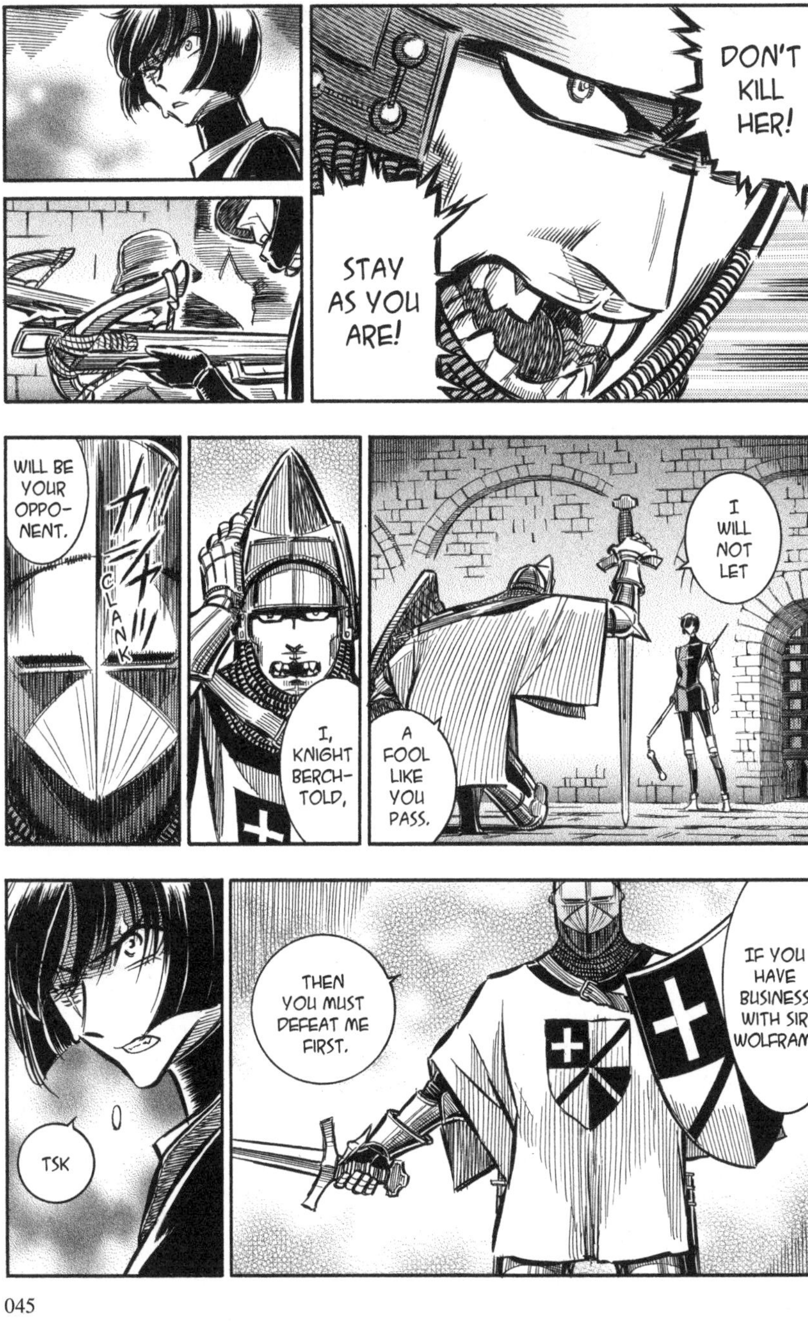
DON'T KILL HER!
STAY AS YOU ARE!
I WILL NOT LET
A FOOL LIKE YOU PASS.
I, KNIGHT BERCH-TOLD,
WILL BE YOUR OPPO-NENT.
CLANK
IF YOU HAVE BUSINESS WITH SIR WOLFRAM,
THEN YOU MUST DEFEAT ME FIRST.
TSK

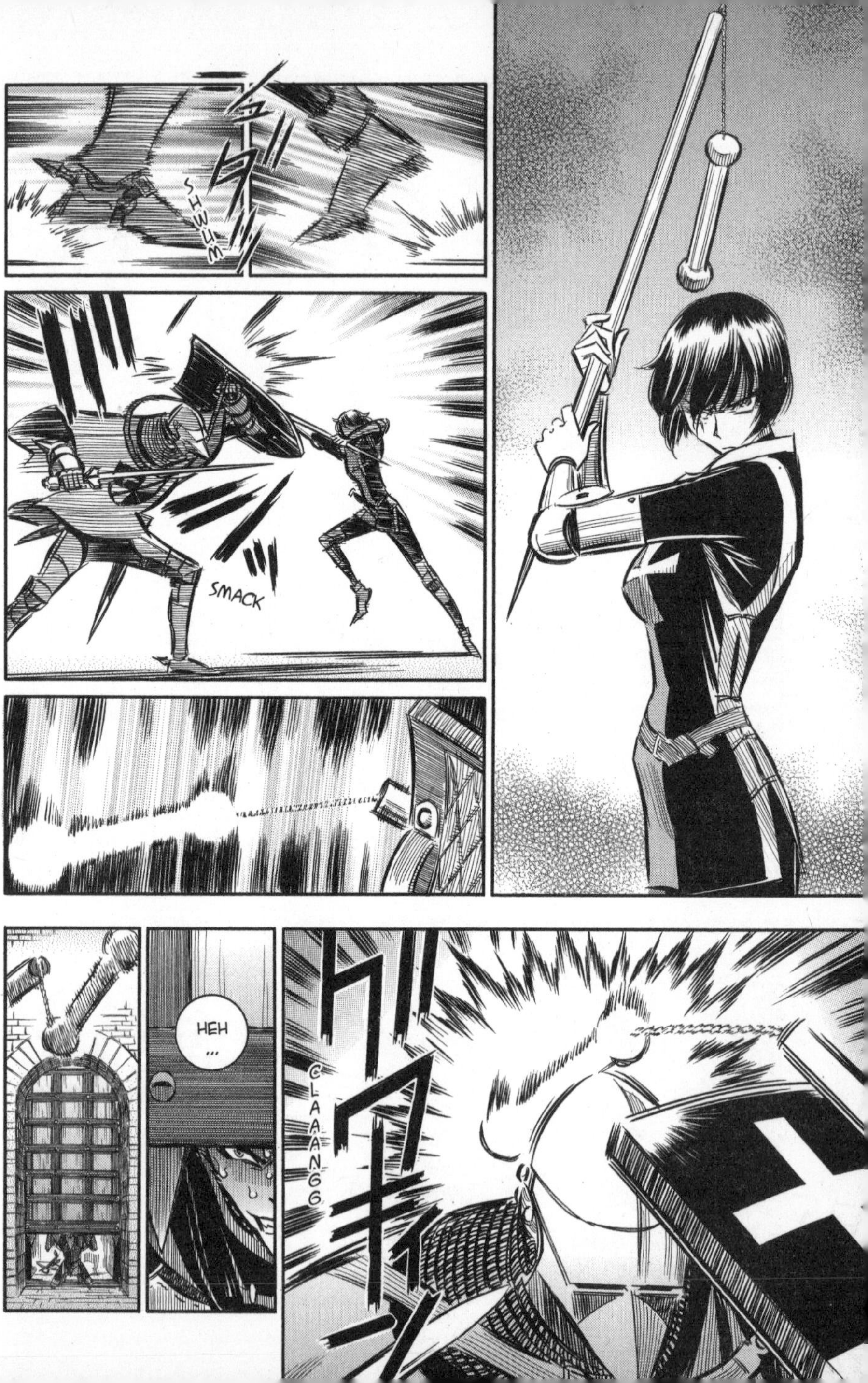
SHWUM
SMACK
CLAAAANGG
HEH ...

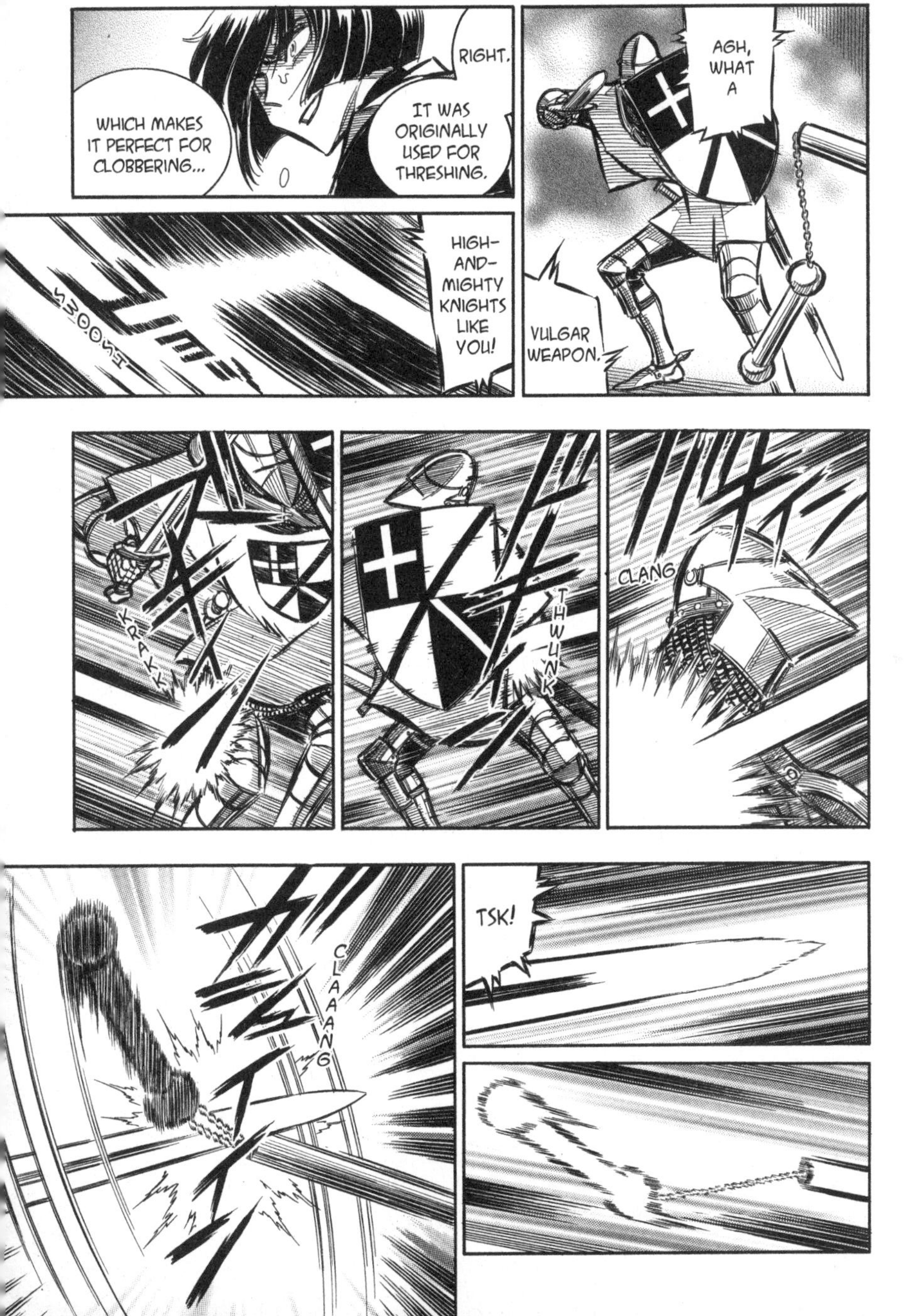
AGH, WHAT A
VULGAR WEAPON.
RIGHT.
IT WAS ORIGINALLY USED FOR THRESHING.
WHICH MAKES IT PERFECT FOR CLOBBERING...
HIGH-AND-MIGHTY KNIGHTS LIKE YOU!
CLANG
THWUNK
KRAKK
TSK!
CLAAAANG

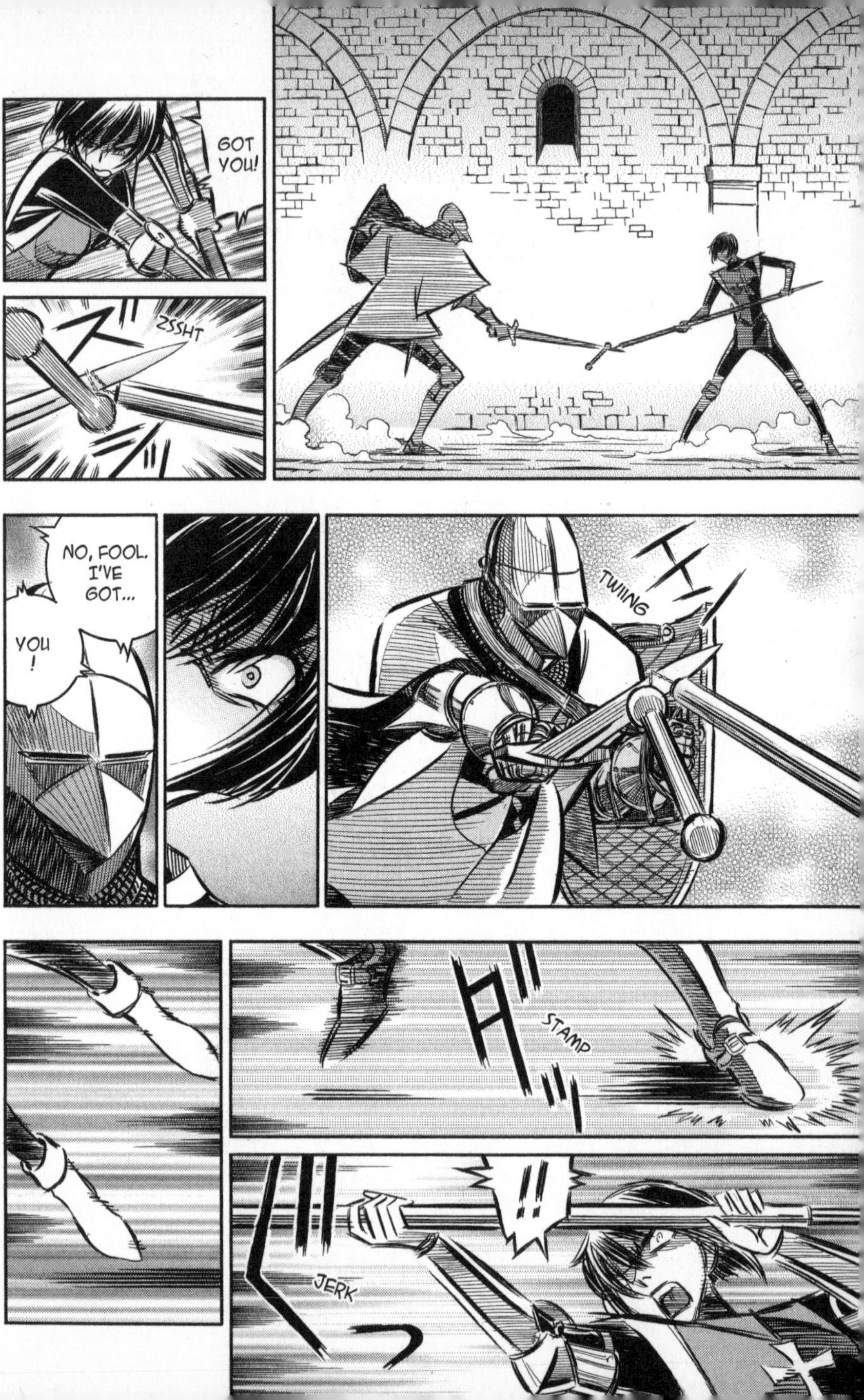

GOT YOU!
ZSSHT
TWIING
NO, FOOL. I'VE GOT...
YOU!
STAMP
!!
JERK

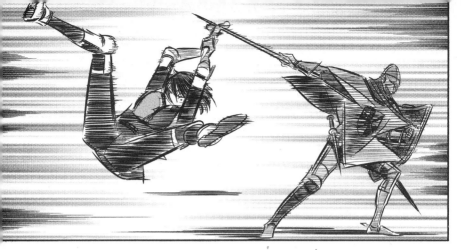

THUD

THUD

OH
N—

NGH

NKKH

BARBARA!

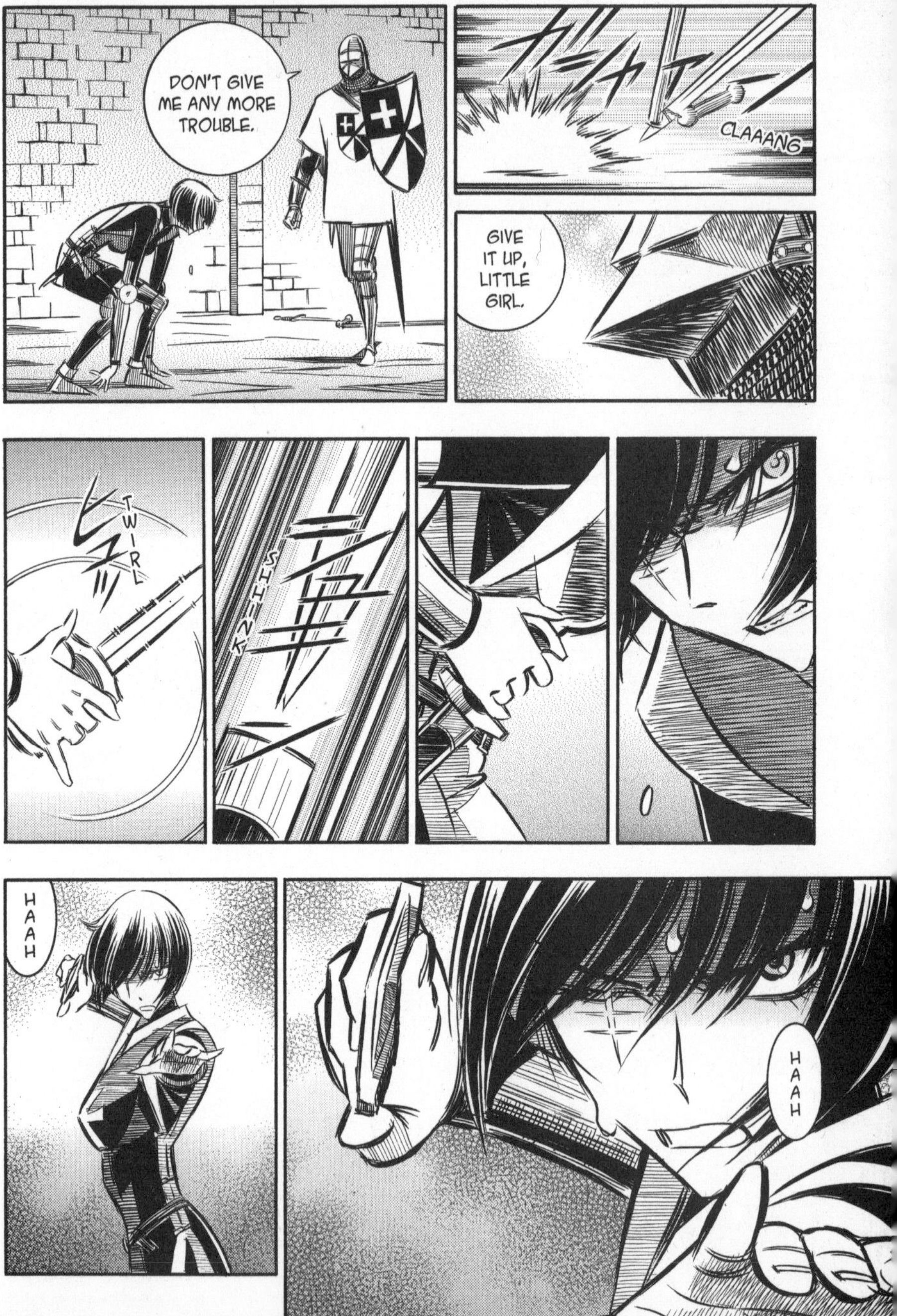
CLAAANG
GIVE IT UP, LITTLE GIRL.
DON'T GIVE ME ANY MORE TROUBLE.
SHIIINK
TWIRL
HAAH
HAAH

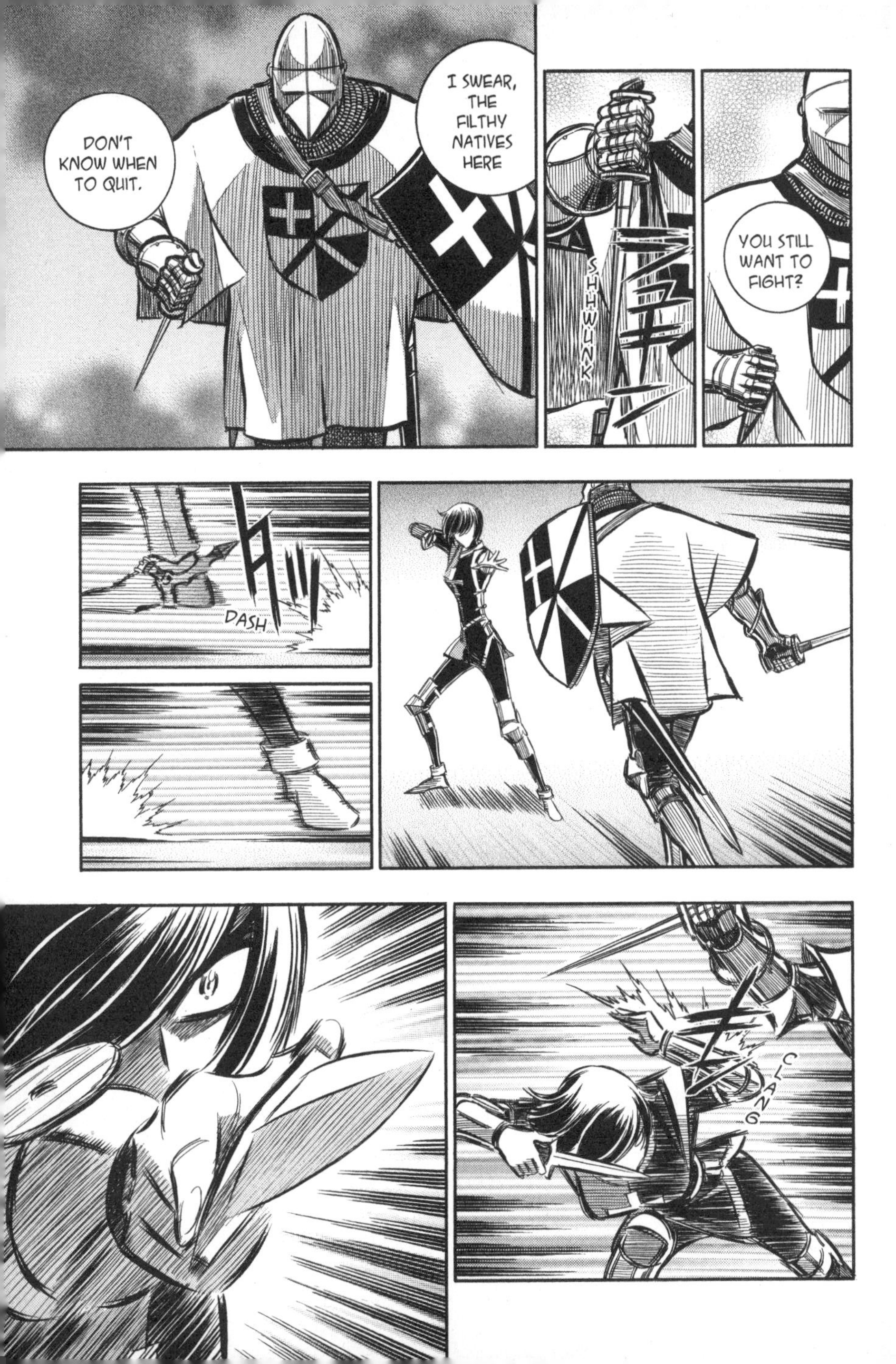
YOU STILL WANT TO FIGHT?
SHHWUNK
I SWEAR, THE FILTHY NATIVES HERE
DON'T KNOW WHEN TO QUIT.
DASH
CLANG

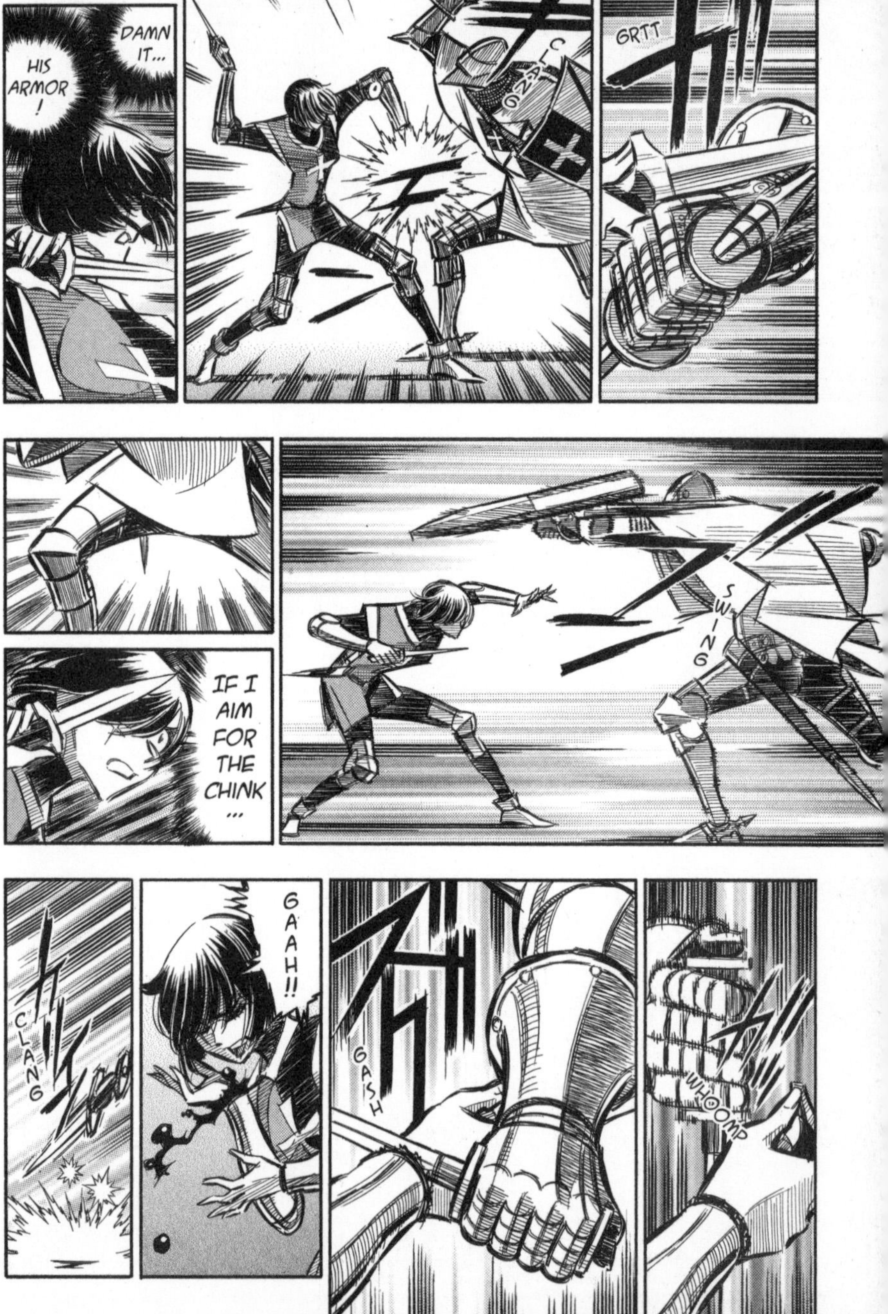
GRTT
CLANG
DAMN IT...
HIS ARMOR!
SWING
IF I AIM FOR THE CHINK...
WHOOMP
GASH
GAAH!!
CLANG

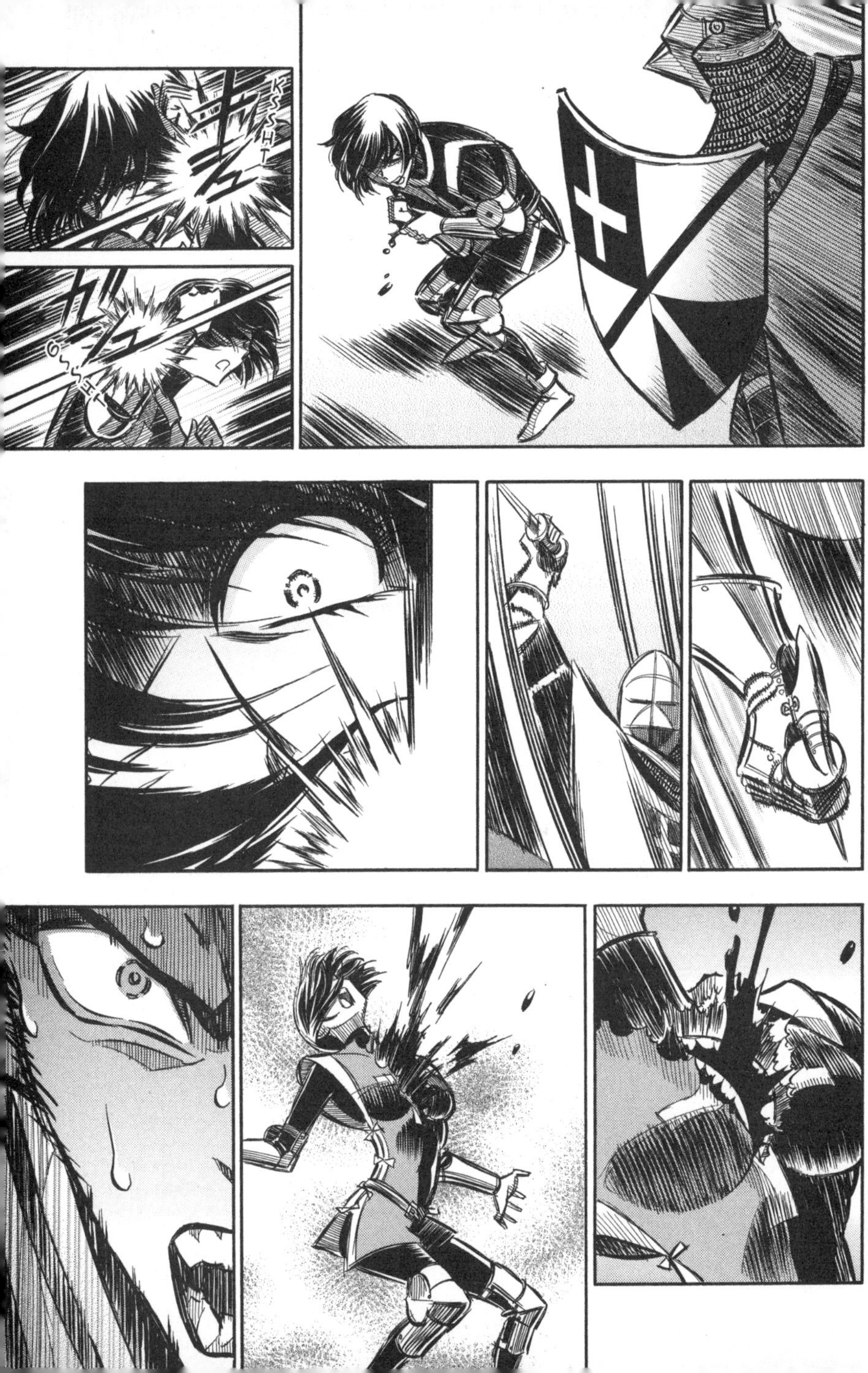
KSSHT
GSSHT

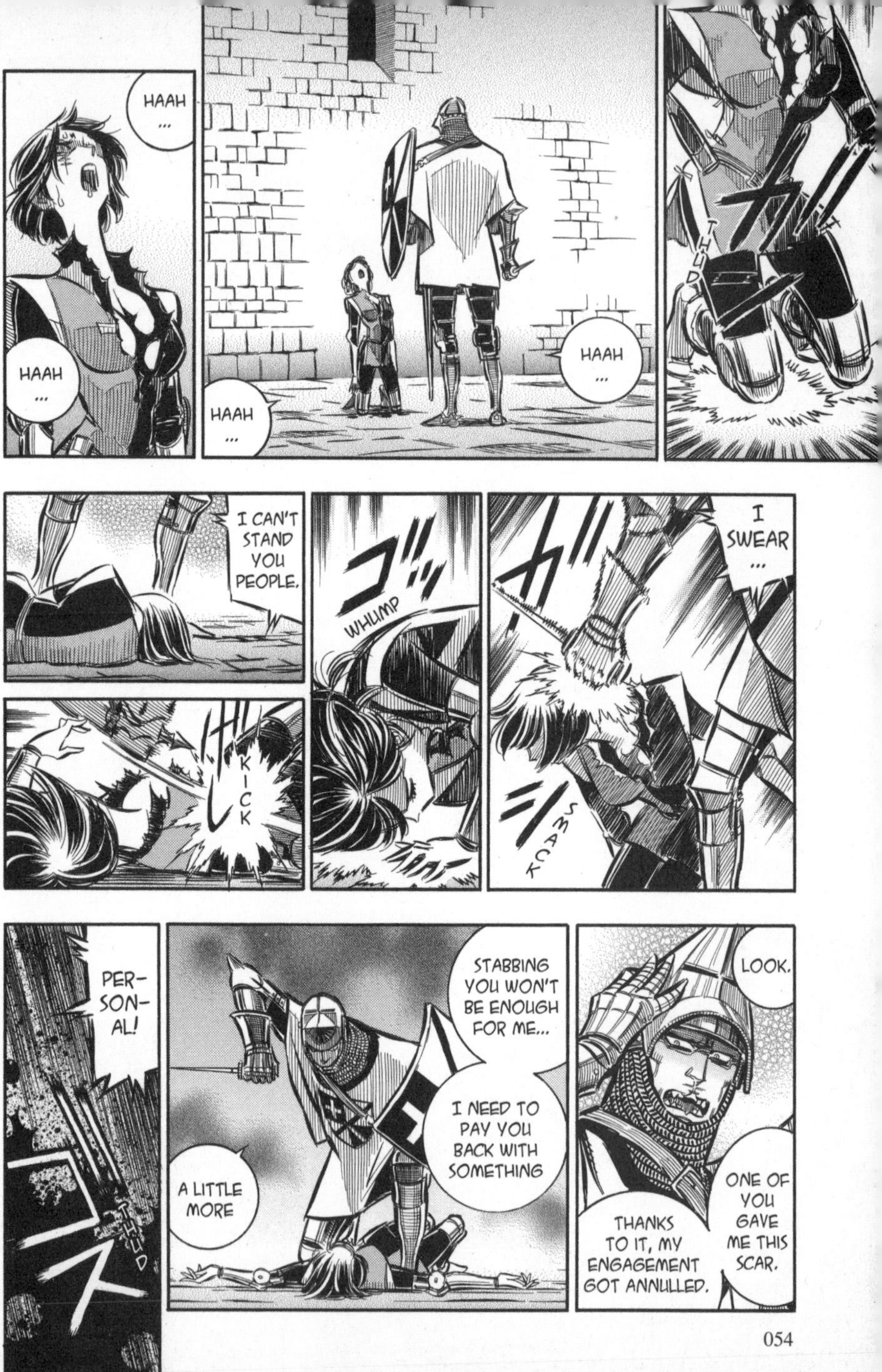
THUD
HAAH ...
HAAH ...
HAAH ...
HAAH ...
I SWEAR ...
SMACK
WHUMP
I CAN'T STAND YOU PEOPLE.
KICK
LOOK.
ONE OF YOU GAVE ME THIS SCAR.
THANKS TO IT, MY ENGAGEMENT GOT ANNULLED.
STABBING YOU WON'T BE ENOUGH FOR ME...
I NEED TO PAY YOU BACK WITH SOMETHING
A LITTLE MORE
PER-SON-AL!
THUD

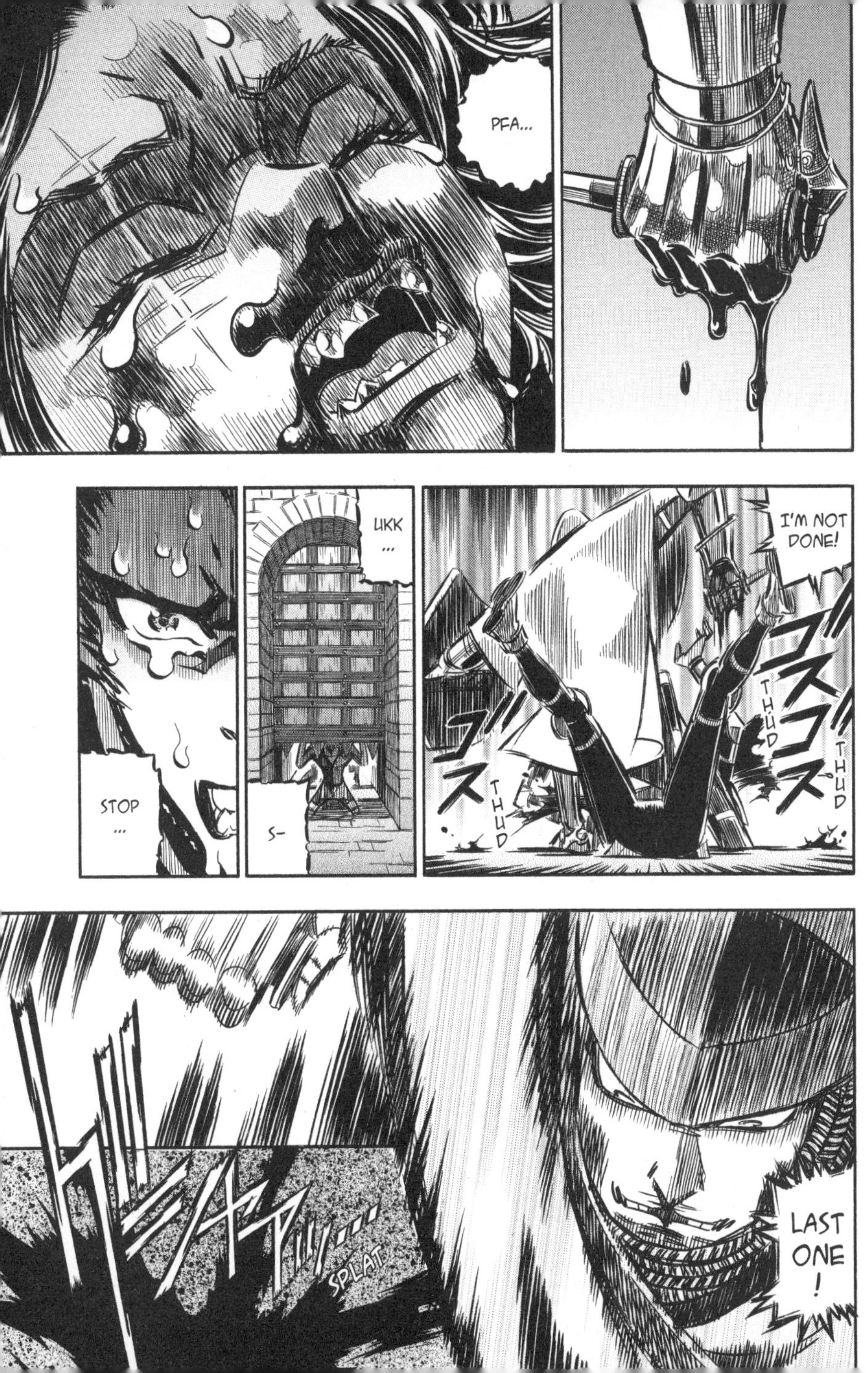
PFA...
I'M NOT DONE!
THUD
THUD
THUD
UKK ...
S-
STOP ...
LAST ONE !
SPLAT

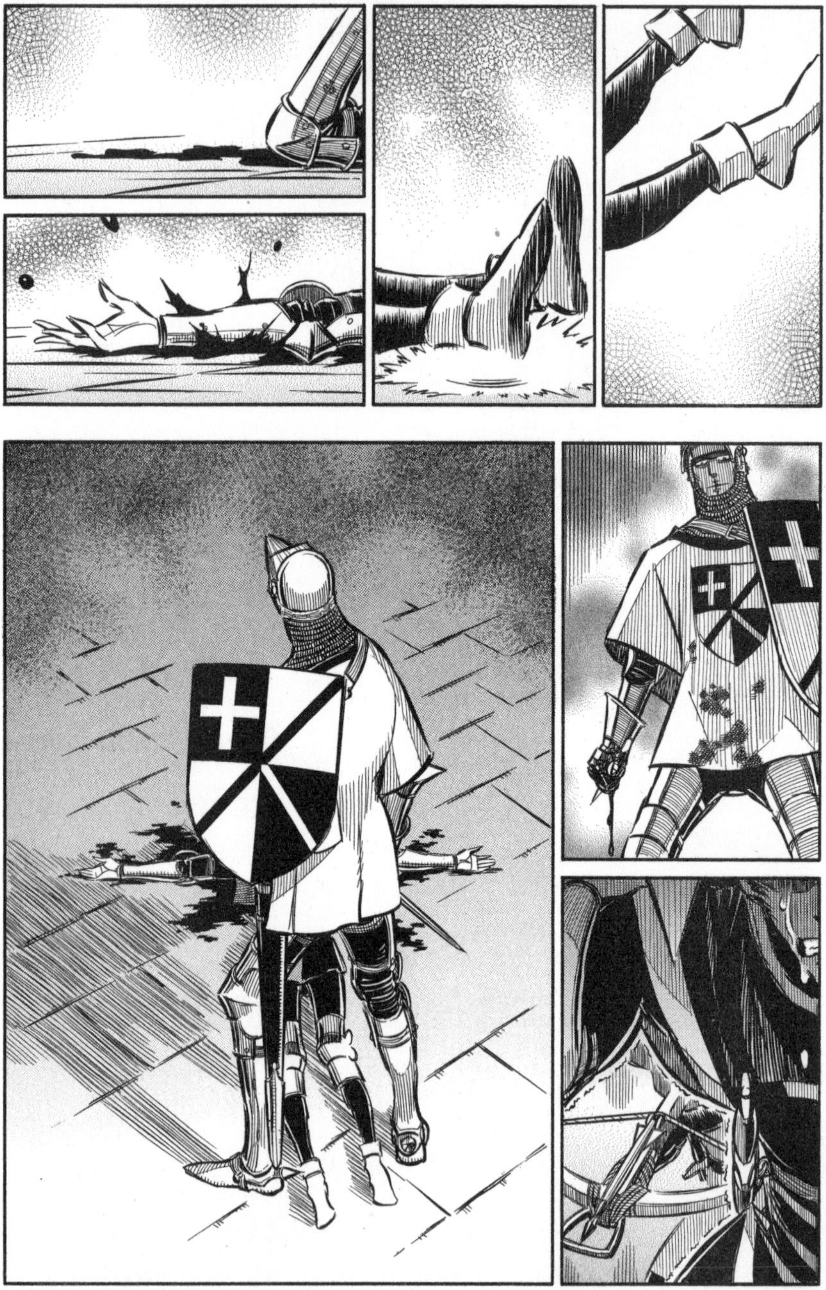

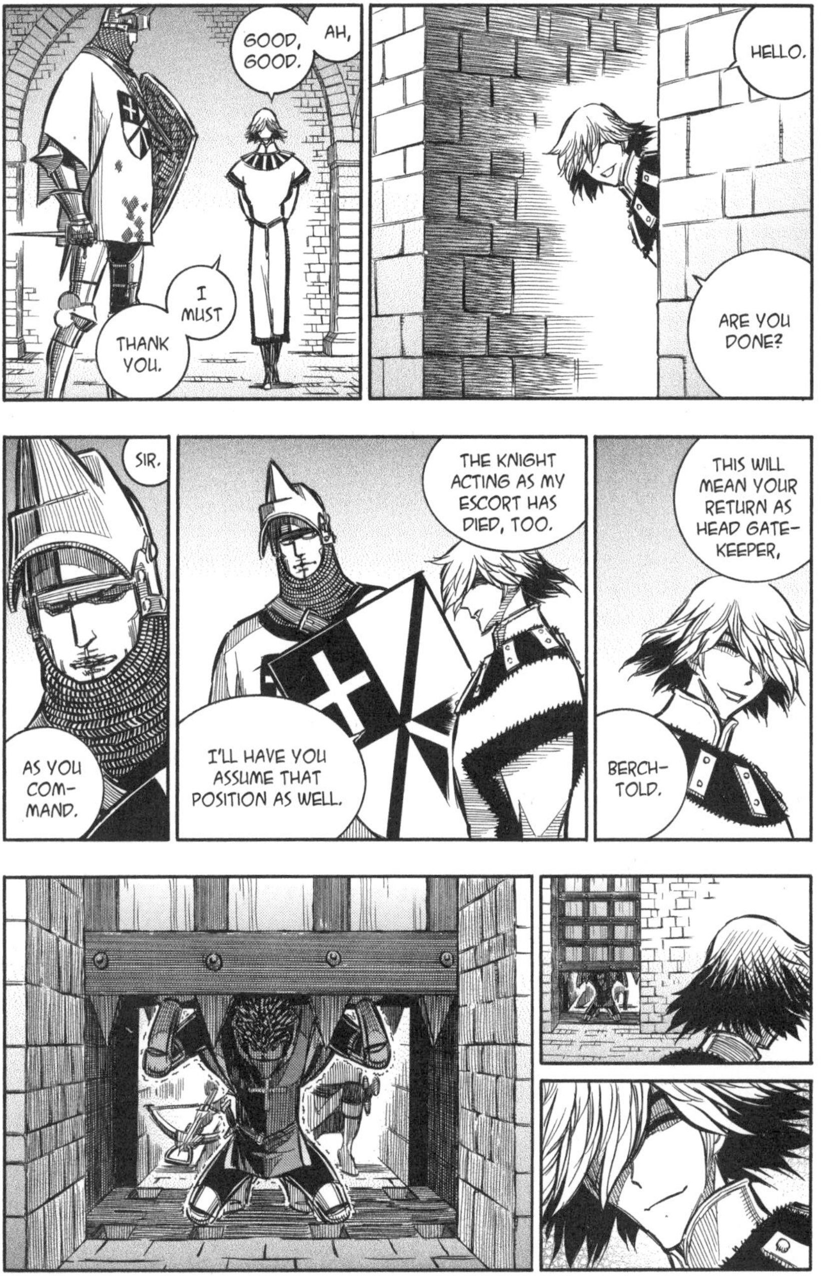
HELLO.
ARE YOU DONE?
AH,
GOOD, GOOD.
I MUST THANK YOU.
THIS WILL MEAN YOUR RETURN AS HEAD GATE-KEEPER,
BERCH-TOLD.
THE KNIGHT ACTING AS MY ESCORT HAS DIED, TOO.
I'LL HAVE YOU ASSUME THAT POSITION AS WELL.
SIR.
AS YOU COM-MAND.

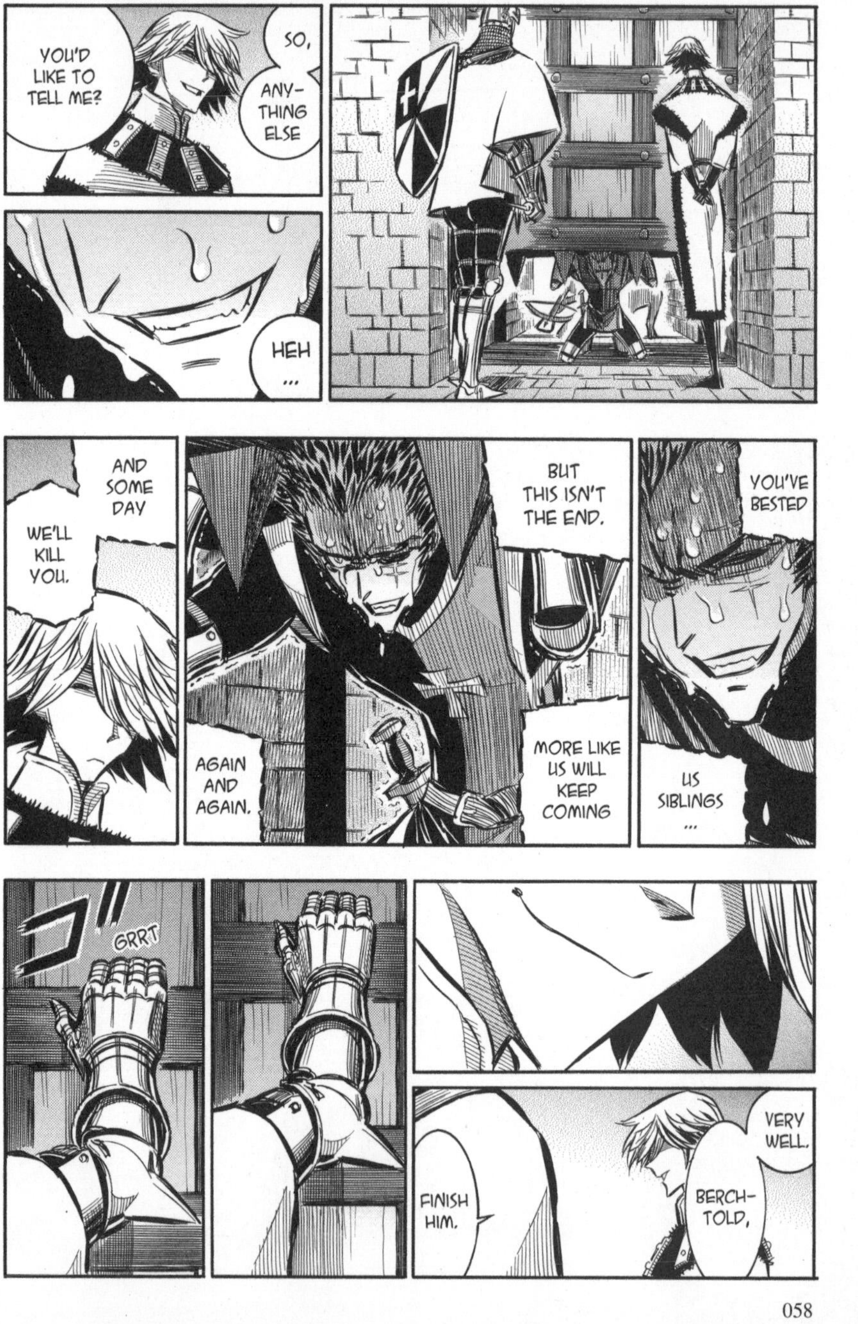
SO, ANY-THING ELSE
YOU'D LIKE TO TELL ME?
HEH ...
YOU'VE BESTED
US SIBLINGS ...
BUT THIS ISN'T THE END.
MORE LIKE US WILL KEEP COMING
AGAIN AND AGAIN.
AND SOME DAY
WE'LL KILL YOU.
VERY WELL.
BERCH-TOLD,
FINISH HIM.
GRRT

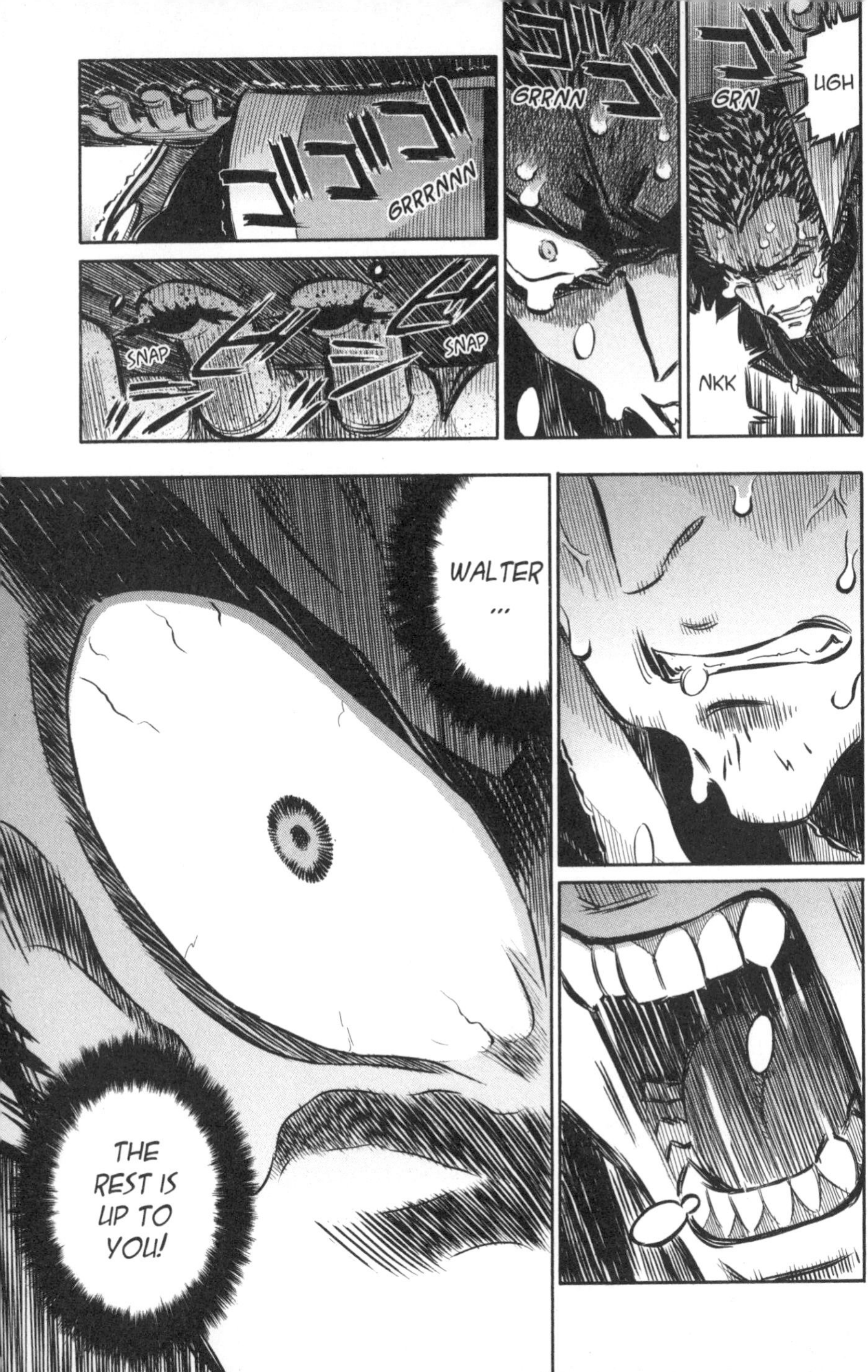
UGH
GRN
NKK
GRRNN
GRRRNNN
SNAP
SNAP
WALTER ...
THE REST IS UP TO YOU!

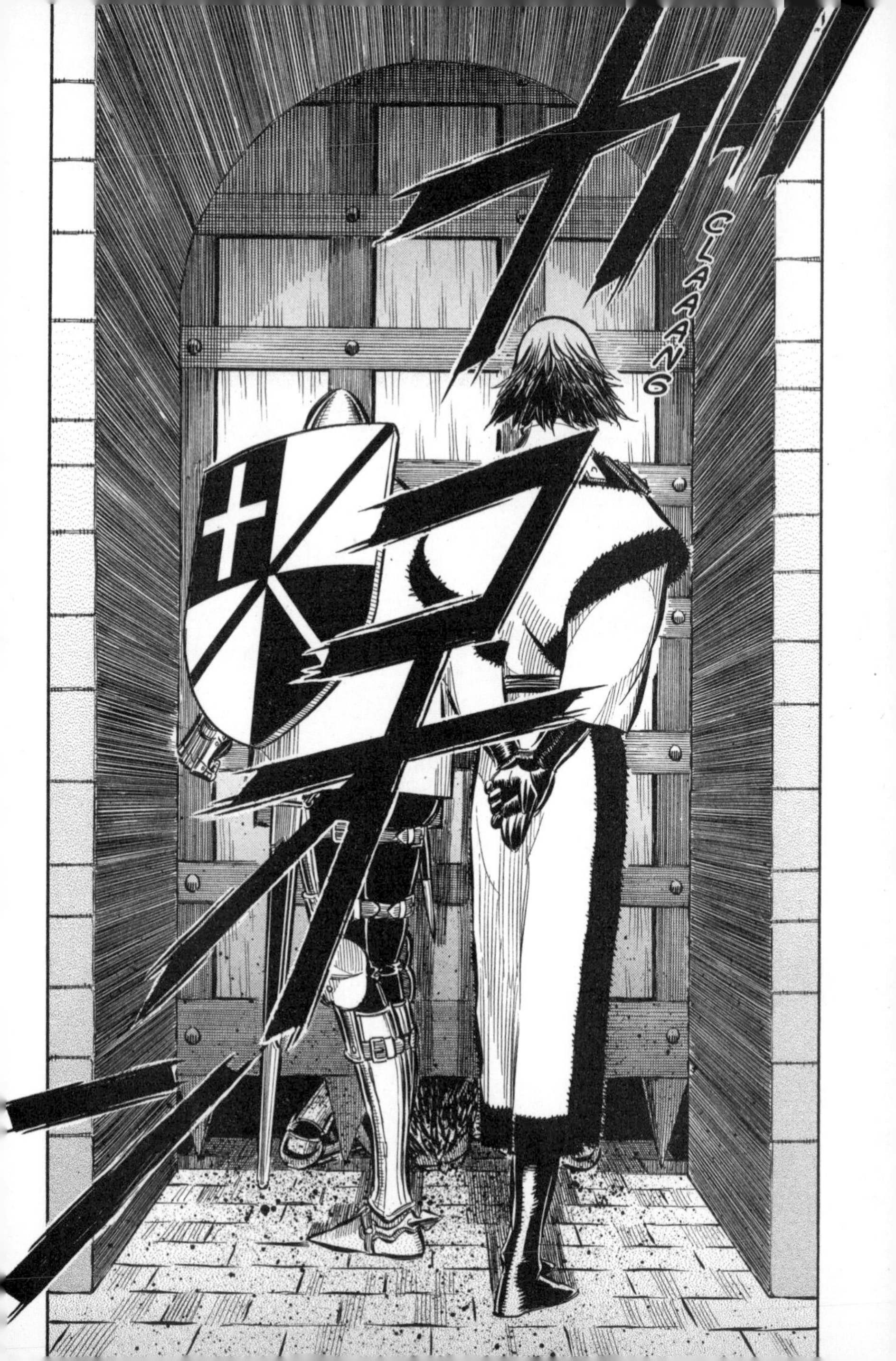
CLAAAANG

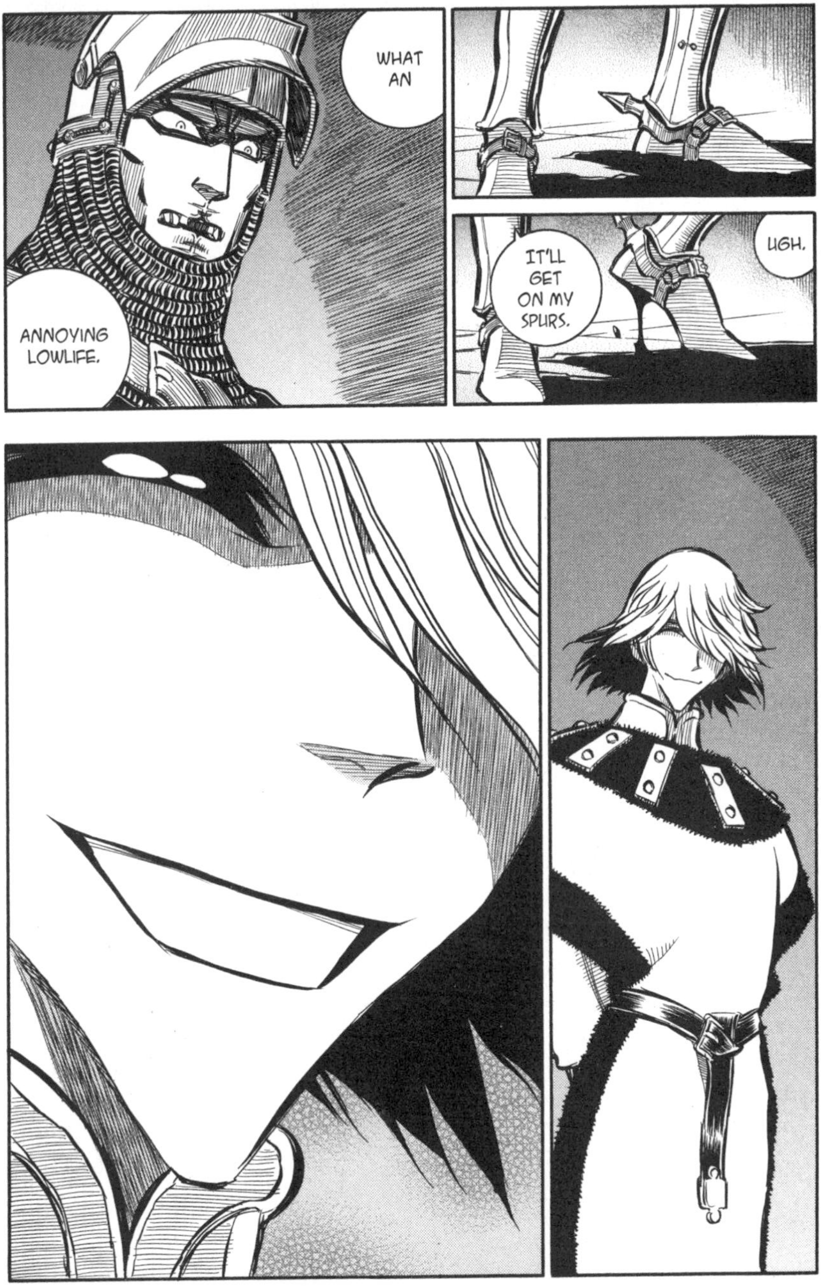
UGH.
IT'LL GET ON MY SPURS.
WHAT AN
ANNOYING LOWLIFE.

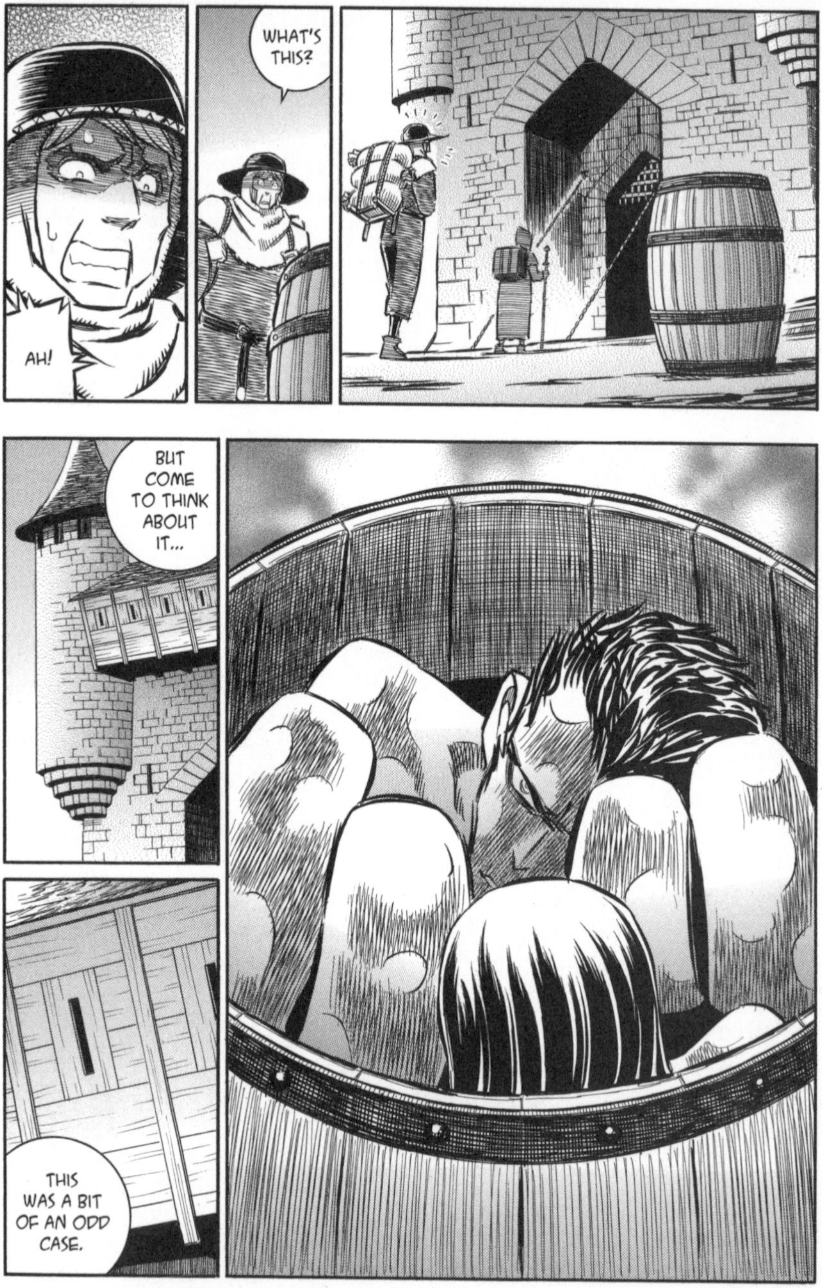
WHAT'S THIS?
AH!
BUT COME TO THINK ABOUT IT...
THIS WAS A BIT OF AN ODD CASE.

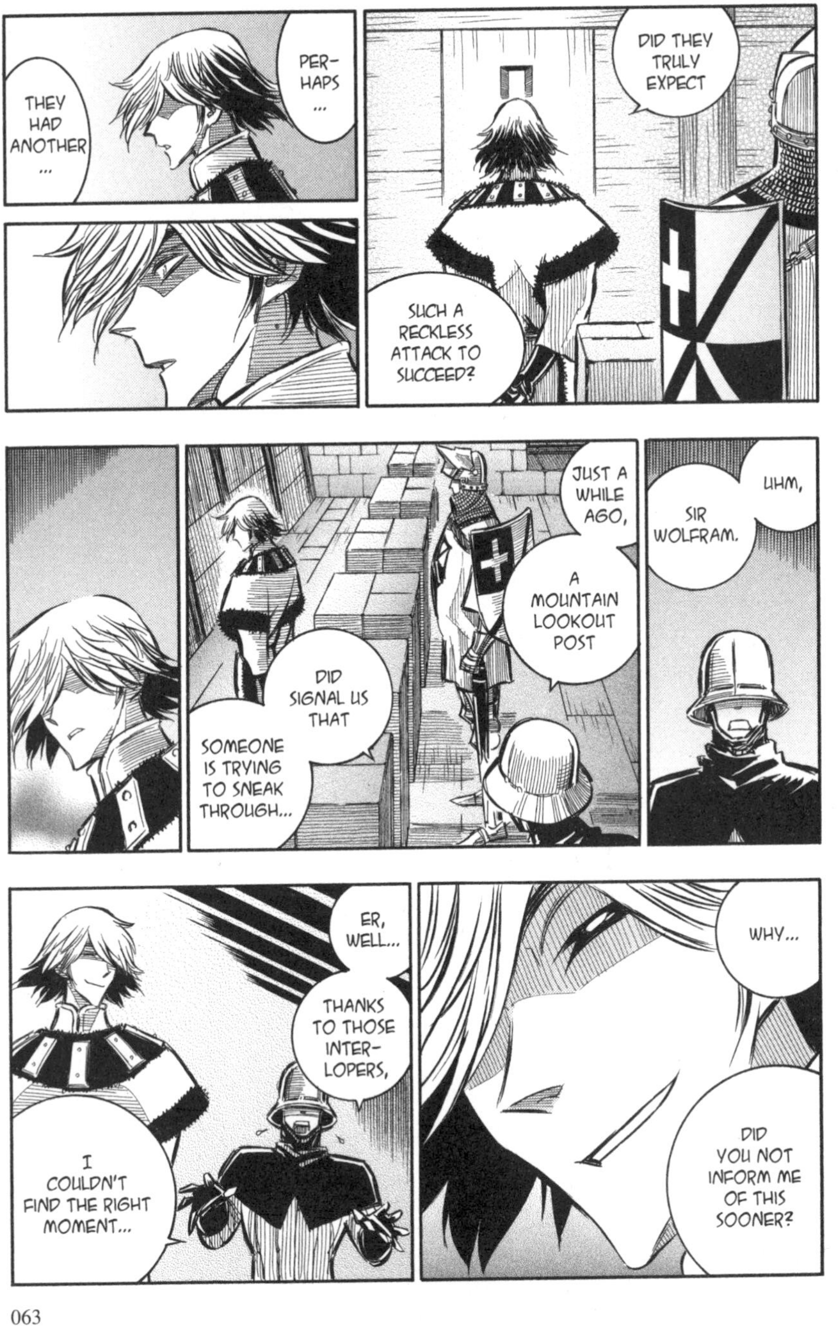
DID THEY TRULY EXPECT
SUCH A RECKLESS ATTACK TO SUCCEED?
PER-HAPS ...
THEY HAD ANOTHER ...
UHM,
SIR WOLFRAM.
JUST A WHILE AGO,
A MOUNTAIN LOOKOUT POST
DID SIGNAL US THAT
SOMEONE IS TRYING TO SNEAK THROUGH...
WHY...
DID YOU NOT INFORM ME OF THIS SOONER?
ER, WELL...
THANKS TO THOSE INTER-LOPERS,
I COULDN'T FIND THE RIGHT MOMENT...

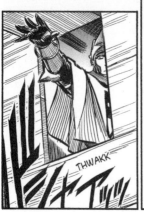

AAA AAA AGH
THWAKK
WE'RE HEADING OUT.
SUSPEND PROCESSING FOR THE DAY.
THEY GOT ME.
I DO HOPE THAT IT'S NOT AN IRREDEEMABLE BLUNDER.

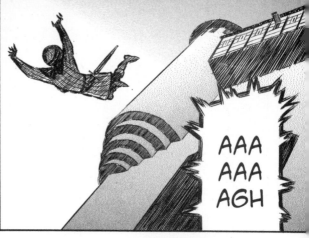

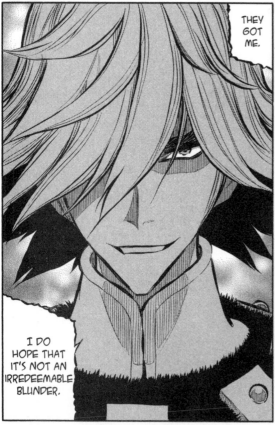

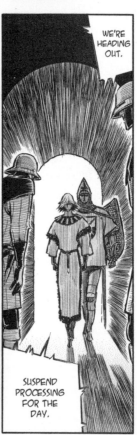

Chapter Eight END

Chapter Nine: Walter and the Comrades in Fate

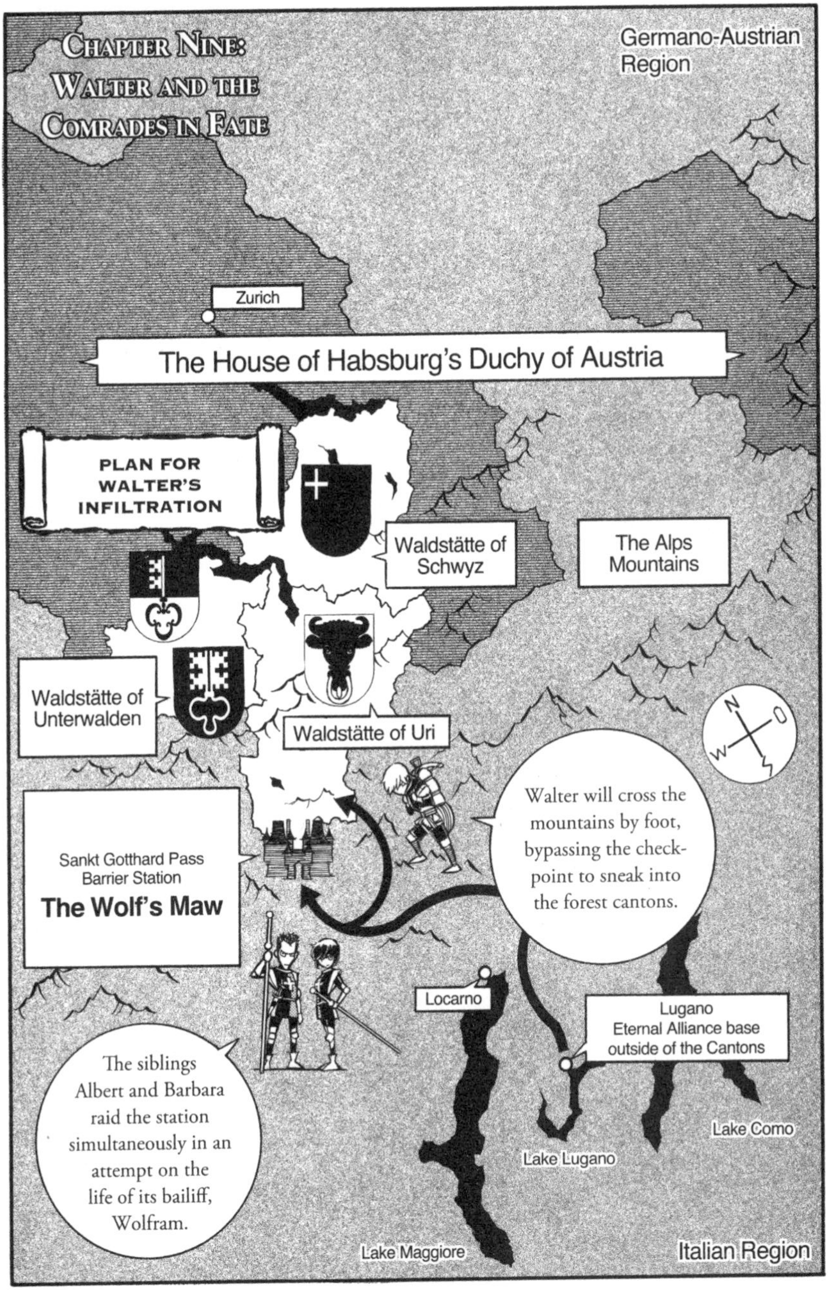
Germano-Austrian Region
Zurich
The House of Habsburg's Duchy of Austria
PLAN FOR WALTER'S INFILTRATION
Waldstätte of Schwyz
The Alps Mountains
Waldstätte of Unterwalden
Waldstätte of Uri
Sankt Gotthard Pass Barrier Station
The Wolf's Maw
Walter will cross the mountains by foot, bypassing the check-point to sneak into the forest cantons.
Locarno
Lugano Eternal Alliance base outside of the Cantons
The siblings Albert and Barbara raid the station simultaneously in an attempt on the life of its bailiff, Wolfram.
Lake Como
Lake Lugano
Lake Maggiore
Italian Region

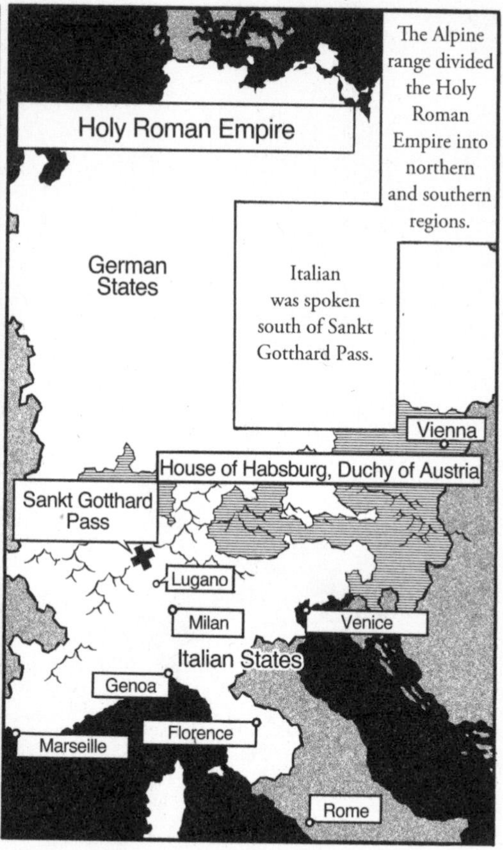
The Alpine range divided the Holy Roman Empire into northern and southern regions.
Holy Roman Empire
Italian was spoken south of Sankt Gotthard Pass.
German States
Vienna
House of Habsburg, Duchy of Austria
Sankt Gotthard Pass
Lugano
Venice
Milan
Italian States
Genoa
Florence
Marseille
Rome

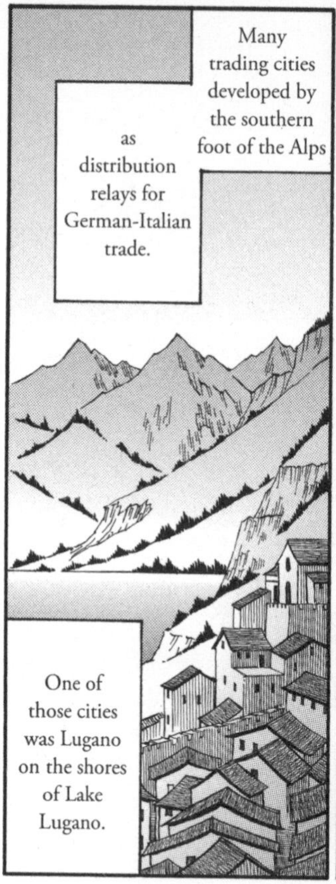
Many trading cities developed by the southern foot of the Alps
as distribution relays for German-Italian trade.
One of those cities was Lugano on the shores of Lake Lugano.

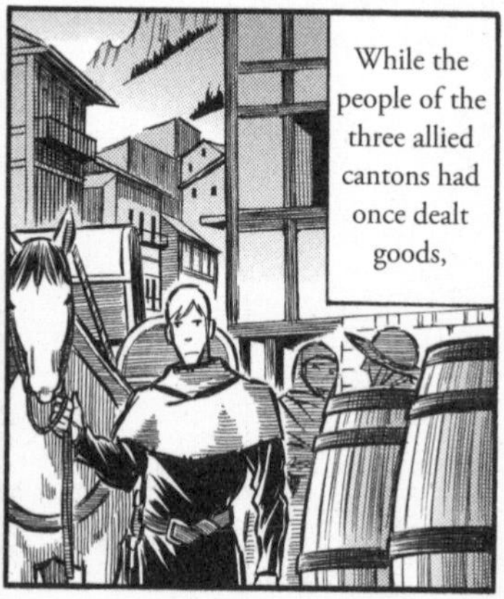
While the people of the three allied cantons had once dealt goods,

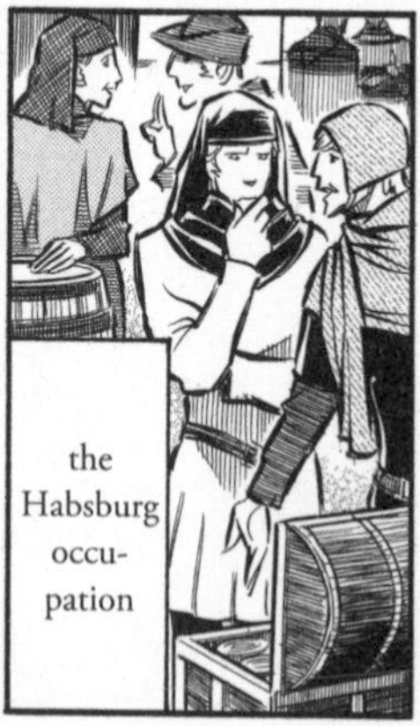
the Habsburg occu-pation

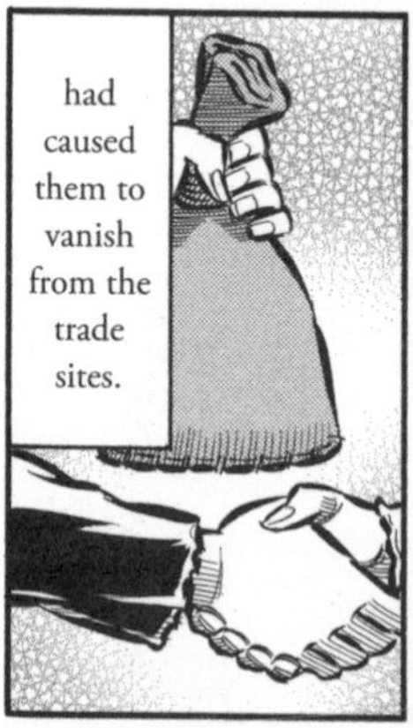
had caused them to vanish from the trade sites.

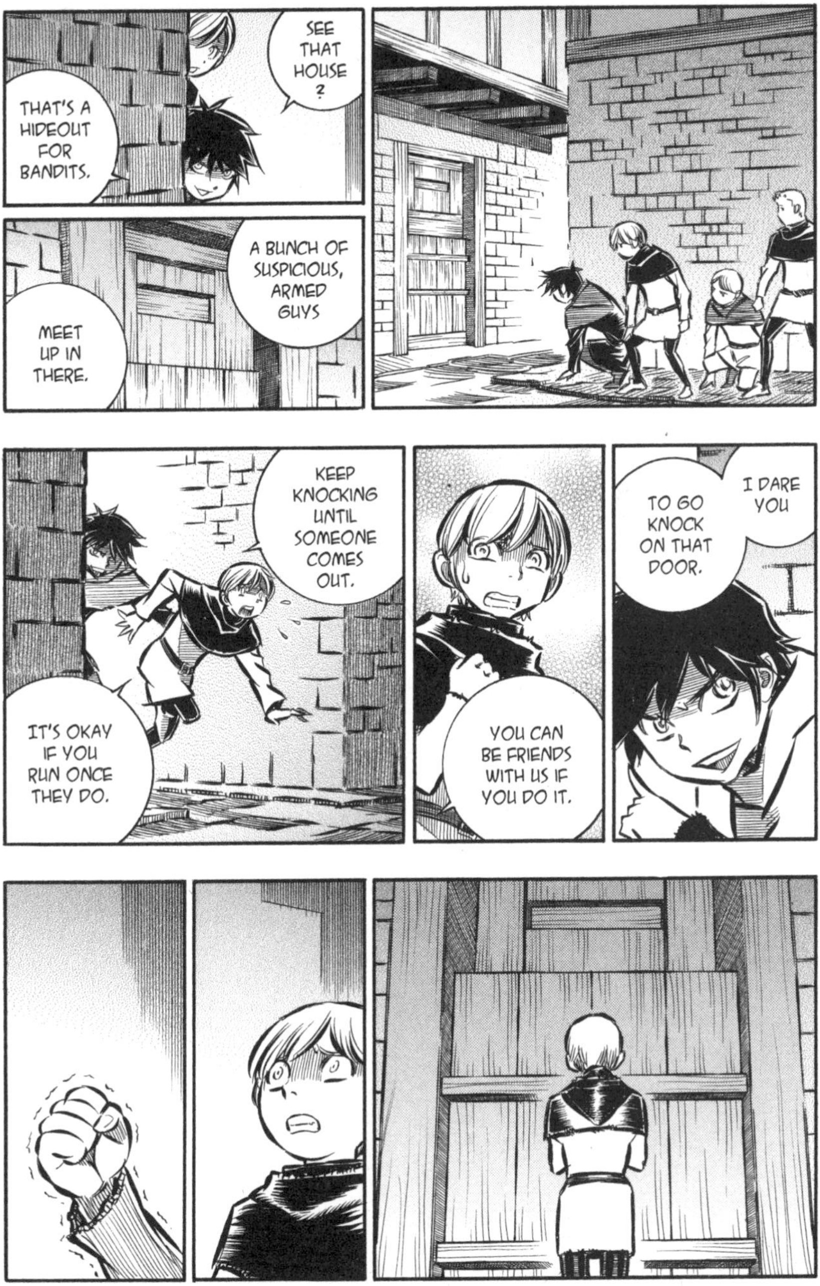
SEE THAT HOUSE?
THAT'S A HIDEOUT FOR BANDITS.
A BUNCH OF SUSPICIOUS, ARMED GUYS
MEET UP IN THERE.
I DARE YOU
TO GO KNOCK ON THAT DOOR.
YOU CAN BE FRIENDS WITH US IF YOU DO IT.
KEEP KNOCKING UNTIL SOMEONE COMES OUT.
IT'S OKAY IF YOU RUN ONCE THEY DO.

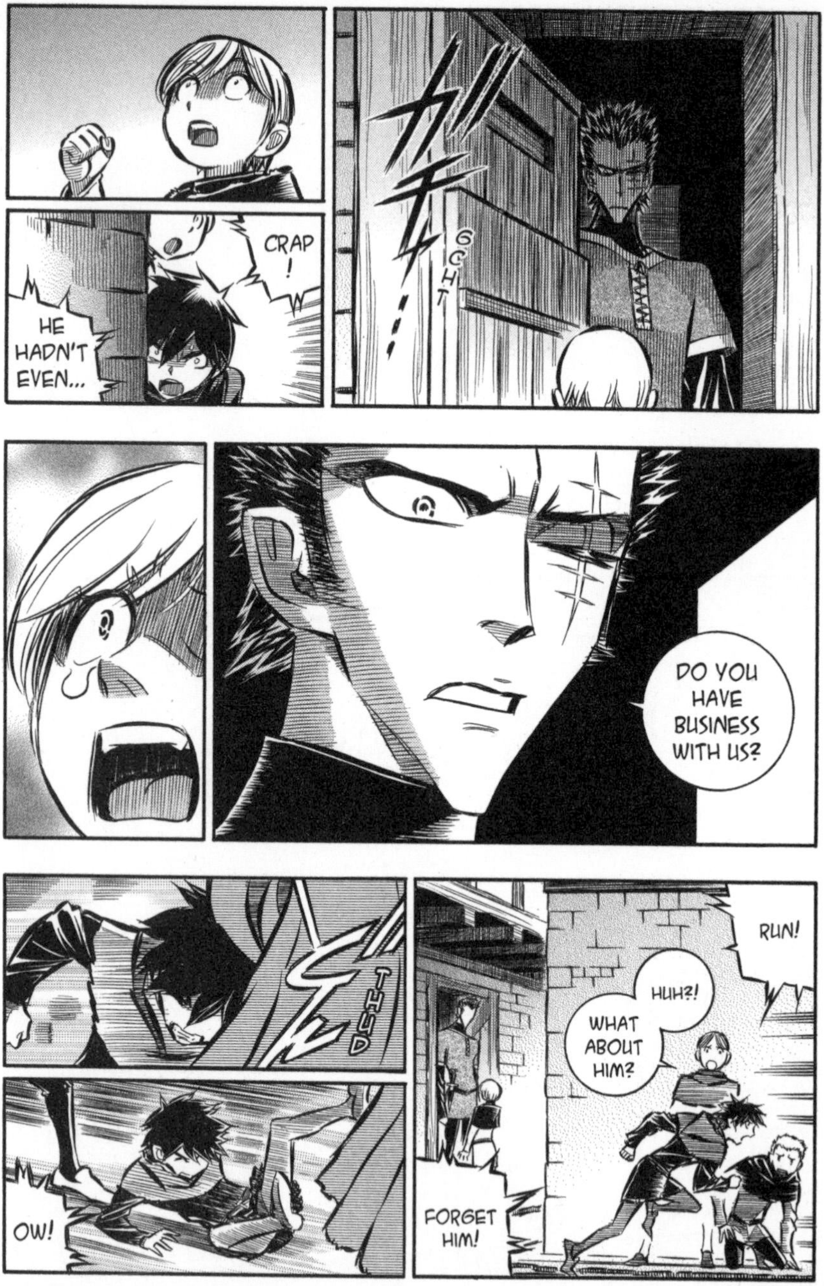
GCHT
CRAP!
HE HADN'T EVEN...
DO YOU HAVE BUSINESS WITH US?
RUN!
HUH?!
WHAT ABOUT HIM?
FORGET HIM!
THUD
OW!

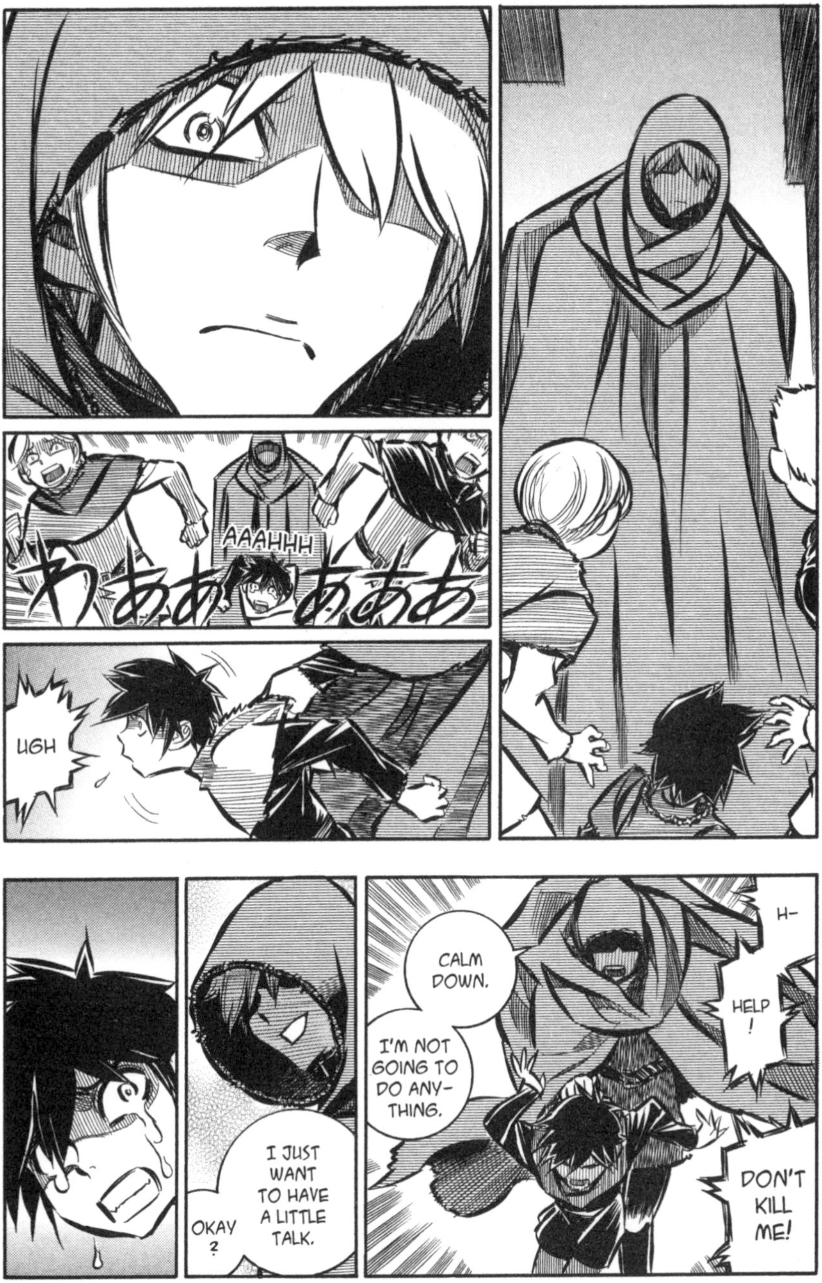
わああ
AAAHHH
あああ
UGH
H-
HELP!
CALM DOWN.
I'M NOT GOING TO DO ANYTHING.
DON'T KILL ME!
I JUST WANT TO HAVE A LITTLE TALK.
OKAY?

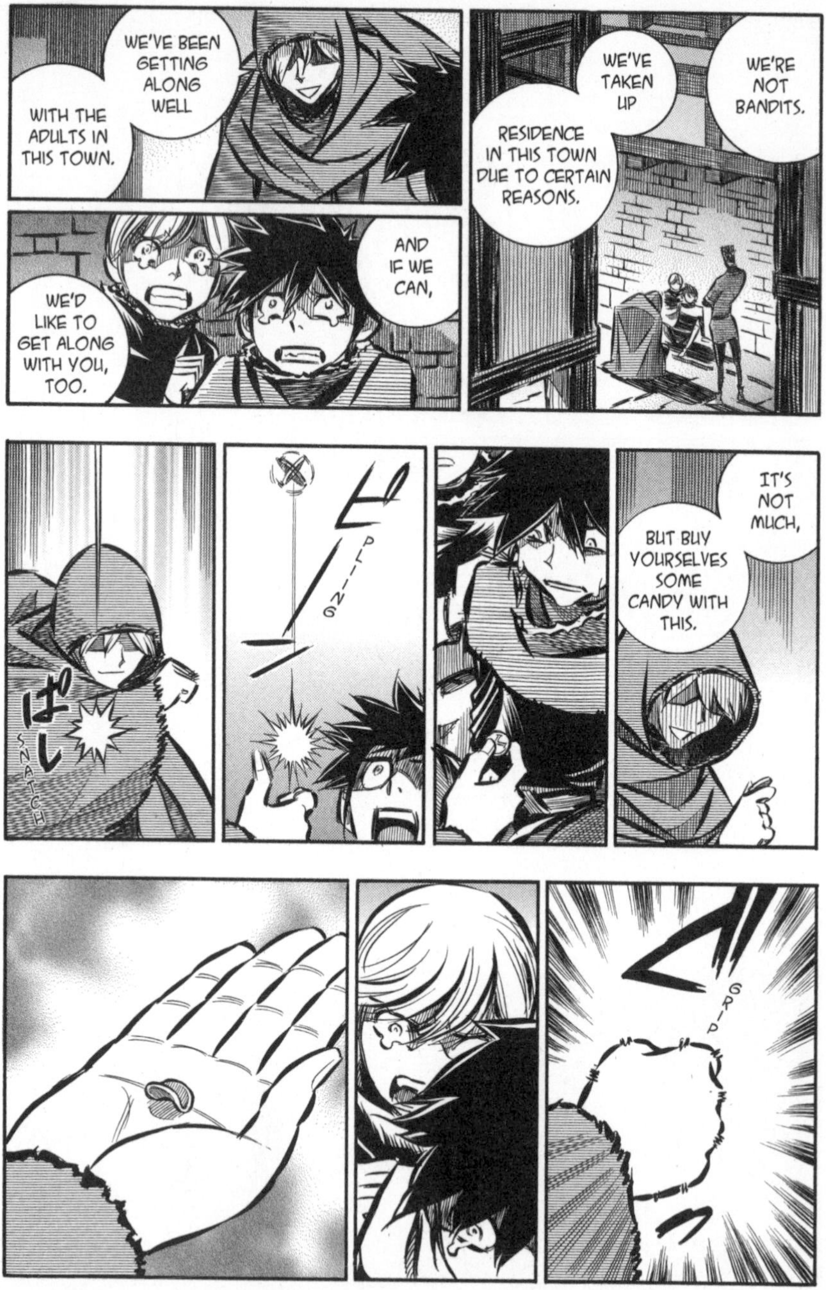
WE'RE NOT BANDITS.
WE'VE TAKEN UP
RESIDENCE IN THIS TOWN DUE TO CERTAIN REASONS.
WE'VE BEEN GETTING ALONG WELL
WITH THE ADULTS IN THIS TOWN.
AND IF WE CAN,
WE'D LIKE TO GET ALONG WITH YOU, TOO.
IT'S NOT MUCH,
BUT BUY YOURSELVES SOME CANDY WITH THIS.
PLING
ぱし
SNATCH
GRIP

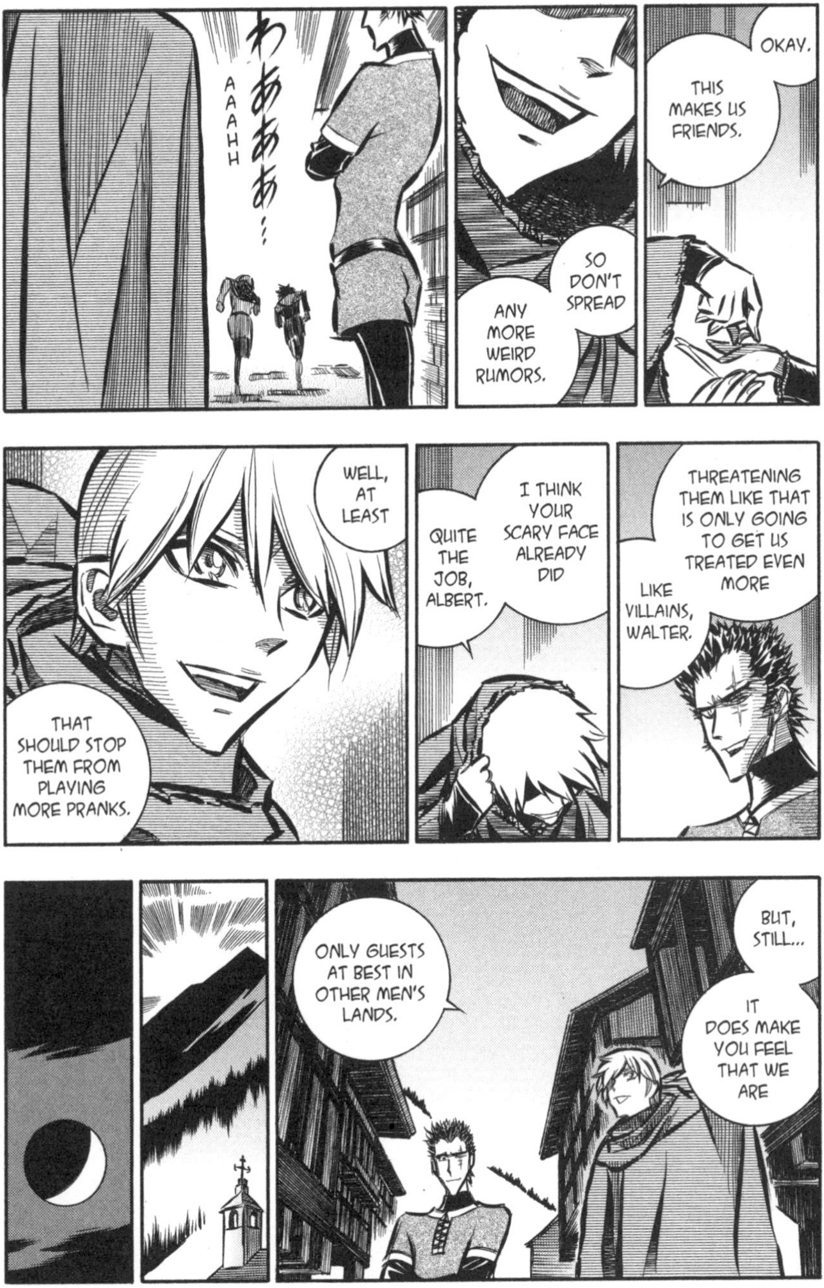

OKAY.
THIS MAKES US FRIENDS.
SO DON'T SPREAD
ANY MORE WEIRD RUMORS.
わあああ!!
AAAAHH
THREATENING THEM LIKE THAT IS ONLY GOING TO GET US TREATED EVEN MORE
LIKE VILLAINS, WALTER.
I THINK YOUR SCARY FACE ALREADY DID
QUITE THE JOB, ALBERT.
WELL, AT LEAST
THAT SHOULD STOP THEM FROM PLAYING MORE PRANKS.
BUT, STILL...
IT DOES MAKE YOU FEEL THAT WE ARE
ONLY GUESTS AT BEST IN OTHER MEN'S LANDS.

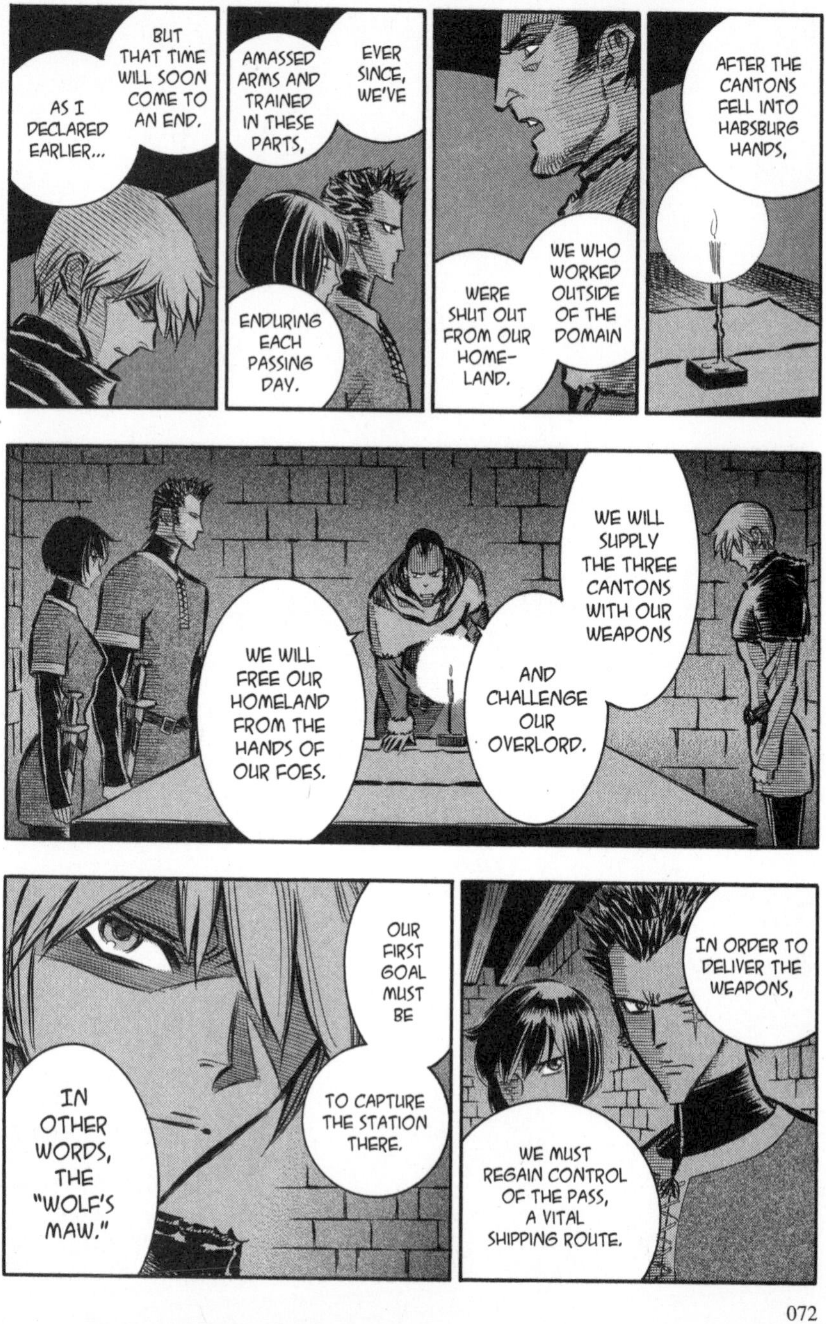
AFTER THE CANTONS FELL INTO HABSBURG HANDS,
WE WHO WORKED OUTSIDE OF THE DOMAIN
WERE SHUT OUT FROM OUR HOME-LAND.
EVER SINCE, WE'VE
AMASSED ARMS AND TRAINED IN THESE PARTS,
ENDURING EACH PASSING DAY.
BUT THAT TIME WILL SOON COME TO AN END.
AS I DECLARED EARLIER...
WE WILL SUPPLY THE THREE CANTONS WITH OUR WEAPONS
AND CHALLENGE OUR OVERLORD.
WE WILL FREE OUR HOMELAND FROM THE HANDS OF OUR FOES.
IN ORDER TO DELIVER THE WEAPONS,
WE MUST REGAIN CONTROL OF THE PASS, A VITAL SHIPPING ROUTE.
OUR FIRST GOAL MUST BE
TO CAPTURE THE STATION THERE.
IN OTHER WORDS, THE "WOLF'S MAW."

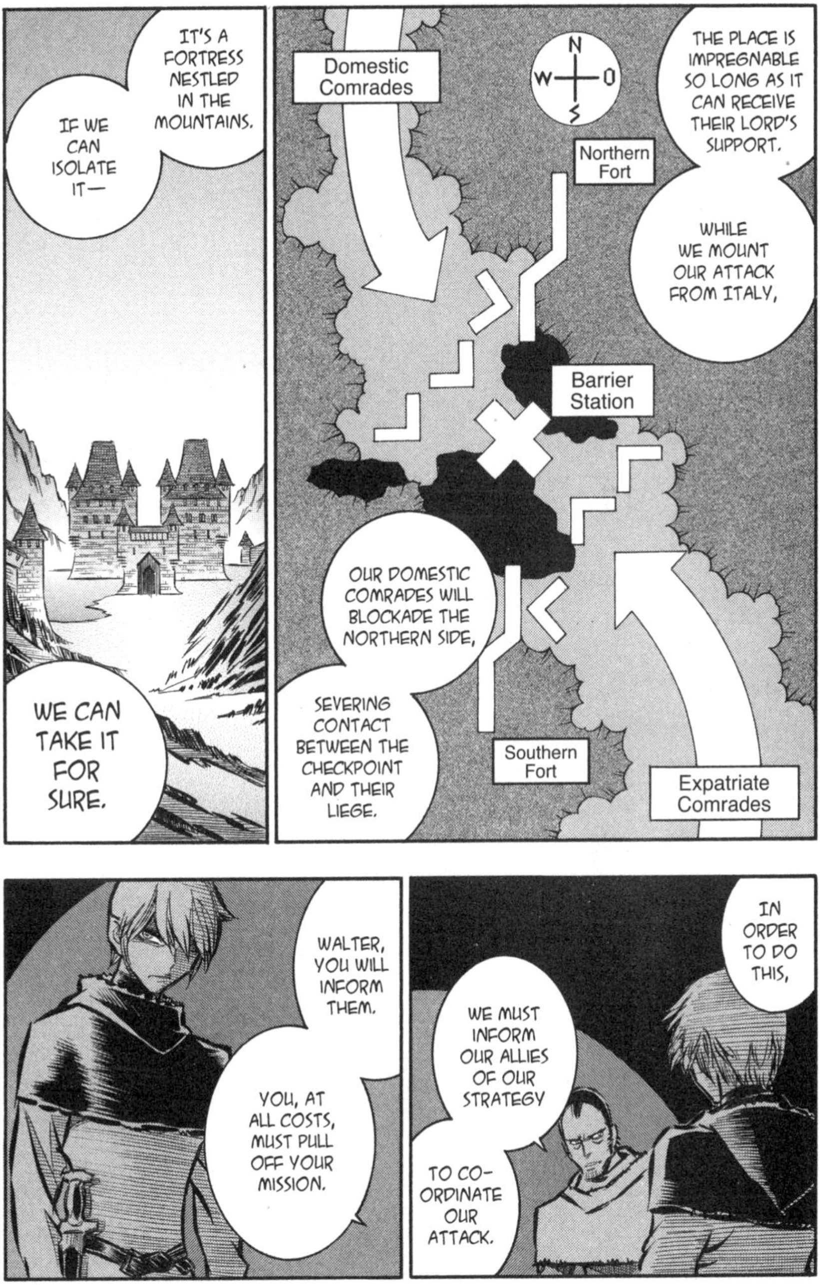
THE PLACE IS IMPREGNABLE SO LONG AS IT CAN RECEIVE THEIR LORD'S SUPPORT.
WHILE WE MOUNT OUR ATTACK FROM ITALY,
N
W
O
S
Domestic Comrades
Northern Fort
Barrier Station
OUR DOMESTIC COMRADES WILL BLOCKADE THE NORTHERN SIDE,
SEVERING CONTACT BETWEEN THE CHECKPOINT AND THEIR LIEGE.
Southern Fort
Expatriate Comrades
IT'S A FORTRESS NESTLED IN THE MOUNTAINS.
IF WE CAN ISOLATE IT—
WE CAN TAKE IT FOR SURE.
IN ORDER TO DO THIS,
WE MUST INFORM OUR ALLIES OF OUR STRATEGY
TO CO-ORDINATE OUR ATTACK.
WALTER, YOU WILL INFORM THEM.
YOU, AT ALL COSTS, MUST PULL OFF YOUR MISSION.

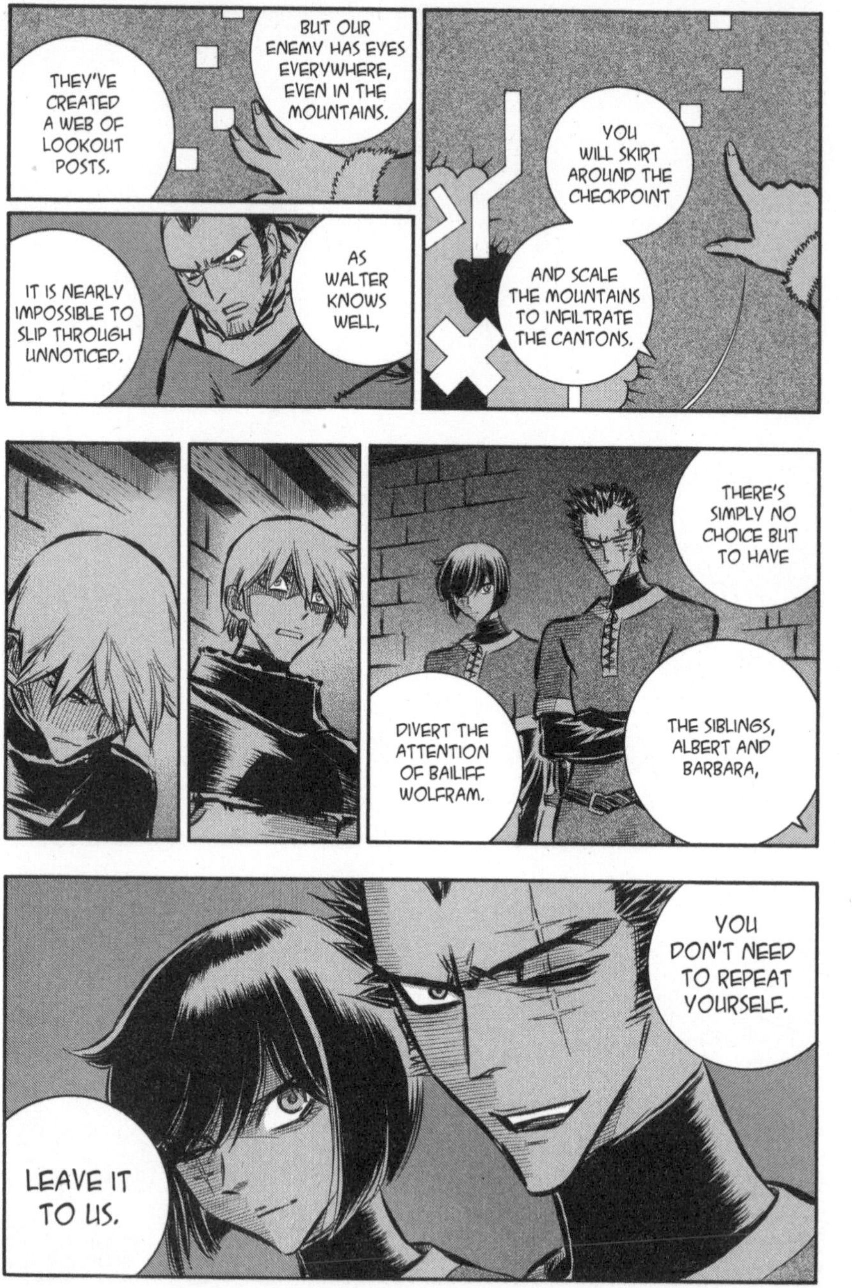
YOU WILL SKIRT AROUND THE CHECKPOINT
AND SCALE THE MOUNTAINS TO INFILTRATE THE CANTONS.
BUT OUR ENEMY HAS EYES EVERYWHERE, EVEN IN THE MOUNTAINS.
THEY'VE CREATED A WEB OF LOOKOUT POSTS.
AS WALTER KNOWS WELL,
IT IS NEARLY IMPOSSIBLE TO SLIP THROUGH UNNOTICED.
THERE'S SIMPLY NO CHOICE BUT TO HAVE
THE SIBLINGS, ALBERT AND BARBARA,
DIVERT THE ATTENTION OF BAILIFF WOLFRAM.
YOU DON'T NEED TO REPEAT YOURSELF.
LEAVE IT TO US.

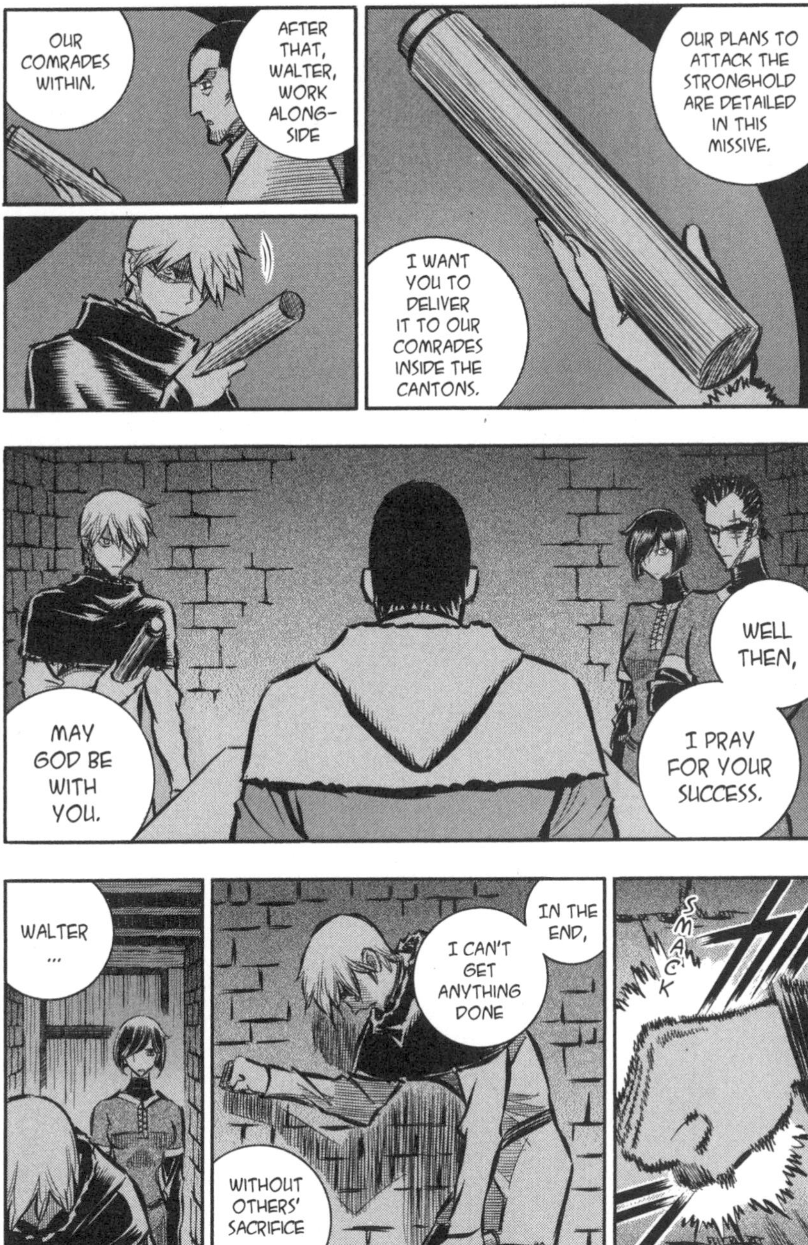
OUR PLANS TO ATTACK THE STRONGHOLD ARE DETAILED IN THIS MISSIVE.
I WANT YOU TO DELIVER IT TO OUR COMRADES INSIDE THE CANTONS.
AFTER THAT, WALTER, WORK ALONG-SIDE
OUR COMRADES WITHIN.
WELL THEN,
I PRAY FOR YOUR SUCCESS.
MAY GOD BE WITH YOU.
SMACK
IN THE END,
I CAN'T GET ANYTHING DONE
WITHOUT OTHERS' SACRIFICE ...
WALTER ...

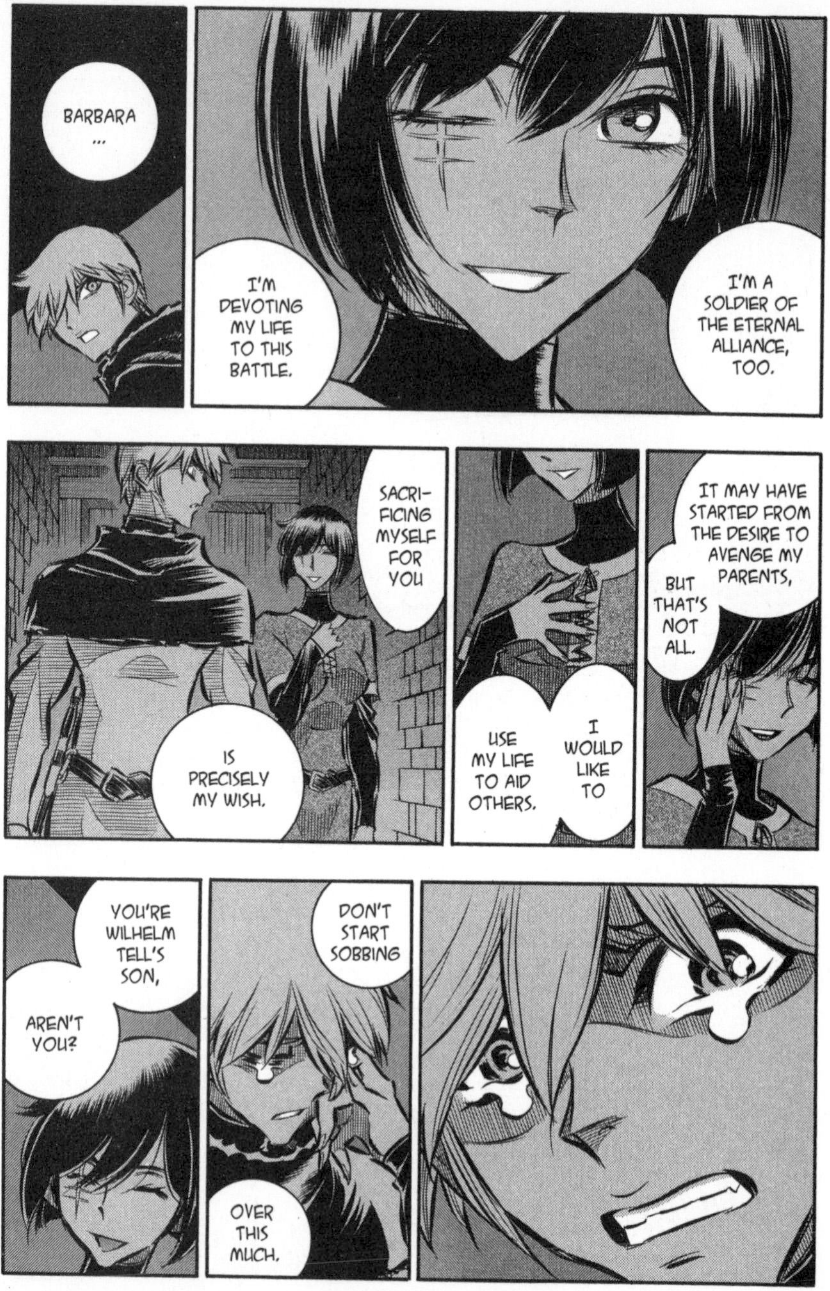
I'M A SOLDIER OF THE ETERNAL ALLIANCE, TOO.
I'M DEVOTING MY LIFE TO THIS BATTLE.
BARBARA ...
IT MAY HAVE STARTED FROM THE DESIRE TO AVENGE MY PARENTS,
BUT THAT'S NOT ALL.
I WOULD LIKE TO
USE MY LIFE TO AID OTHERS.
SACRI-FICING MYSELF FOR YOU
IS PRECISELY MY WISH.
DON'T START SOBBING
OVER THIS MUCH.
YOU'RE WILHELM TELL'S SON,
AREN'T YOU?

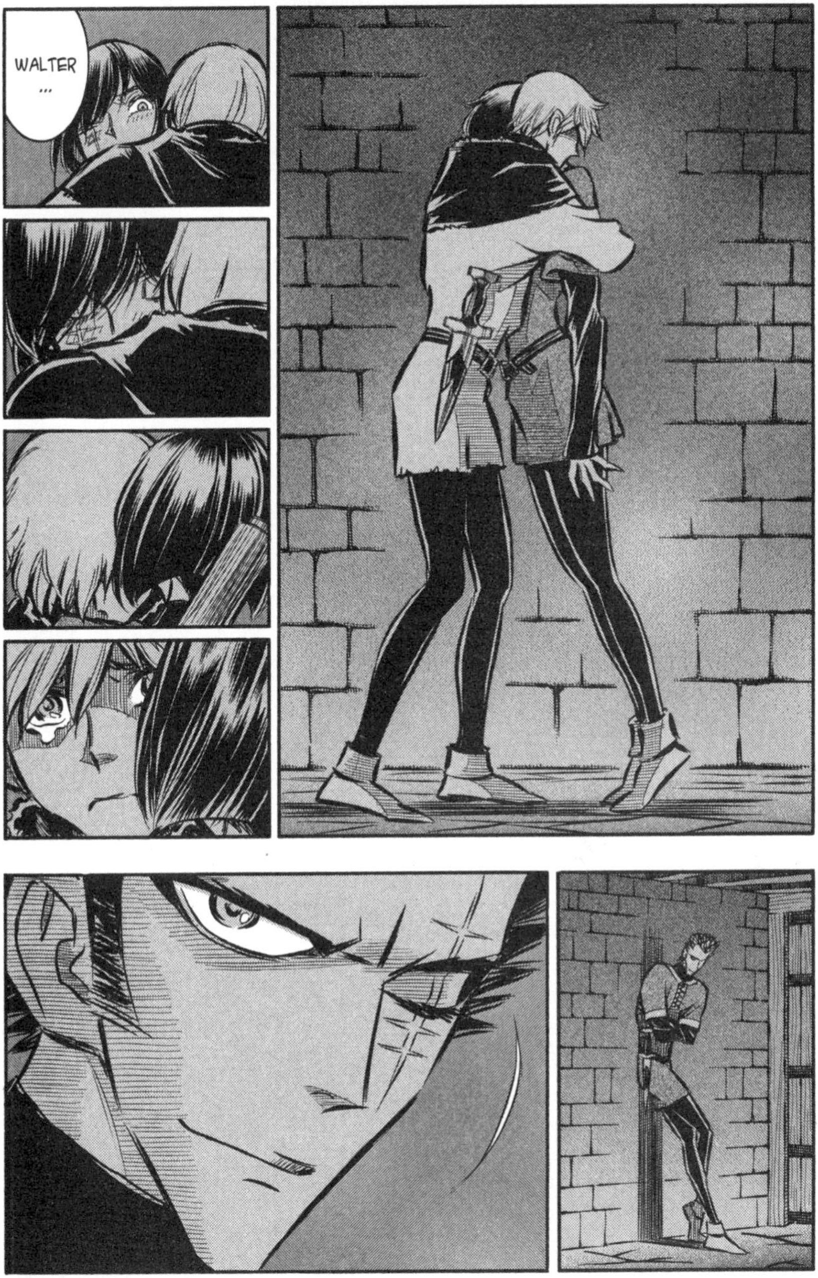
WALTER ...

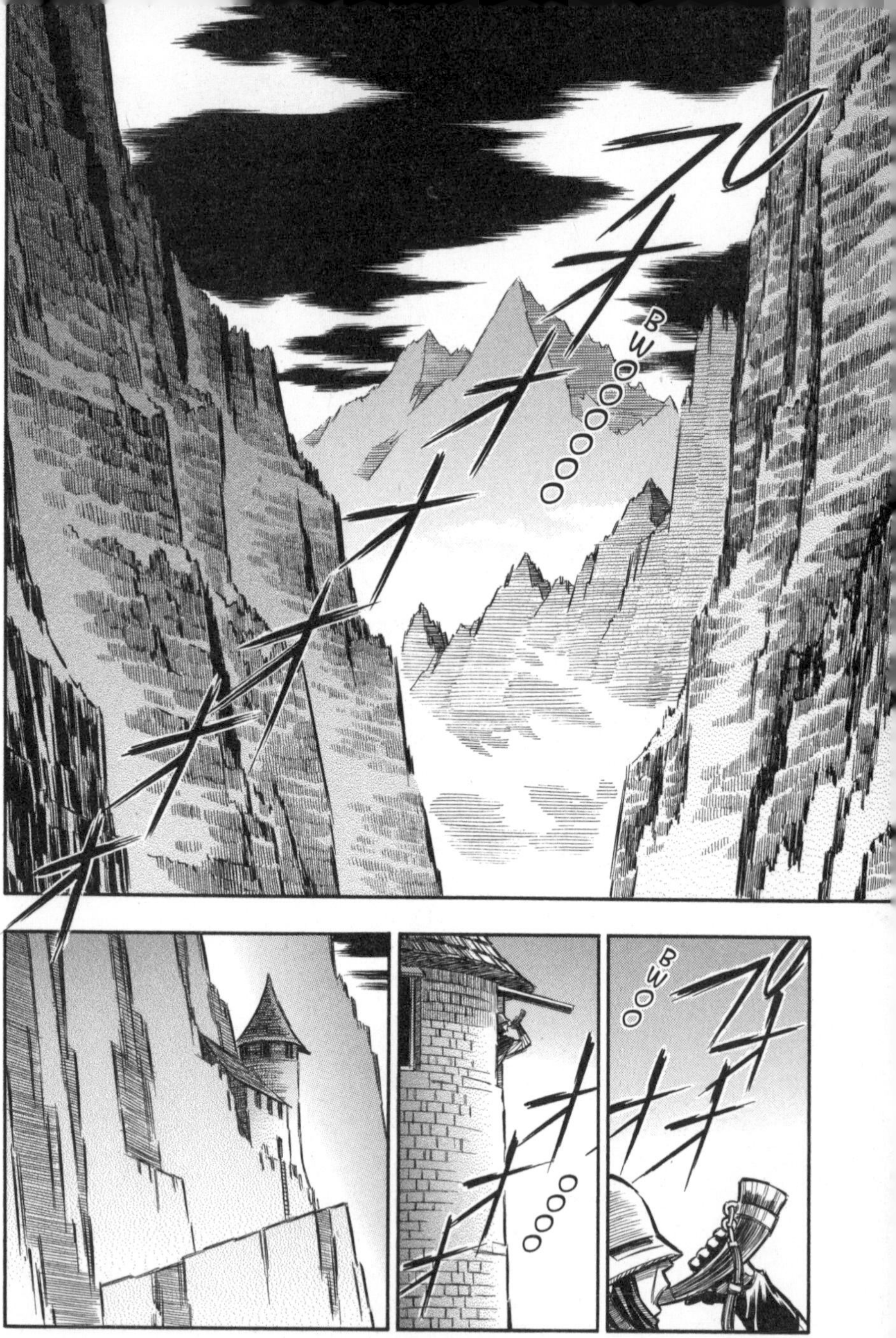

BWOOOOOOOO
BWOO
OOOO

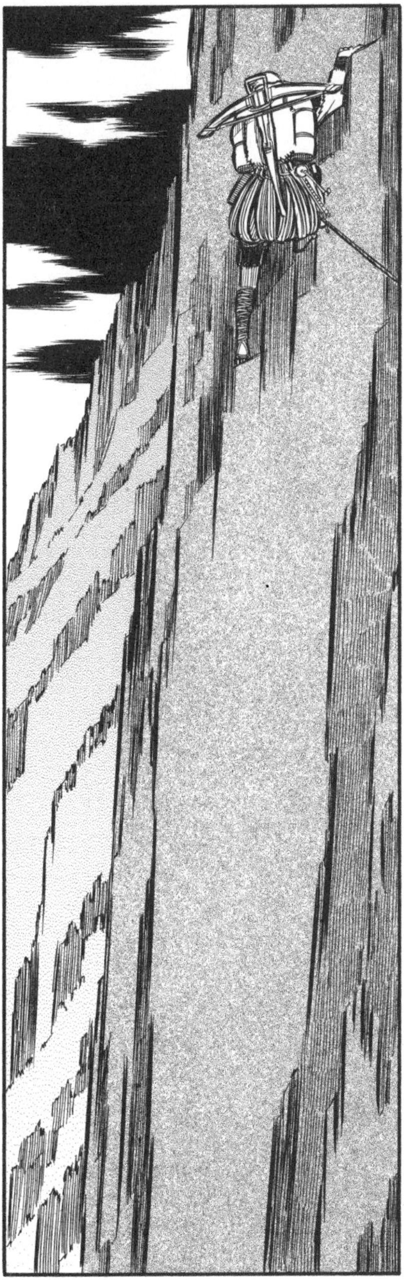
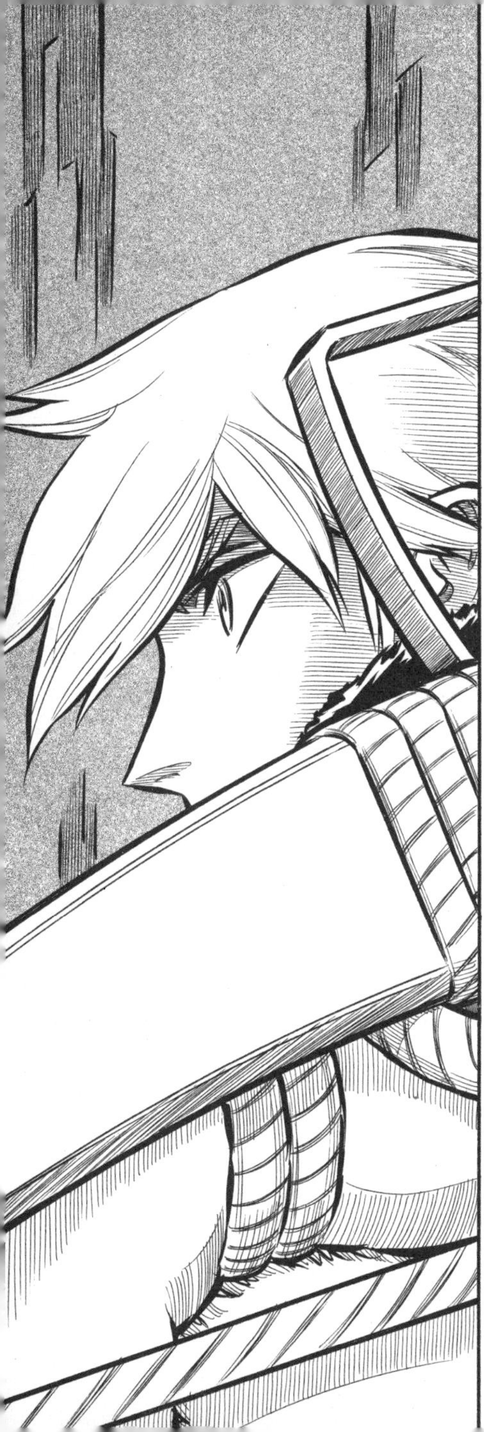

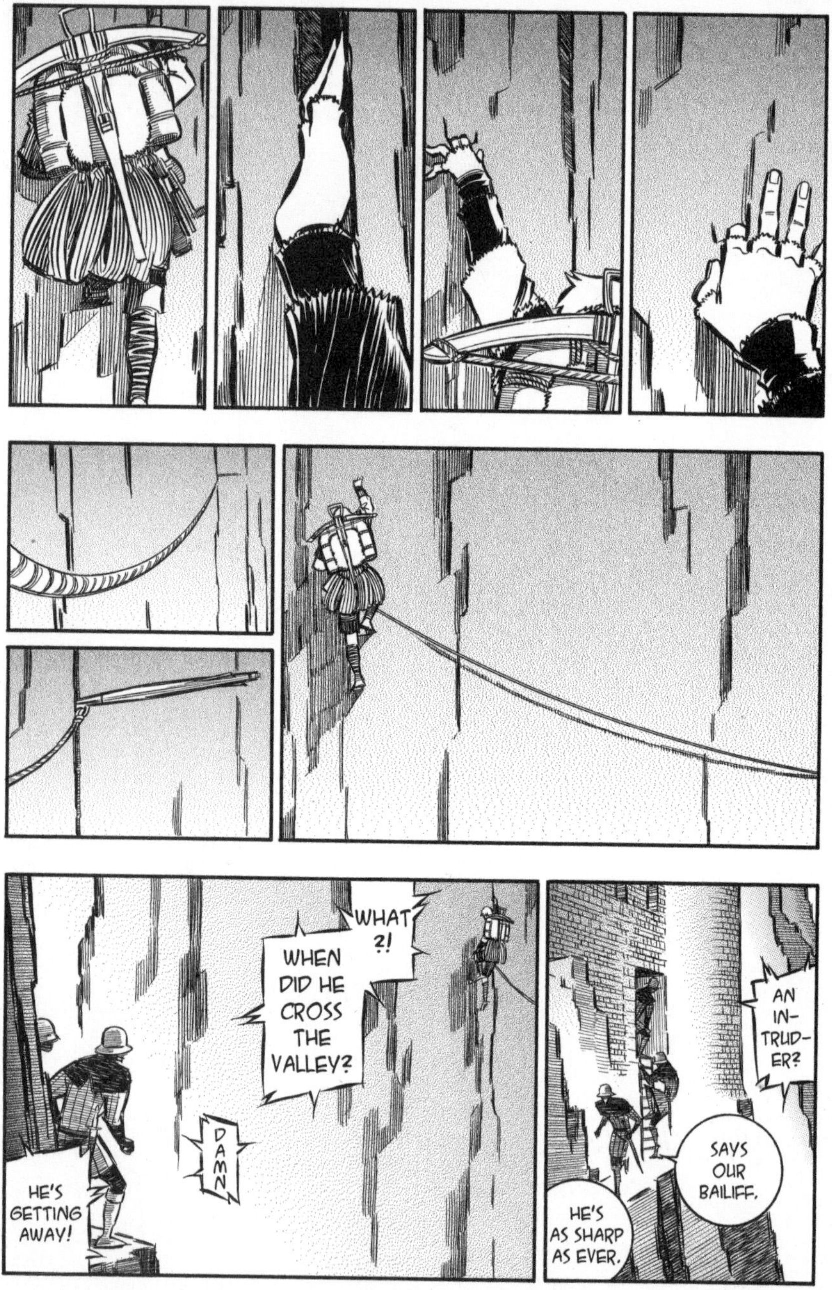
AN INTRUDER?
SAYS OUR BAILIFF.
HE'S AS SHARP AS EVER.
WHAT?!
WHEN DID HE CROSS THE VALLEY?
DAMN
HE'S GETTING AWAY!

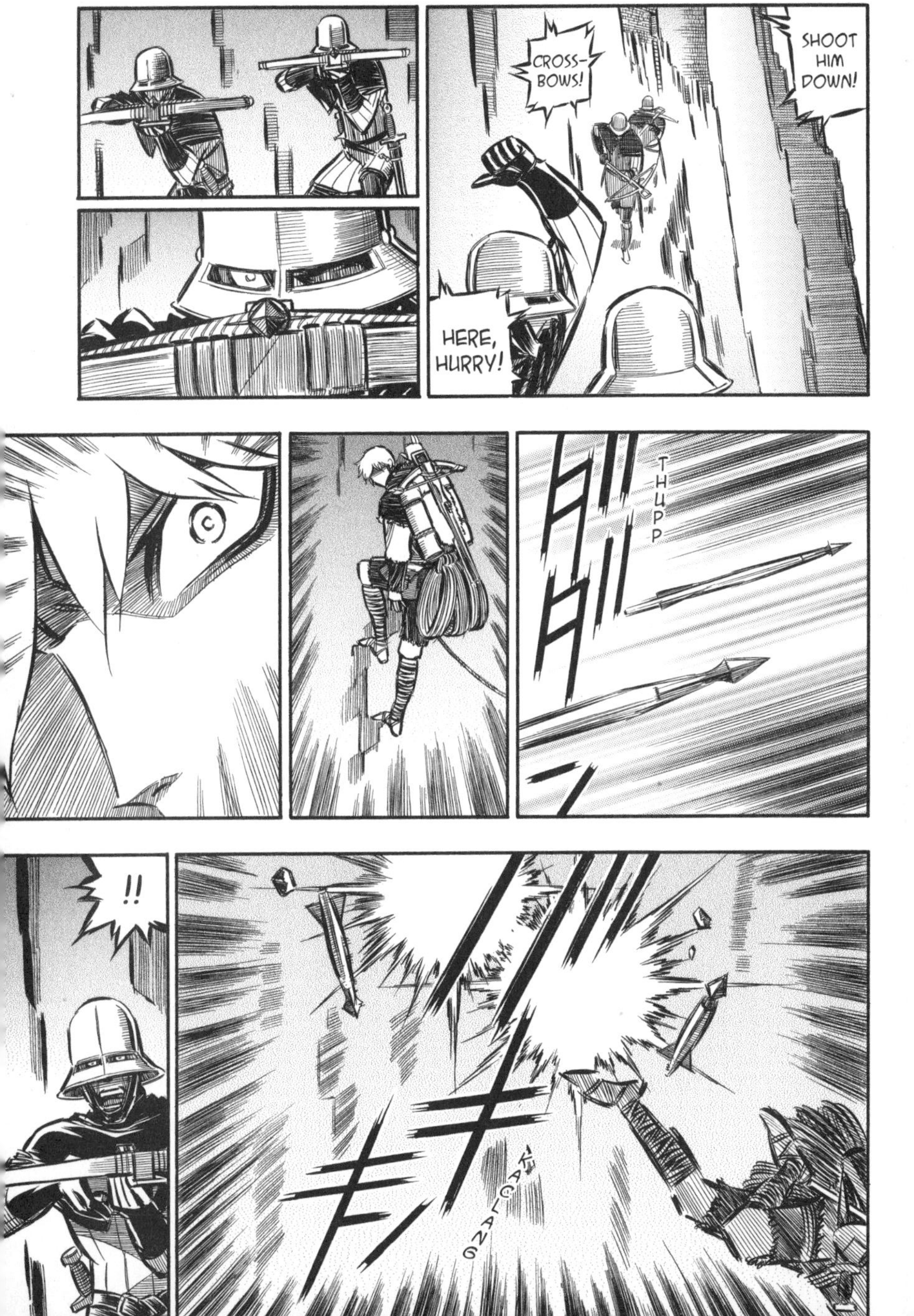
SHOOT HIM DOWN!
CROSS-BOWS!
HERE, HURRY!
THUPP
KACLANG
!!

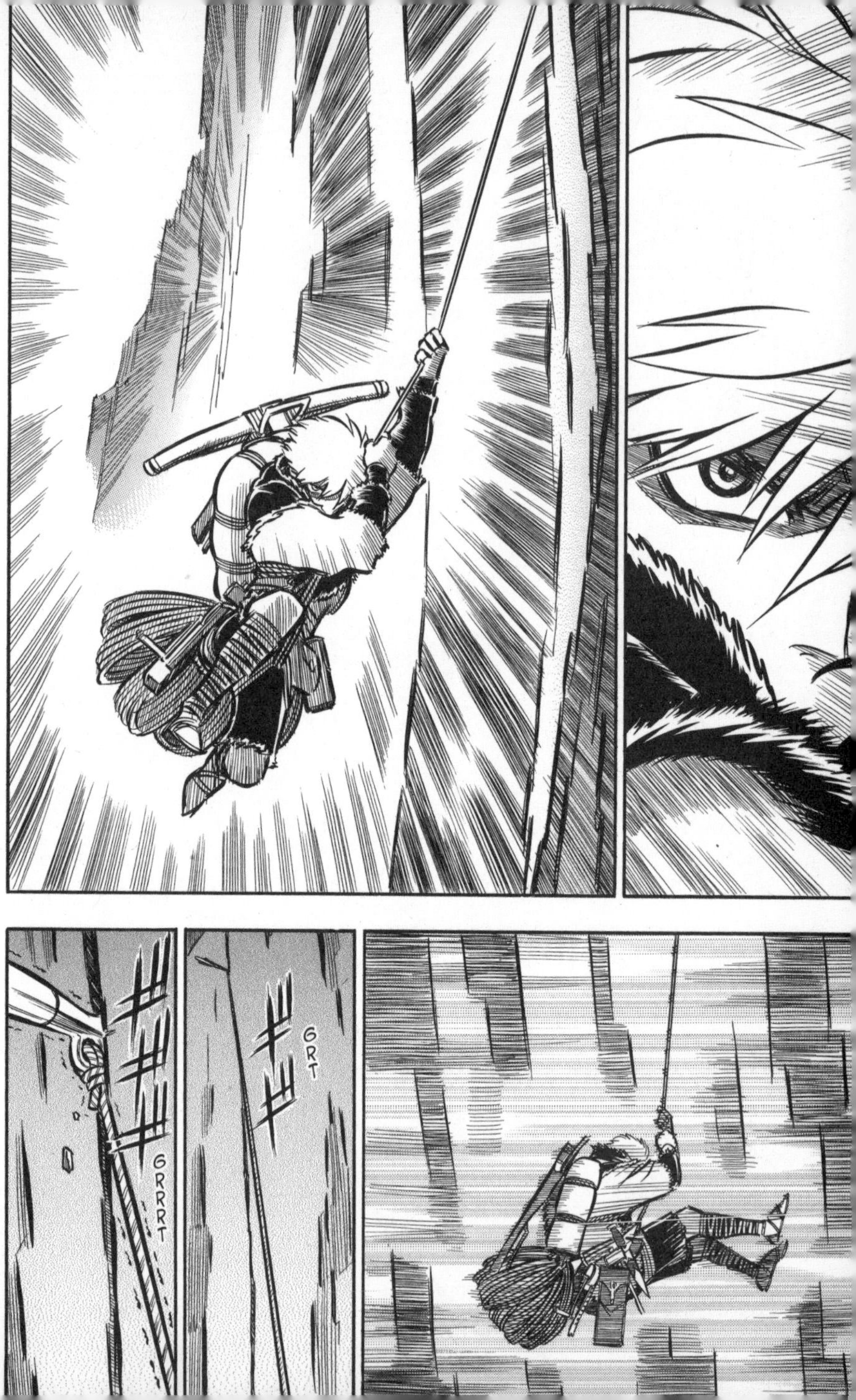
GRT
GRRRT

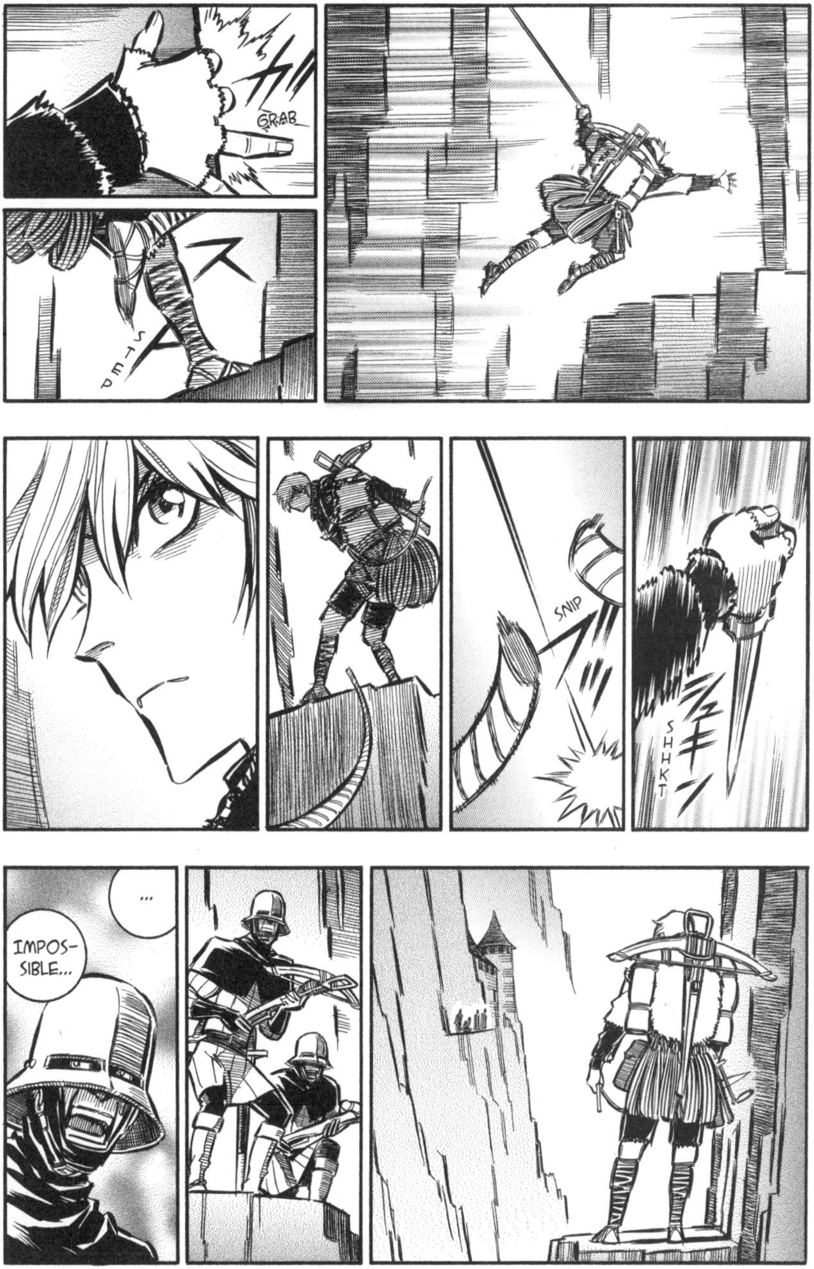
GRAB
STEP
SHHKT
SNIP
...
IMPOS-SIBLE...

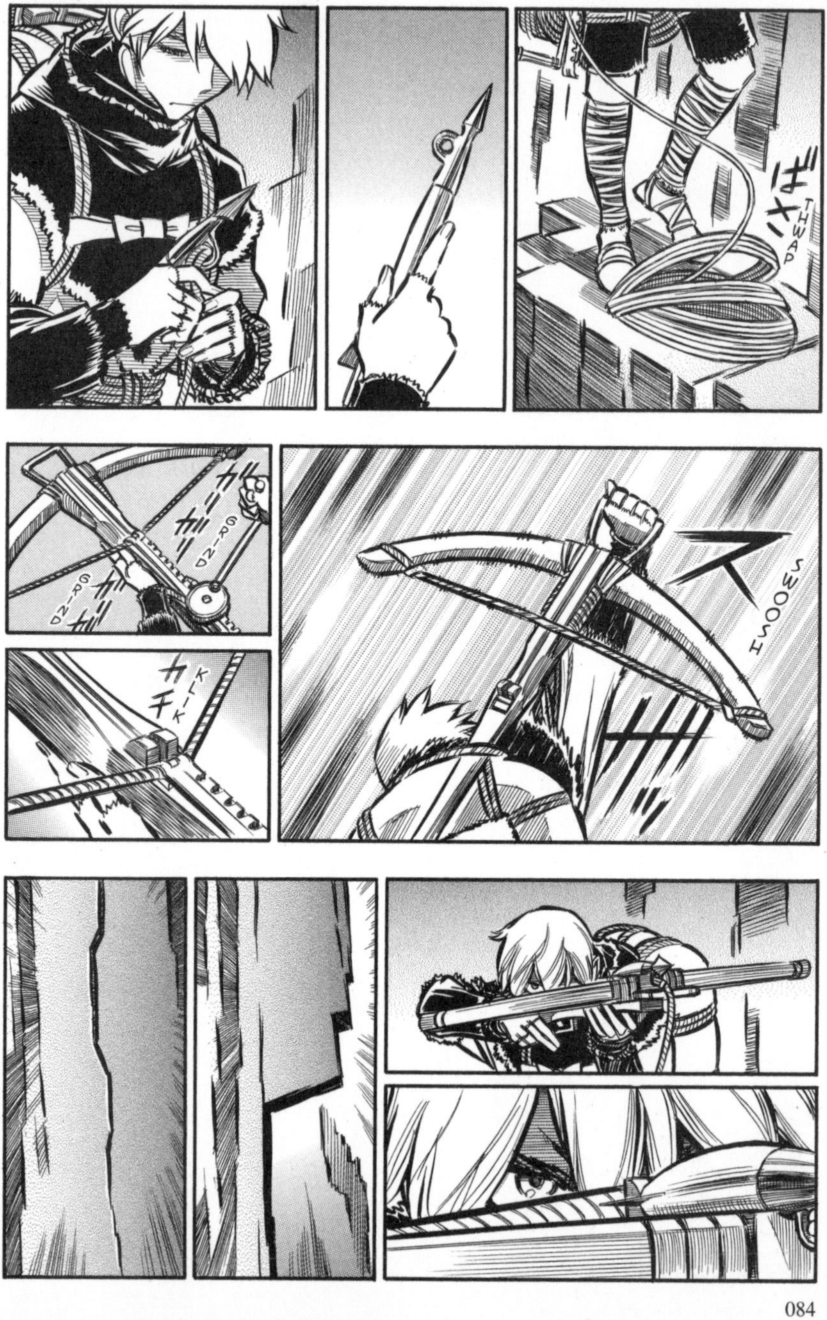
THWAP
SWOOSH
GRIND
GRIND
KLIK

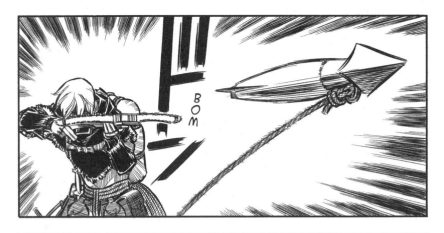

BOM

THWINK

O-KAY.

ZSHK

TUG TUG TUG

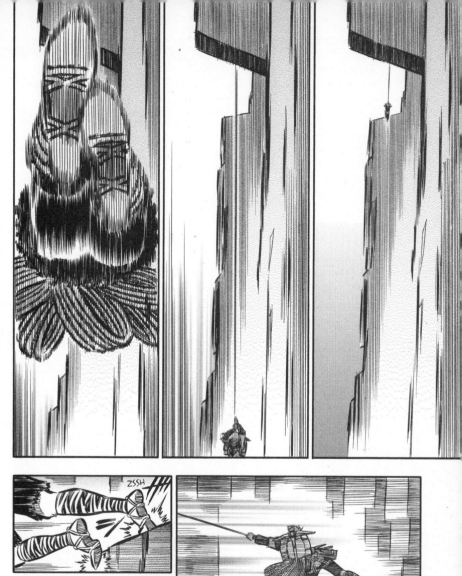

ZSSH

PHEW
...

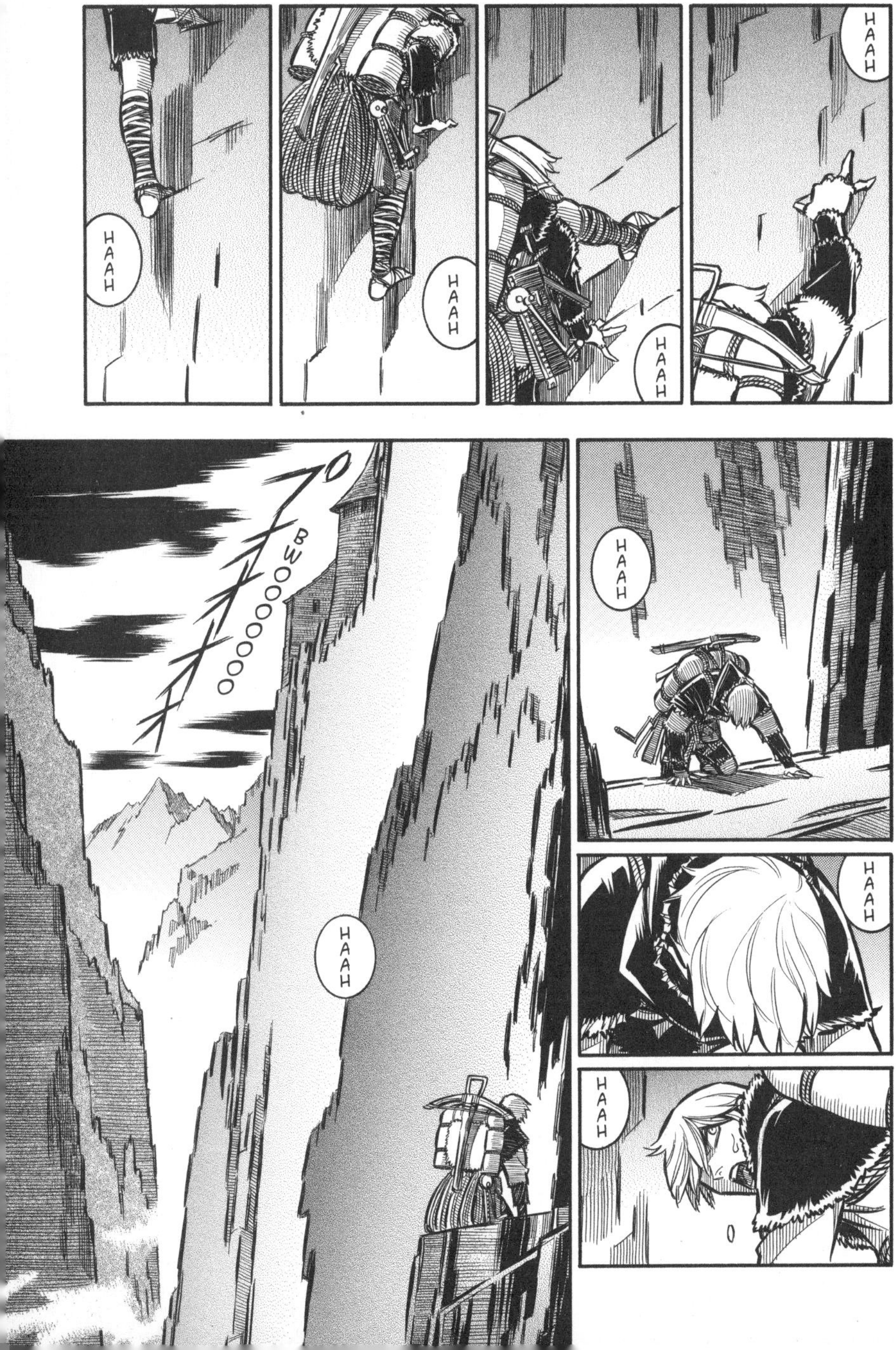
HAAH
HAAH
HAAH
HAAH
HAAH
HAAH
HAAH
BWOOOOOOOO
HAAH

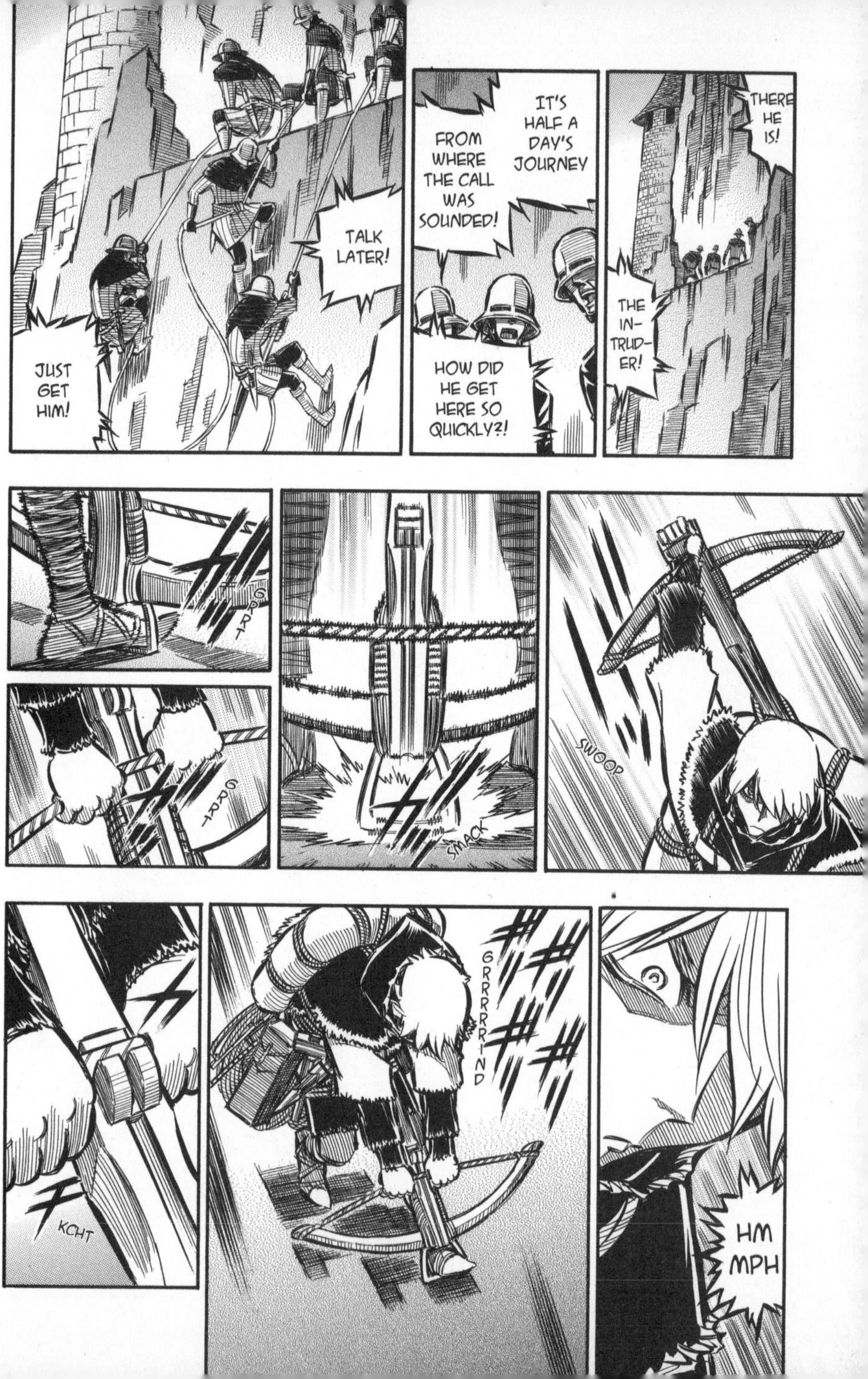
THERE HE IS!
THE IN-TRUD-ER!
IT'S HALF A DAY'S JOURNEY
FROM WHERE THE CALL WAS SOUNDED!
HOW DID HE GET HERE SO QUICKLY?!
TALK LATER!
JUST GET HIM!
SWOOP
SMACK
GRRT
GRRT
HM MPH
GRRRRRIND
KCHT

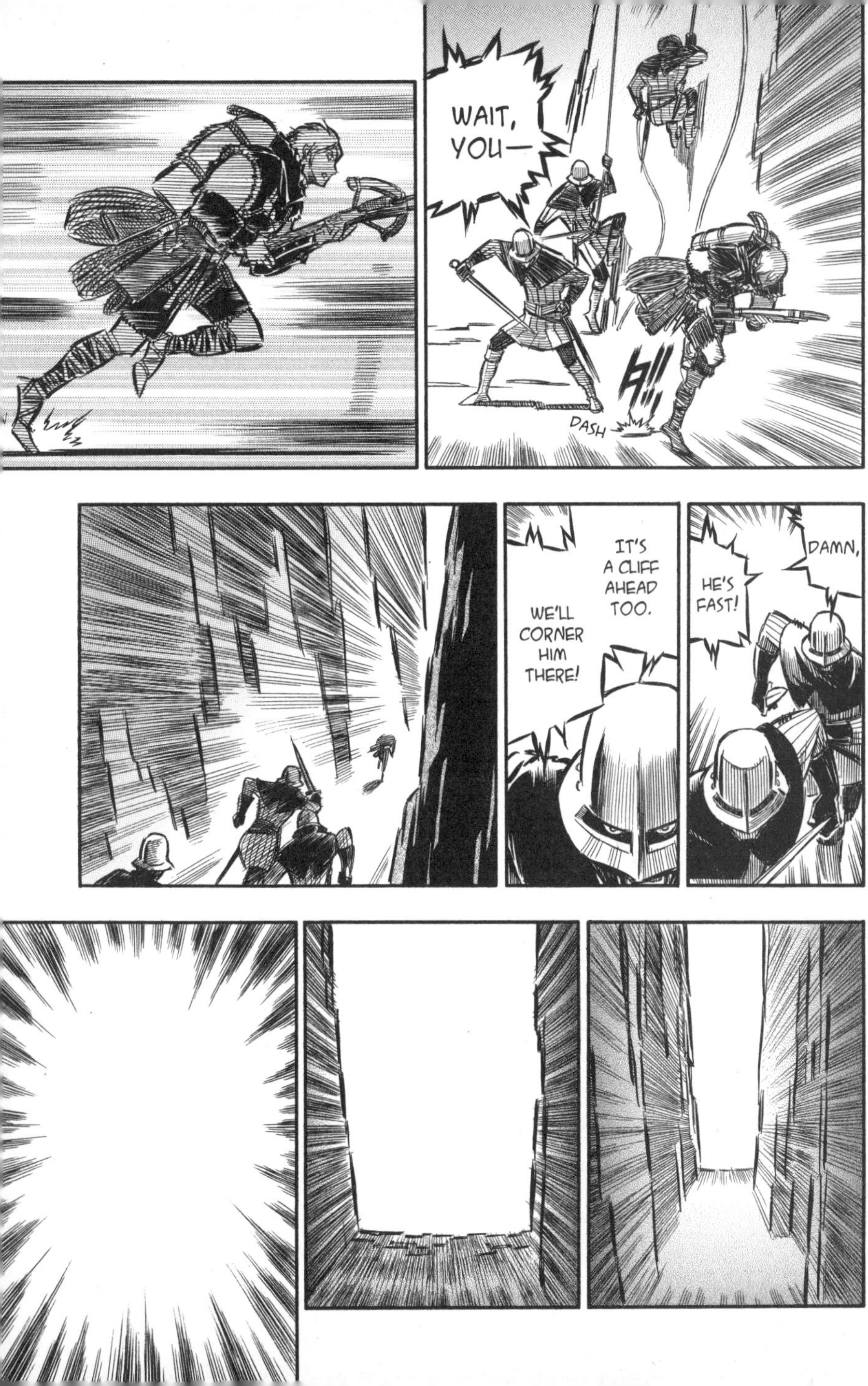
WAIT, YOU—
DASH
DAMN, HE'S FAST!
IT'S A CLIFF AHEAD TOO.
WE'LL CORNER HIM THERE!

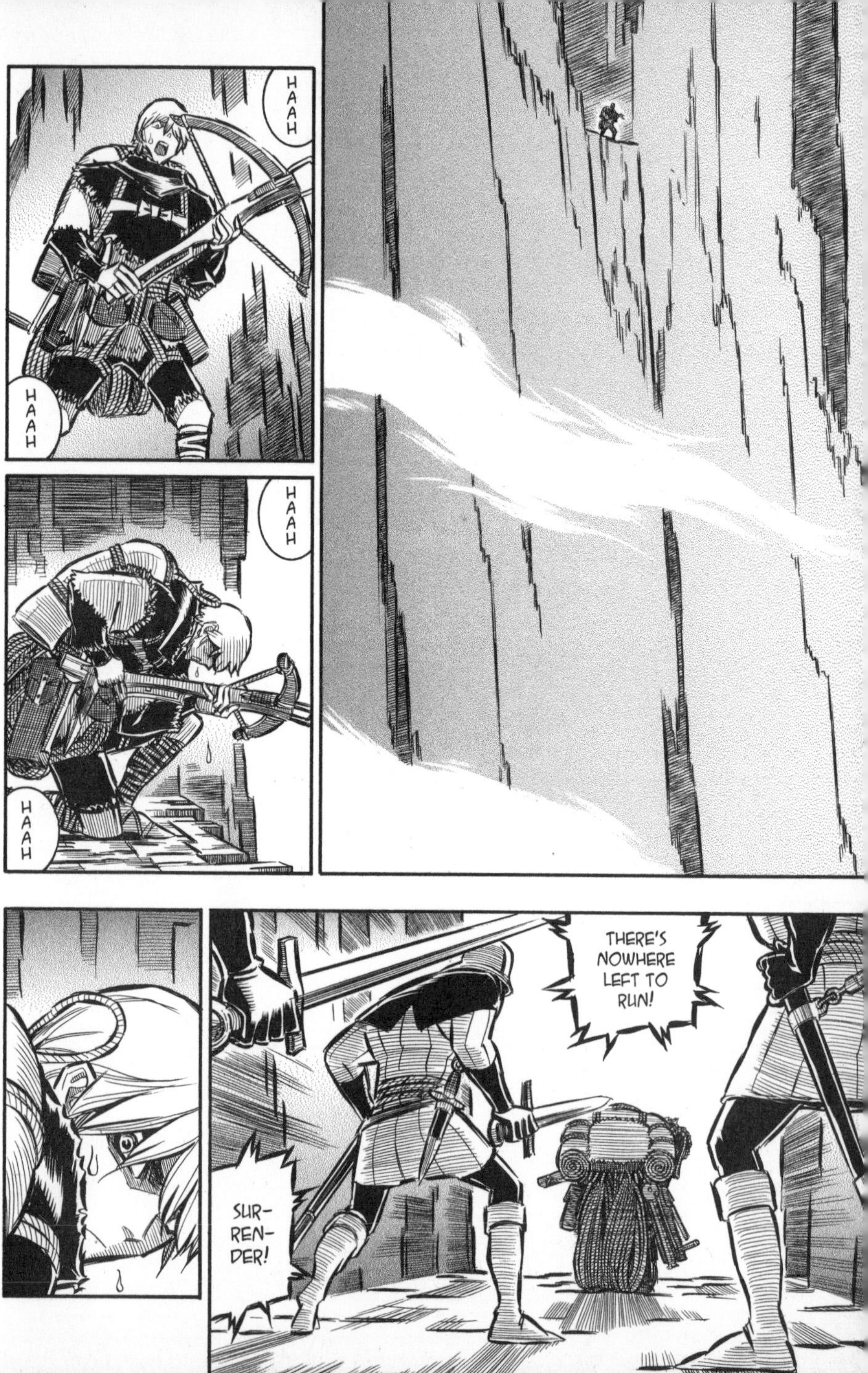
HAAH
HAAH
HAAH
HAAH
THERE'S NOWHERE LEFT TO RUN!
SUR-REN-DER!

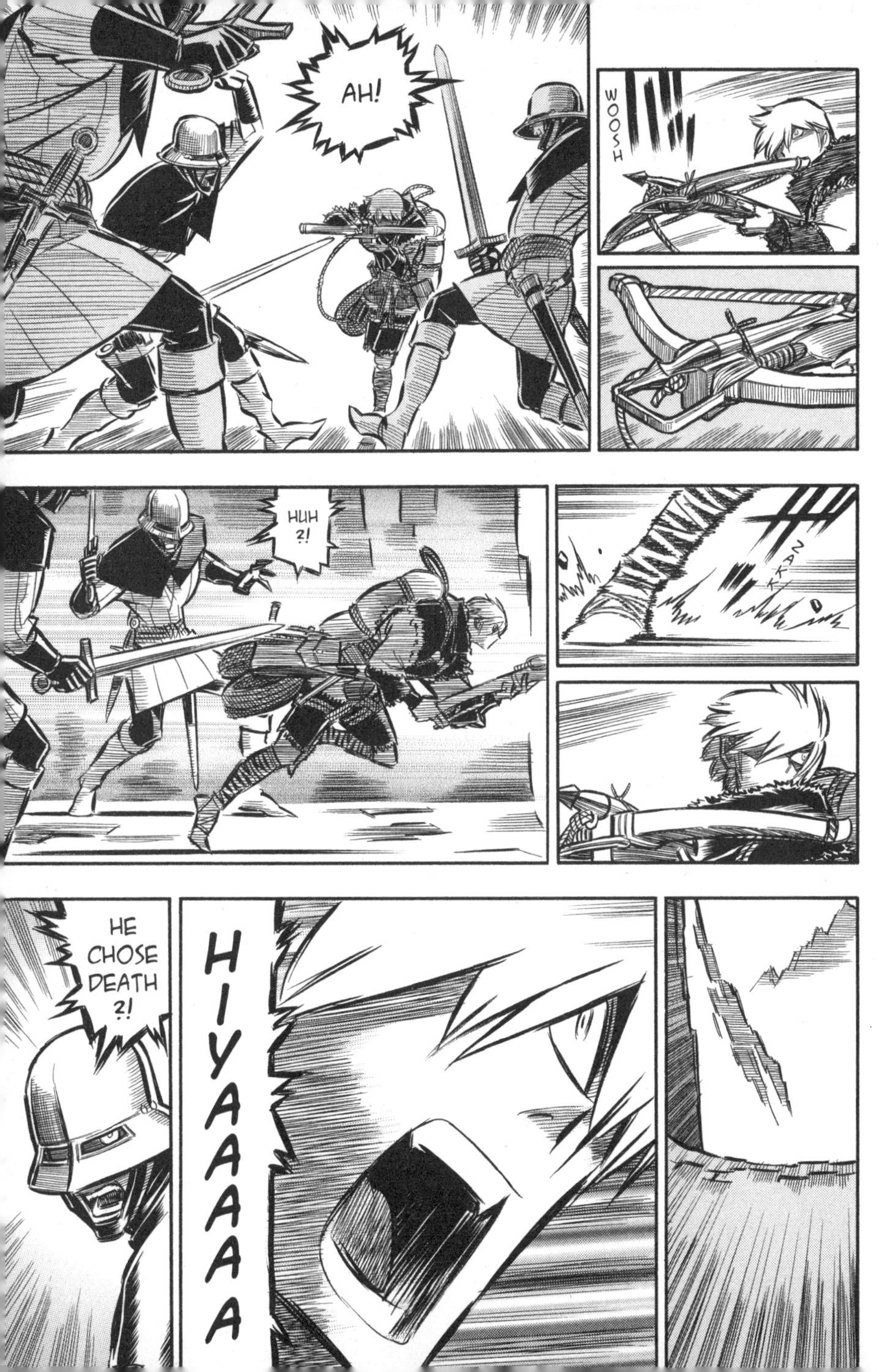
WOOSH
AH!
ZAKK
HUH ?!
HIYAAAAA
HE CHOSE DEATH ?!

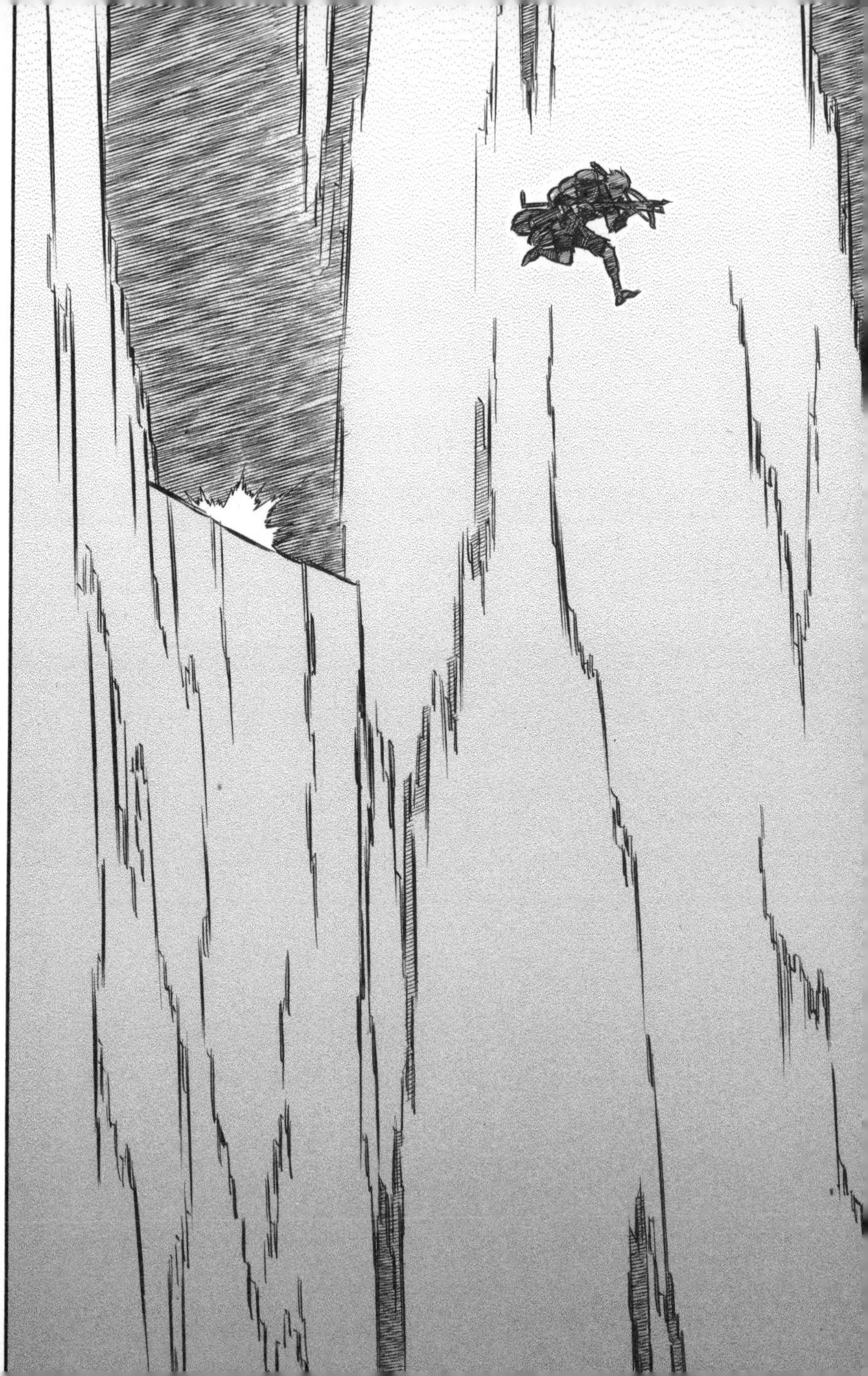

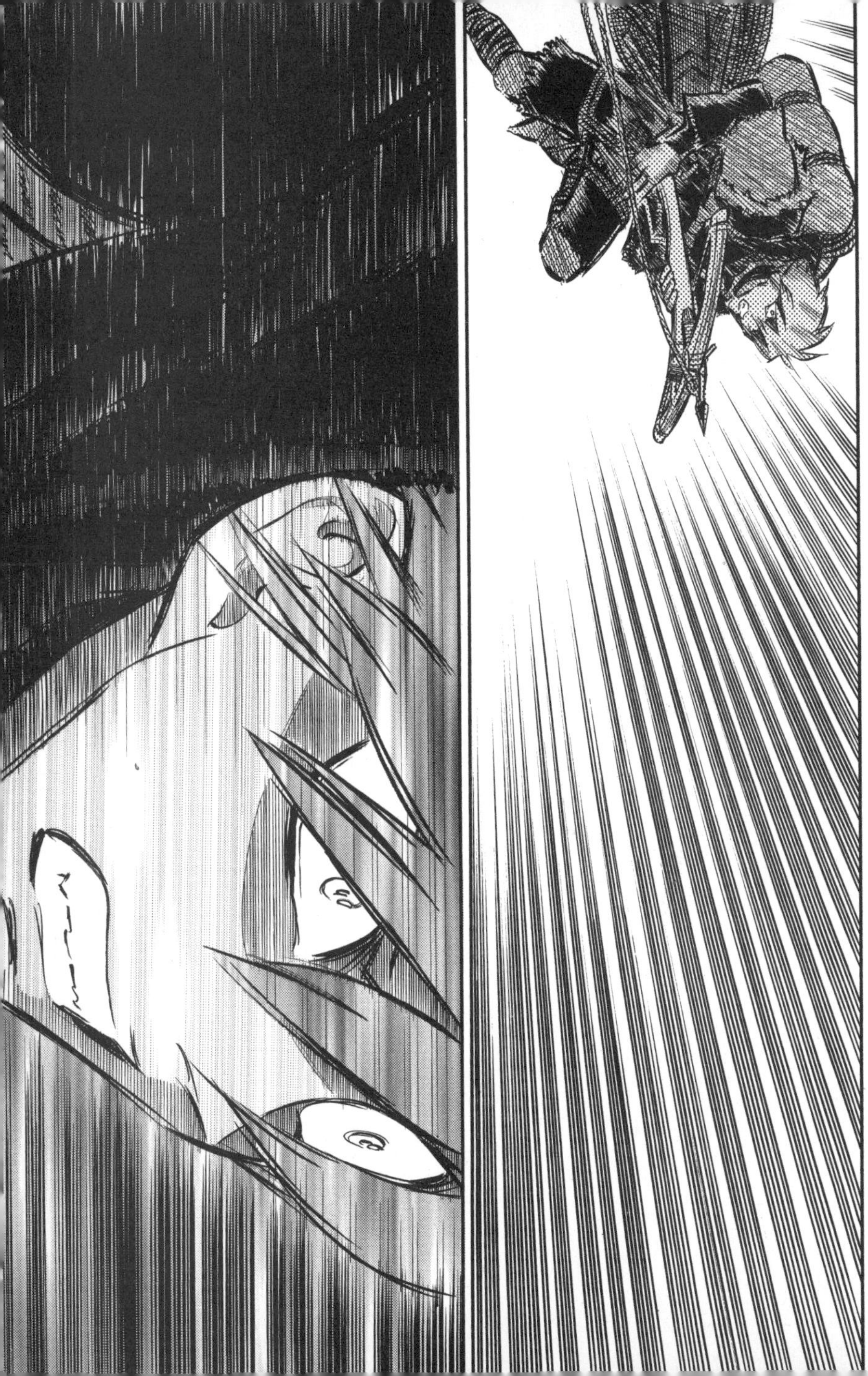

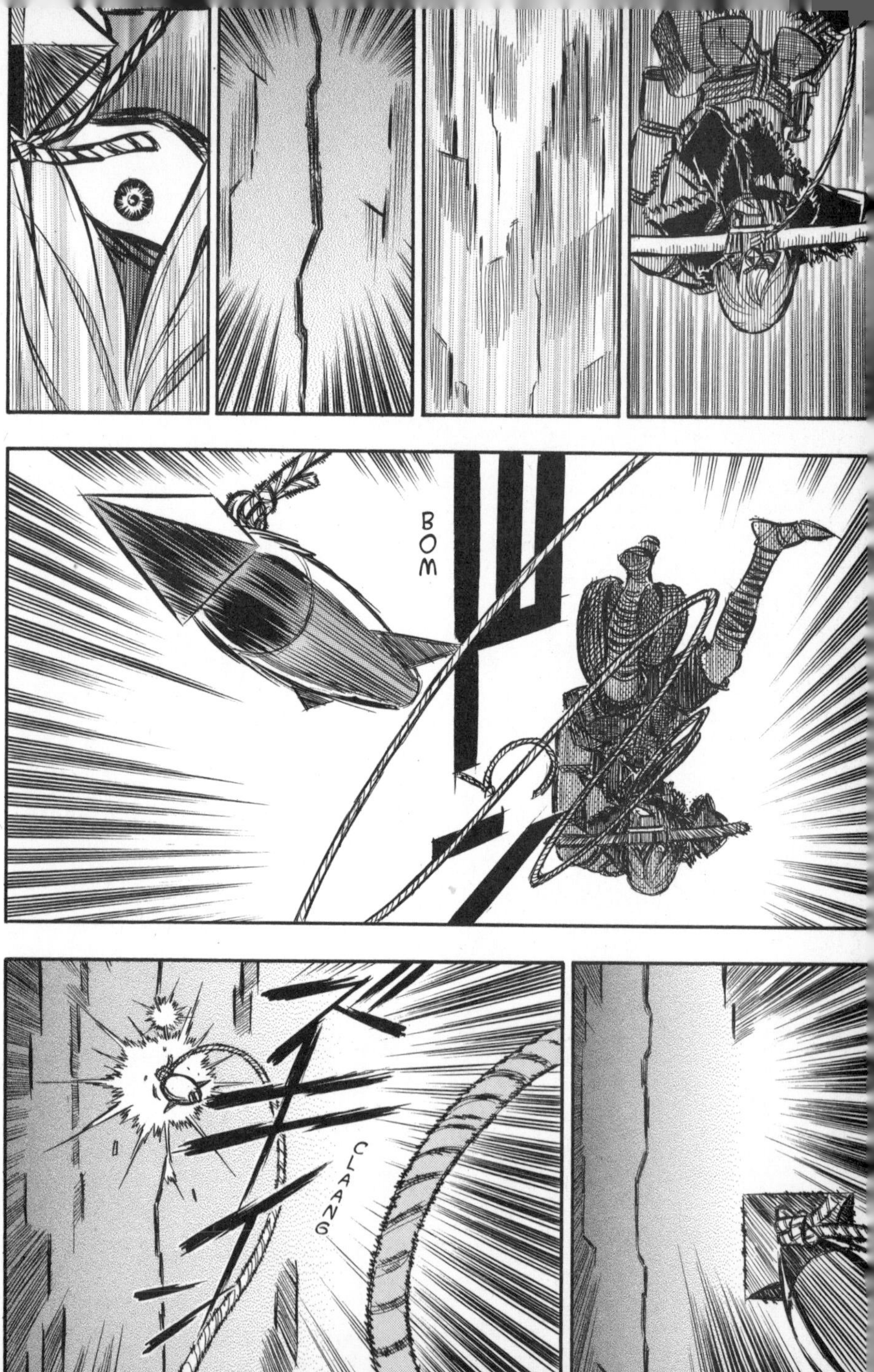
BOM
CLAANG

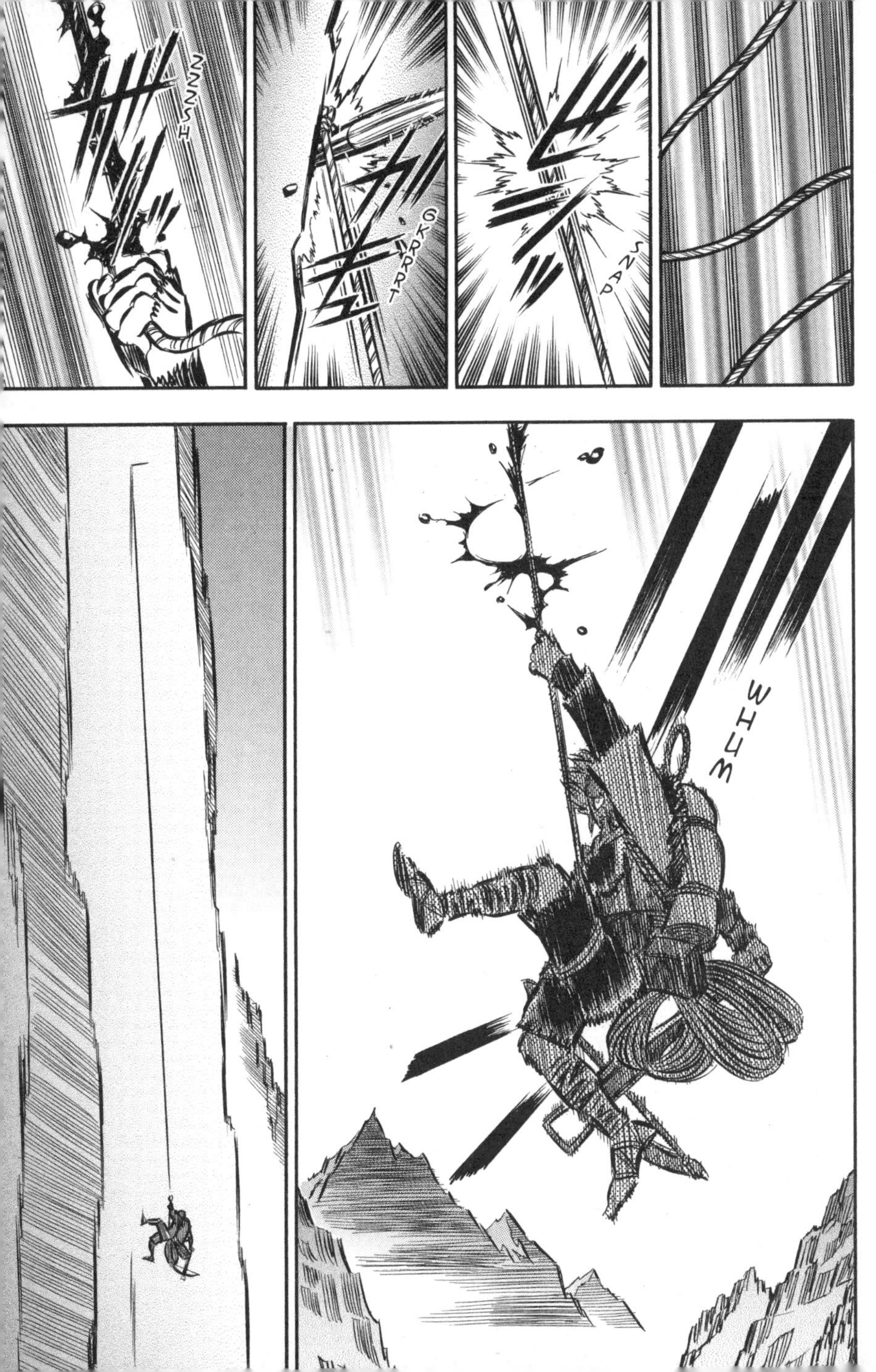
SNAP
GKRRRT
ZZZSH
WHUM

THUNK
PHEW...
CLANG
CLANG
YANK
TOSS

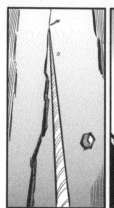

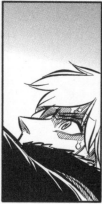

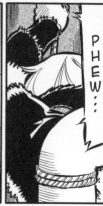

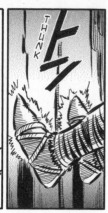

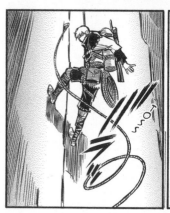

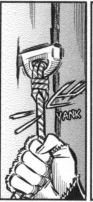

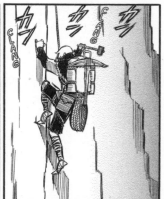

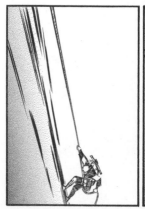

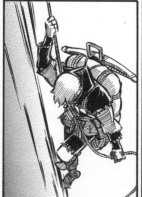

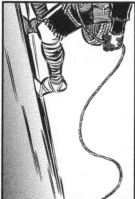

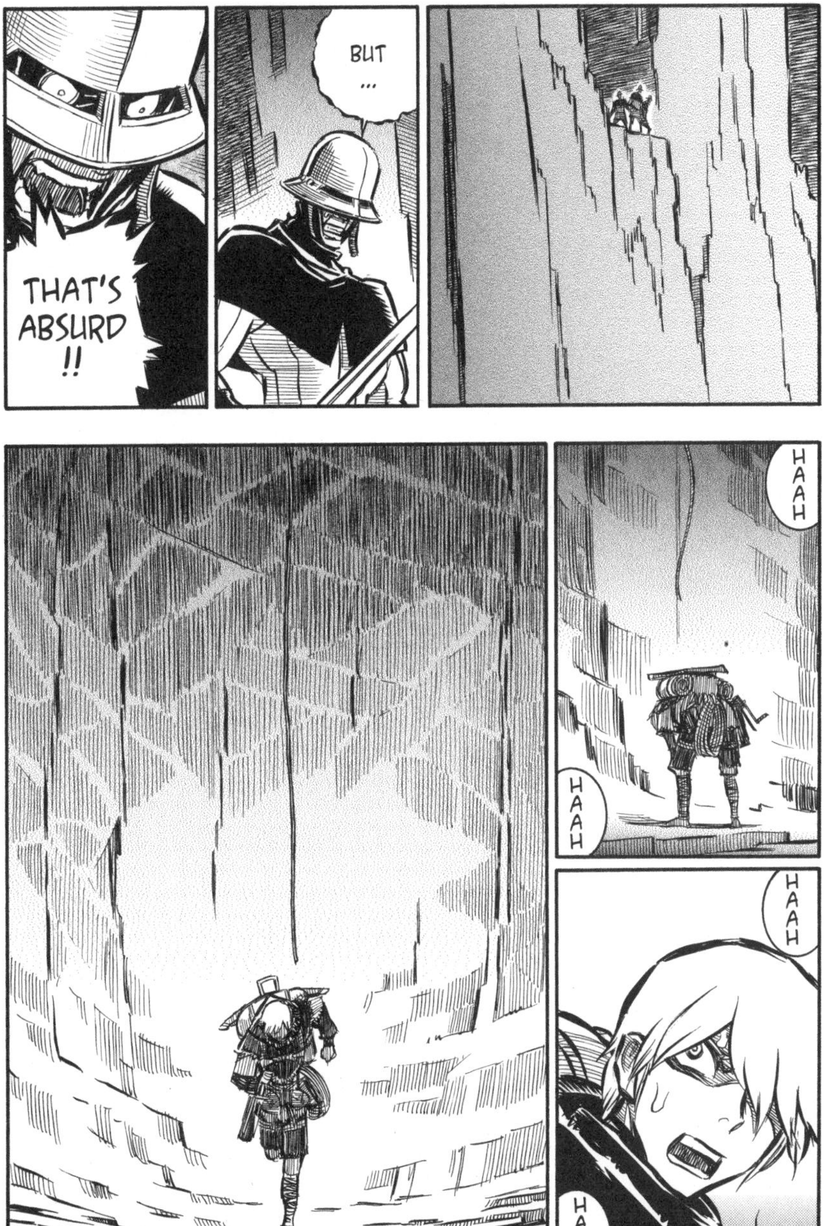
BUT ...
THAT'S ABSURD !!
HAAH
HAAH
HAAH
HAAH

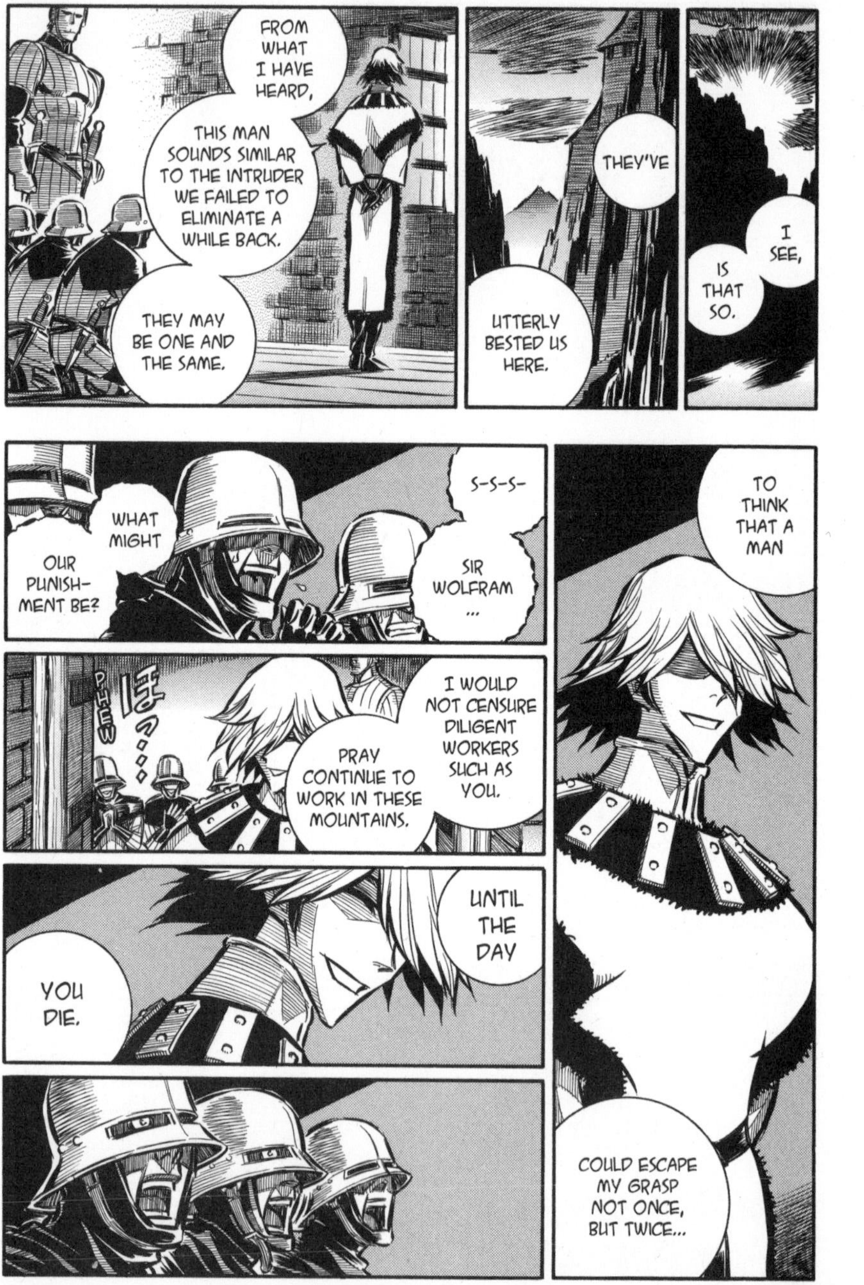
I SEE,
IS THAT SO.
THEY'VE
UTTERLY BESTED US HERE.
FROM WHAT I HAVE HEARD,
THIS MAN SOUNDS SIMILAR TO THE INTRUDER WE FAILED TO ELIMINATE A WHILE BACK.
THEY MAY BE ONE AND THE SAME.
TO THINK THAT A MAN
COULD ESCAPE MY GRASP NOT ONCE, BUT TWICE...
S-S-S-
SIR WOLFRAM ...
WHAT MIGHT
OUR PUNISH-MENT BE?
I WOULD NOT CENSURE DILIGENT WORKERS SUCH AS YOU.
PRAY CONTINUE TO WORK IN THESE MOUNTAINS.
ほっ
PHEW
UNTIL THE DAY
YOU DIE.

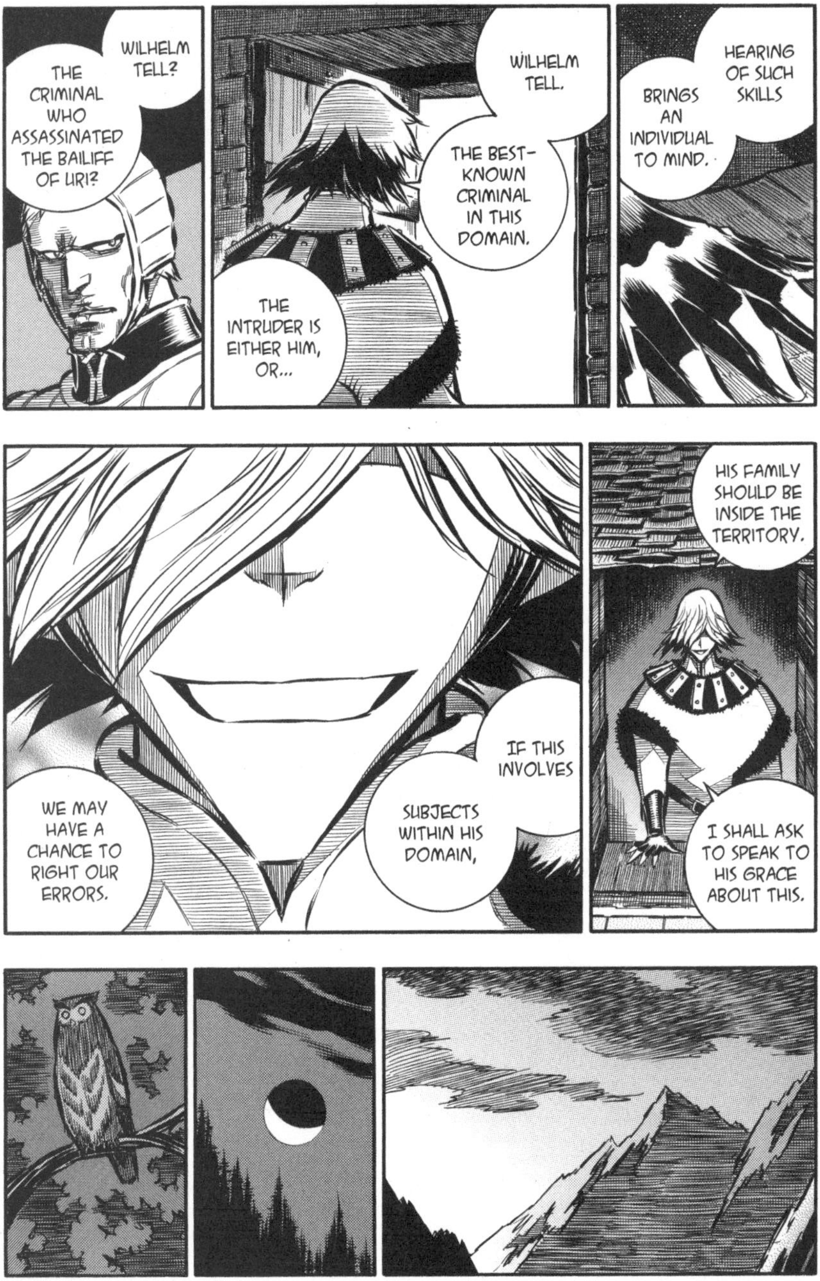
HEARING OF SUCH SKILLS
BRINGS AN INDIVIDUAL TO MIND.
WILHELM TELL.
THE BEST-KNOWN CRIMINAL IN THIS DOMAIN.
THE INTRUDER IS EITHER HIM, OR...
WILHELM TELL?
THE CRIMINAL WHO ASSASSINATED THE BAILIFF OF URI?
HIS FAMILY SHOULD BE INSIDE THE TERRITORY.
I SHALL ASK TO SPEAK TO HIS GRACE ABOUT THIS.
IF THIS INVOLVES
SUBJECTS WITHIN HIS DOMAIN,
WE MAY HAVE A CHANCE TO RIGHT OUR ERRORS.

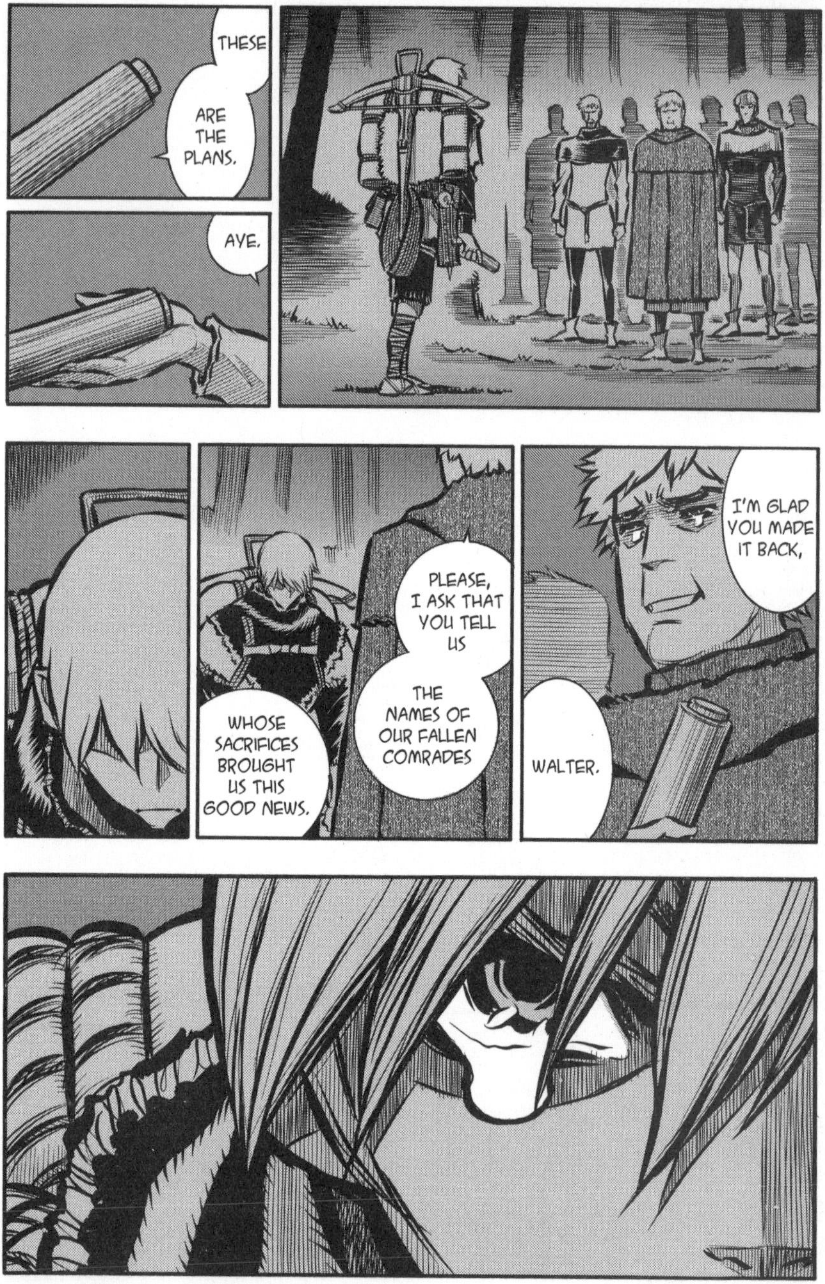
THESE
ARE THE PLANS.
AYE.
I'M GLAD YOU MADE IT BACK,
WALTER.
PLEASE, I ASK THAT YOU TELL US
THE NAMES OF OUR FALLEN COMRADES
WHOSE SACRIFICES BROUGHT US THIS GOOD NEWS.

Chapter Nine END

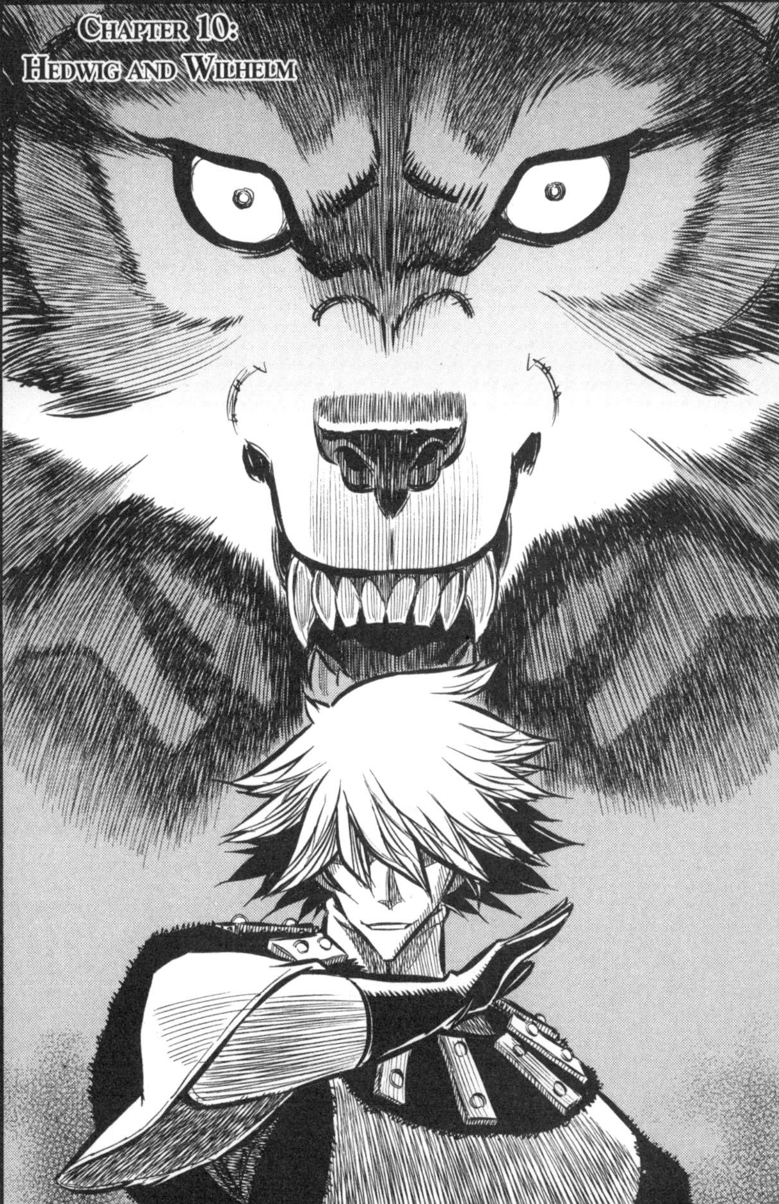
Chapter 10:
Hedwig and Wilhelm

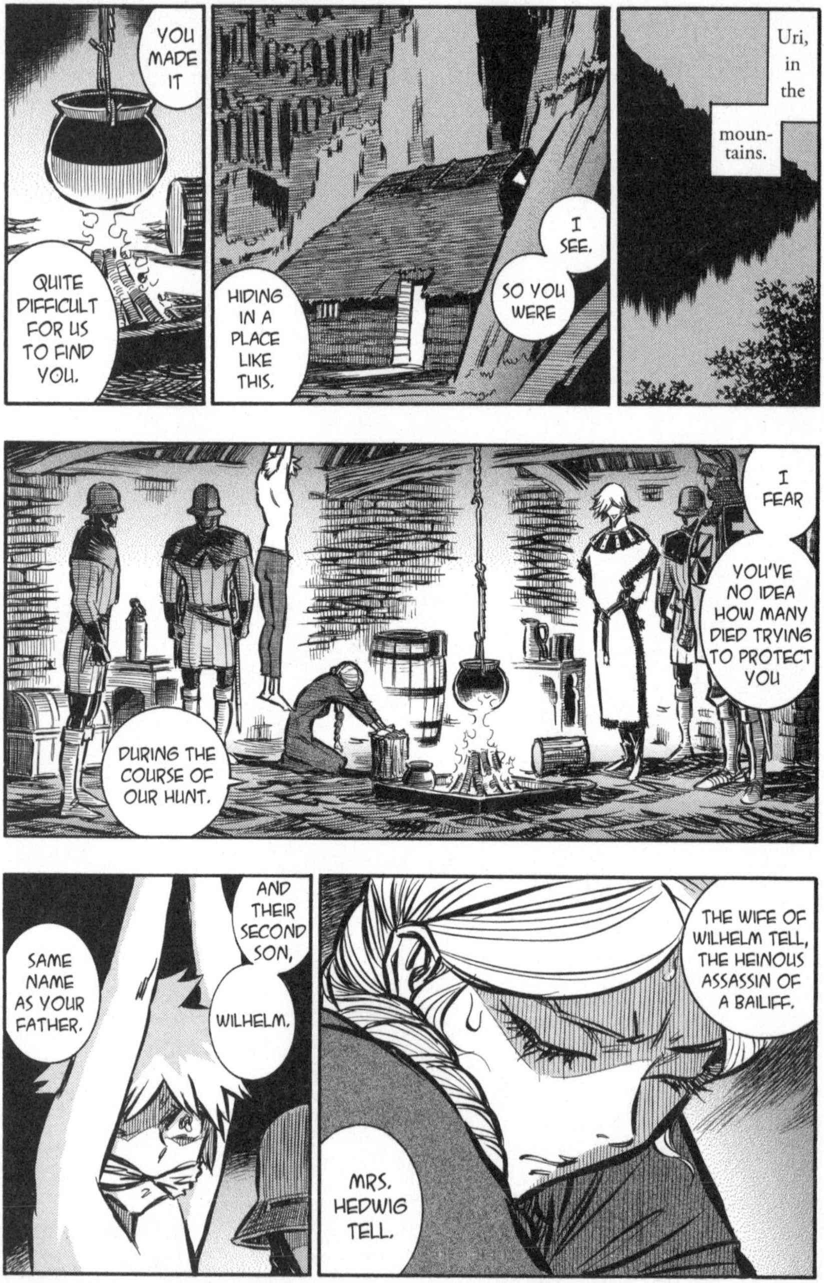
Uri, in the mountains.
I SEE.
SO YOU WERE
HIDING IN A PLACE LIKE THIS.
YOU MADE IT
QUITE DIFFICULT FOR US TO FIND YOU.
I FEAR
YOU'VE NO IDEA HOW MANY DIED TRYING TO PROTECT YOU
DURING THE COURSE OF OUR HUNT.
THE WIFE OF WILHELM TELL, THE HEINOUS ASSASSIN OF A BAILIFF.
MRS. HEDWIG TELL.
AND THEIR SECOND SON,
WILHELM.
SAME NAME AS YOUR FATHER.

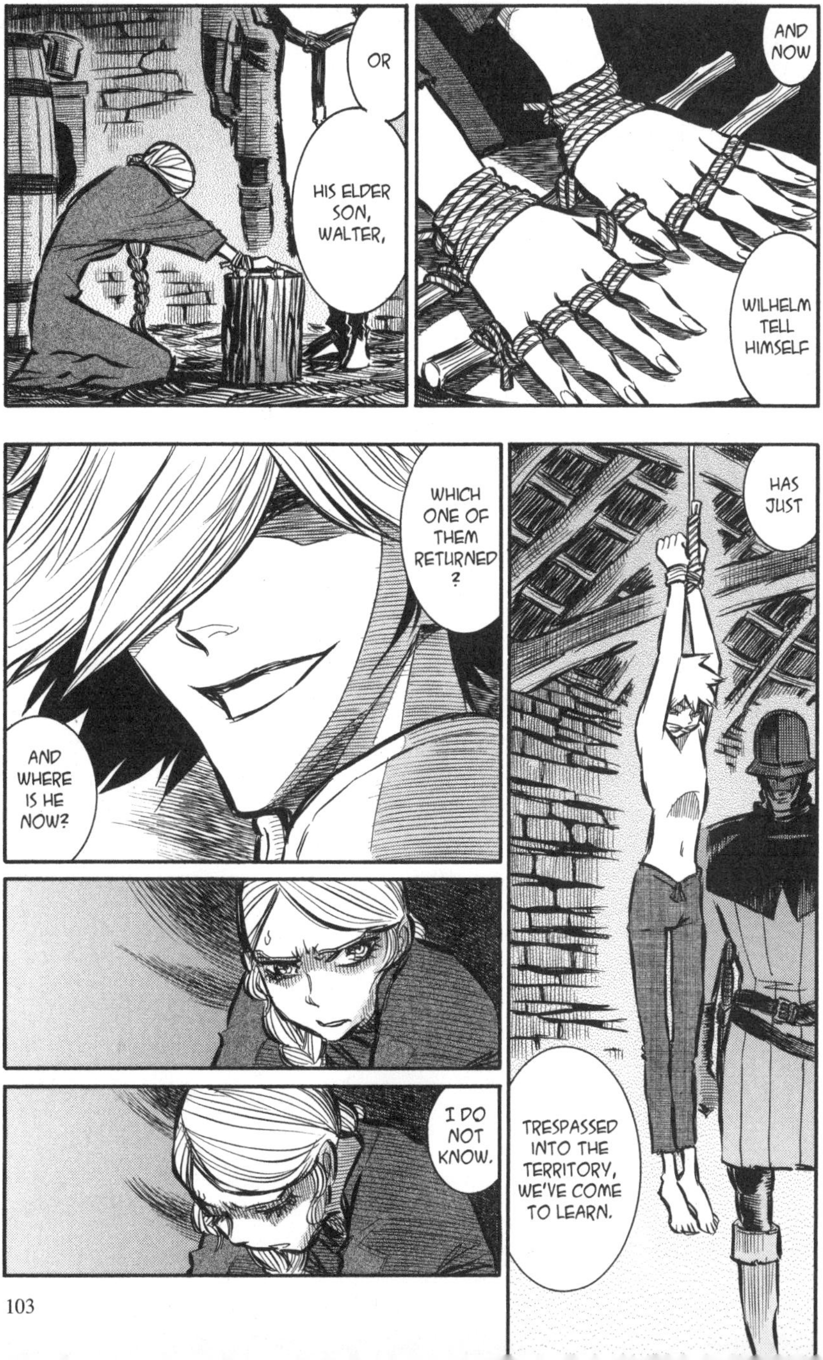
AND NOW
WILHELM TELL HIMSELF
OR
HIS ELDER SON, WALTER,
HAS JUST
TRESPASSED INTO THE TERRITORY, WE'VE COME TO LEARN.
WHICH ONE OF THEM RETURNED?
AND WHERE IS HE NOW?
I DO NOT KNOW.

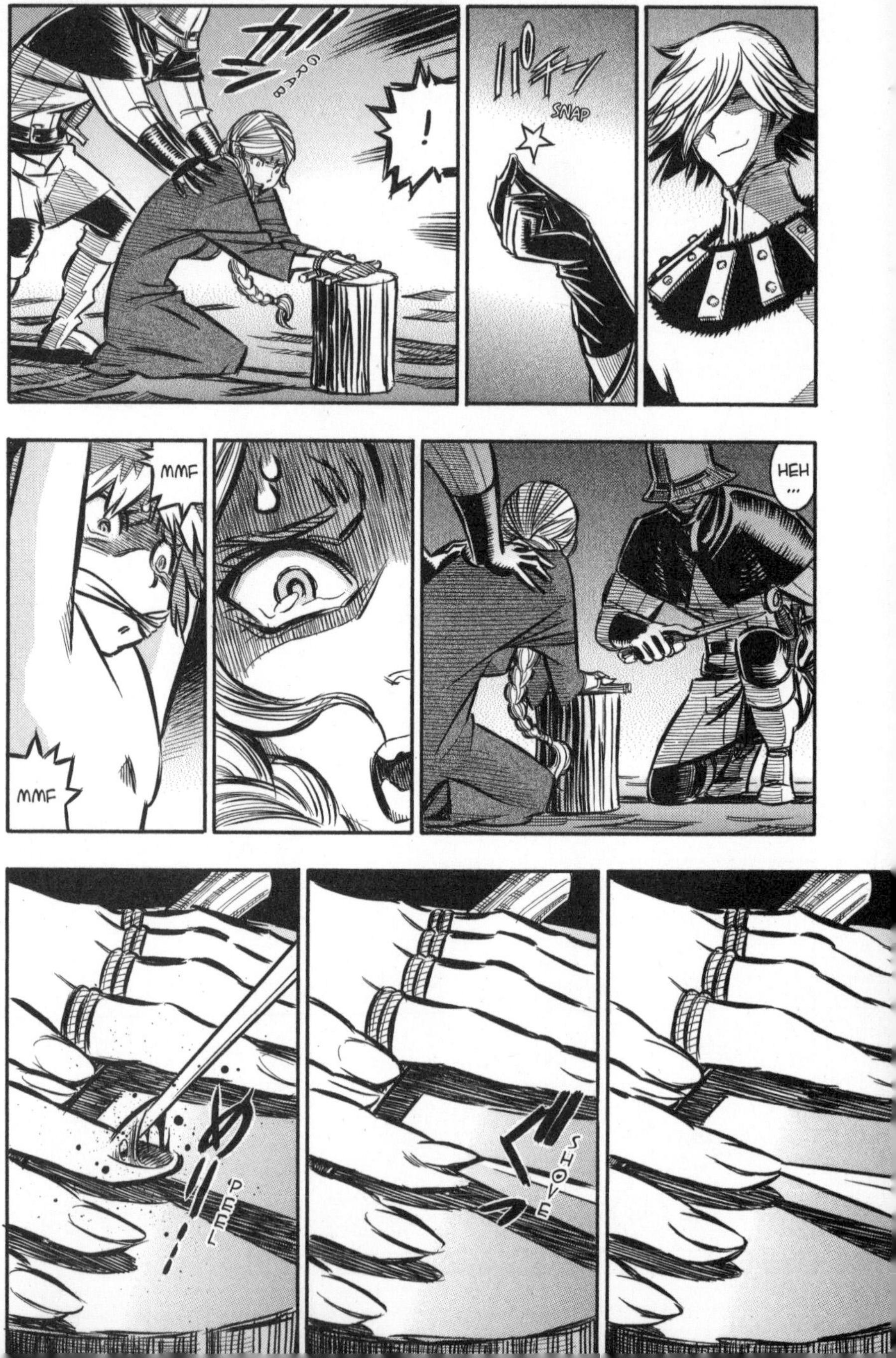

SNAP
GRAB
!
HEH ...
MMF
MMF
SHOVE
PEEL

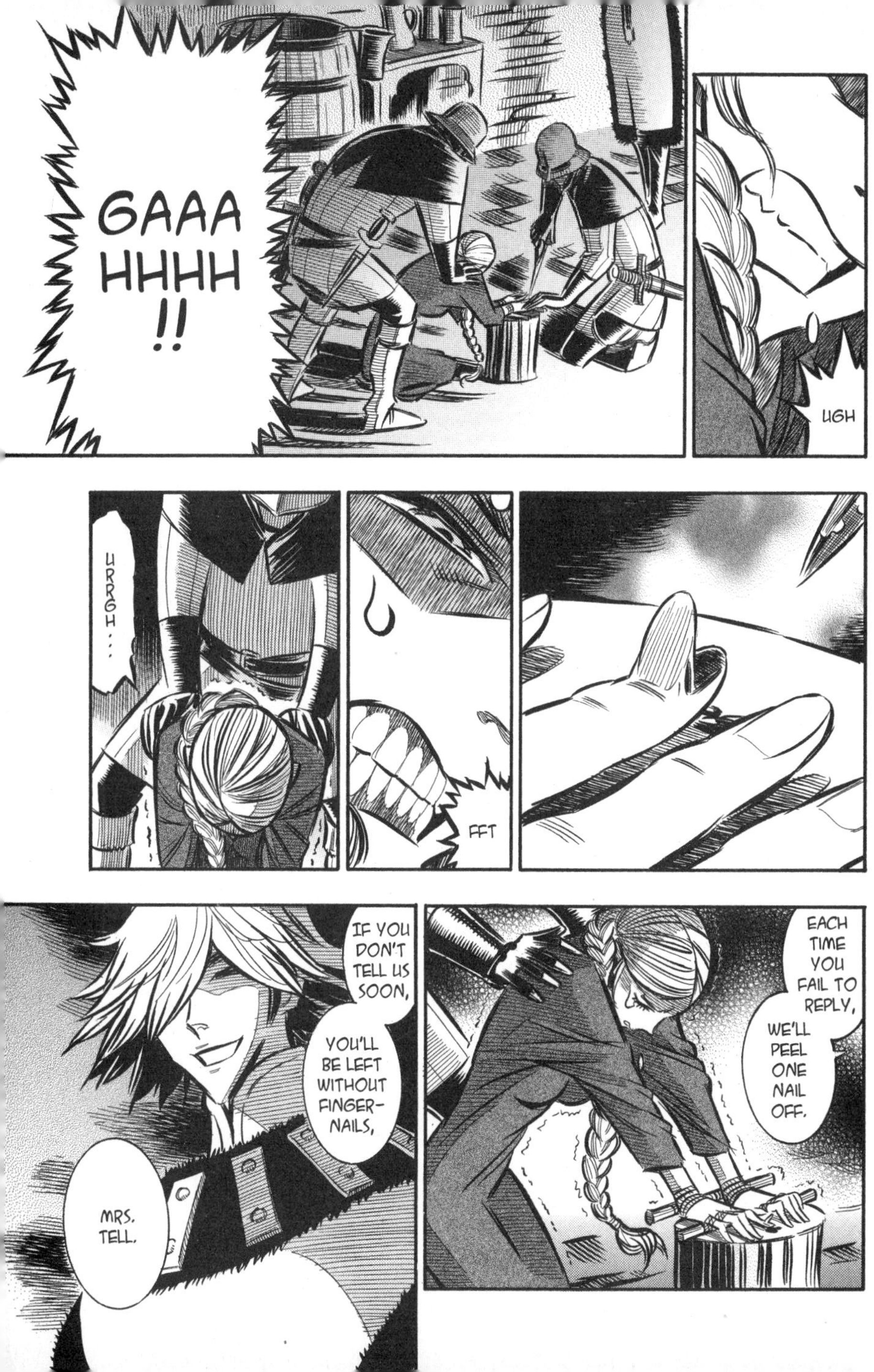
UGH
GAAA HHHH !!
FFT
URRGH...
EACH TIME YOU FAIL TO REPLY,
WE'LL PEEL ONE NAIL OFF.
IF YOU DON'T TELL US SOON,
YOU'LL BE LEFT WITHOUT FINGER-NAILS,
MRS. TELL.

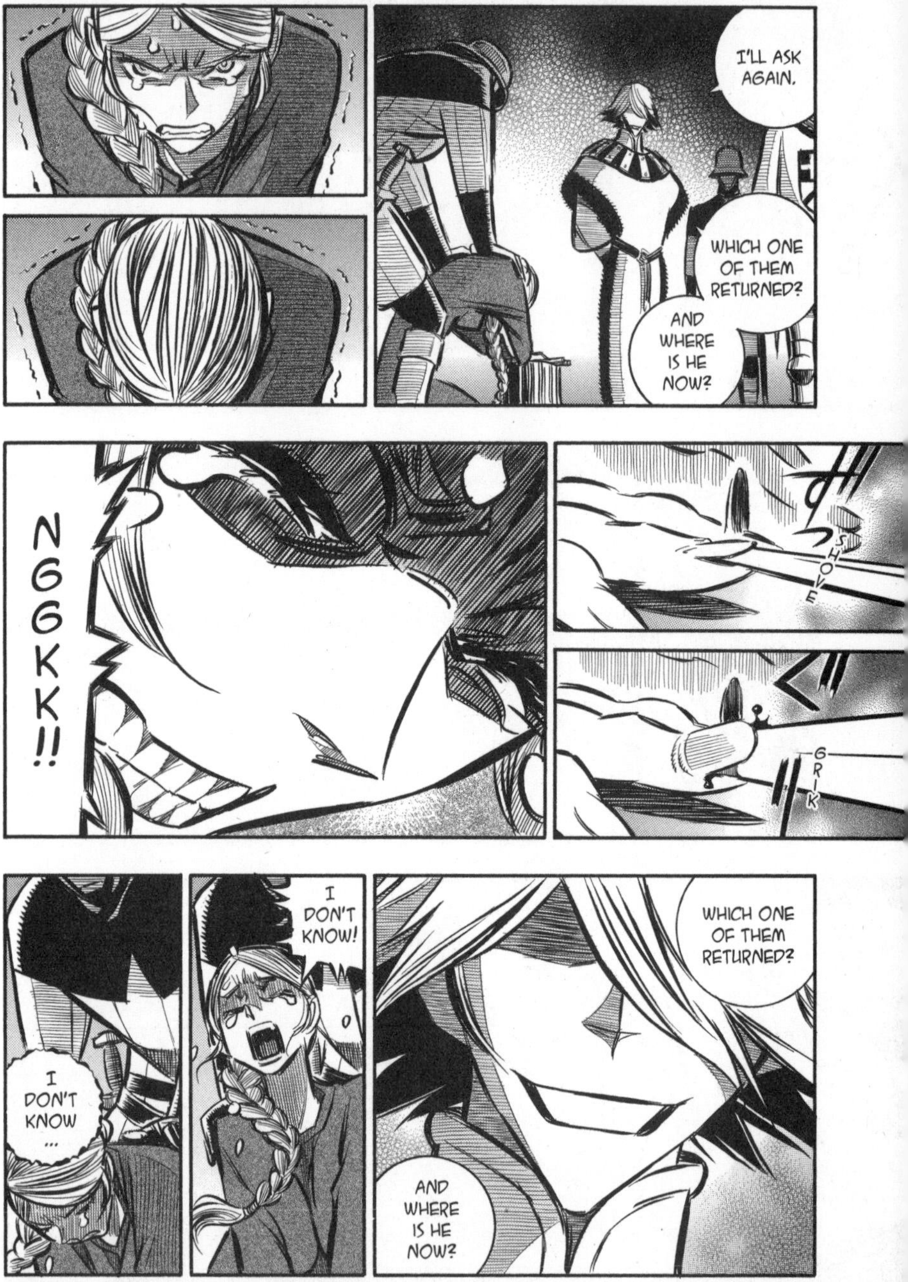
I'LL ASK AGAIN.
WHICH ONE OF THEM RETURNED?
AND WHERE IS HE NOW?
SHOVE
GRIK
NGGKK!!
WHICH ONE OF THEM RETURNED?
AND WHERE IS HE NOW?
I DON'T KNOW!
I DON'T KNOW ...

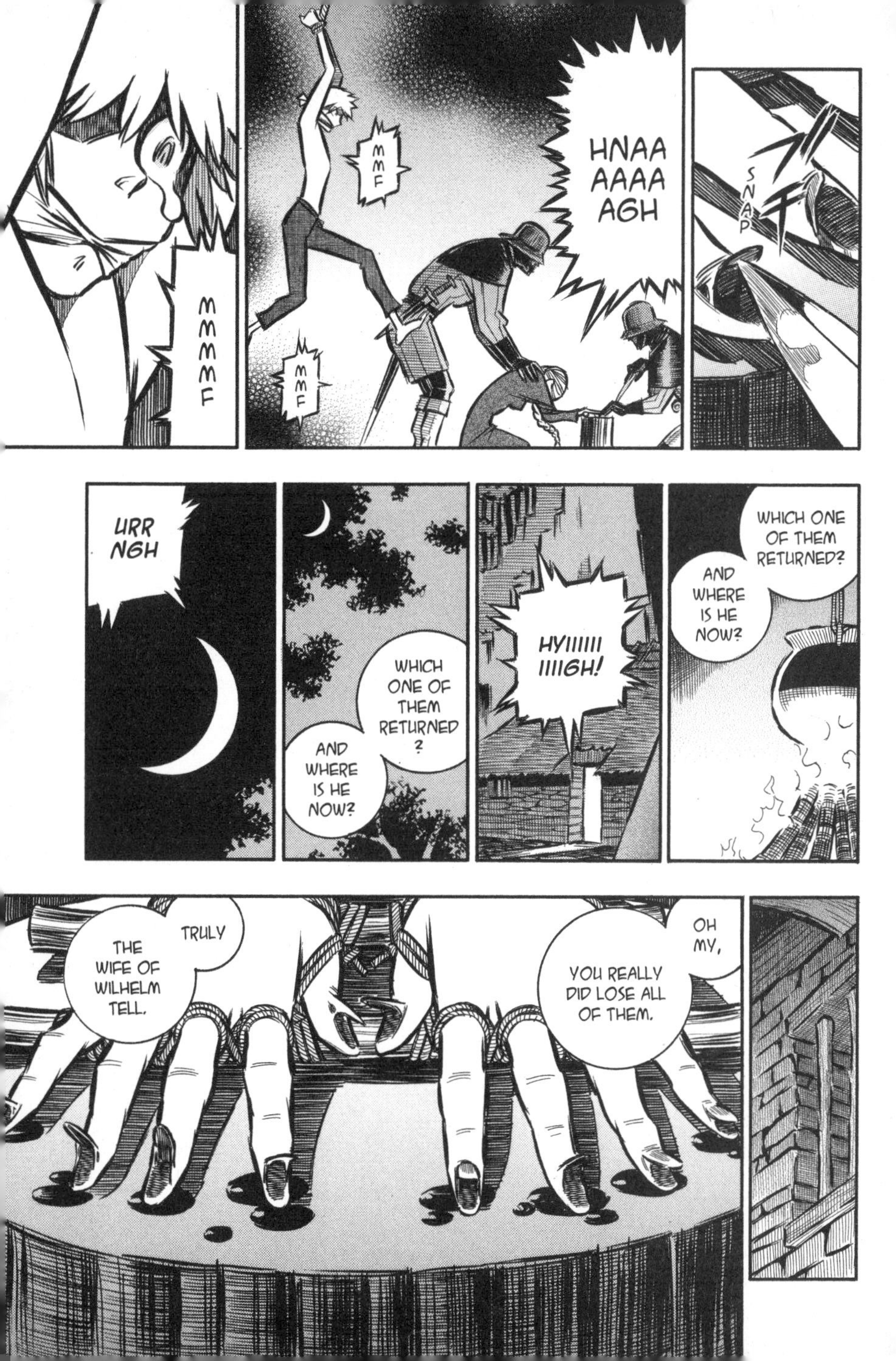
SNAP
HNAA AAAA AGH
MMF
MMF
MMMMMF
WHICH ONE OF THEM RETURNED?
AND WHERE IS HE NOW?
HYIIIIII IIIIGH!
WHICH ONE OF THEM RETURNED?
AND WHERE IS HE NOW?
URR NGH
OH MY,
YOU REALLY DID LOSE ALL OF THEM.
TRULY
THE WIFE OF WILHELM TELL.

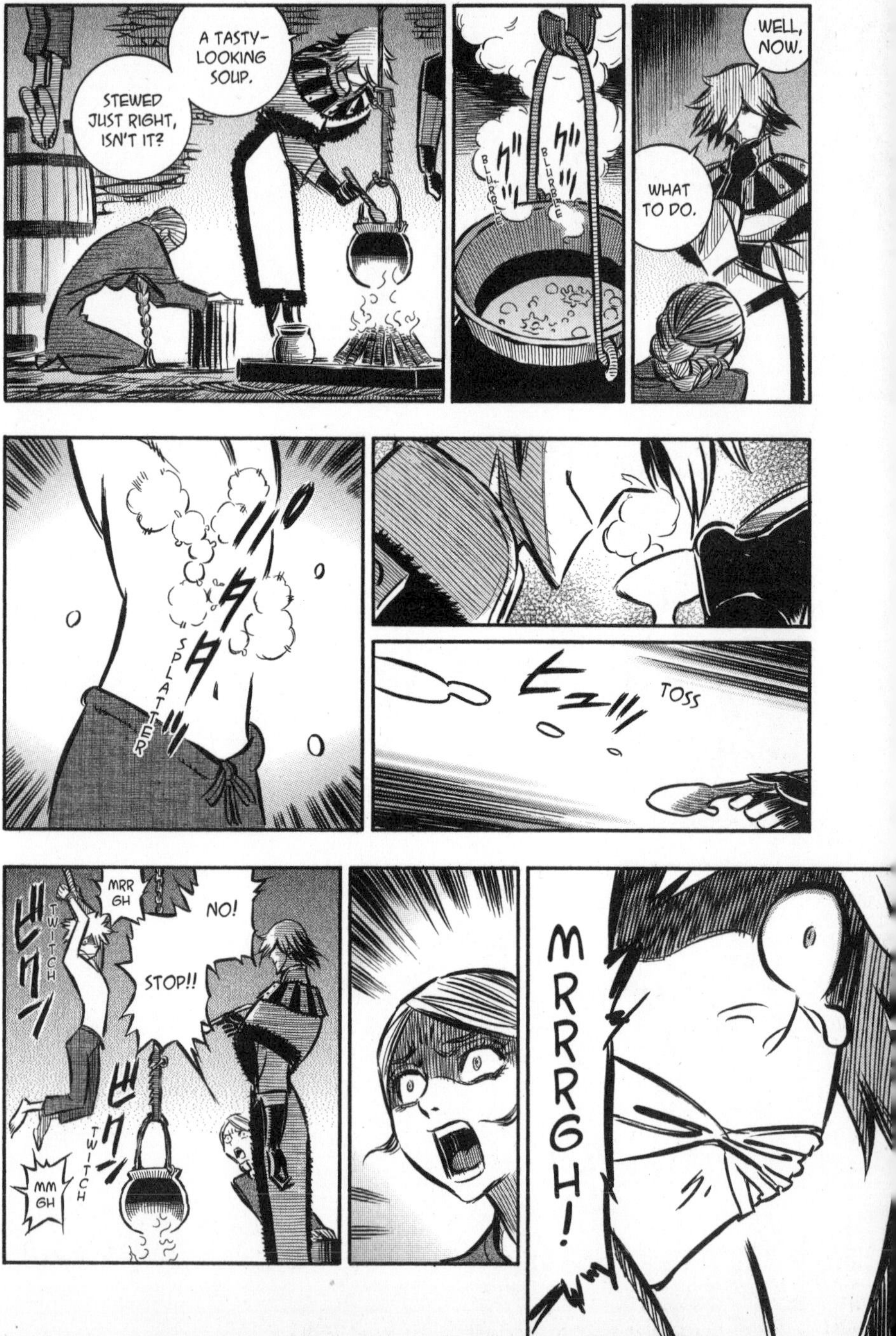
WELL, NOW.
WHAT TO DO.
BLURBLE
BLURBLE
A TASTY-LOOKING SOUP.
STEWED JUST RIGHT, ISN'T IT?
TOSS
SPLATTER
MRRRGH!
NO!
STOP!!
MRRGH
TWITCH
TWITCH
MMGH

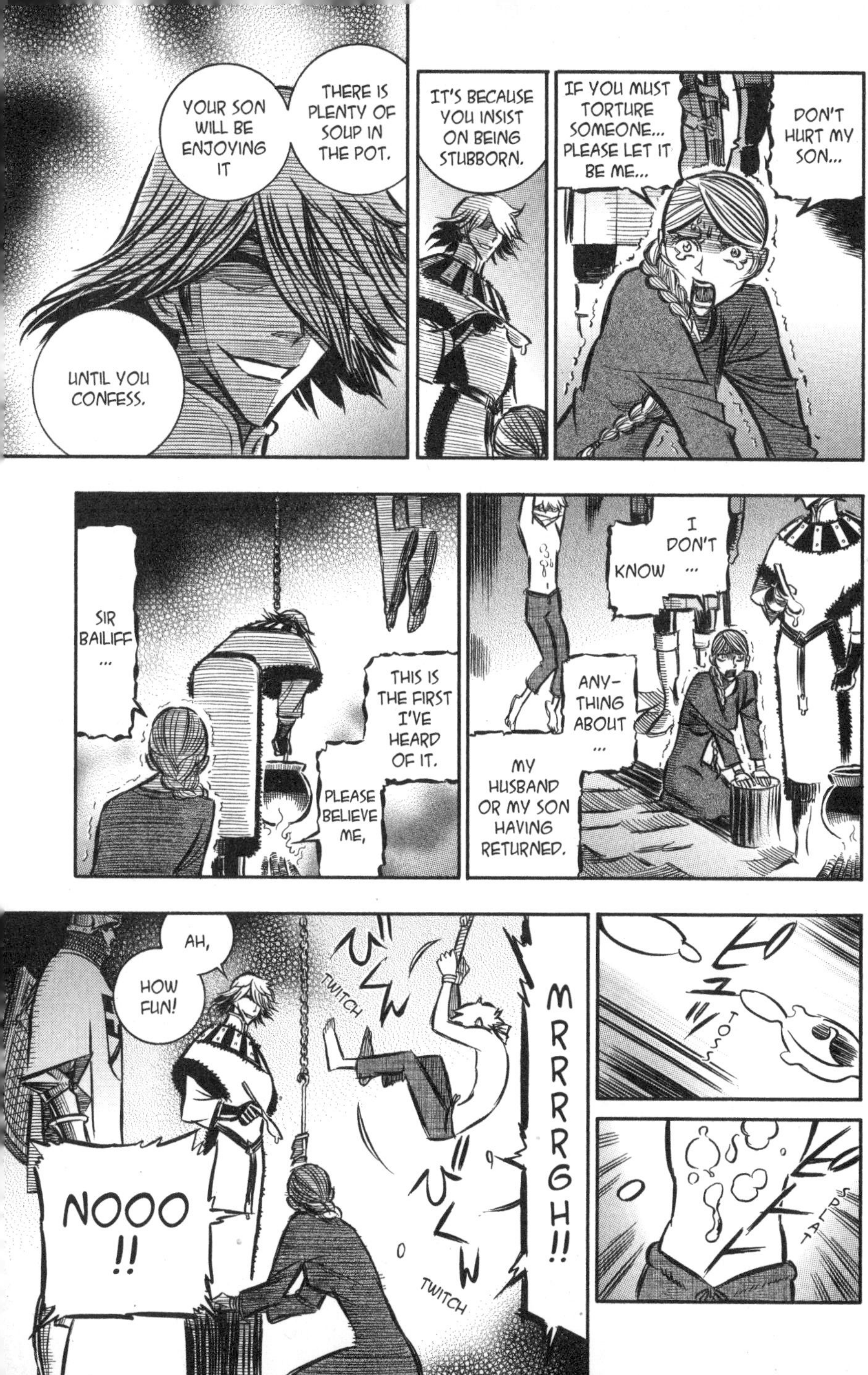
DON'T HURT MY SON...
IF YOU MUST TORTURE SOMEONE... PLEASE LET IT BE ME...
IT'S BECAUSE YOU INSIST ON BEING STUBBORN.
THERE IS PLENTY OF SOUP IN THE POT.
YOUR SON WILL BE ENJOYING IT
UNTIL YOU CONFESS.
I DON'T KNOW ...
ANY-THING ABOUT ...
MY HUSBAND OR MY SON HAVING RETURNED.
SIR BAILIFF ...
THIS IS THE FIRST I'VE HEARD OF IT.
PLEASE BELIEVE ME,
TOSS
SPLAT
MRRRRGH!!
AH, HOW FUN!
TWITCH
NOOO !!
TWITCH

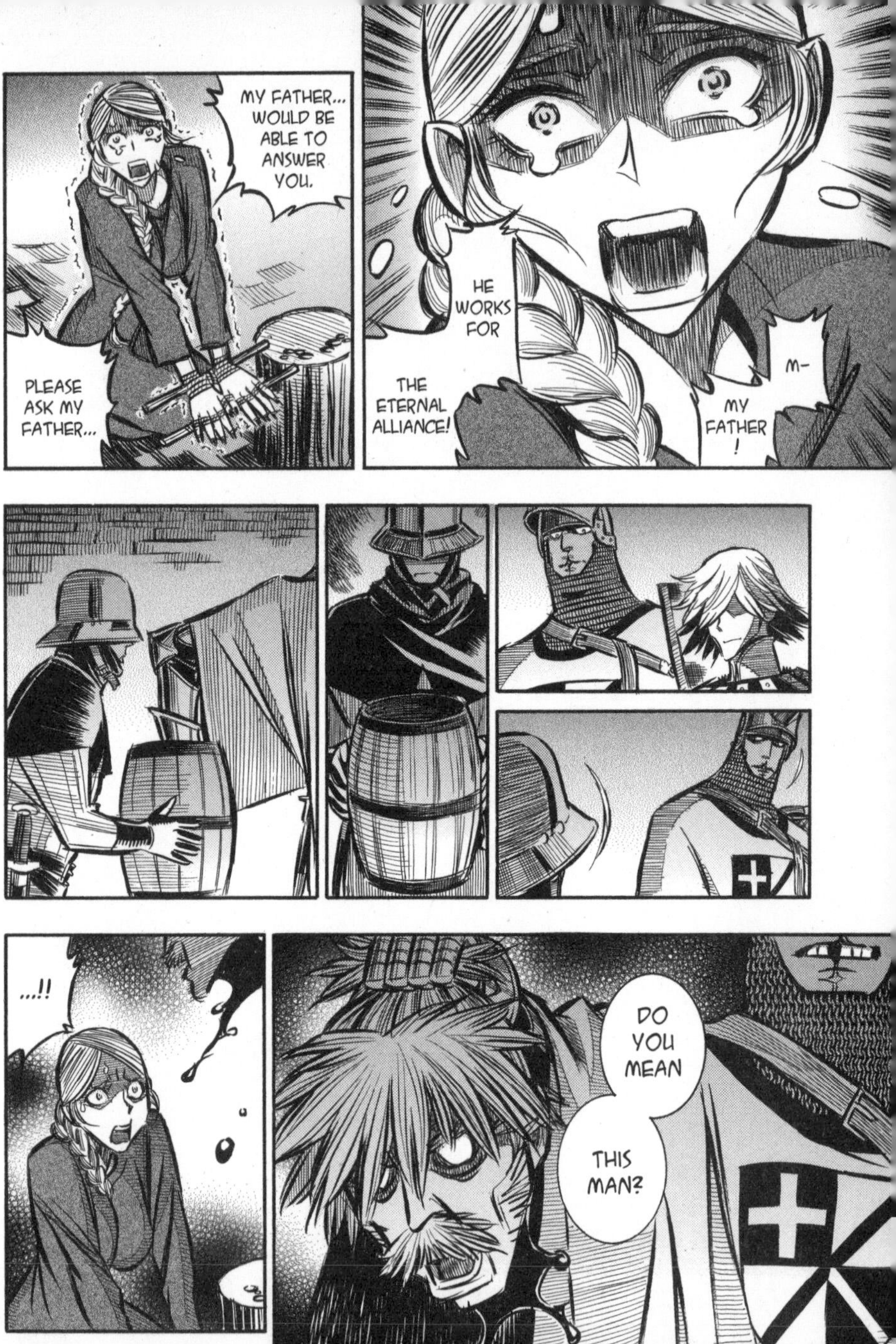
M-
MY FATHER!
HE WORKS FOR
THE ETERNAL ALLIANCE!
MY FATHER... WOULD BE ABLE TO ANSWER YOU.
PLEASE ASK MY FATHER...
DO YOU MEAN
THIS MAN?
...!!

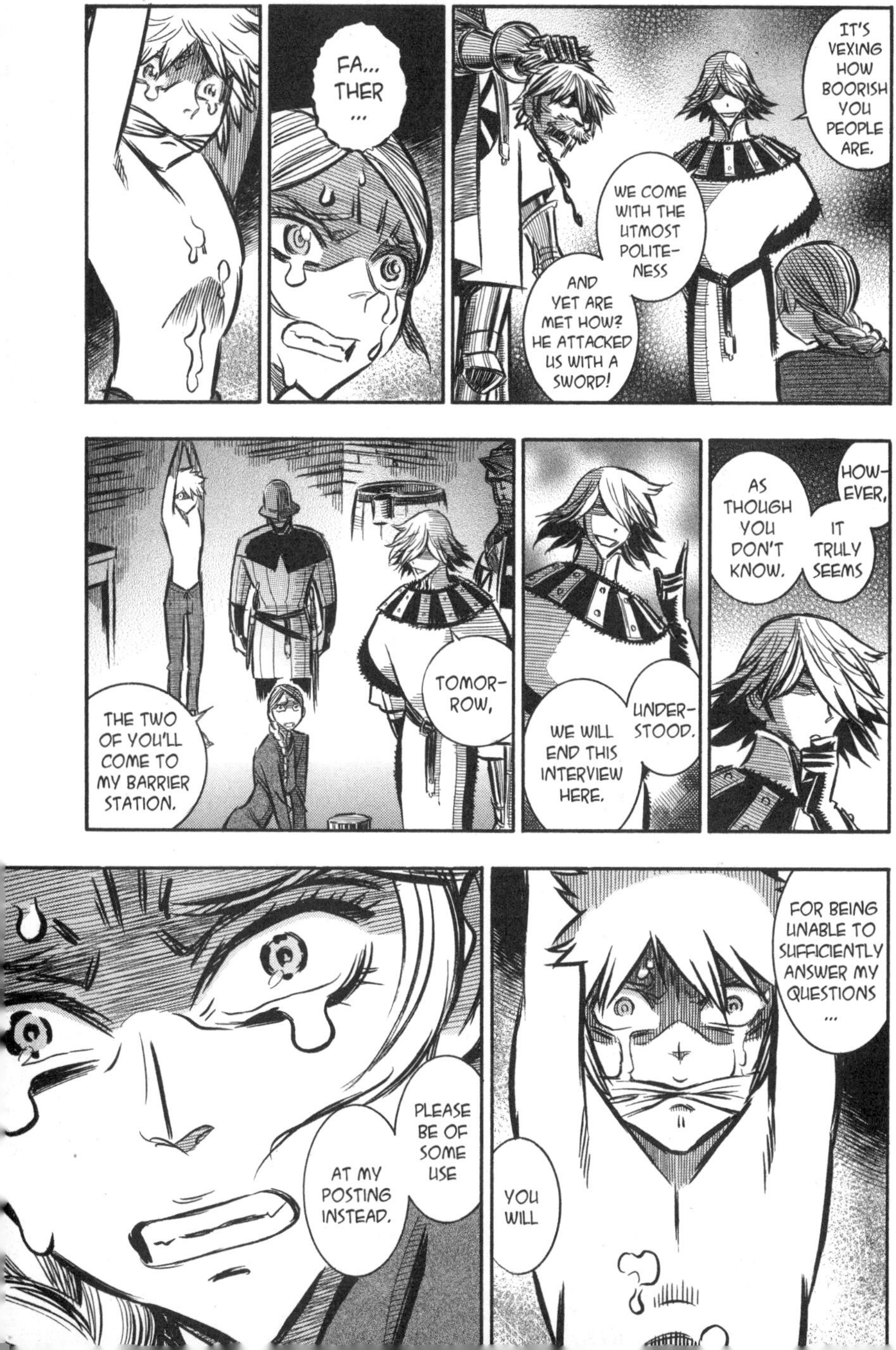
IT'S VEXING HOW BOORISH YOU PEOPLE ARE.
WE COME WITH THE UTMOST POLITE-NESS
AND YET ARE MET HOW? HE ATTACKED US WITH A SWORD!
FA... THER ...
HOW-EVER, IT TRULY SEEMS
AS THOUGH YOU DON'T KNOW.
UNDER-STOOD.
WE WILL END THIS INTERVIEW HERE.
TOMOR-ROW,
THE TWO OF YOU'LL COME TO MY BARRIER STATION.
FOR BEING UNABLE TO SUFFICIENTLY ANSWER MY QUESTIONS ...
YOU WILL
PLEASE BE OF SOME USE
AT MY POSTING INSTEAD.

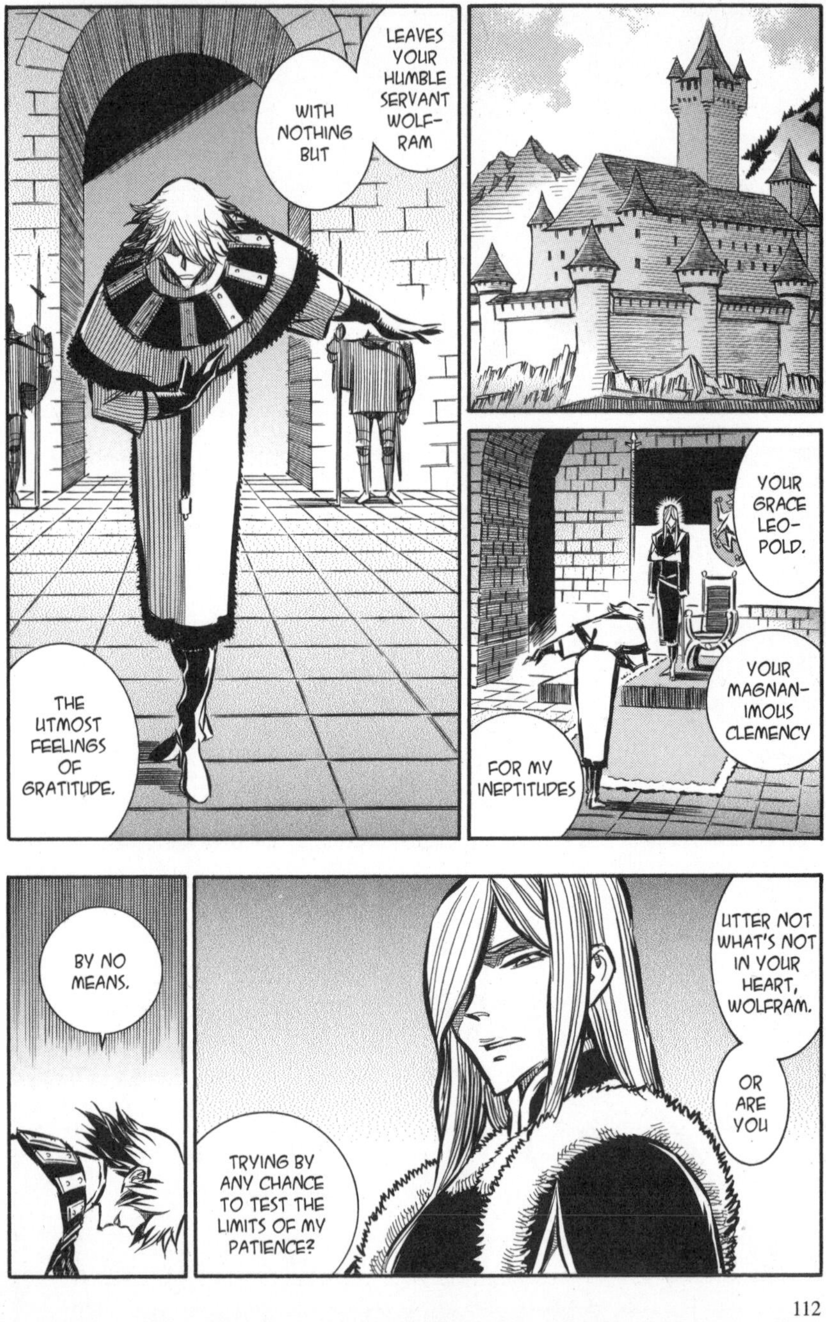
YOUR GRACE LEOPOLD.
YOUR MAGNANIMOUS CLEMENCY
FOR MY INEPTITUDES
LEAVES YOUR HUMBLE SERVANT WOLFRAM
WITH NOTHING BUT
THE UTMOST FEELINGS OF GRATITUDE.
UTTER NOT WHAT'S NOT IN YOUR HEART, WOLFRAM.
OR ARE YOU
TRYING BY ANY CHANCE TO TEST THE LIMITS OF MY PATIENCE?
BY NO MEANS.

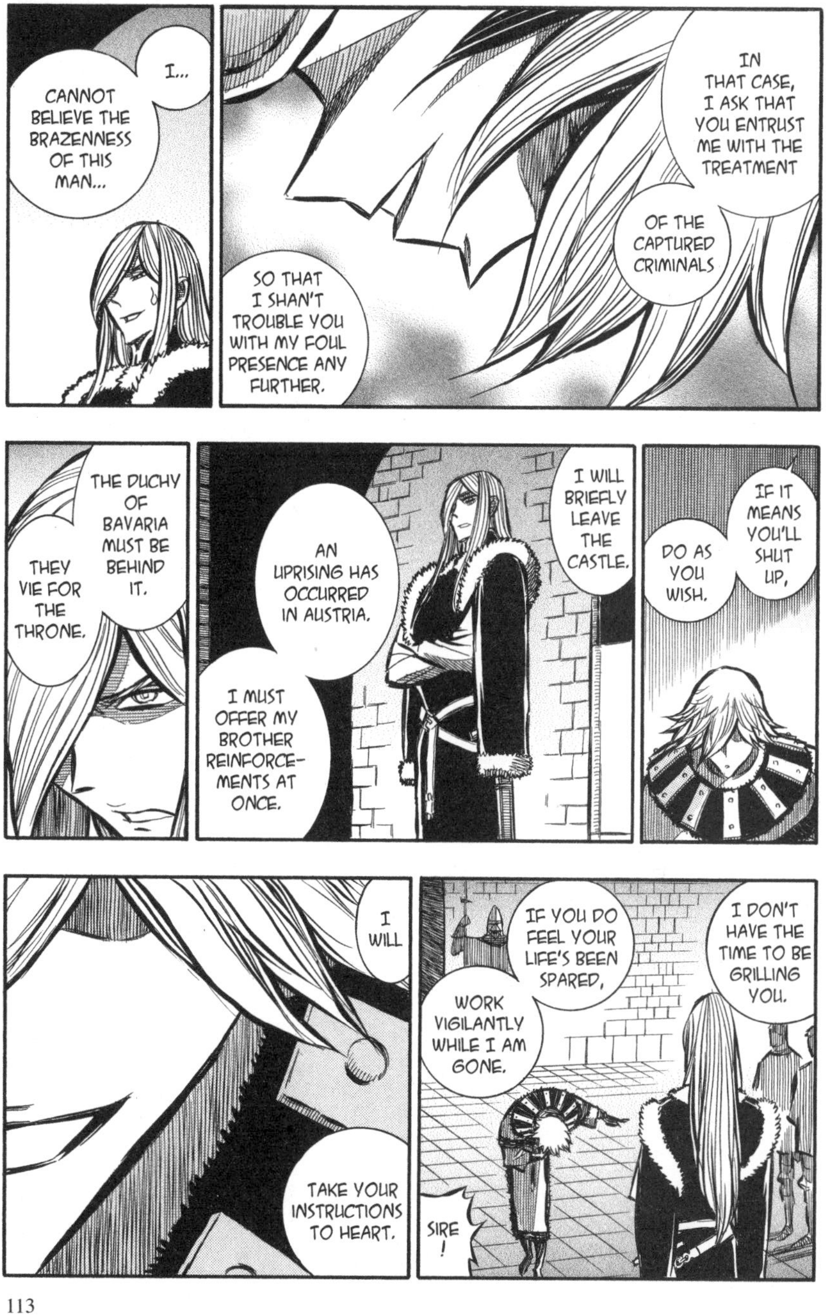
IN THAT CASE, I ASK THAT YOU ENTRUST ME WITH THE TREATMENT
OF THE CAPTURED CRIMINALS
SO THAT I SHAN'T TROUBLE YOU WITH MY FOUL PRESENCE ANY FURTHER.
I...
CANNOT BELIEVE THE BRAZENNESS OF THIS MAN...
IF IT MEANS YOU'LL SHUT UP,
DO AS YOU WISH.
I WILL BRIEFLY LEAVE THE CASTLE.
AN UPRISING HAS OCCURRED IN AUSTRIA.
I MUST OFFER MY BROTHER REINFORCE-MENTS AT ONCE.
THE DUCHY OF BAVARIA MUST BE BEHIND IT.
THEY VIE FOR THE THRONE.
I DON'T HAVE THE TIME TO BE GRILLING YOU.
IF YOU DO FEEL YOUR LIFE'S BEEN SPARED,
WORK VIGILANTLY WHILE I AM GONE.
SIRE!
I WILL
TAKE YOUR INSTRUCTIONS TO HEART.

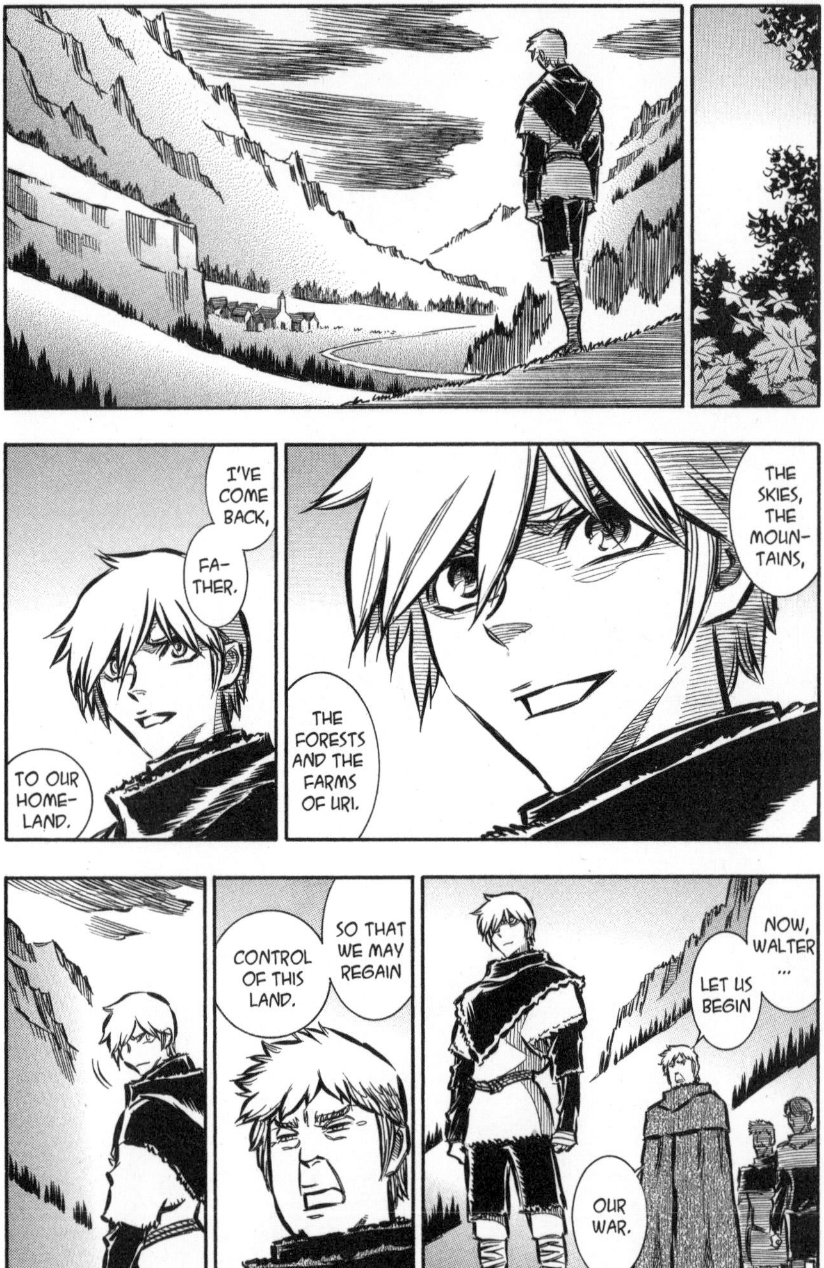
THE SKIES, THE MOUNTAINS,
THE FORESTS AND THE FARMS OF URI.
I'VE COME BACK,
FATHER.
TO OUR HOMELAND.
NOW, WALTER ...
LET US BEGIN
OUR WAR.
SO THAT WE MAY REGAIN
CONTROL OF THIS LAND.

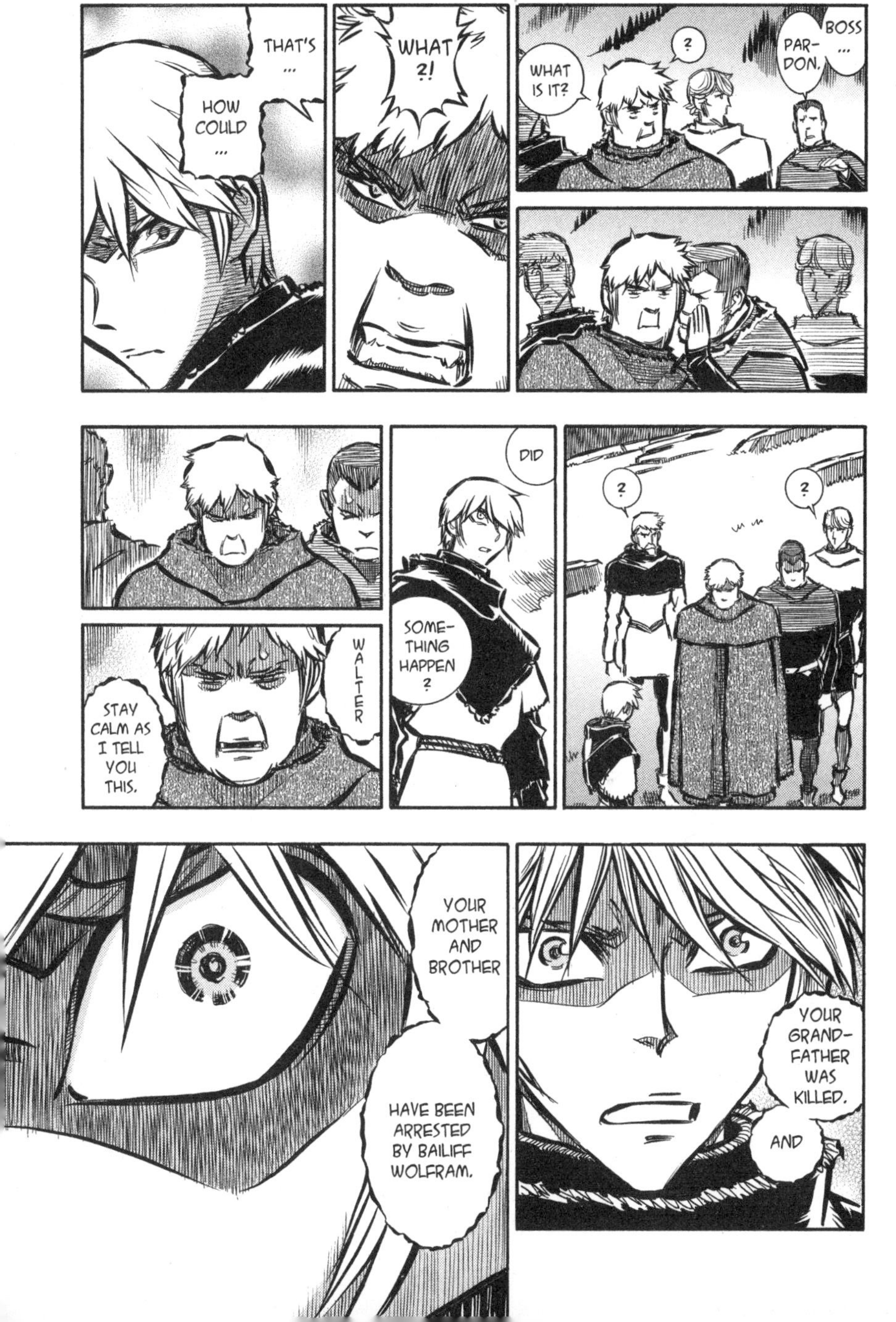
BOSS ...
PAR-DON.
?
WHAT IS IT?
WHAT ?!
THAT'S ...
HOW COULD ...
?
?
DID
SOME-THING HAPPEN ?
WALTER
STAY CALM AS I TELL YOU THIS.
YOUR GRAND-FATHER WAS KILLED.
AND
YOUR MOTHER AND BROTHER
HAVE BEEN ARRESTED BY BAILIFF WOLFRAM.

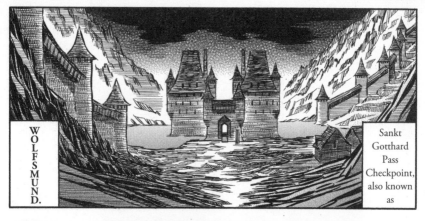

Sankt Gotthard Pass Checkpoint, also known as
WOLFSMUND.
WE WILL NOW CONDUCT THE EXECUTION
OF THE REBEL WILHELM TELL'S FAMILY,
HIS WIFE AND THEIR CHILD!

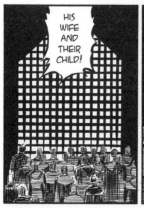

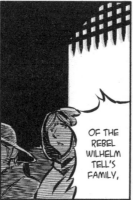

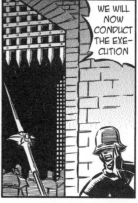

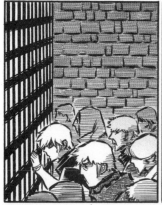

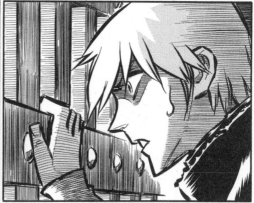

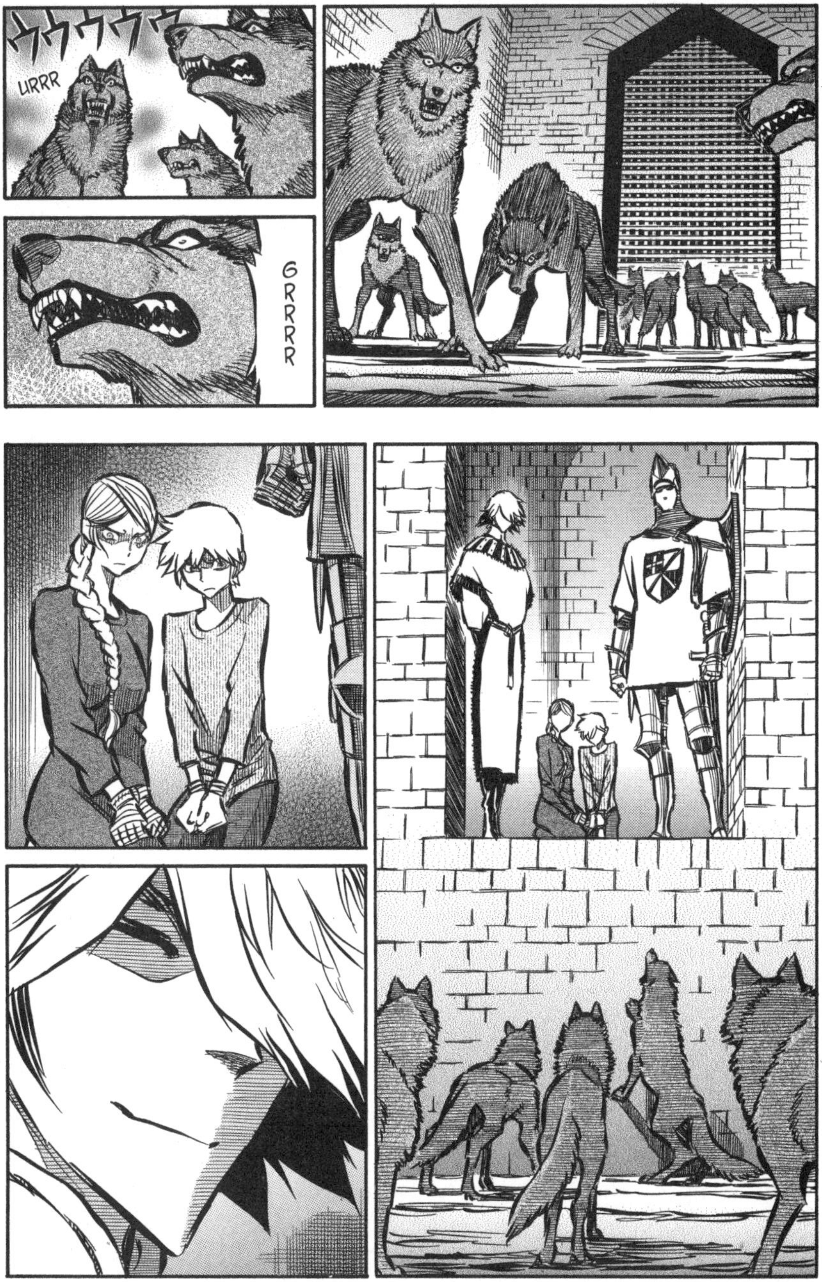
ウウウウウ
URRR
GRRRR

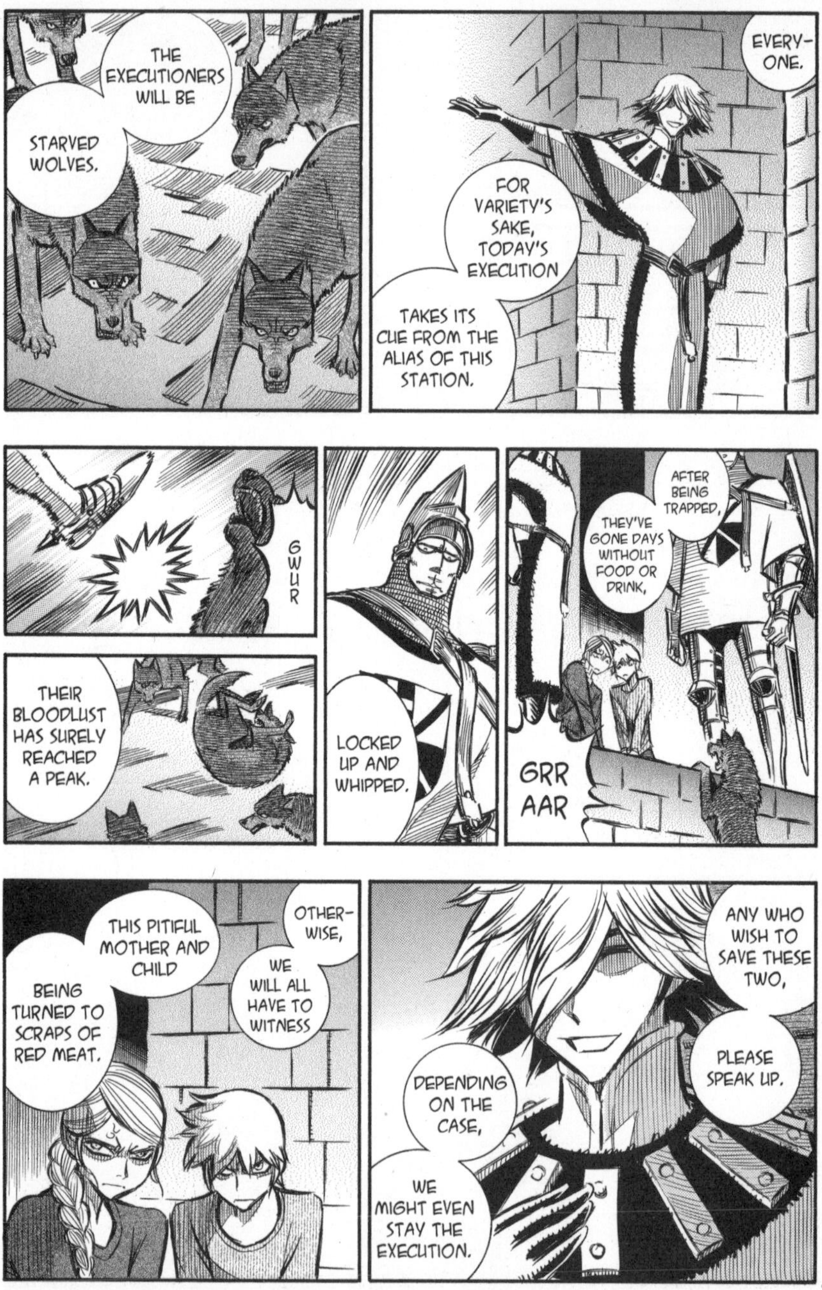
EVERY-ONE.
FOR VARIETY'S SAKE, TODAY'S EXECUTION
TAKES ITS CUE FROM THE ALIAS OF THIS STATION.
THE EXECUTIONERS WILL BE
STARVED WOLVES.
AFTER BEING TRAPPED,
THEY'VE GONE DAYS WITHOUT FOOD OR DRINK,
GRR AAR
LOCKED UP AND WHIPPED.
GWUR
THEIR BLOODLUST HAS SURELY REACHED A PEAK.
ANY WHO WISH TO SAVE THESE TWO,
PLEASE SPEAK UP.
DEPENDING ON THE CASE,
WE MIGHT EVEN STAY THE EXECUTION.
OTHER-WISE,
WE WILL ALL HAVE TO WITNESS
THIS PITIFUL MOTHER AND CHILD
BEING TURNED TO SCRAPS OF RED MEAT.

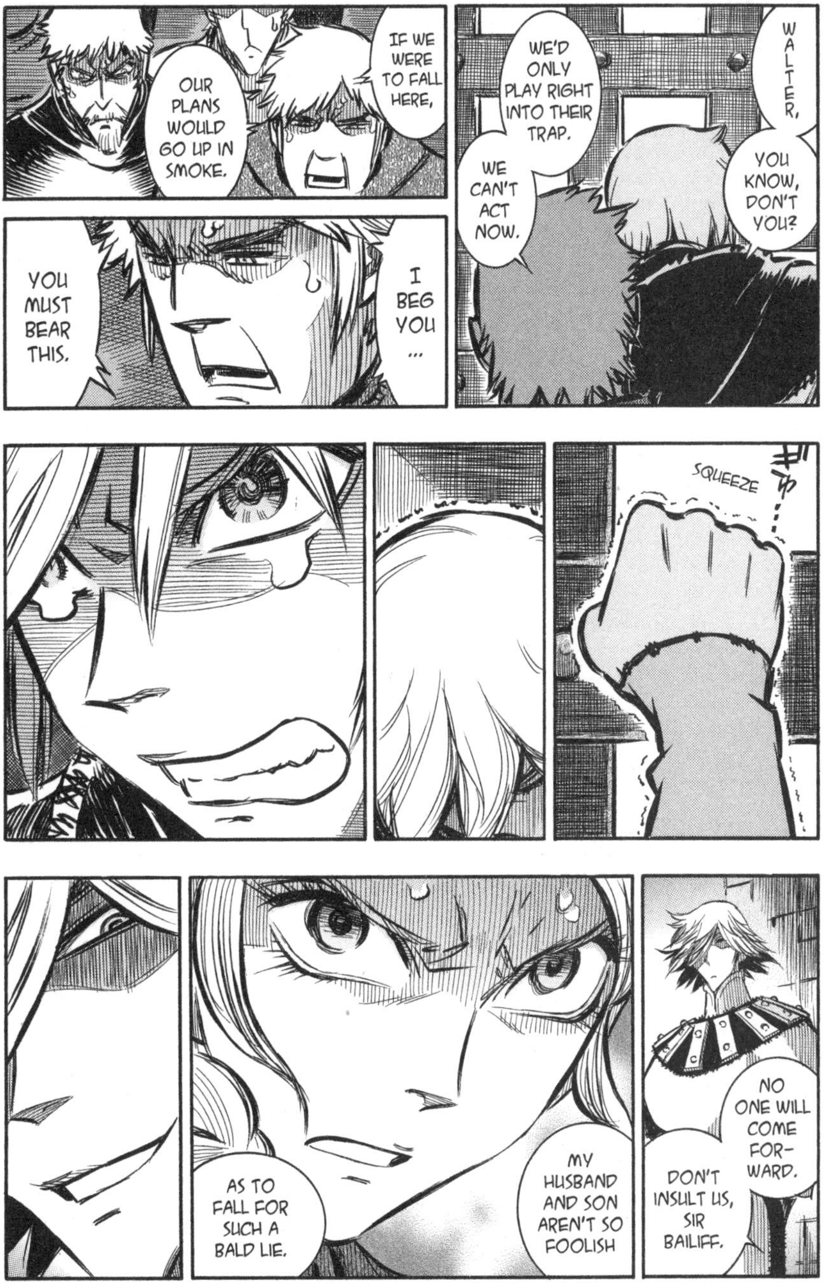
WALTER,
YOU KNOW, DON'T YOU?
WE'D ONLY PLAY RIGHT INTO THEIR TRAP.
WE CAN'T ACT NOW.
IF WE WERE TO FALL HERE,
OUR PLANS WOULD GO UP IN SMOKE.
I BEG YOU ...
YOU MUST BEAR THIS.
SQUEEZE
NO ONE WILL COME FOR-WARD.
DON'T INSULT US, SIR BAILIFF.
MY HUSBAND AND SON AREN'T SO FOOLISH
AS TO FALL FOR SUCH A BALD LIE.

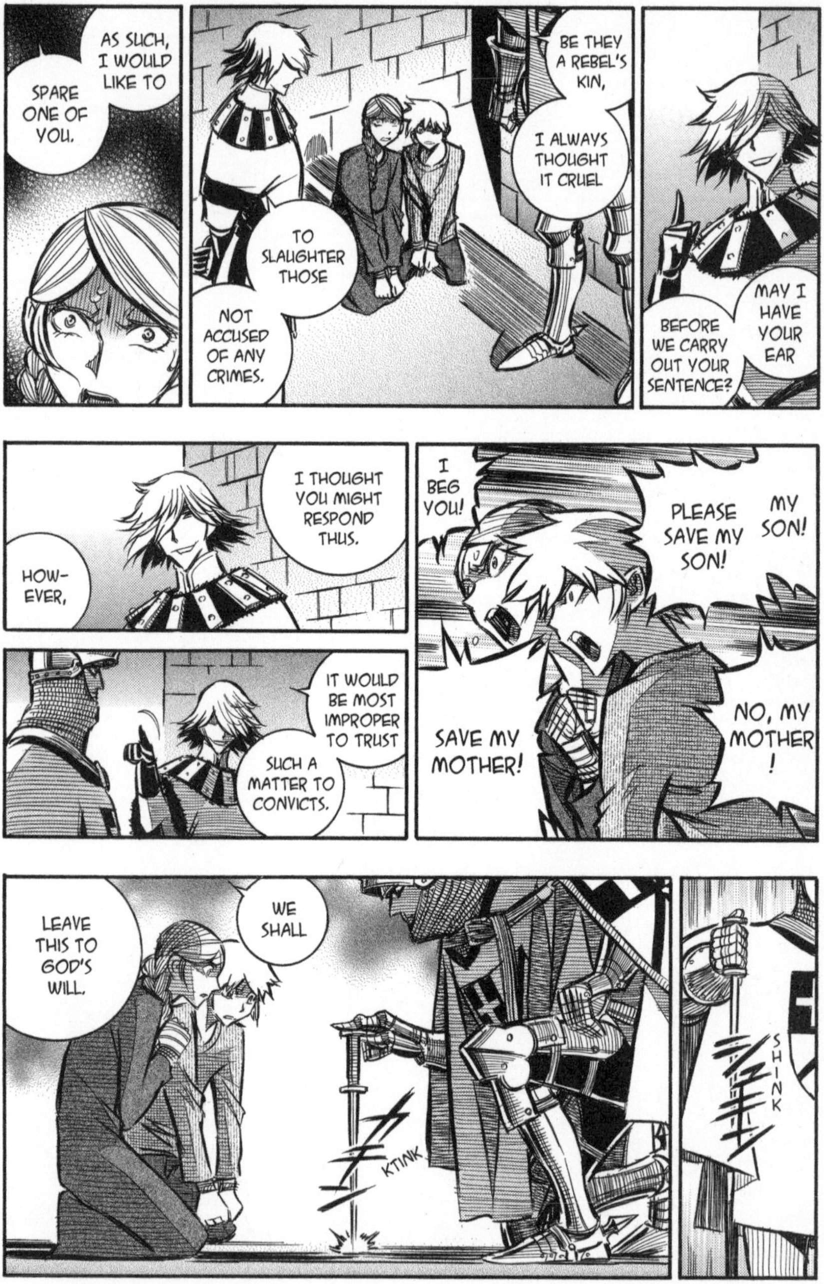
MAY I HAVE YOUR EAR
BEFORE WE CARRY OUT YOUR SENTENCE?
BE THEY A REBEL'S KIN,
I ALWAYS THOUGHT IT CRUEL
TO SLAUGHTER THOSE
NOT ACCUSED OF ANY CRIMES.
AS SUCH, I WOULD LIKE TO
SPARE ONE OF YOU.
MY SON!
PLEASE SAVE MY SON!
I BEG YOU!
NO, MY MOTHER!
SAVE MY MOTHER!
I THOUGHT YOU MIGHT RESPOND THUS.
HOW-EVER,
IT WOULD BE MOST IMPROPER TO TRUST
SUCH A MATTER TO CONVICTS.
SHINK
WE SHALL
LEAVE THIS TO GOD'S WILL.
KTINK

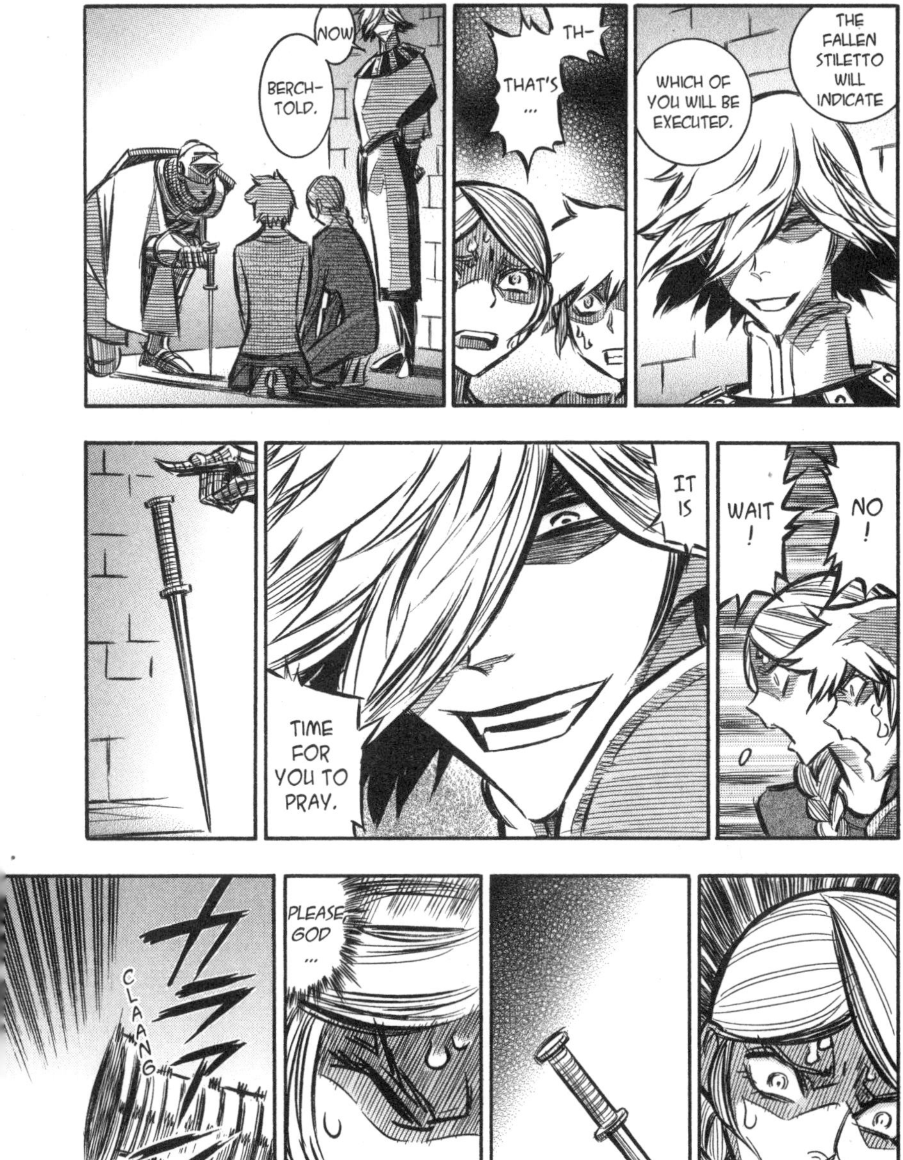
THE FALLEN STILETTO WILL INDICATE
WHICH OF YOU WILL BE EXECUTED.
TH-
THAT'S ...
NOW
BERCH-TOLD.
NO!
WAIT!
IT IS
TIME FOR YOU TO PRAY.
PLEASE, GOD ...
CLAAANG

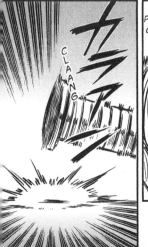

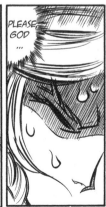

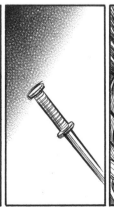

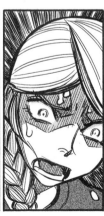

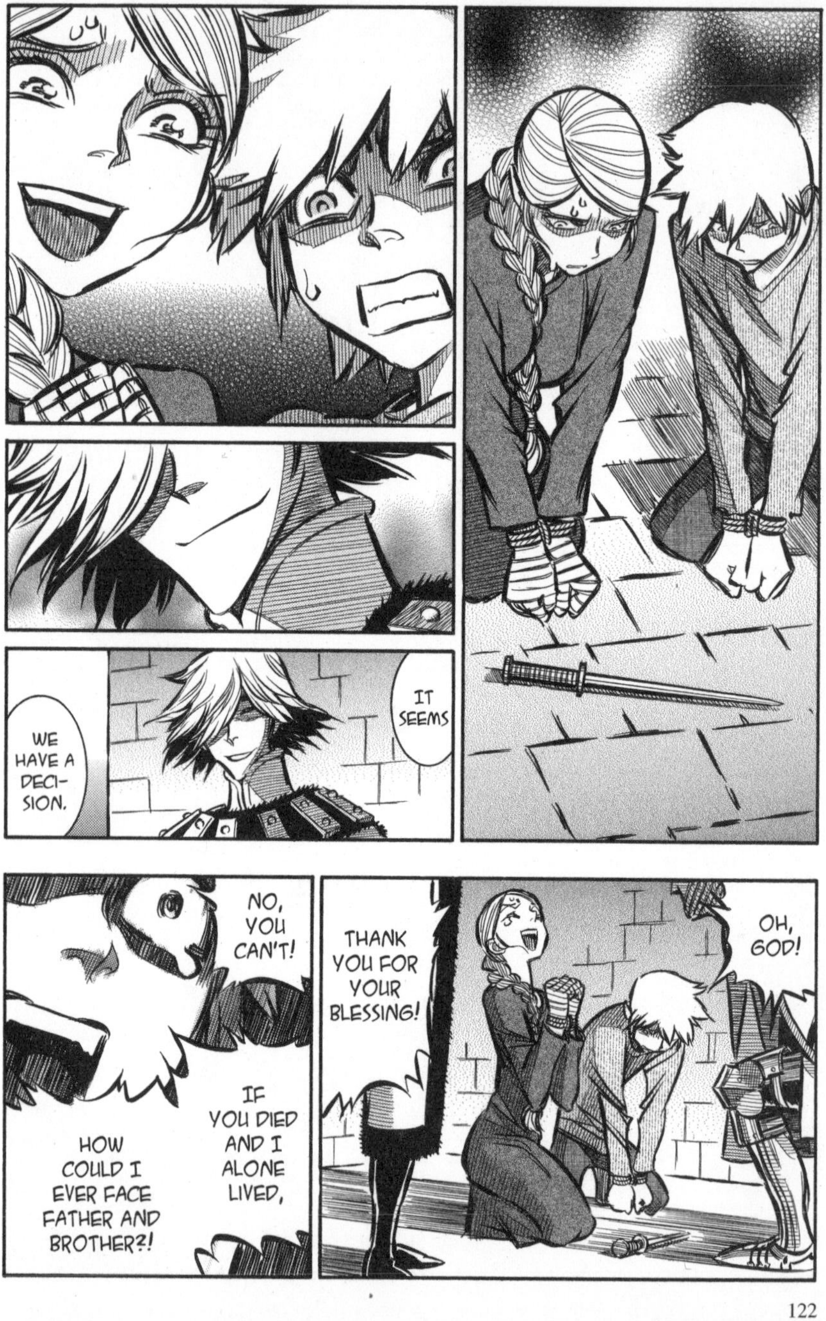
IT SEEMS
WE HAVE A DECISION.
OH, GOD!
THANK YOU FOR YOUR BLESSING!
NO, YOU CAN'T!
IF YOU DIED AND I ALONE LIVED,
HOW COULD I EVER FACE FATHER AND BROTHER?!

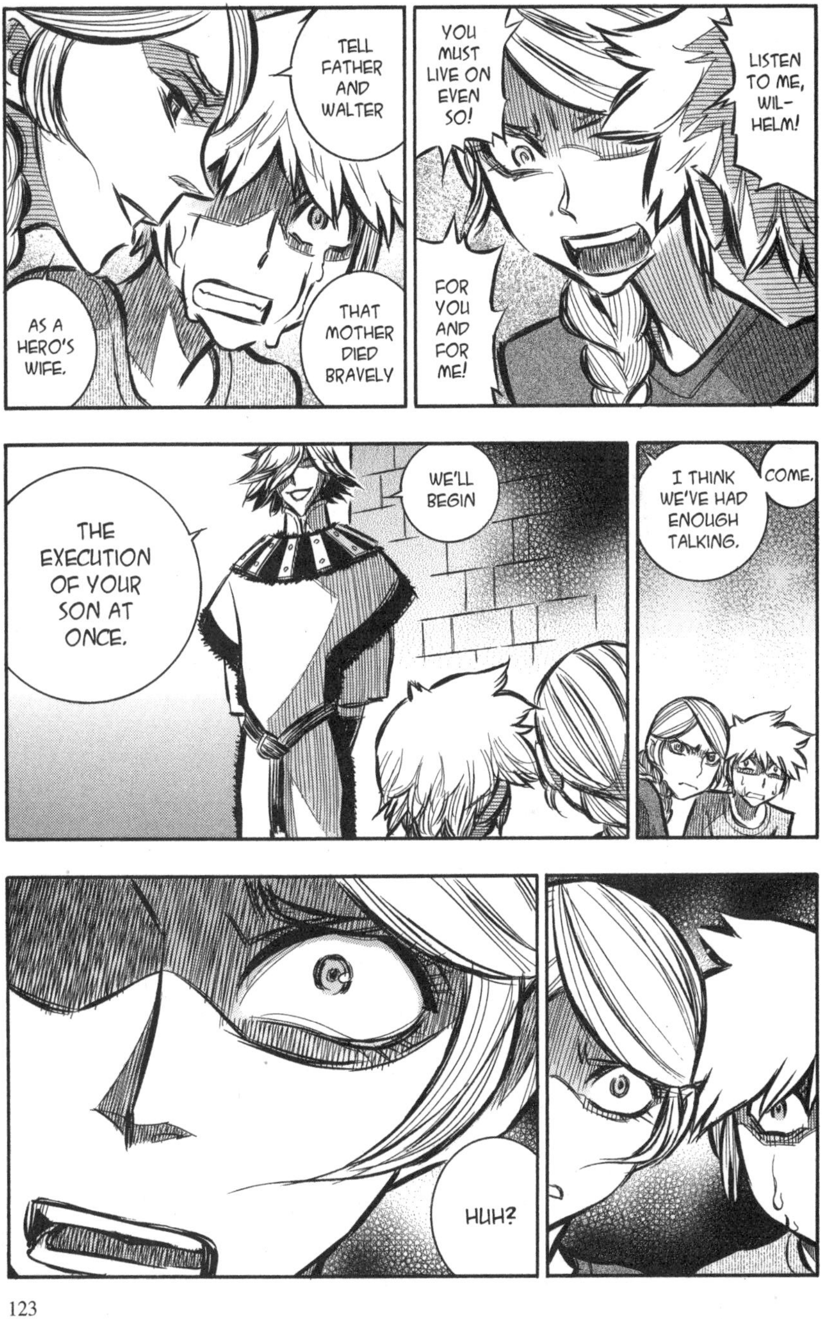
LISTEN TO ME, WIL-HELM!
YOU MUST LIVE ON EVEN SO!
FOR YOU AND FOR ME!
TELL FATHER AND WALTER
THAT MOTHER DIED BRAVELY
AS A HERO'S WIFE.
COME.
I THINK WE'VE HAD ENOUGH TALKING.
WE'LL BEGIN
THE EXECUTION OF YOUR SON AT ONCE.
HUH?

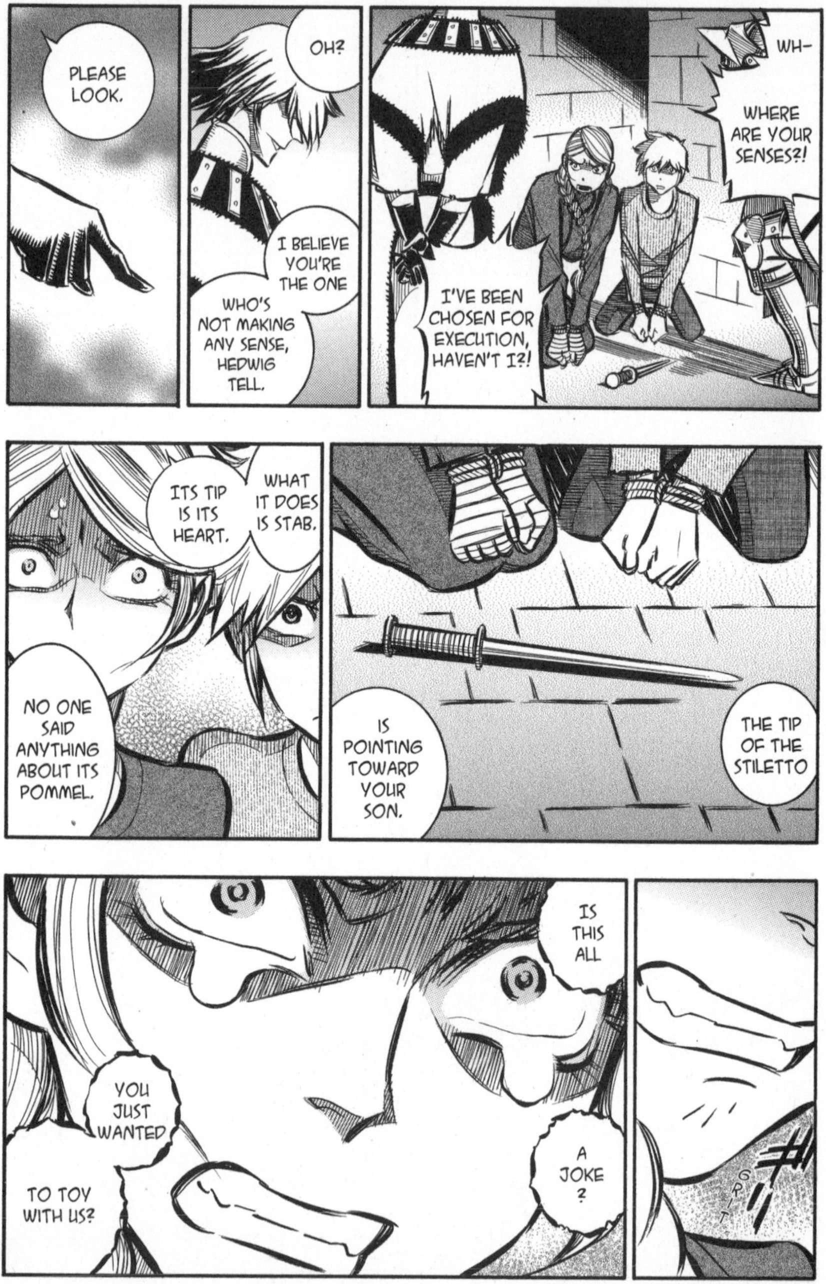
WH-
WHERE ARE YOUR SENSES?!
I'VE BEEN CHOSEN FOR EXECUTION, HAVEN'T I?!
OH?
I BELIEVE YOU'RE THE ONE
WHO'S NOT MAKING ANY SENSE, HEDWIG TELL.
PLEASE LOOK.
THE TIP OF THE STILETTO
IS POINTING TOWARD YOUR SON.
WHAT IT DOES IS STAB.
ITS TIP IS ITS HEART.
NO ONE SAID ANYTHING ABOUT ITS POMMEL.
GRIT
IS THIS ALL
A JOKE?
YOU JUST WANTED
TO TOY WITH US?

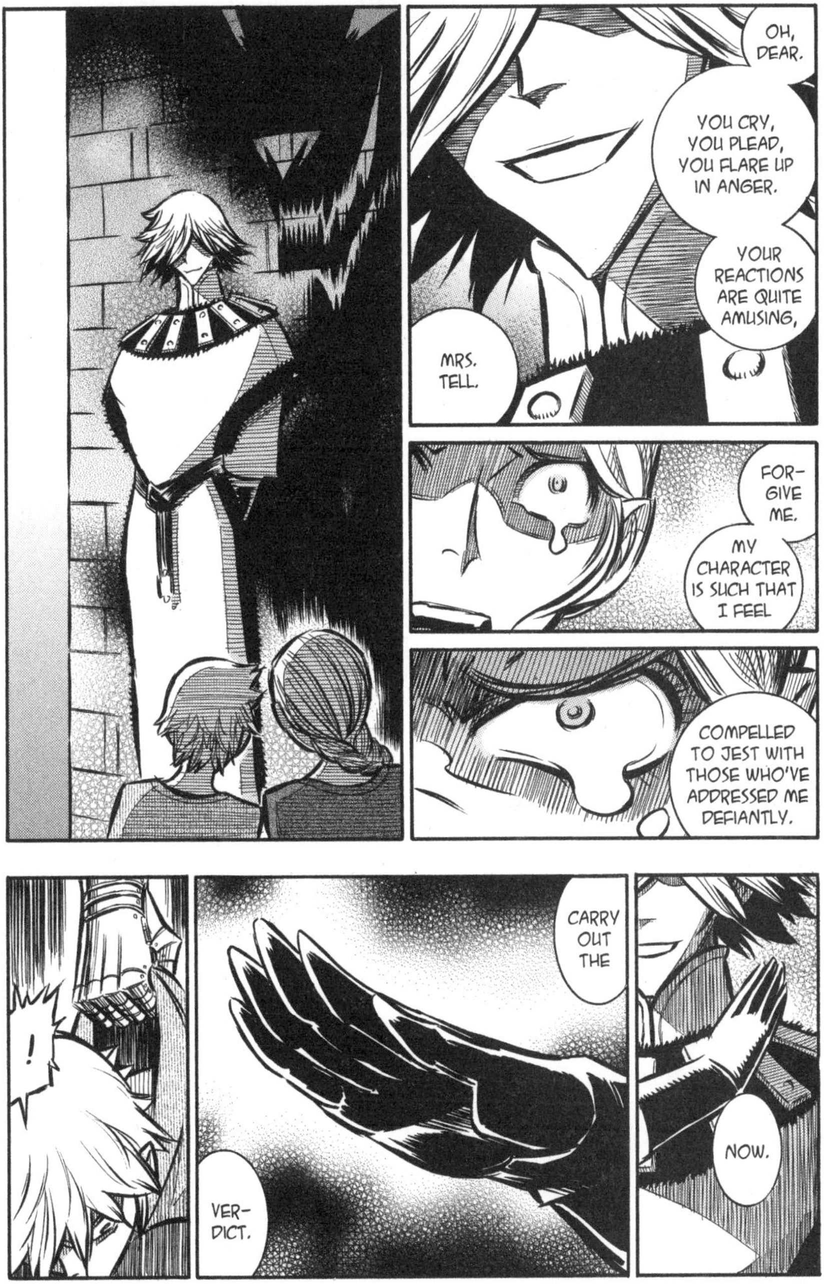
OH, DEAR.
YOU CRY, YOU PLEAD, YOU FLARE UP IN ANGER.
YOUR REACTIONS ARE QUITE AMUSING,
MRS. TELL.
FOR-GIVE ME.
MY CHARACTER IS SUCH THAT I FEEL
COMPELLED TO JEST WITH THOSE WHO'VE ADDRESSED ME DEFIANTLY.
NOW.
CARRY OUT THE
VERDICT.
!

THUD

UGH

NOOOO

WILHELM

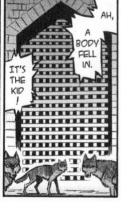

AH, A BODY FELL IN.

IT'S THE KID!

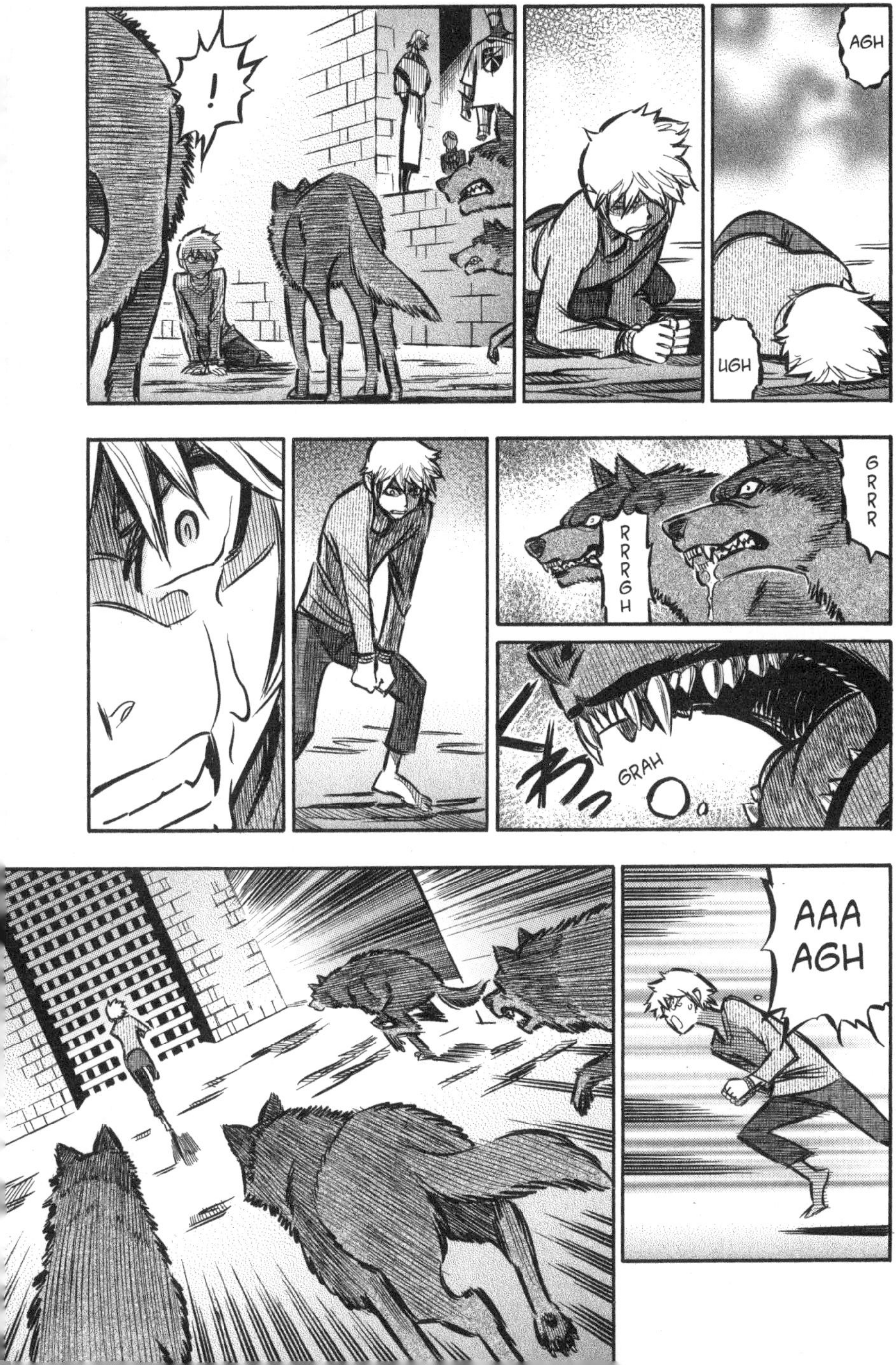
AGH
UGH
!
GRRR
RRRGH
GRAH
AAA AGH

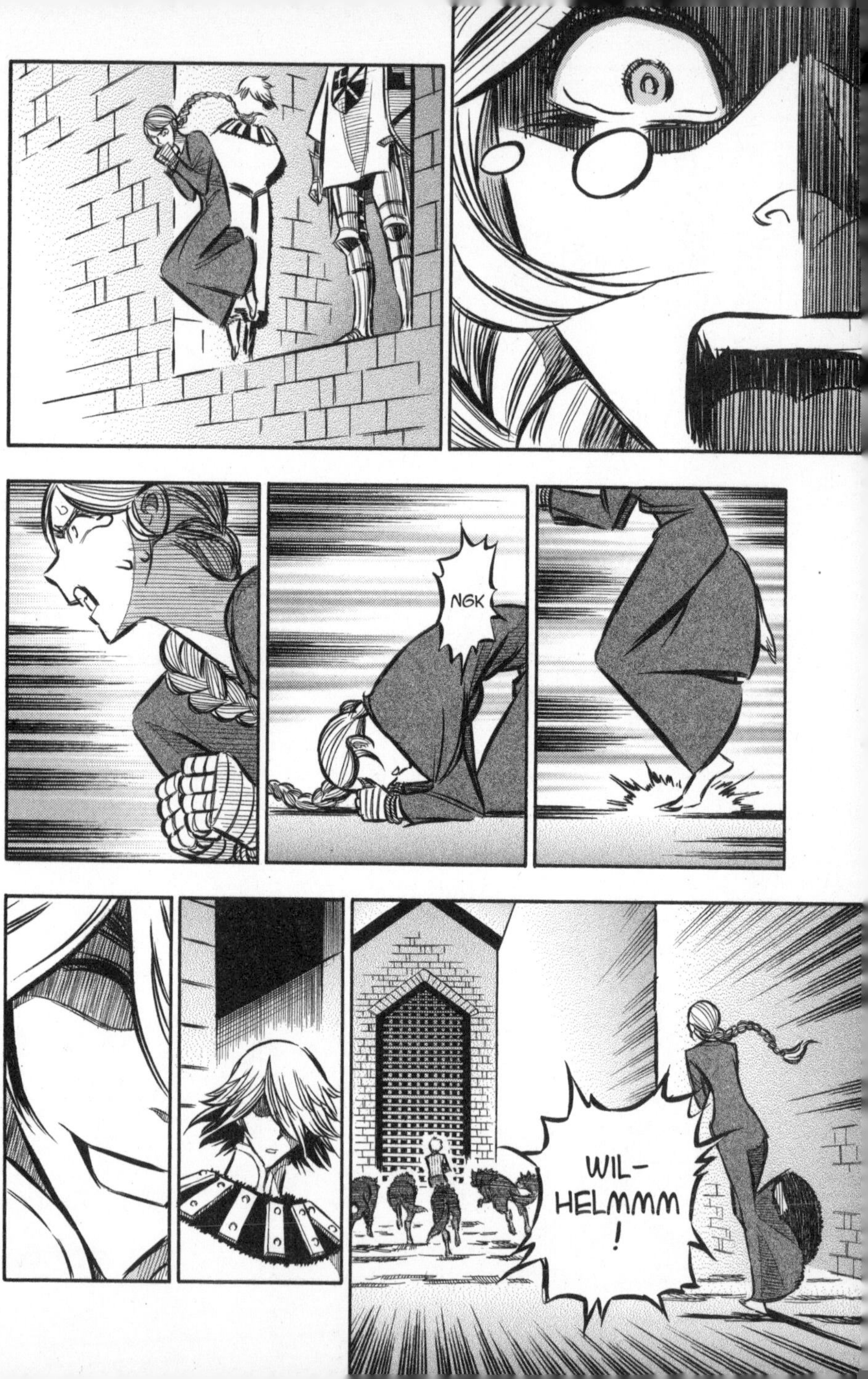
NGK
WIL-
HELMMM
!

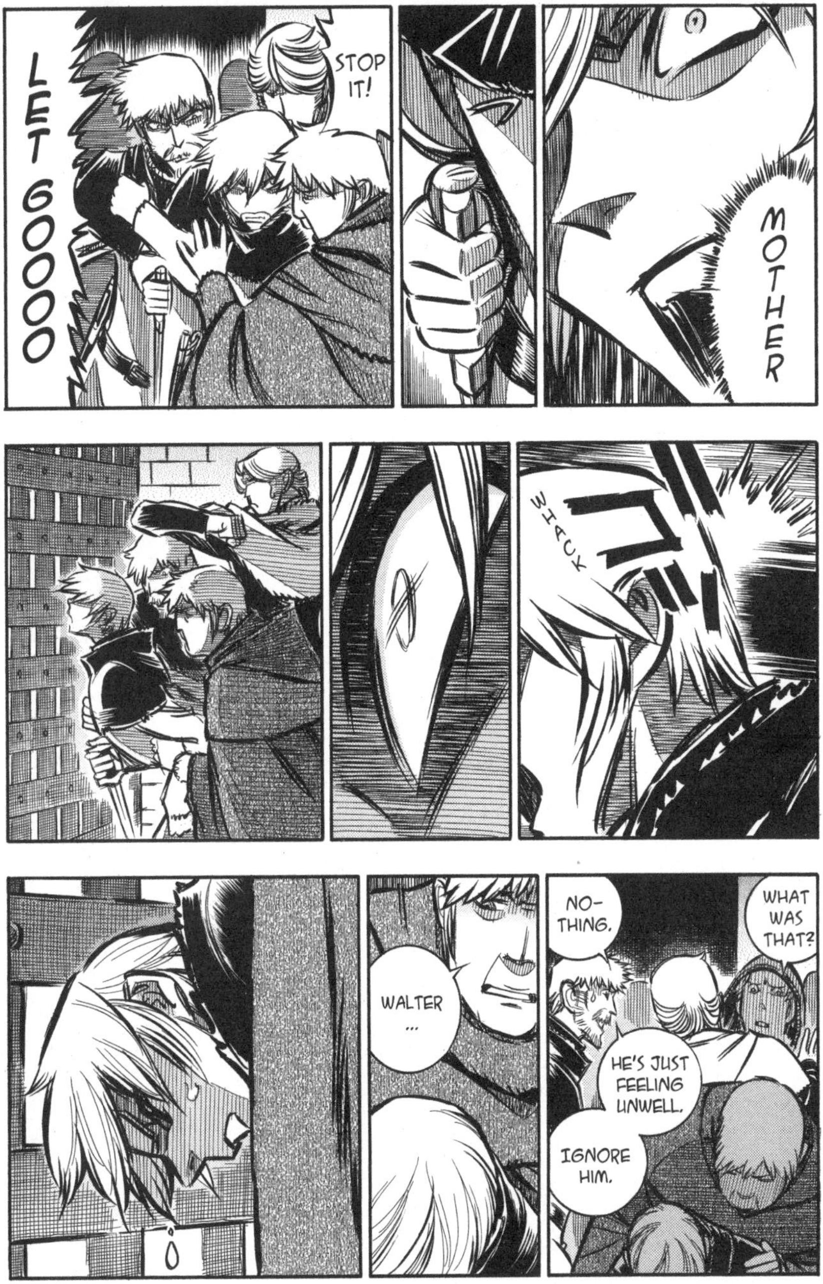
MOTHER
STOP IT!
LET GOOOOO
WHACK
WHAT WAS THAT?
NO-THING.
HE'S JUST FEELING UNWELL.
IGNORE HIM.
WALTER ...

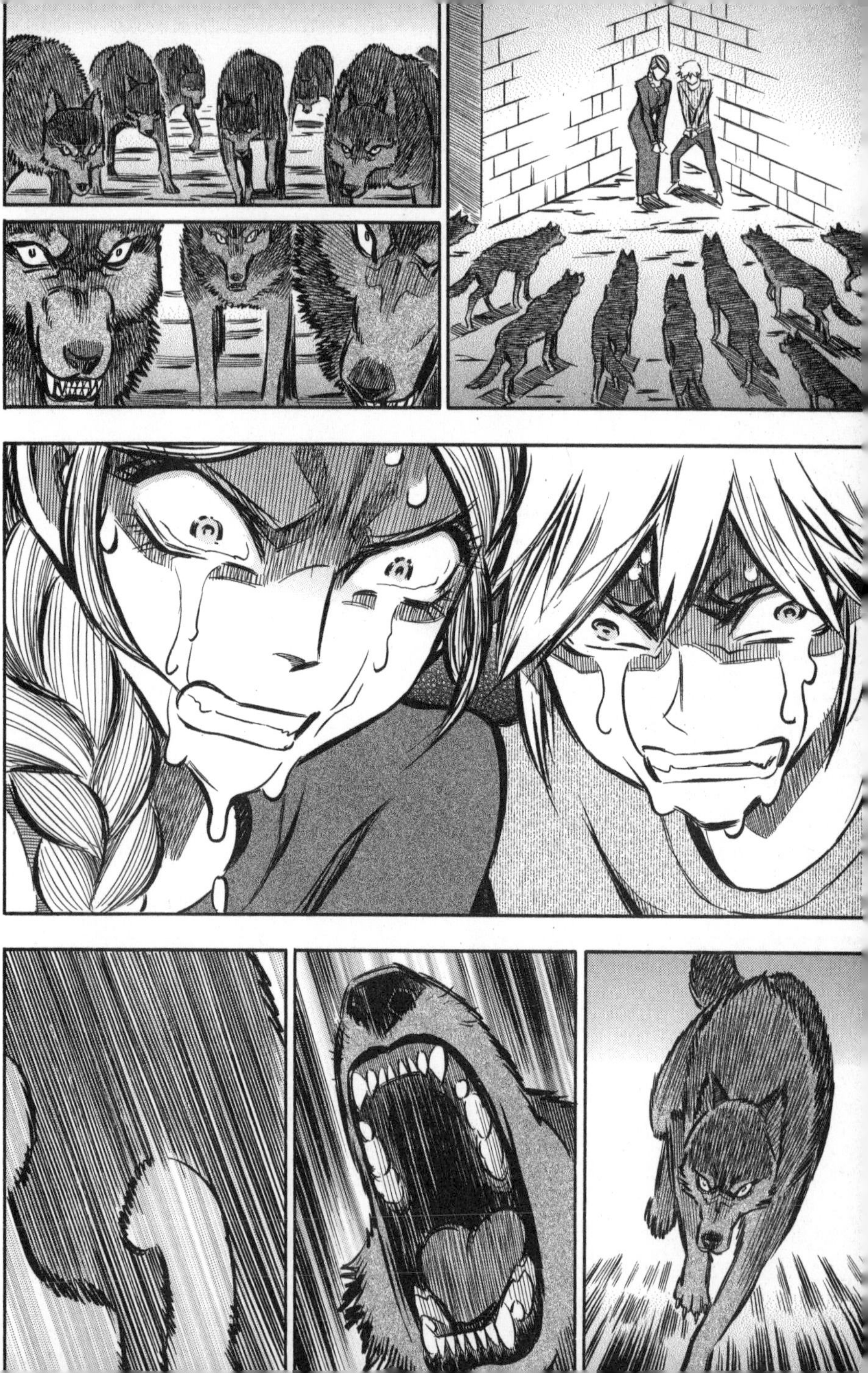

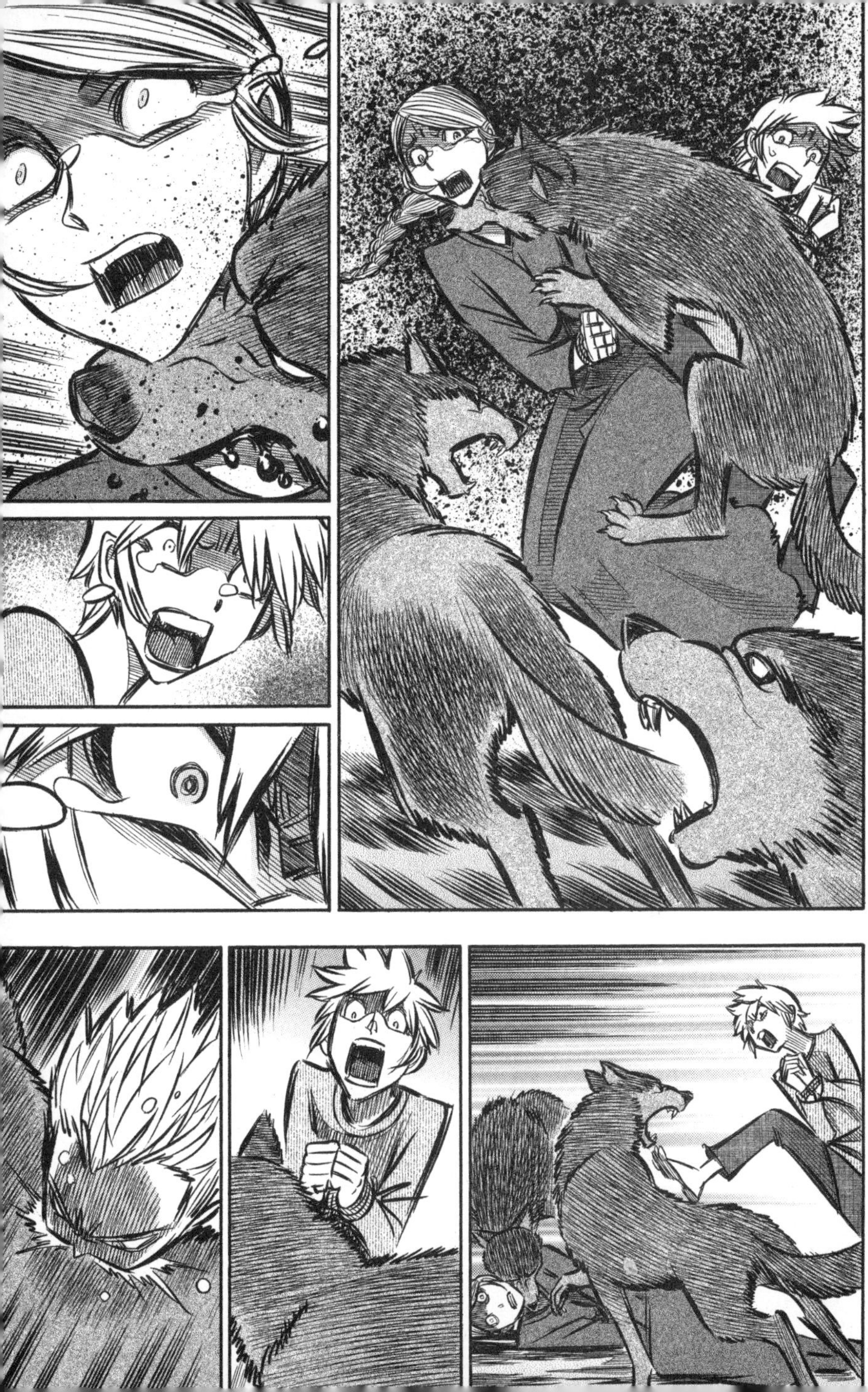

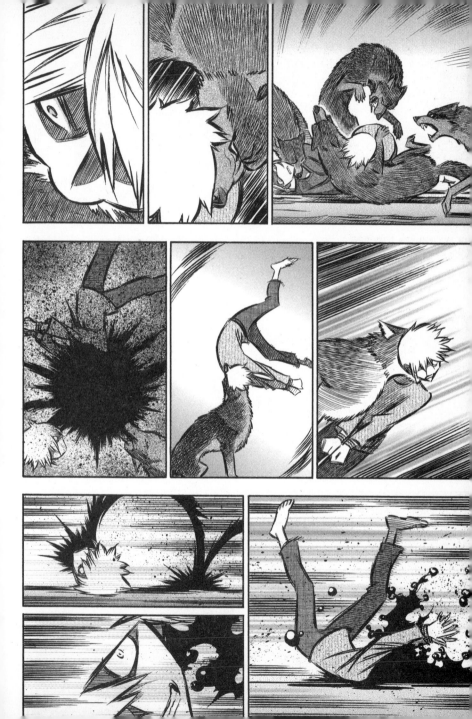

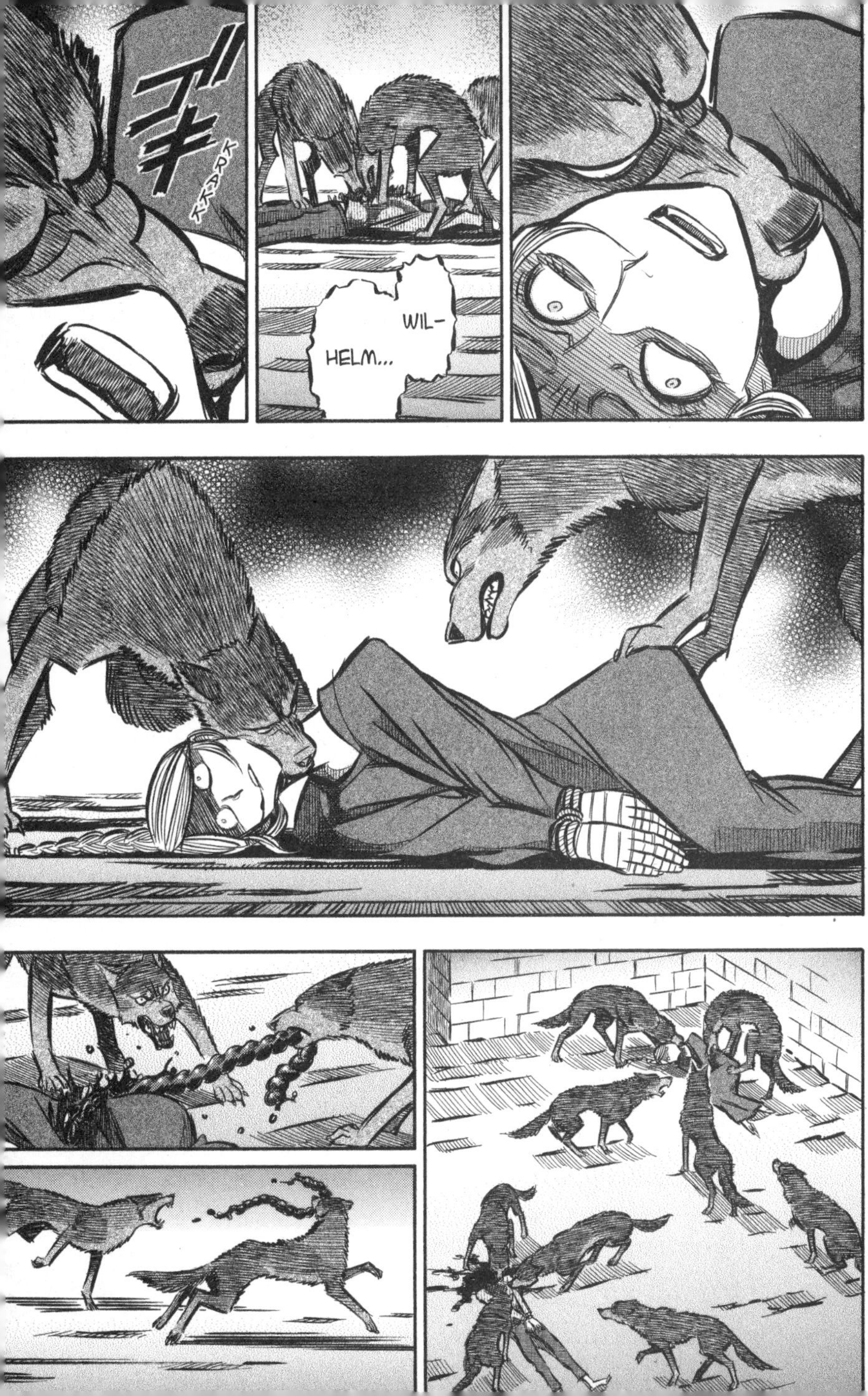
ゴキ
KRAK
WIL-
HELM...

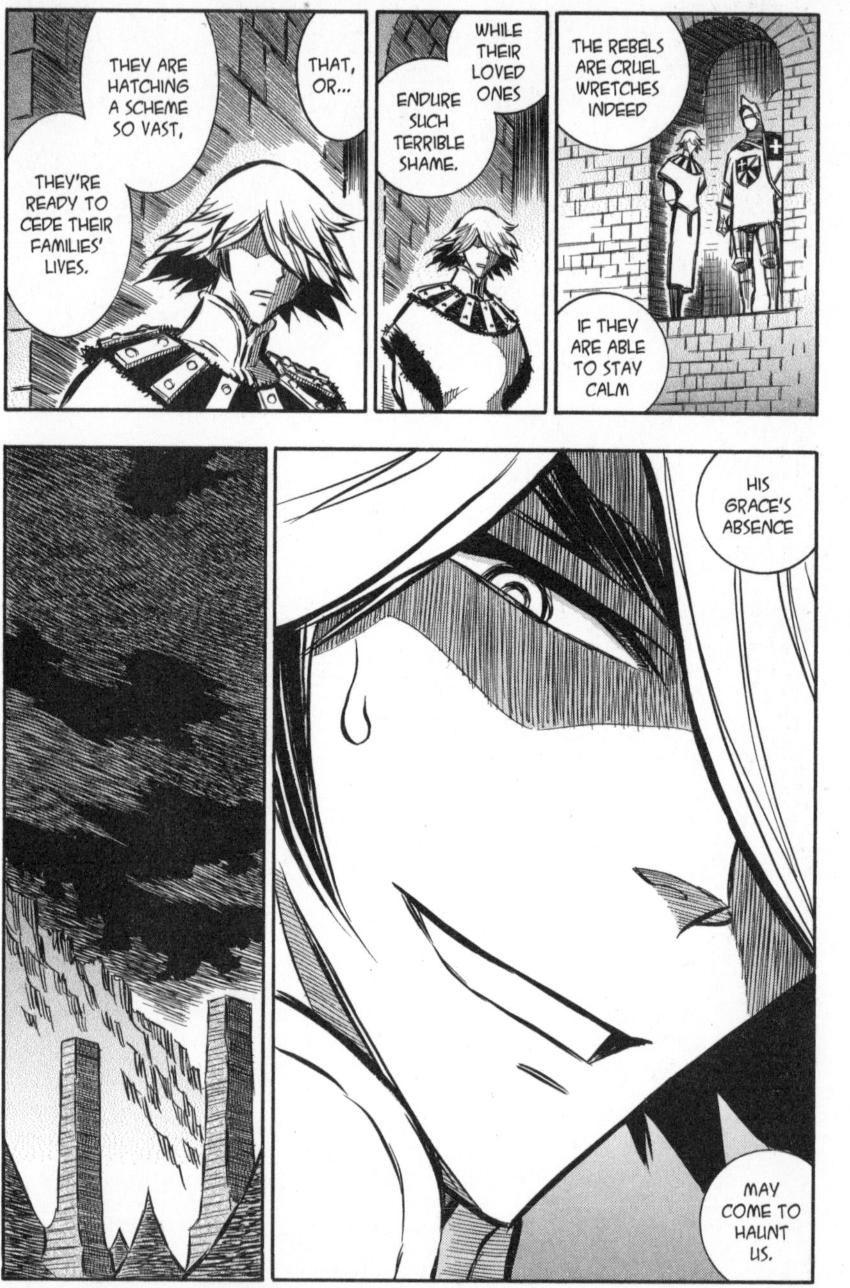
THE REBELS ARE CRUEL WRETCHES INDEED
IF THEY ARE ABLE TO STAY CALM
WHILE THEIR LOVED ONES
ENDURE SUCH TERRIBLE SHAME.
THAT, OR...
THEY ARE HATCHING A SCHEME SO VAST,
THEY'RE READY TO CEDE THEIR FAMILIES' LIVES.
HIS GRACE'S ABSENCE
MAY COME TO HAUNT US.

Chapter Ten END

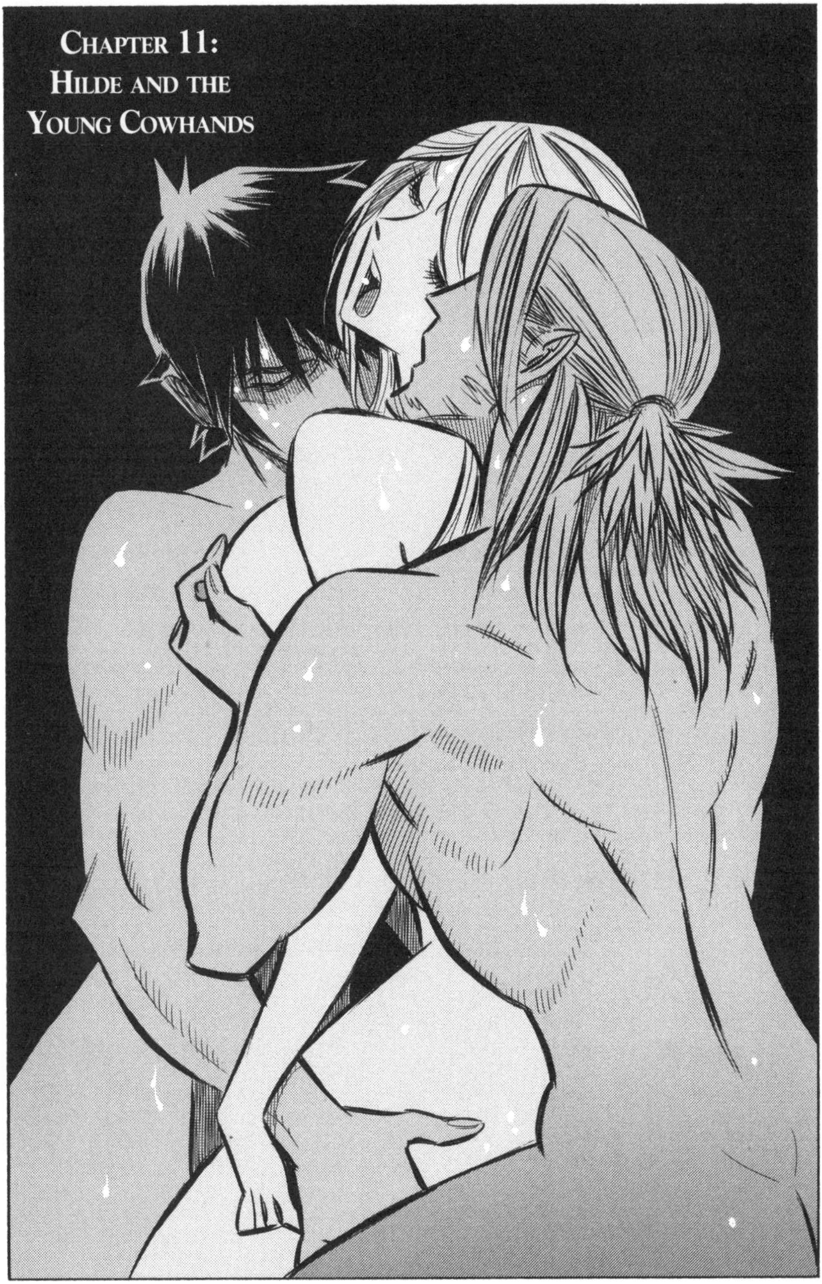
Chapter 11:
Hilde and the
Young Cowhands

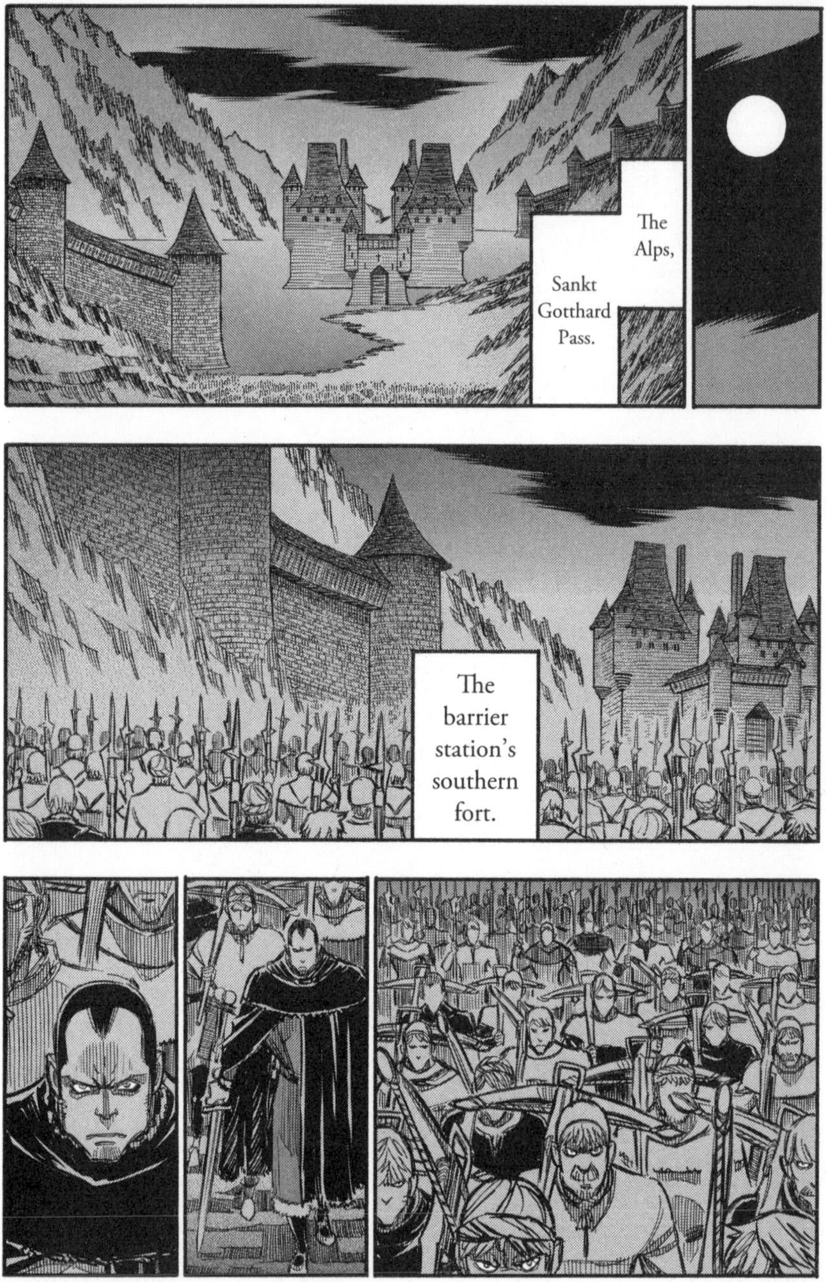
The Alps,
Sankt Gotthard Pass.
The barrier station's southern fort.

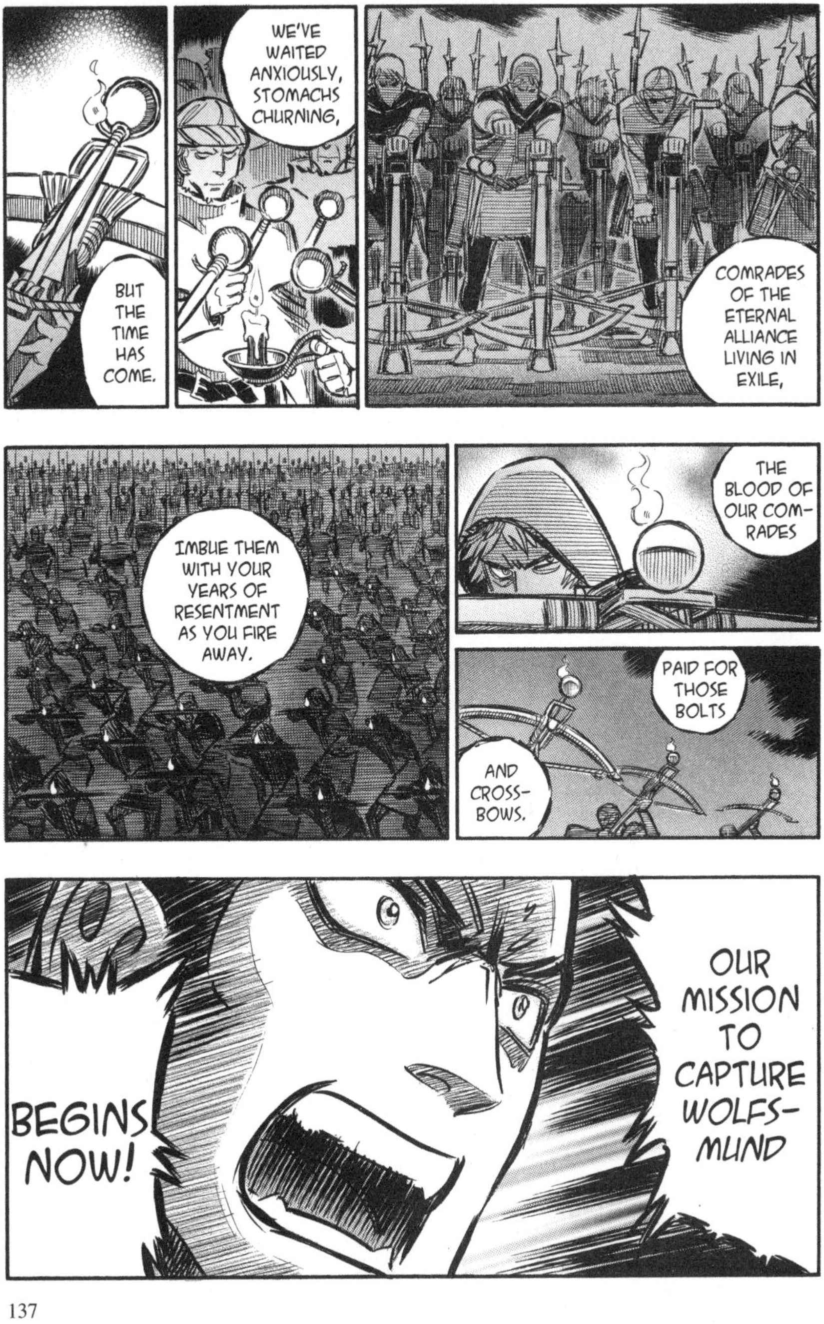
COMRADES OF THE ETERNAL ALLIANCE LIVING IN EXILE,
WE'VE WAITED ANXIOUSLY, STOMACHS CHURNING,
BUT THE TIME HAS COME.
THE BLOOD OF OUR COM-RADES
PAID FOR THOSE BOLTS
AND CROSS-BOWS.
IMBUE THEM WITH YOUR YEARS OF RESENTMENT AS YOU FIRE AWAY.
OUR MISSION TO CAPTURE WOLFS-MUND
BEGINS NOW!

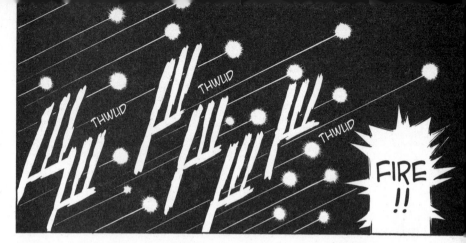

THWUD THWUD THWUD

FIRE!!

BOOM

KAKAK

KAKAK

CLANG

A—AN ENEMY RAID!

WE'RE UNDER ATTACK!!

FOES?!

WH—

WHAT, A FIRE?!

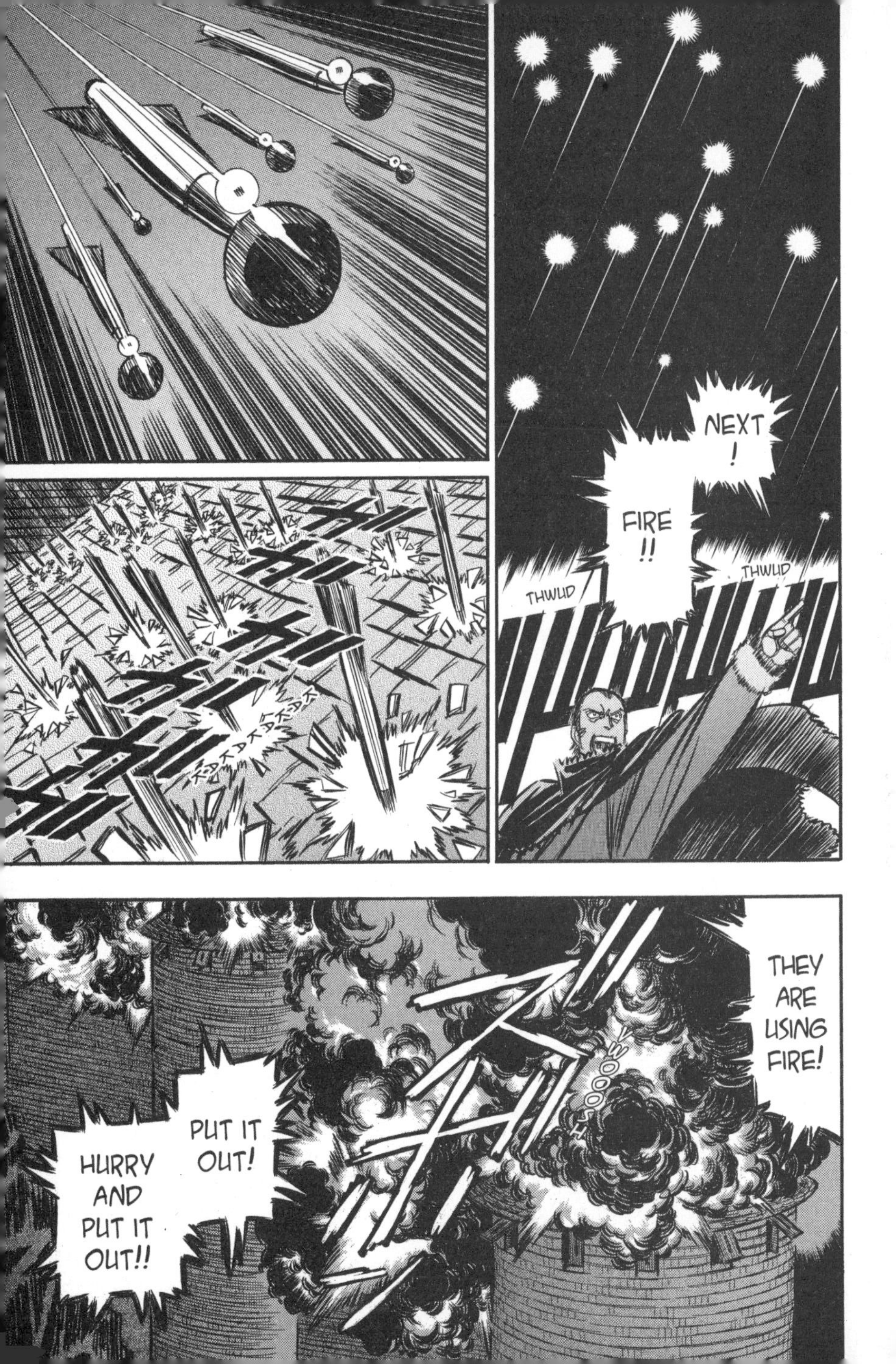

NEXT!
FIRE!!
THWUD
THWUD
KAKAKAKAKAK
THEY ARE USING FIRE!
WOOOSH
PUT IT OUT!
HURRY AND PUT IT OUT!!

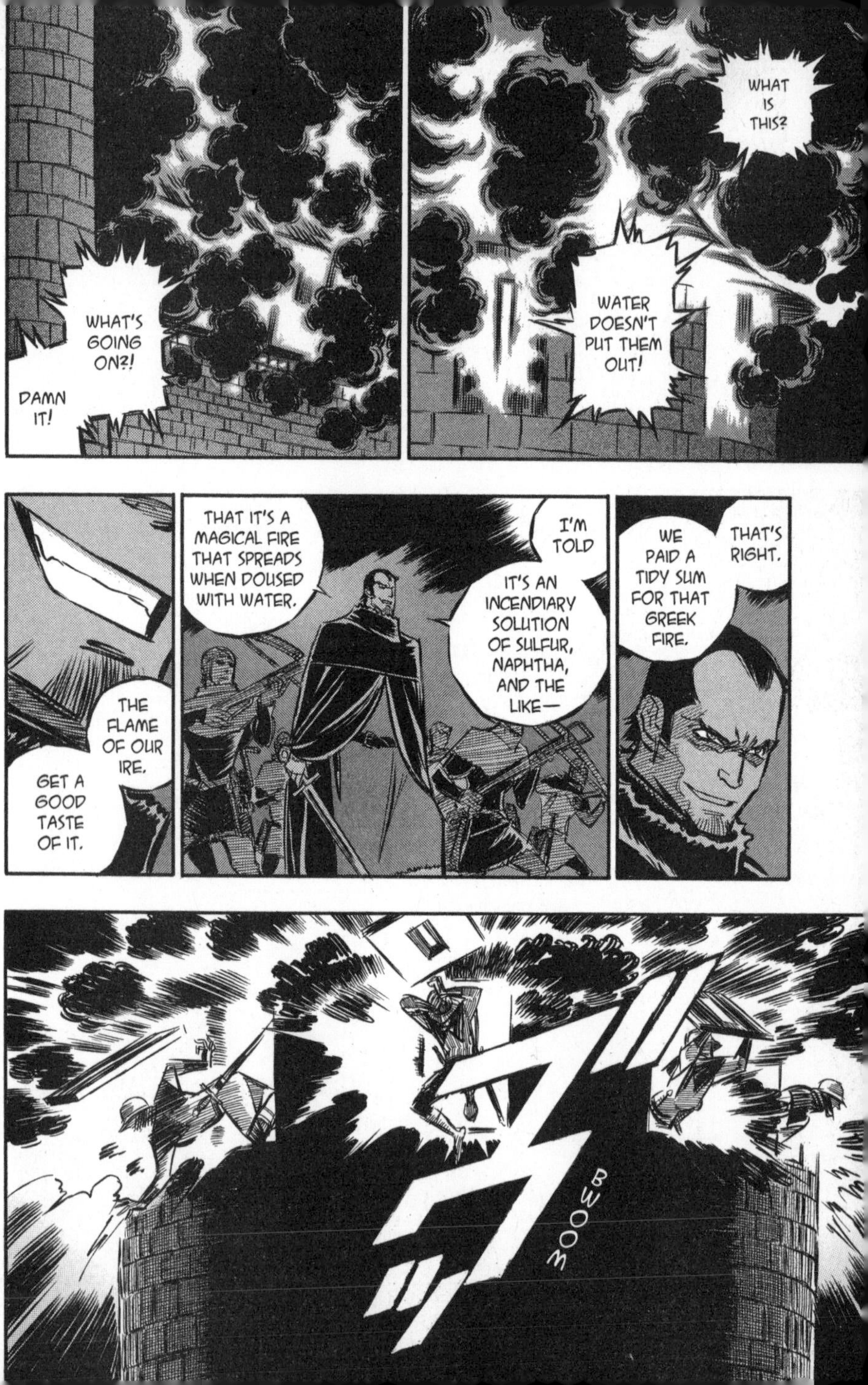
WHAT IS THIS?
WATER DOESN'T PUT THEM OUT!
WHAT'S GOING ON?!
DAMN IT!
THAT'S RIGHT.
WE PAID A TIDY SUM FOR THAT GREEK FIRE.
I'M TOLD
IT'S AN INCENDIARY SOLUTION OF SULFUR, NAPHTHA, AND THE LIKE—
THAT IT'S A MAGICAL FIRE THAT SPREADS WHEN DOUSED WITH WATER.
THE FLAME OF OUR IRE.
GET A GOOD TASTE OF IT.
BWOOM

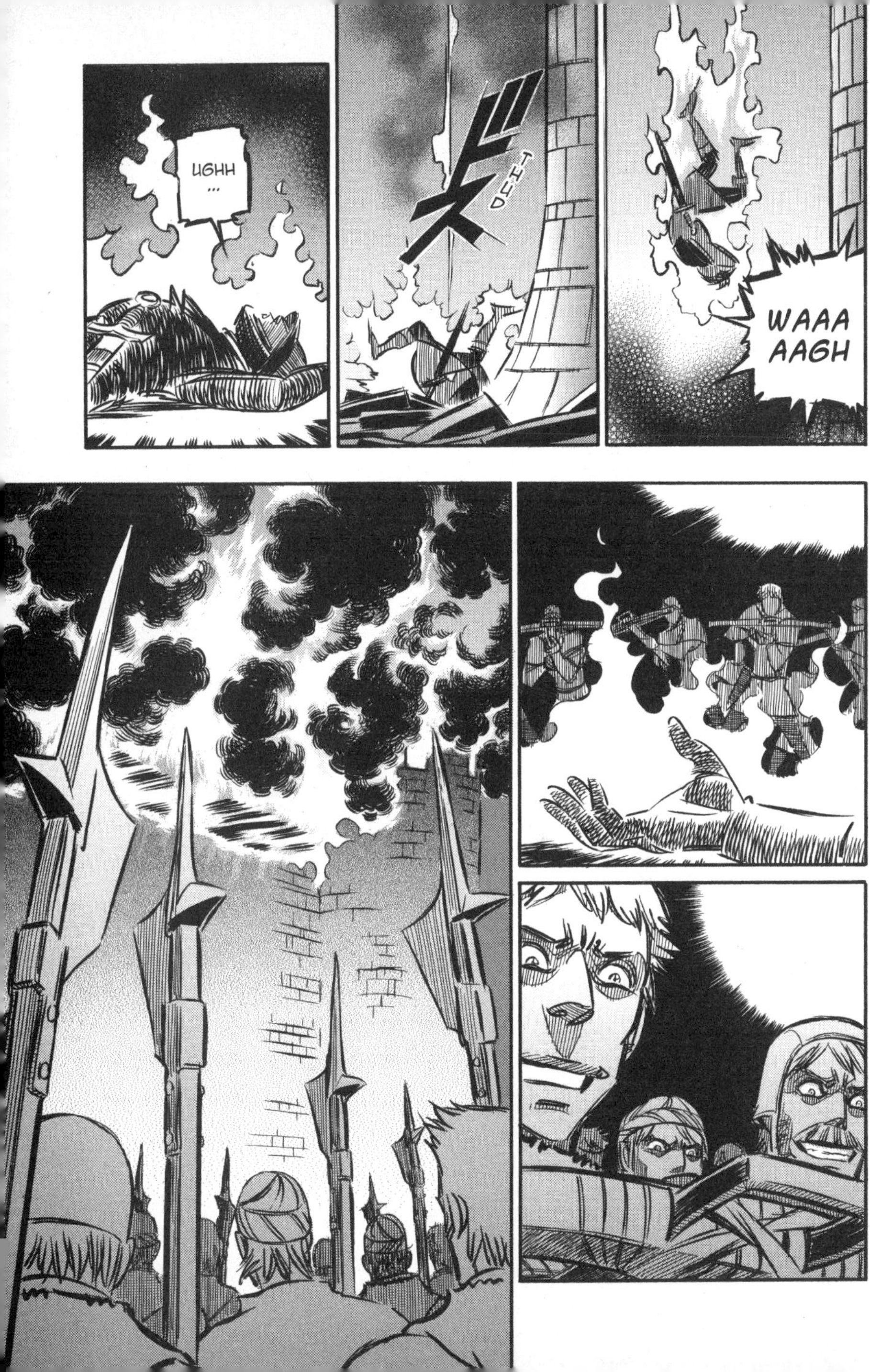
WAAA AAGH
ドス
THUD
UGHH ...

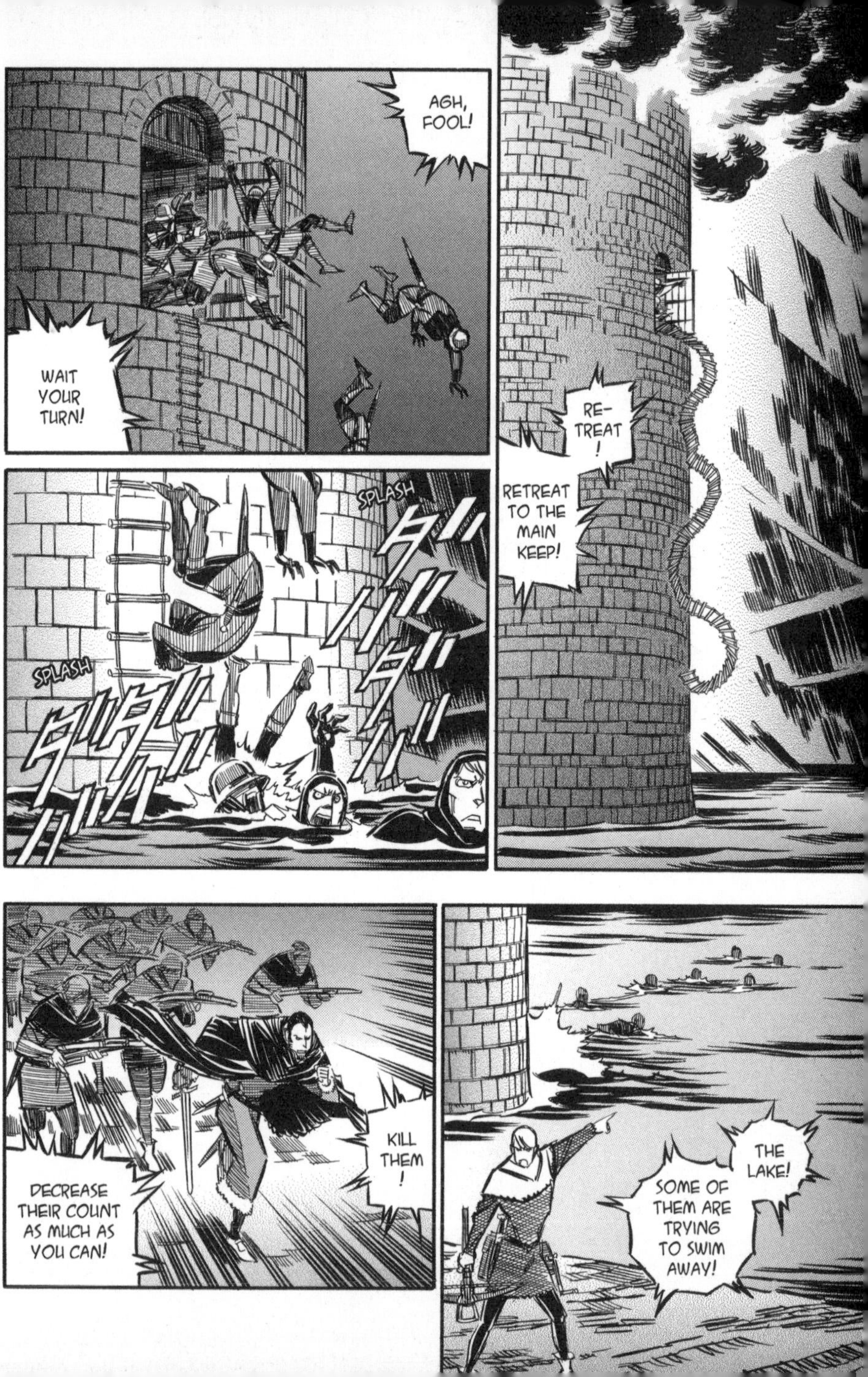
RE-TREAT!
RETREAT TO THE MAIN KEEP!
AGH, FOOL!
WAIT YOUR TURN!
SPLASH
SPLASH
THE LAKE!
SOME OF THEM ARE TRYING TO SWIM AWAY!
KILL THEM!
DECREASE THEIR COUNT AS MUCH AS YOU CAN!

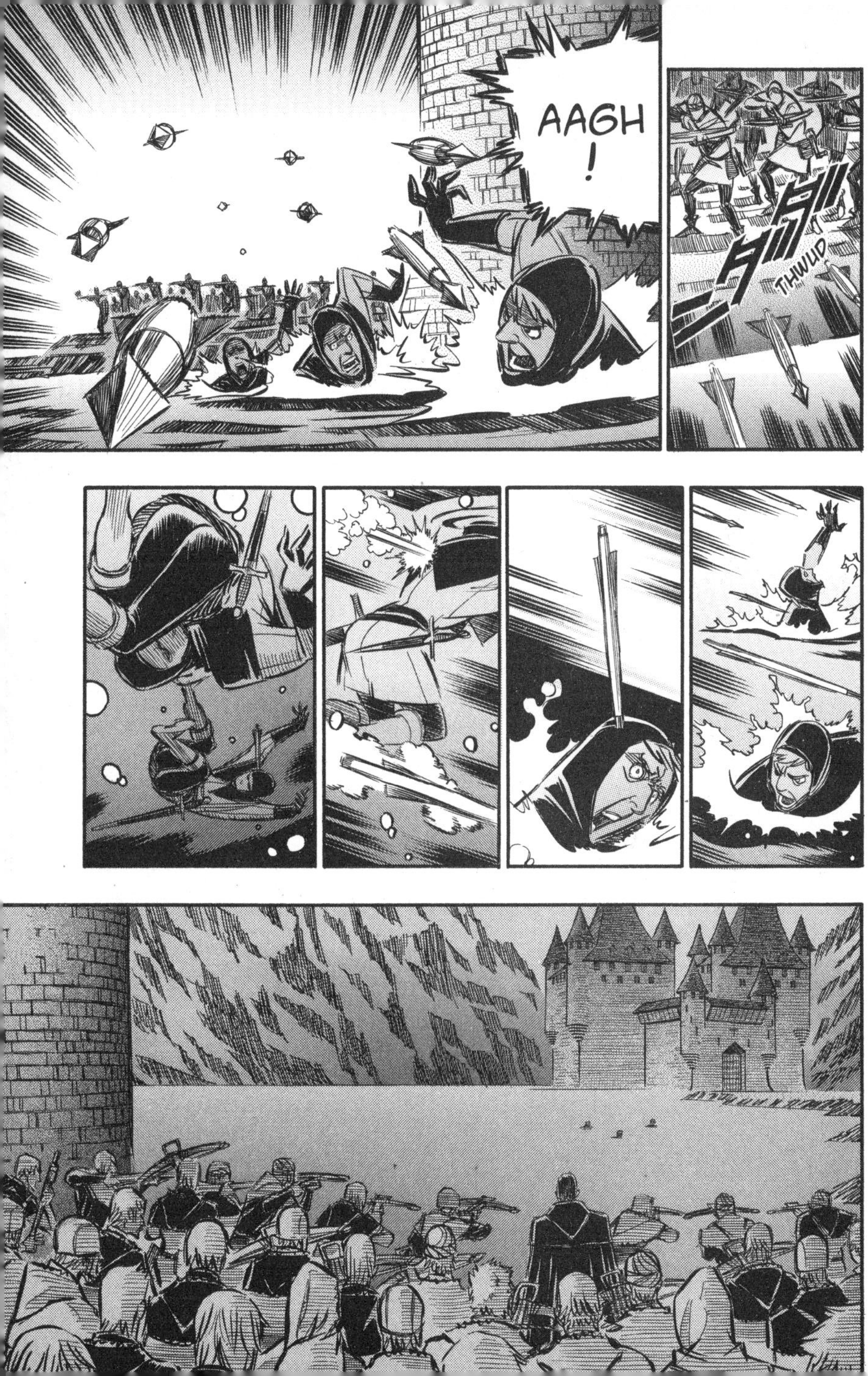
THWUD
AAGH!

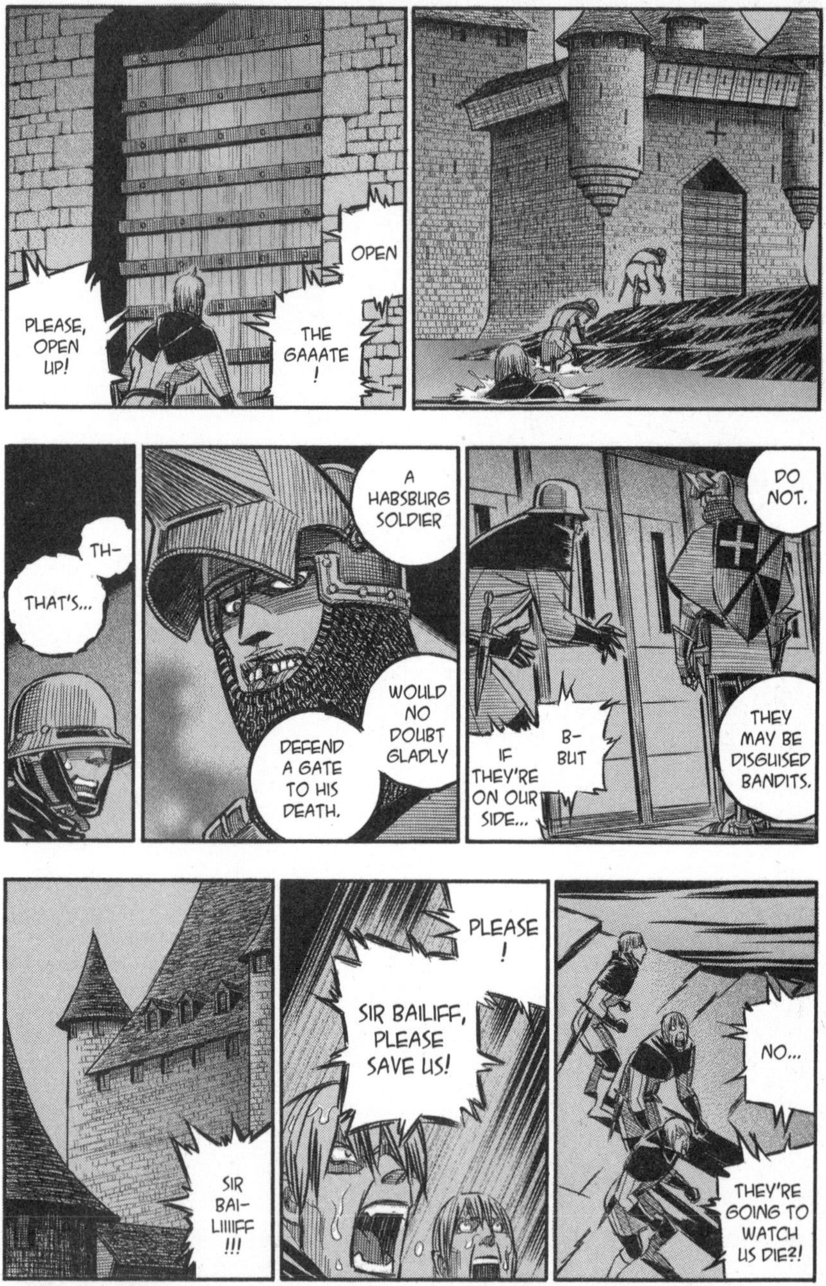
OPEN THE GAAATE!
PLEASE, OPEN UP!
DO NOT.
THEY MAY BE DISGUISED BANDITS.
B-BUT IF THEY'RE ON OUR SIDE...
A HABSBURG SOLDIER
WOULD NO DOUBT GLADLY
DEFEND A GATE TO HIS DEATH.
TH-
THAT'S...
NO...
THEY'RE GOING TO WATCH US DIE?!
PLEASE!
SIR BAILIFF, PLEASE SAVE US!
SIR BAI-LIIIIFF!!!

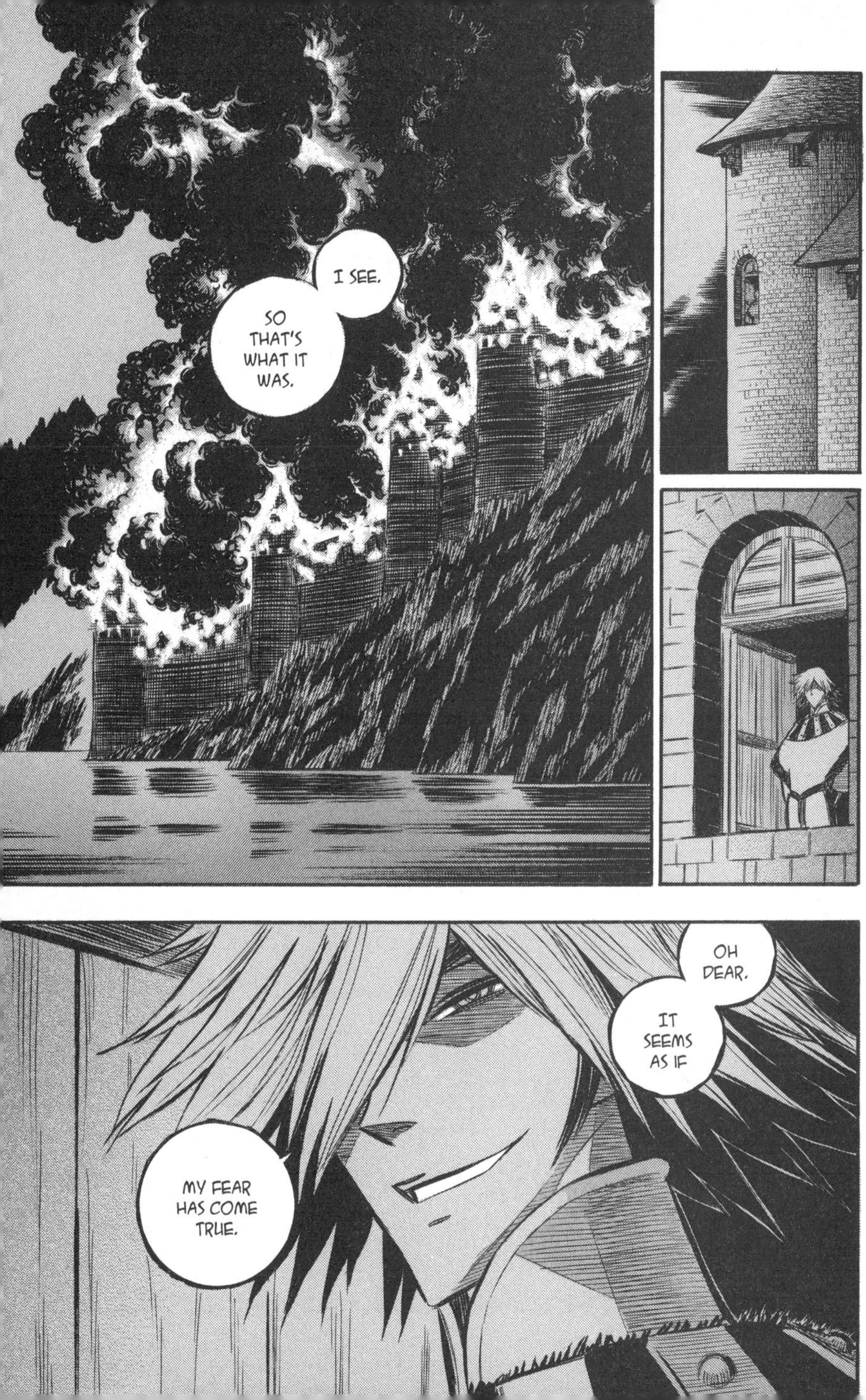
I SEE.
SO THAT'S WHAT IT WAS.
OH DEAR.
IT SEEMS AS IF
MY FEAR HAS COME TRUE.

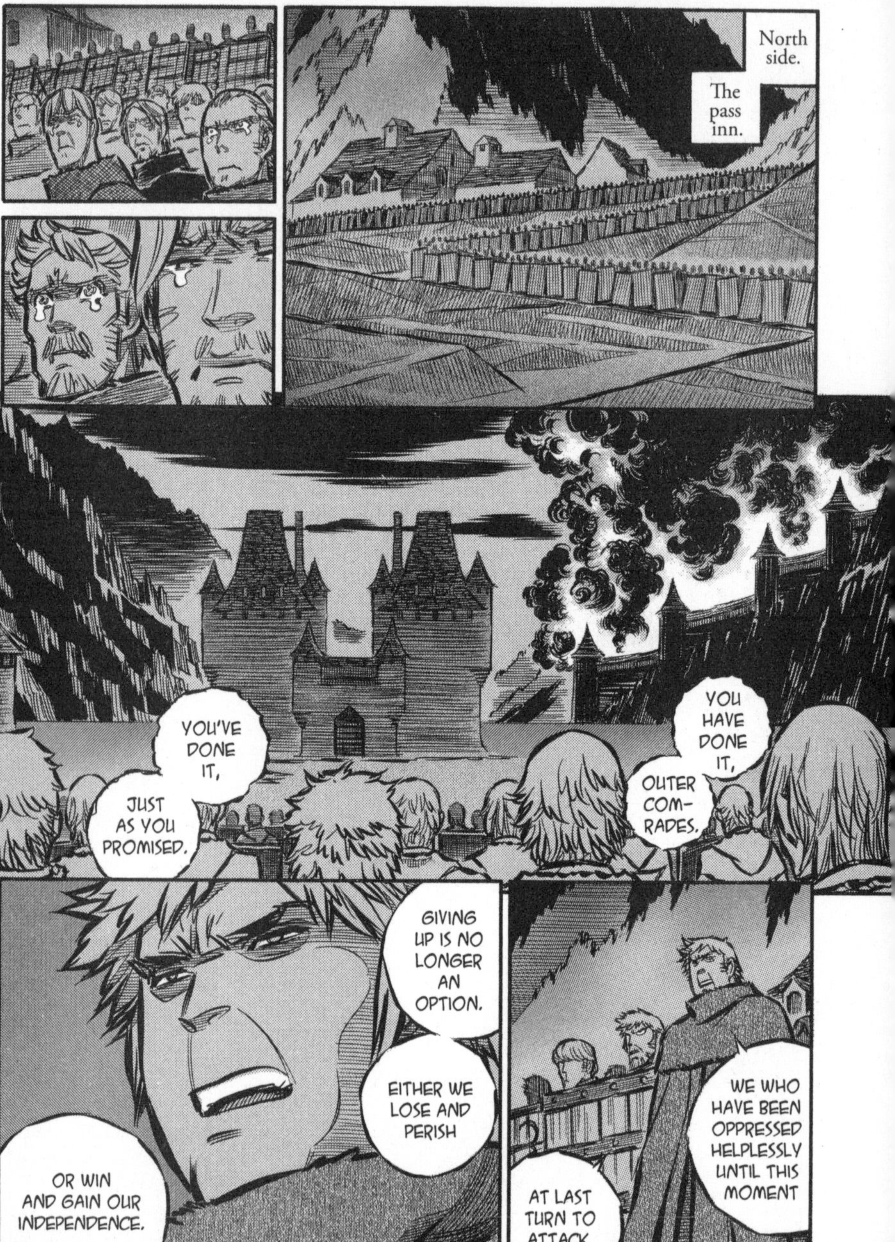
North side.
The pass inn.
YOU HAVE DONE IT,
OUTER COM-RADES.
YOU'VE DONE IT,
JUST AS YOU PROMISED.
WE WHO HAVE BEEN OPPRESSED HELPLESSLY UNTIL THIS MOMENT
AT LAST TURN TO ATTACK.
GIVING UP IS NO LONGER AN OPTION.
EITHER WE LOSE AND PERISH
OR WIN AND GAIN OUR INDEPENDENCE.

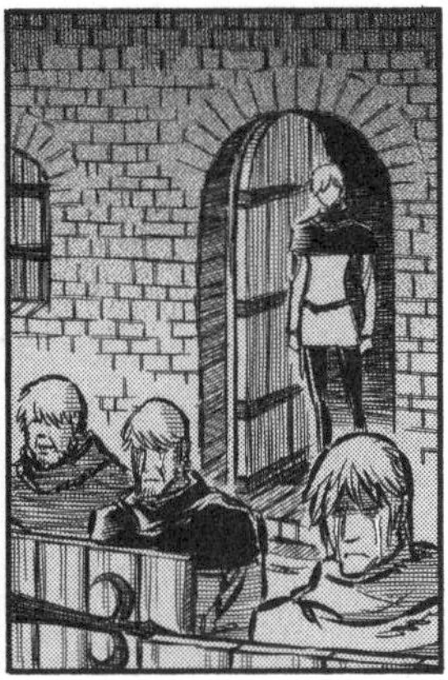

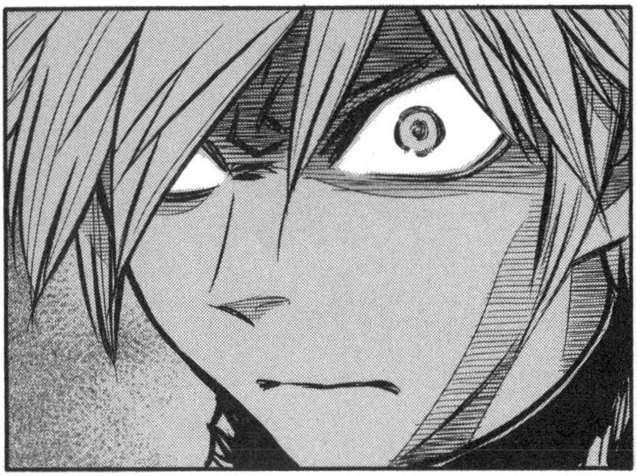

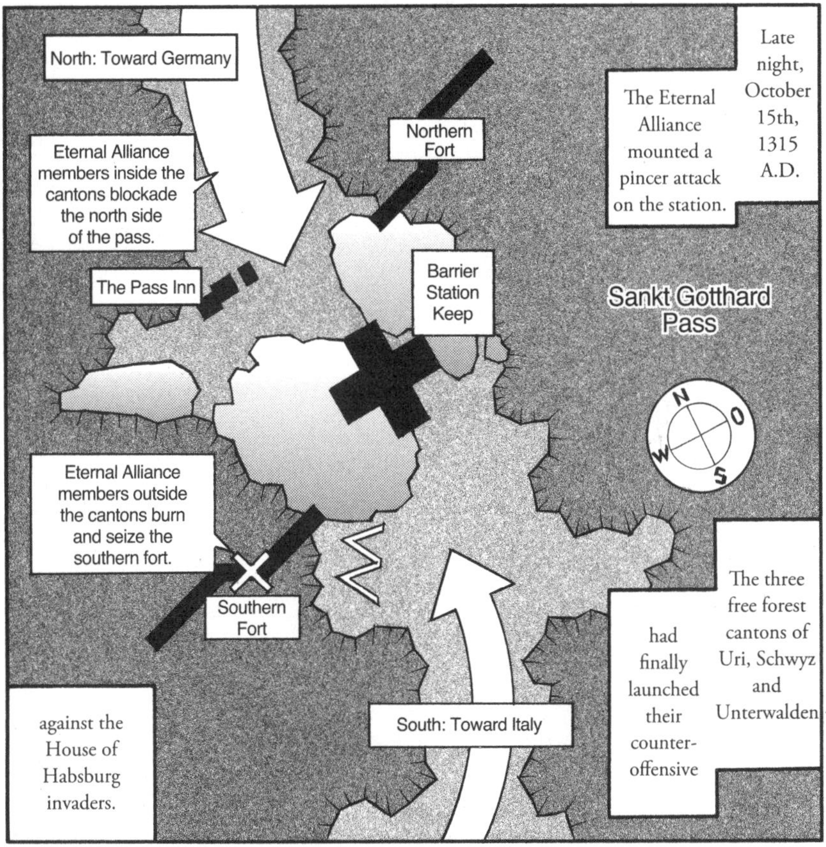

Late night, October 15th, 1315 A.D.
The Eternal Alliance mounted a pincer attack on the station.
Sankt Gotthard Pass
Barrier Station Keep
Northern Fort
North: Toward Germany
Eternal Alliance members inside the cantons blockade the north side of the pass.
The Pass Inn
N
O
W
S
Eternal Alliance members outside the cantons burn and seize the southern fort.
Southern Fort
The three free forest cantons of Uri, Schwyz and Unterwalden
had finally launched their counter-offensive
South: Toward Italy
against the House of Habsburg invaders.

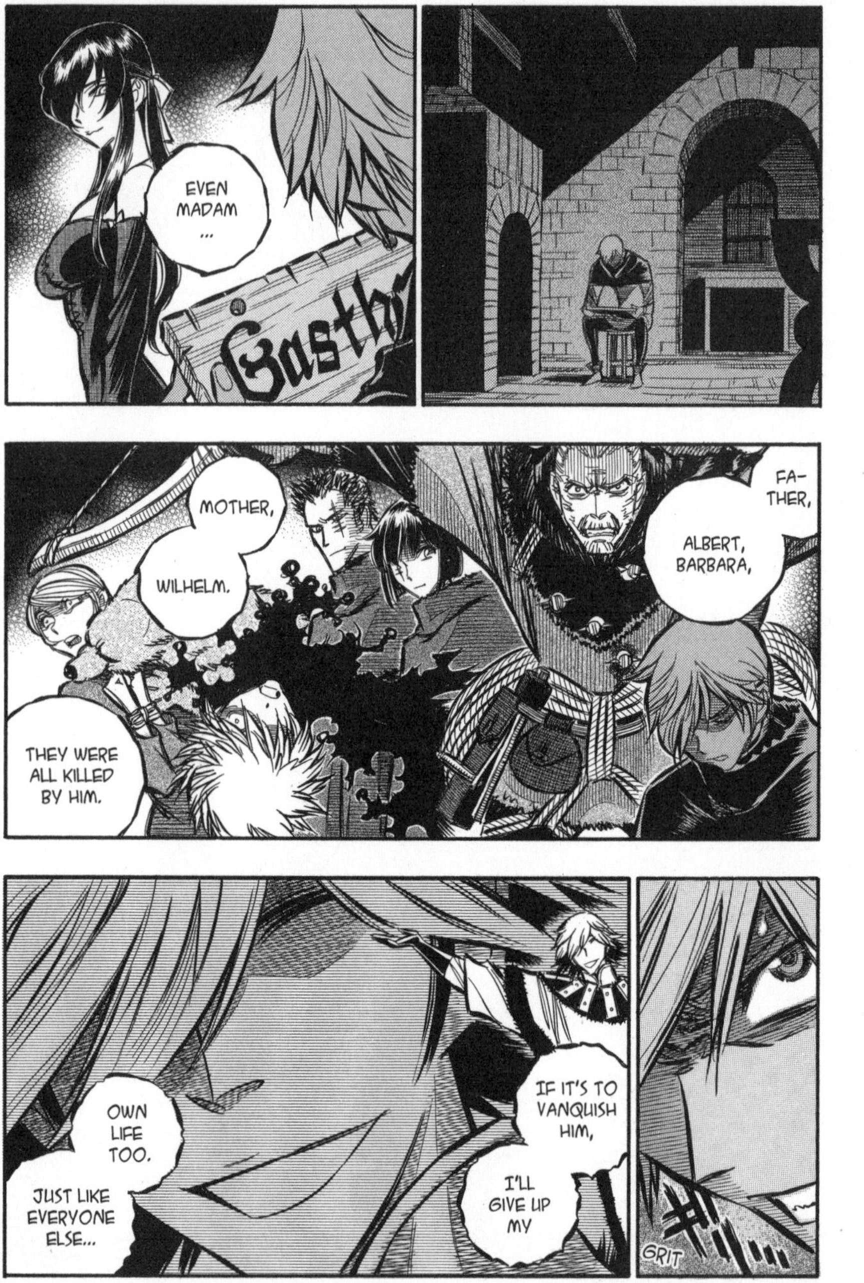
EVEN MADAM ...
FA-THER,
ALBERT, BARBARA,
MOTHER,
WILHELM.
THEY WERE ALL KILLED BY HIM.
GRIT
IF IT'S TO VANQUISH HIM,
I'LL GIVE UP MY
OWN LIFE TOO.
JUST LIKE EVERYONE ELSE...

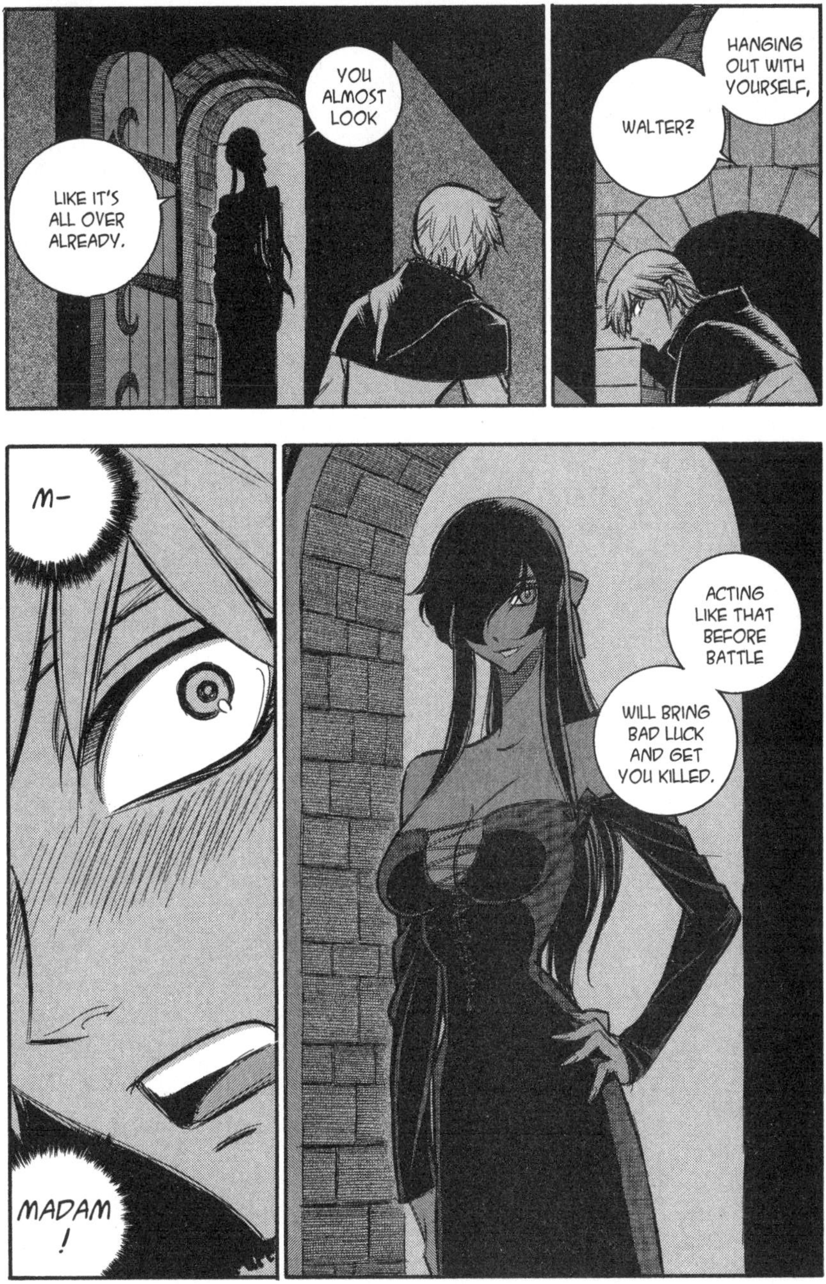
HANGING OUT WITH YOURSELF,
WALTER?
YOU ALMOST LOOK
LIKE IT'S ALL OVER ALREADY.
ACTING LIKE THAT BEFORE BATTLE
WILL BRING BAD LUCK AND GET YOU KILLED.
M-
MADAM!

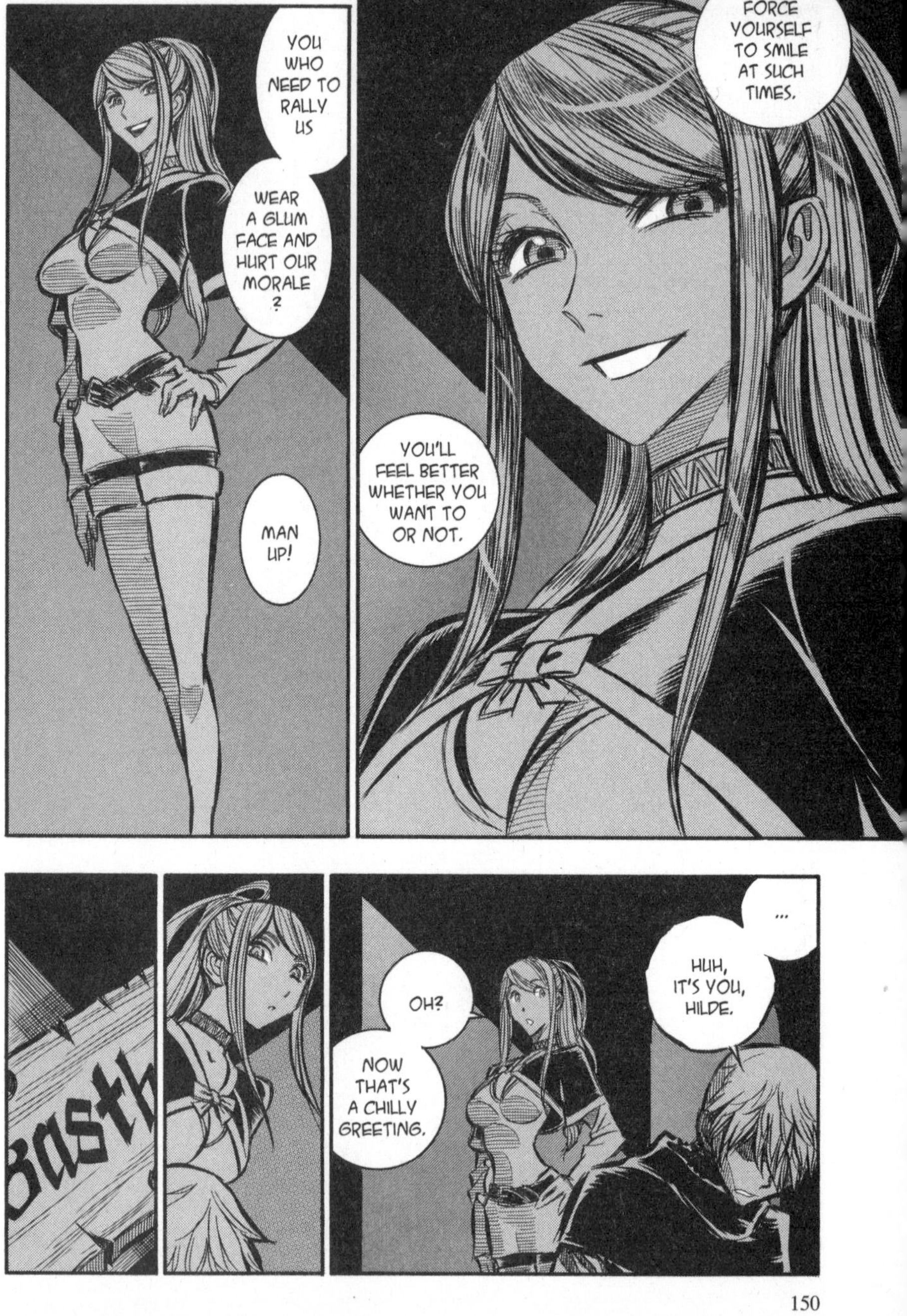
YOU WHO NEED TO RALLY US
WEAR A GLUM FACE AND HURT OUR MORALE?
MAN UP!
FORCE YOURSELF TO SMILE AT SUCH TIMES.
YOU'LL FEEL BETTER WHETHER YOU WANT TO OR NOT.
...
HUH, IT'S YOU, HILDE.
OH?
NOW THAT'S A CHILLY GREETING.

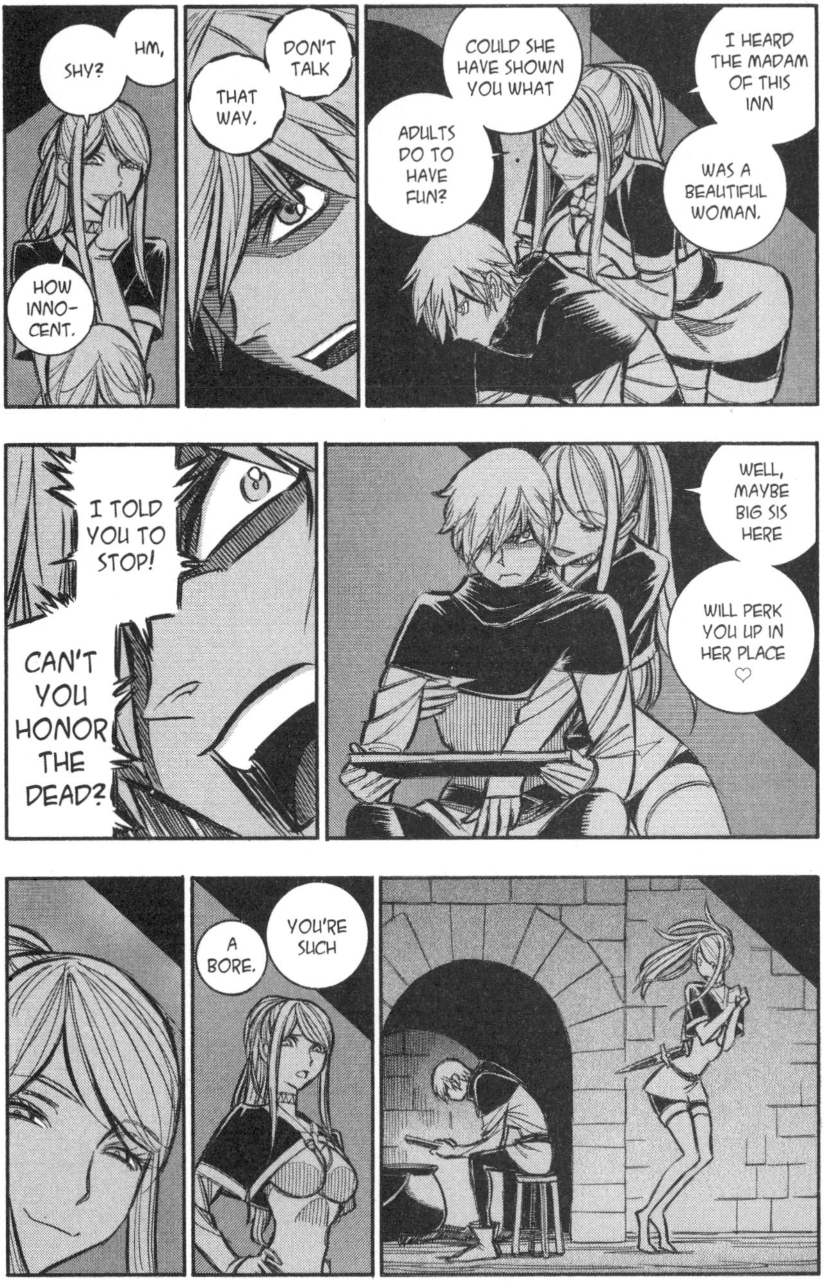
I HEARD THE MADAM OF THIS INN
WAS A BEAUTIFUL WOMAN.
COULD SHE HAVE SHOWN YOU WHAT
ADULTS DO TO HAVE FUN?
DON'T TALK
THAT WAY.
HM,
SHY?
HOW INNO-CENT.
WELL, MAYBE BIG SIS HERE
WILL PERK YOU UP IN HER PLACE ♡
I TOLD YOU TO STOP!
CAN'T YOU HONOR THE DEAD?
YOU'RE SUCH
A BORE.

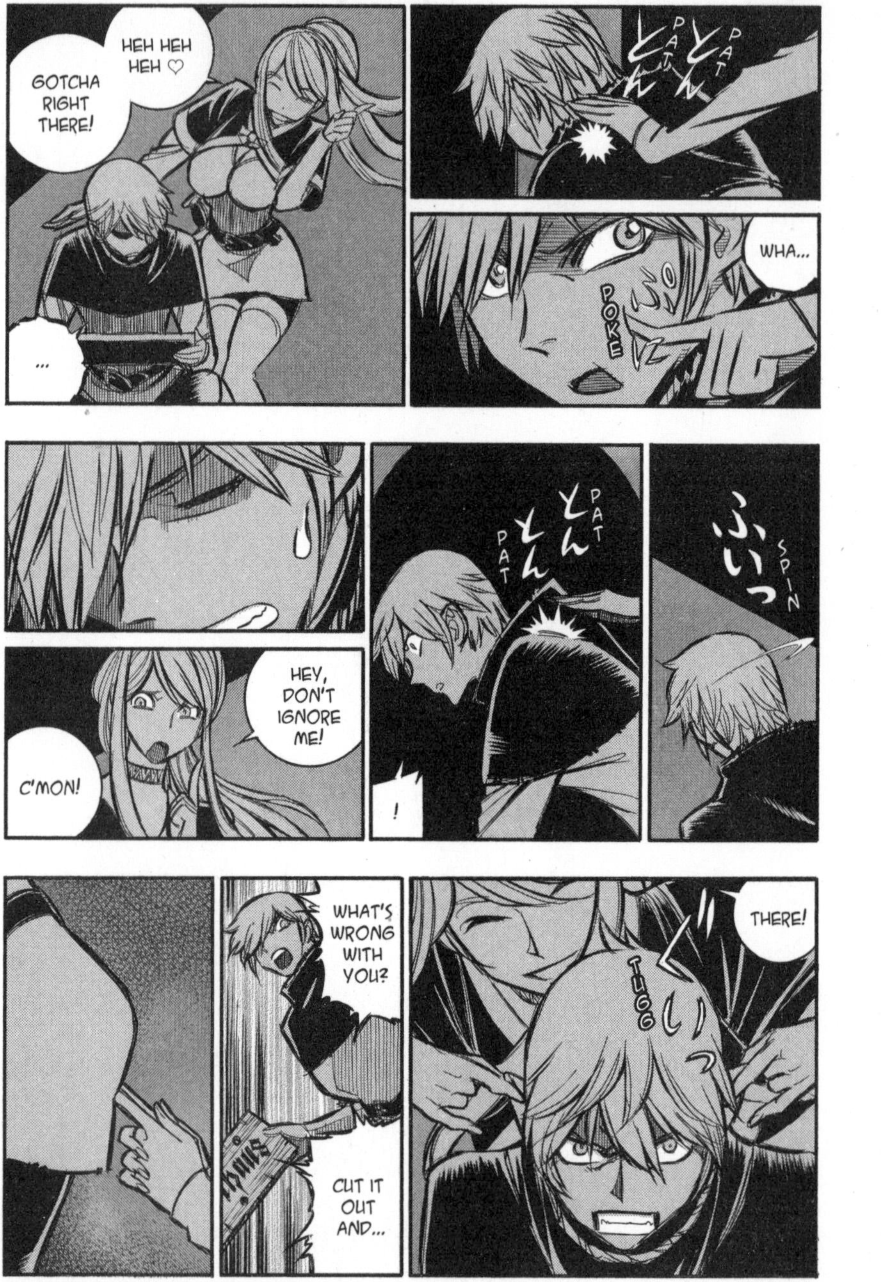
PAT PAT
とん とん
WHA...
POKE
HEH HEH HEH ♡
GOTCHA RIGHT THERE!
...
ふいっ
SPIN
PAT PAT
とん とん
!
HEY, DON'T IGNORE ME!
C'MON!
THERE!
TUGG
WHAT'S WRONG WITH YOU?
CUT IT OUT AND...

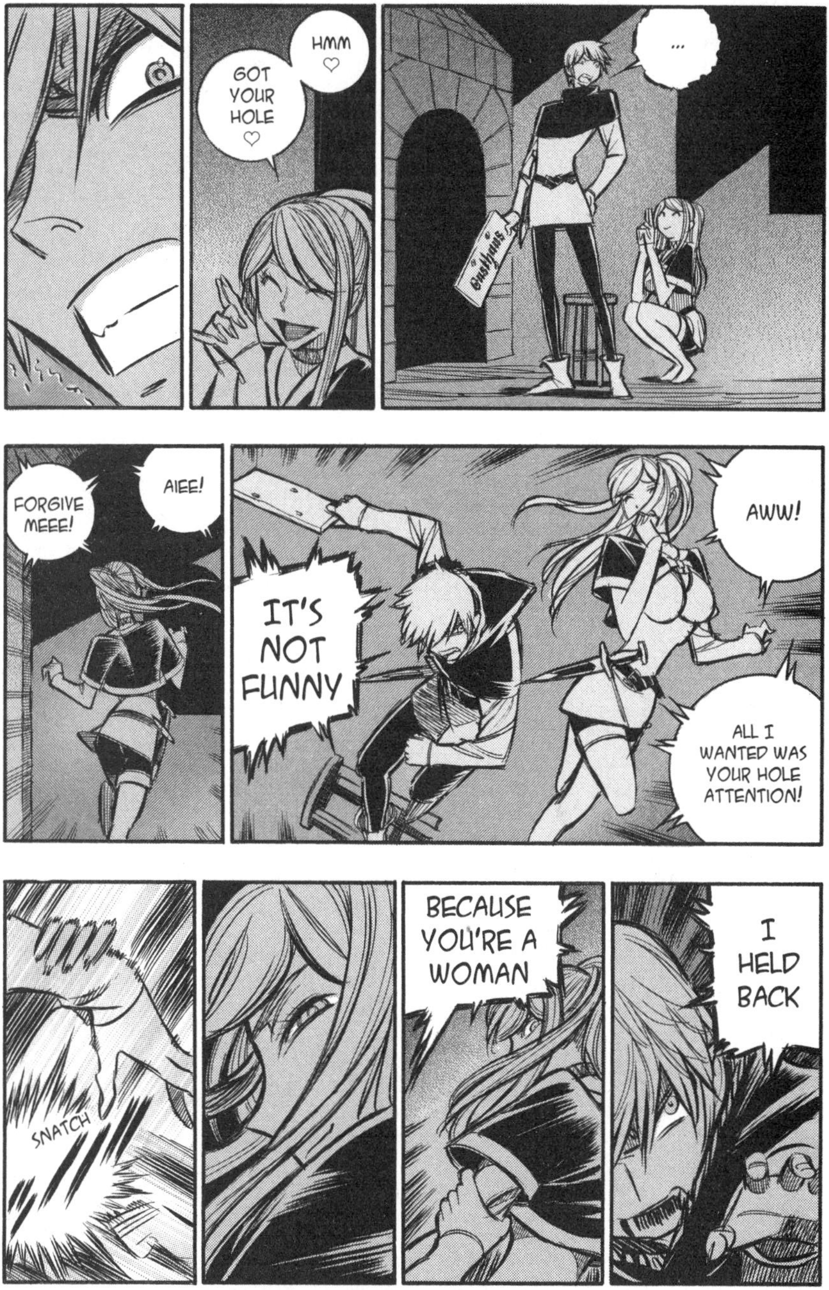
...
HMM ♡
GOT YOUR HOLE ♡
AWW!
IT'S NOT FUNNY
ALL I WANTED WAS YOUR HOLE ATTENTION!
AIEE!
FORGIVE MEEE!
I HELD BACK
BECAUSE YOU'RE A WOMAN
SNATCH

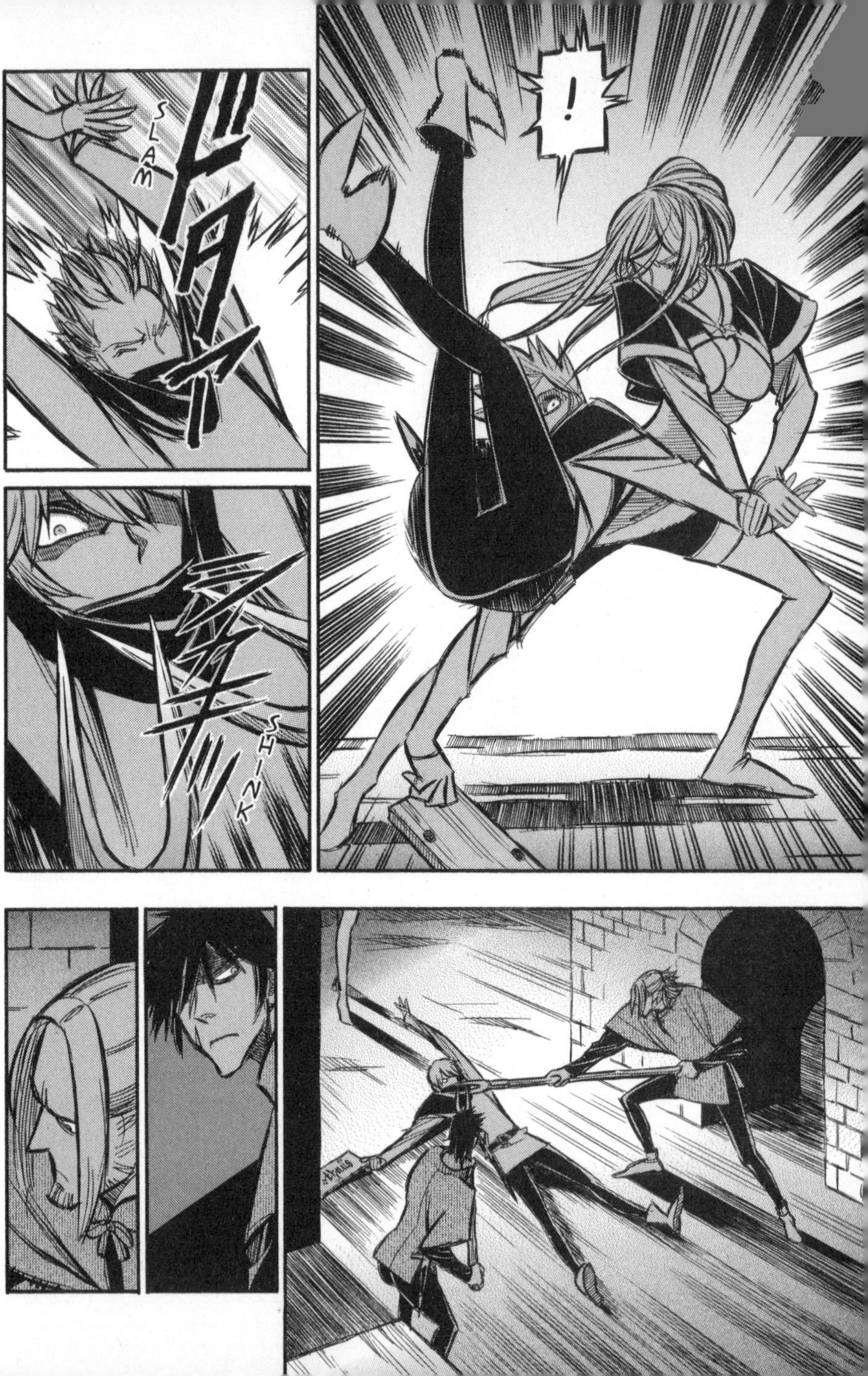
!
SLAM
SHINK

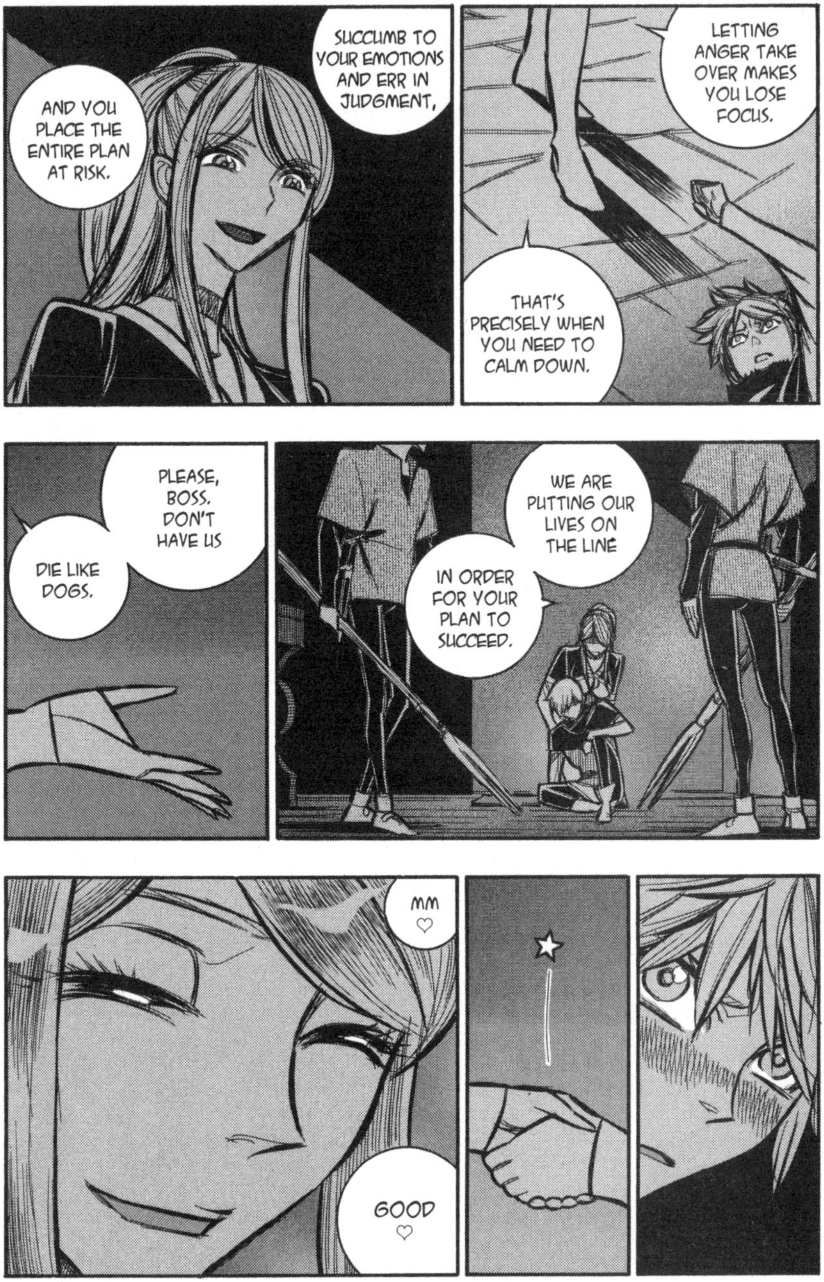
LETTING ANGER TAKE OVER MAKES YOU LOSE FOCUS.
THAT'S PRECISELY WHEN YOU NEED TO CALM DOWN.
SUCCUMB TO YOUR EMOTIONS AND ERR IN JUDGMENT,
AND YOU PLACE THE ENTIRE PLAN AT RISK.
WE ARE PUTTING OUR LIVES ON THE LINE
IN ORDER FOR YOUR PLAN TO SUCCEED.
PLEASE, BOSS. DON'T HAVE US
DIE LIKE DOGS.
MM ♡
GOOD ♡

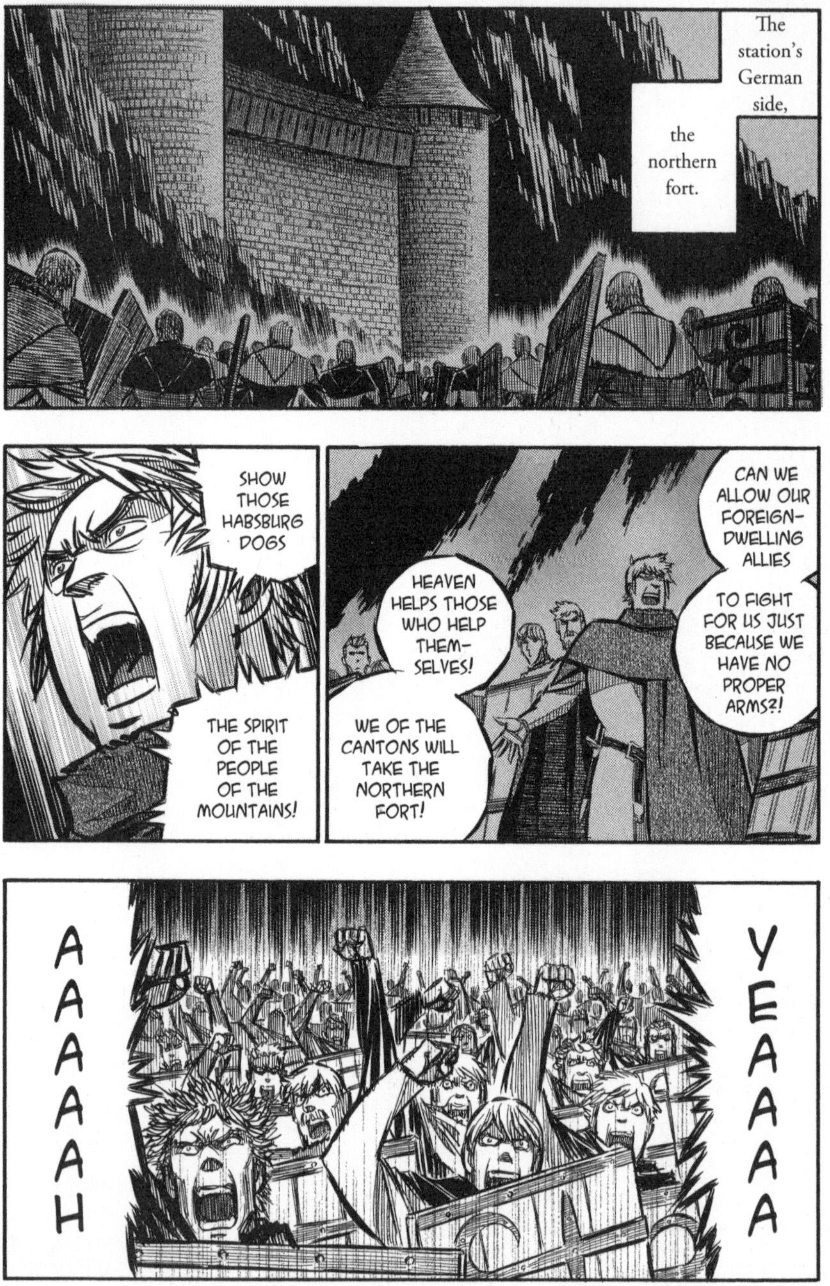
The station's German side,
the northern fort.
CAN WE ALLOW OUR FOREIGN-DWELLING ALLIES
TO FIGHT FOR US JUST BECAUSE WE HAVE NO PROPER ARMS?!
HEAVEN HELPS THOSE WHO HELP THEM-SELVES!
WE OF THE CANTONS WILL TAKE THE NORTHERN FORT!
SHOW THOSE HABSBURG DOGS
THE SPIRIT OF THE PEOPLE OF THE MOUNTAINS!
YEAAAAA
AAAAAAH

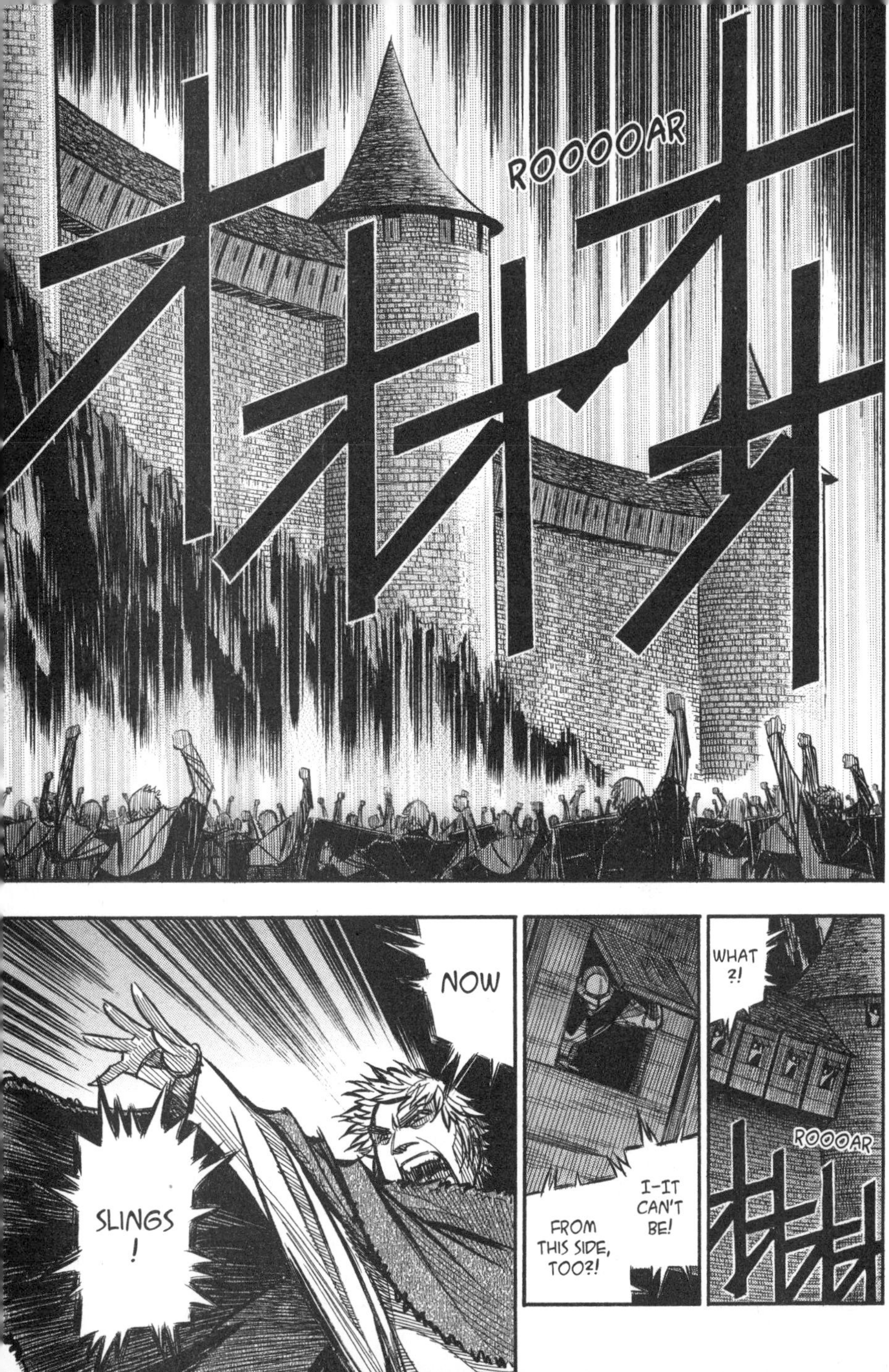
ROOOOAR
WHAT?!
ROOOAR
I-IT CAN'T BE!
FROM THIS SIDE, TOO?!
NOW
SLINGS!

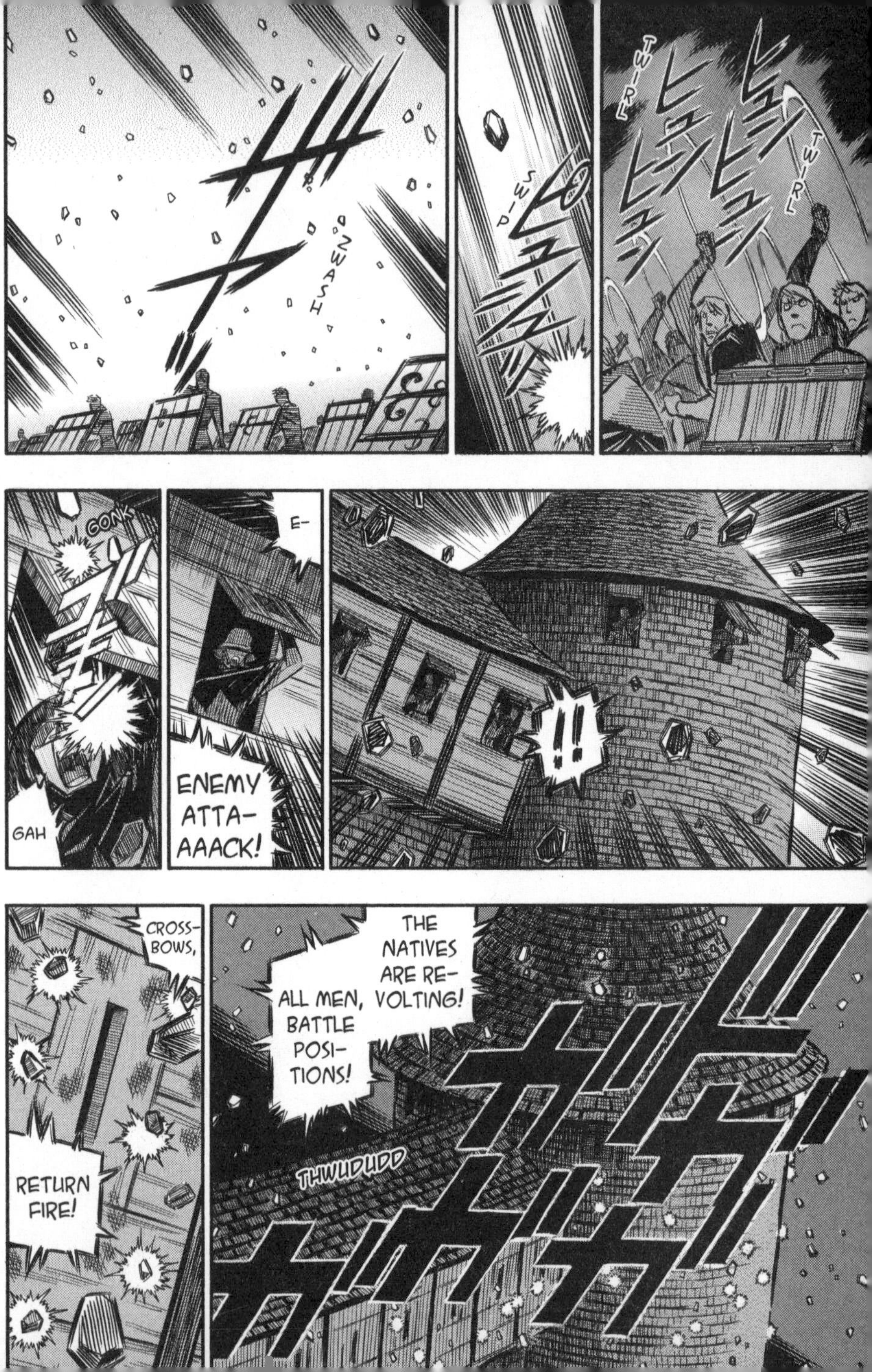
TWIRL
TWIRL
SWIP
ZWASH
!!
E-
ENEMY ATTA-AAACK!
GONK
GAH
THE NATIVES ARE RE-VOLTING!
ALL MEN, BATTLE POSITIONS!
THWUDUDD
CROSS-BOWS,
RETURN FIRE!

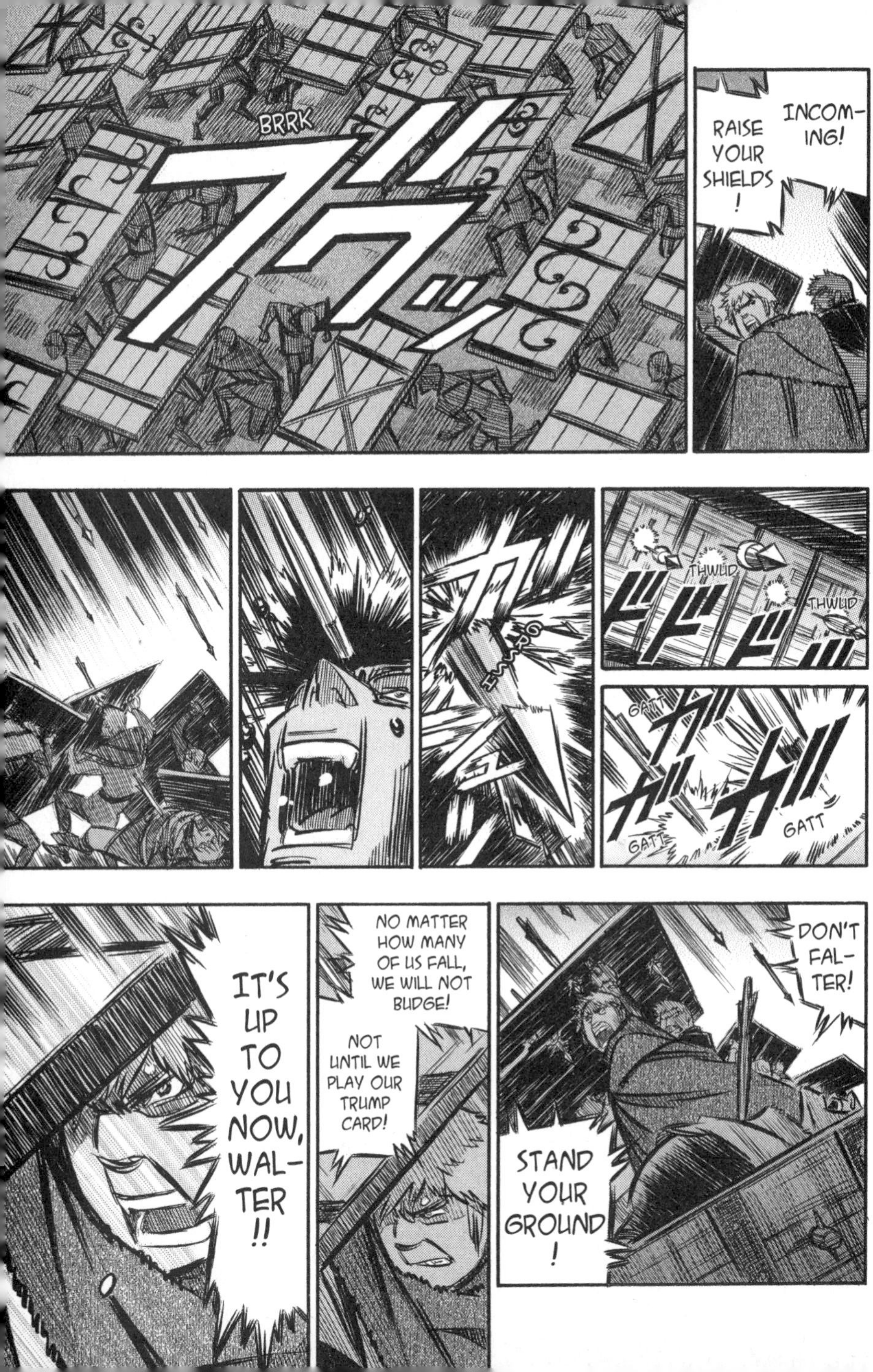
INCOM-ING!
RAISE YOUR SHIELDS!
BRRK
THWUD
THWUD
GATT
GATT
GATT
DON'T FAL-TER!
STAND YOUR GROUND!
NO MATTER HOW MANY OF US FALL, WE WILL NOT BUDGE!
NOT UNTIL WE PLAY OUR TRUMP CARD!
IT'S UP TO YOU NOW, WAL-TER!!

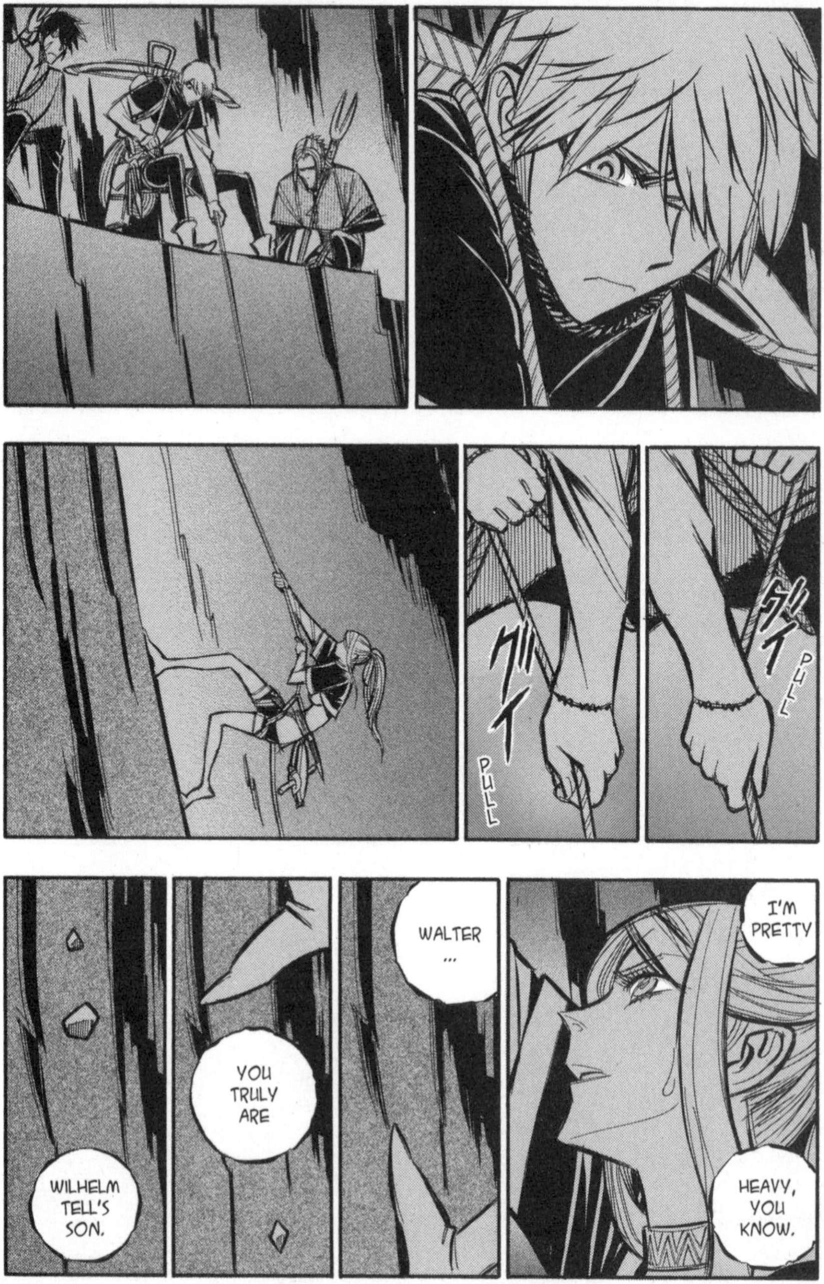
PULL
PULL
I'M PRETTY
HEAVY, YOU KNOW.
WALTER ...
YOU TRULY ARE
WILHELM TELL'S SON.

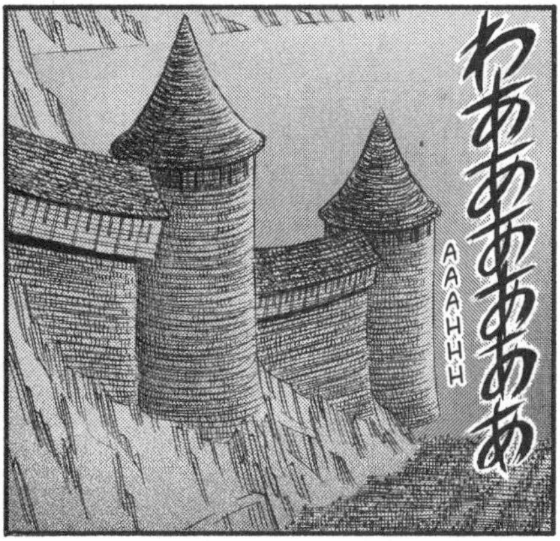
わあああああ
AAAAHHH

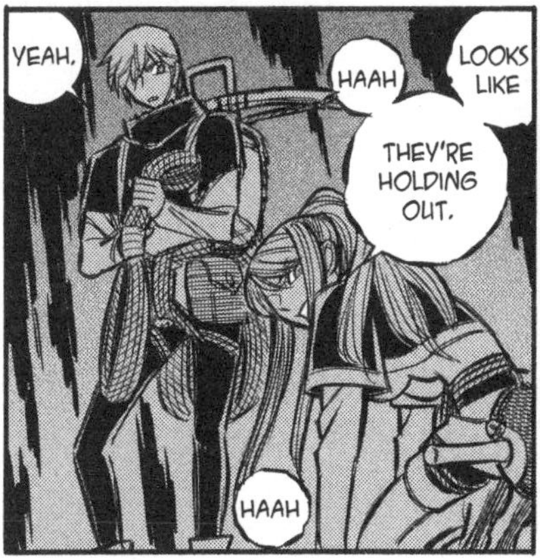
LOOKS LIKE
THEY'RE HOLDING OUT.
HAAH
YEAH.
HAAH

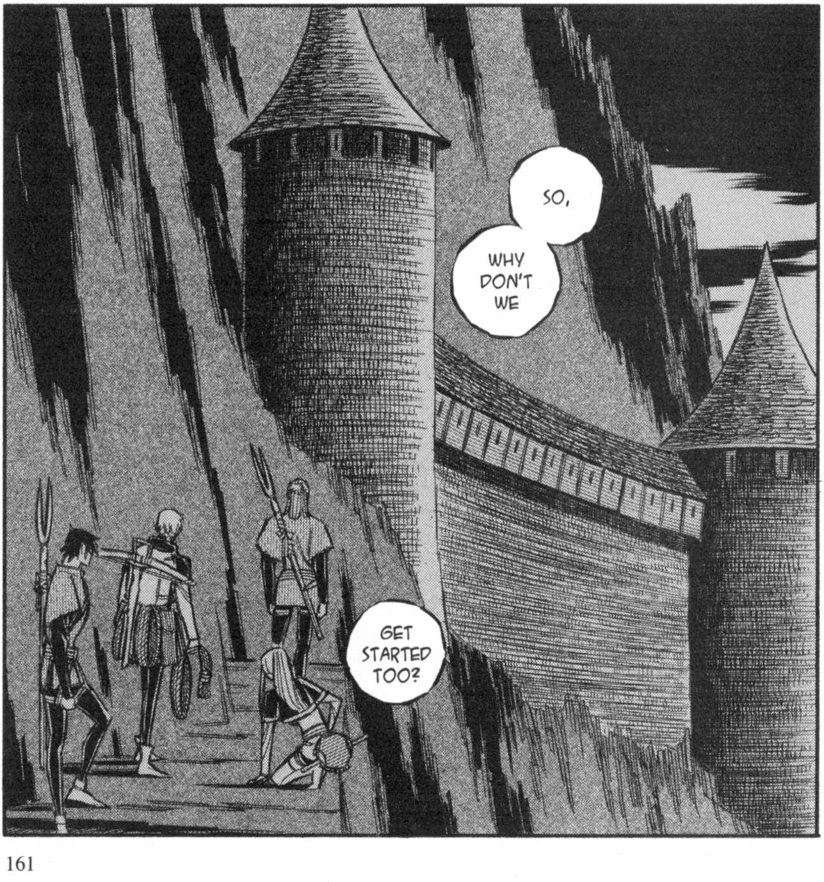
SO,
WHY DON'T WE
GET STARTED TOO?

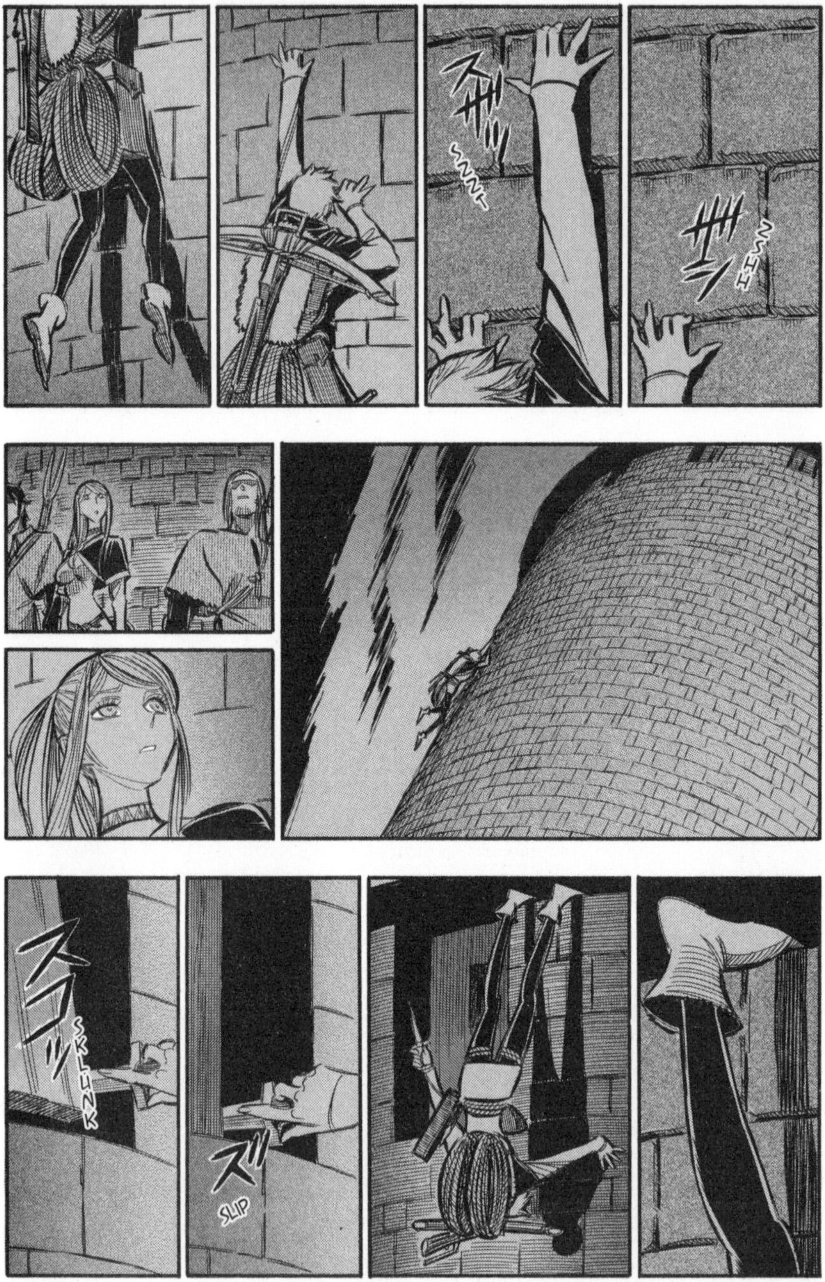
SKLUNK
SLIP

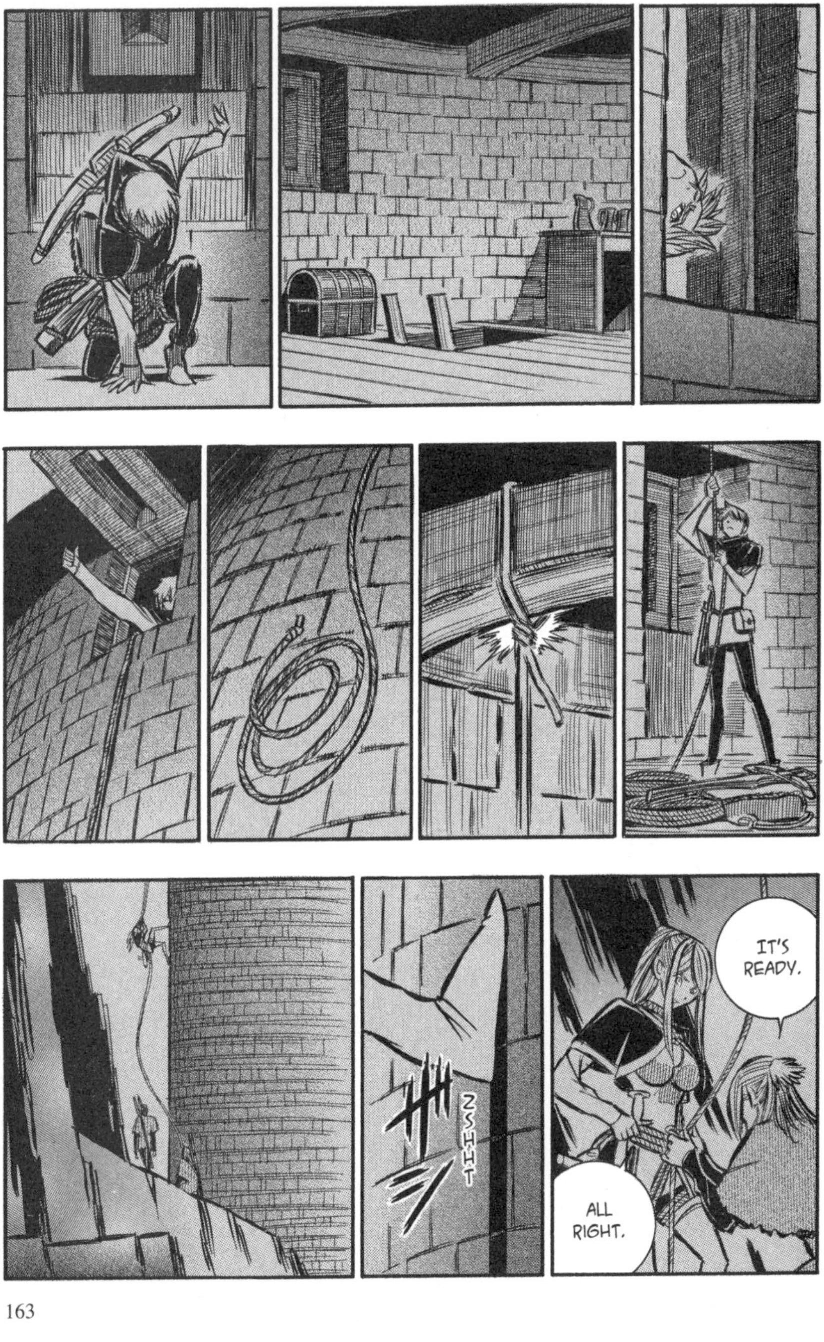
IT'S READY.
ALL RIGHT.
ZSHHT

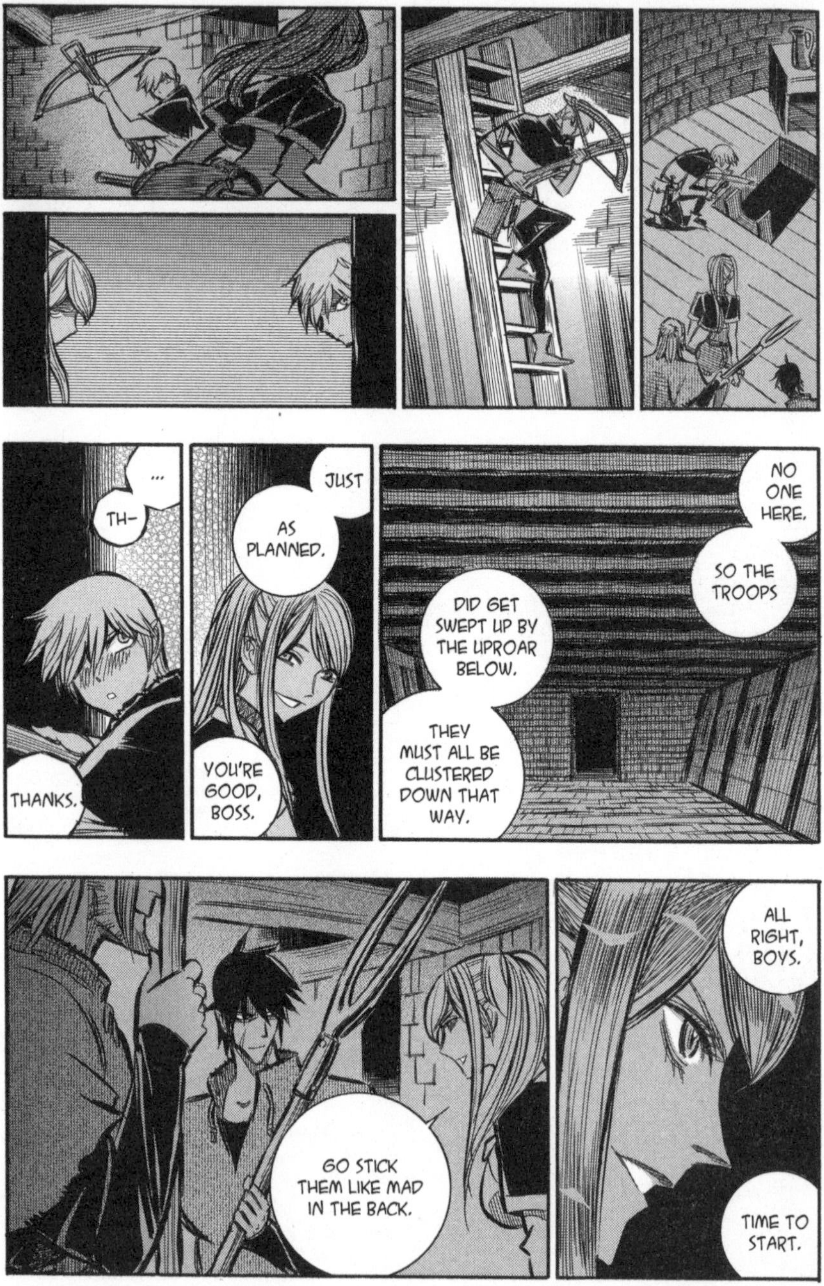
NO ONE HERE.
SO THE TROOPS
DID GET SWEPT UP BY THE UPROAR BELOW.
THEY MUST ALL BE CLUSTERED DOWN THAT WAY.
JUST
AS PLANNED.
YOU'RE GOOD, BOSS.
...
TH-
THANKS.
ALL RIGHT, BOYS.
TIME TO START.
GO STICK THEM LIKE MAD IN THE BACK.

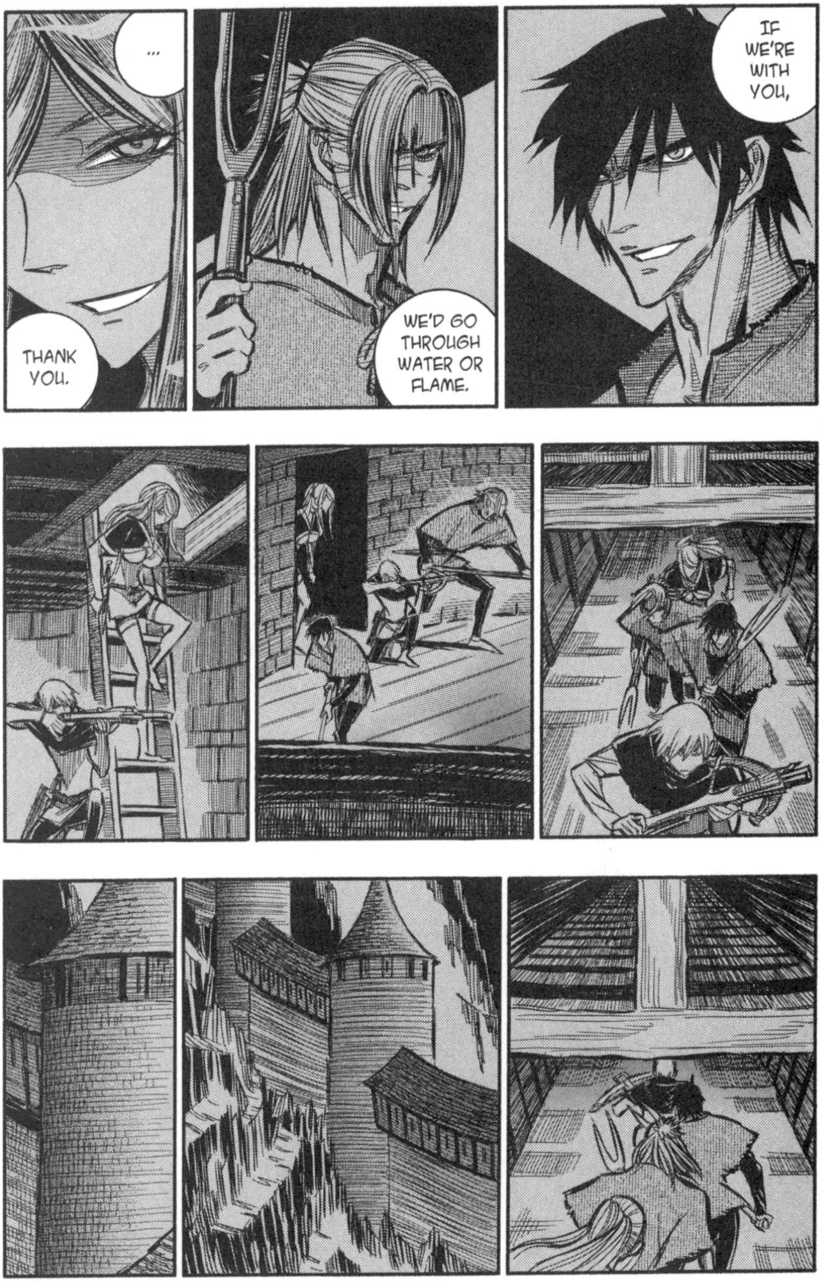
IF WE'RE WITH YOU,
WE'D GO THROUGH WATER OR FLAME.
...
THANK YOU.

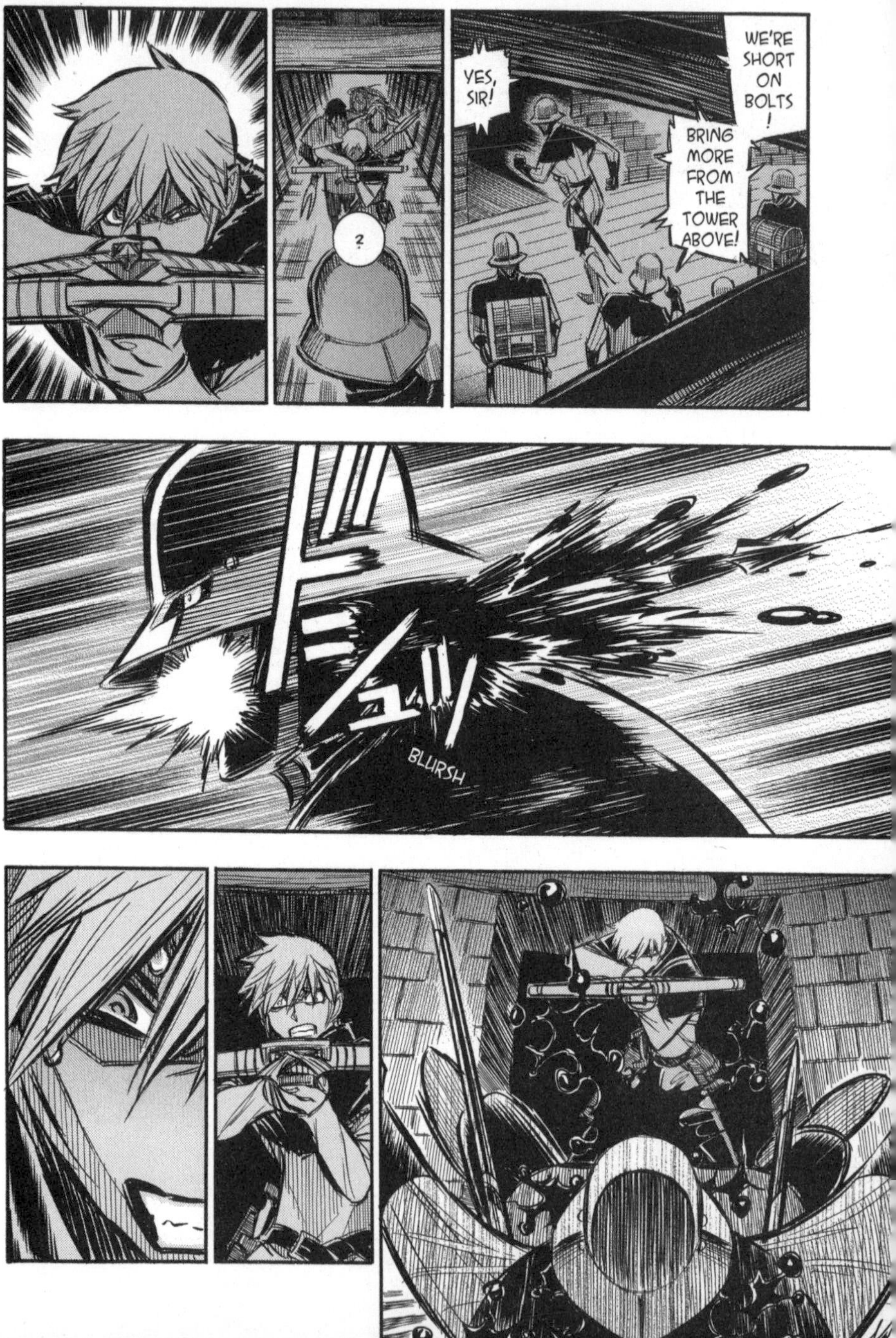
WE'RE SHORT ON BOLTS!
BRING MORE FROM THE TOWER ABOVE!
YES, SIR!
?
BLURSH

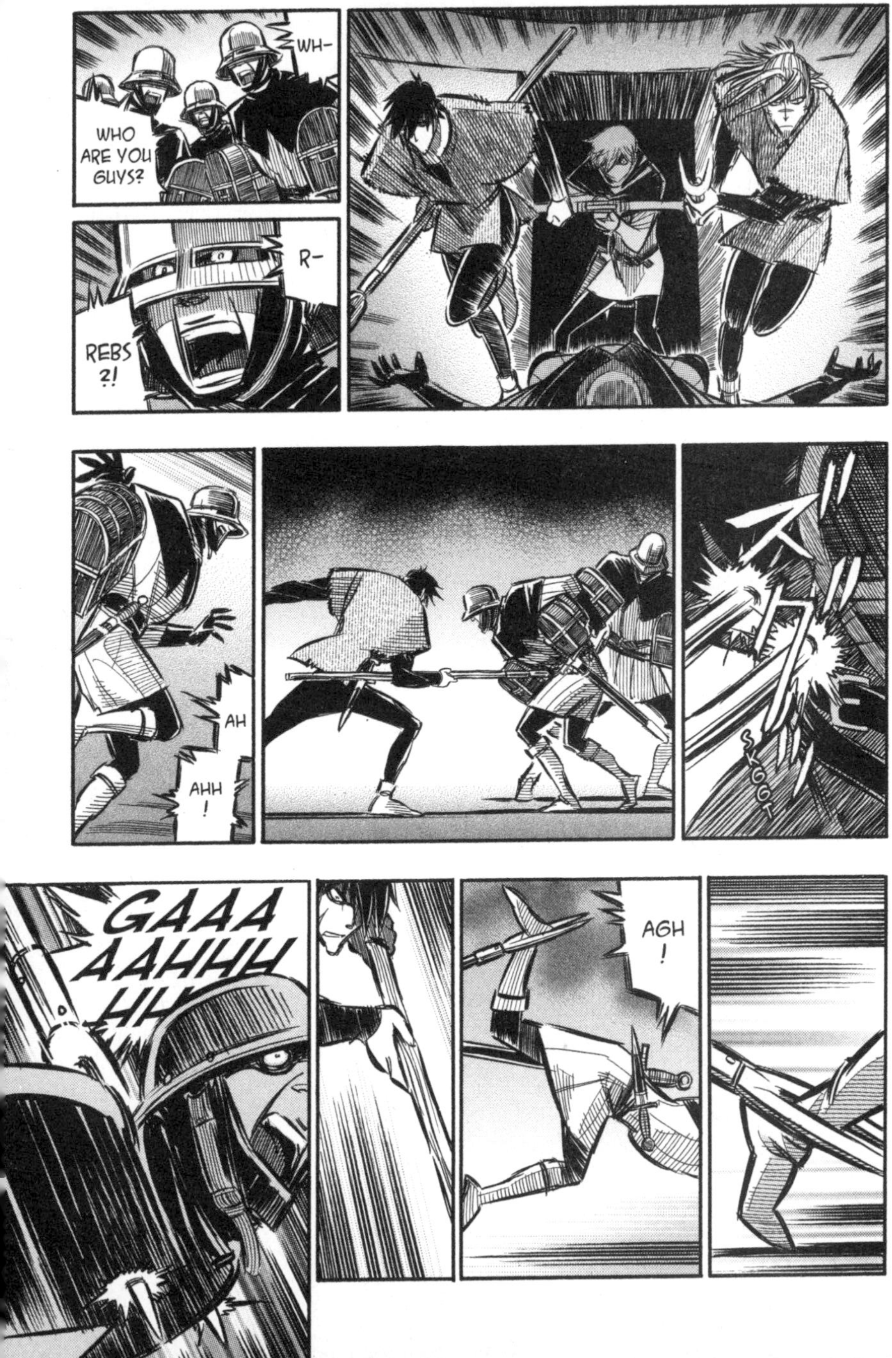
WH-
WHO ARE YOU GUYS?
R-
REBS ?!
SKGGT
AH
AHH !
AGH !
GAAAAAHHHHH

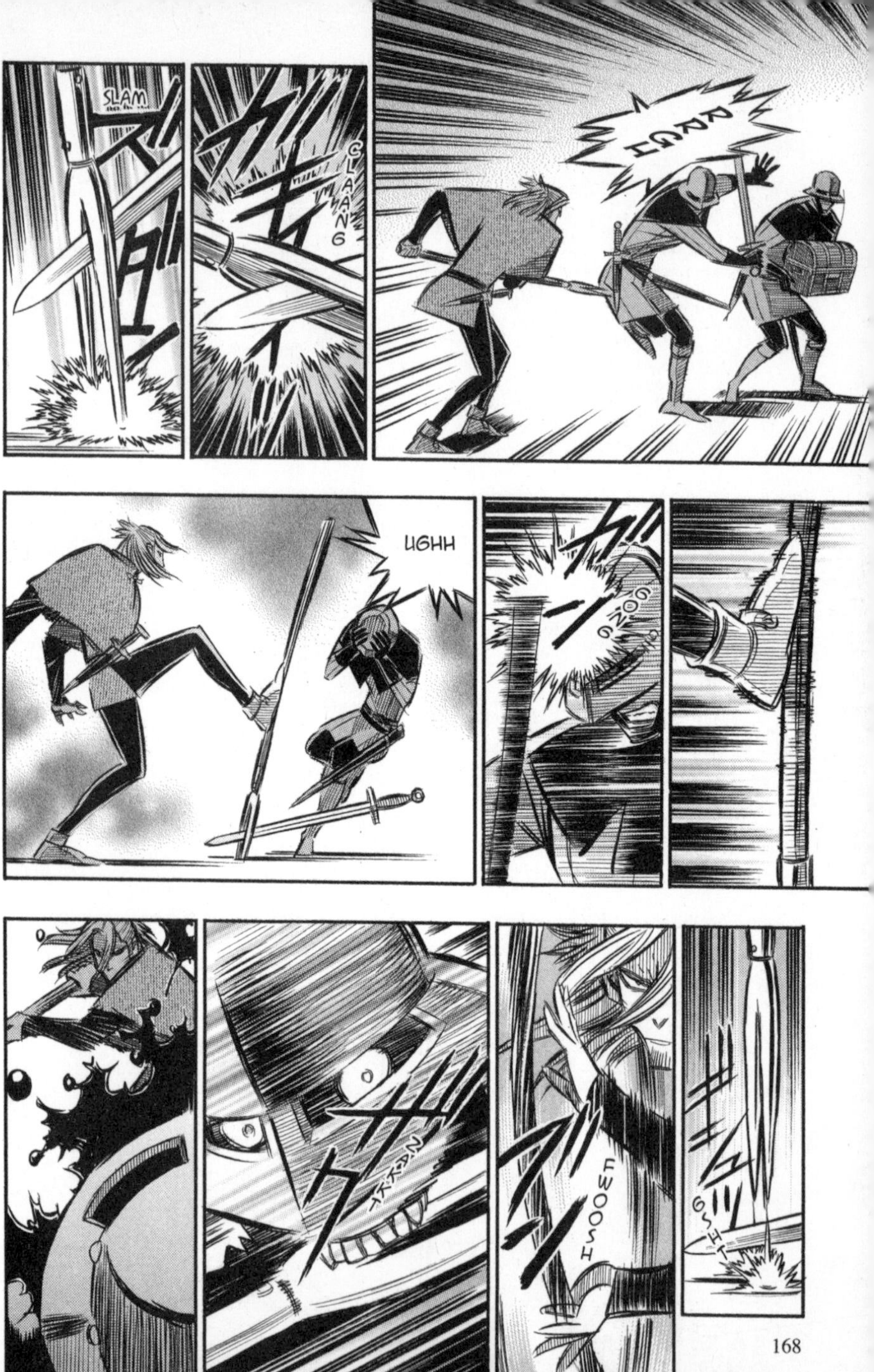
RRGH
CLAAANG
SLAM
GONG
UGHH
GSHT
FWOOSH
TK-KAN

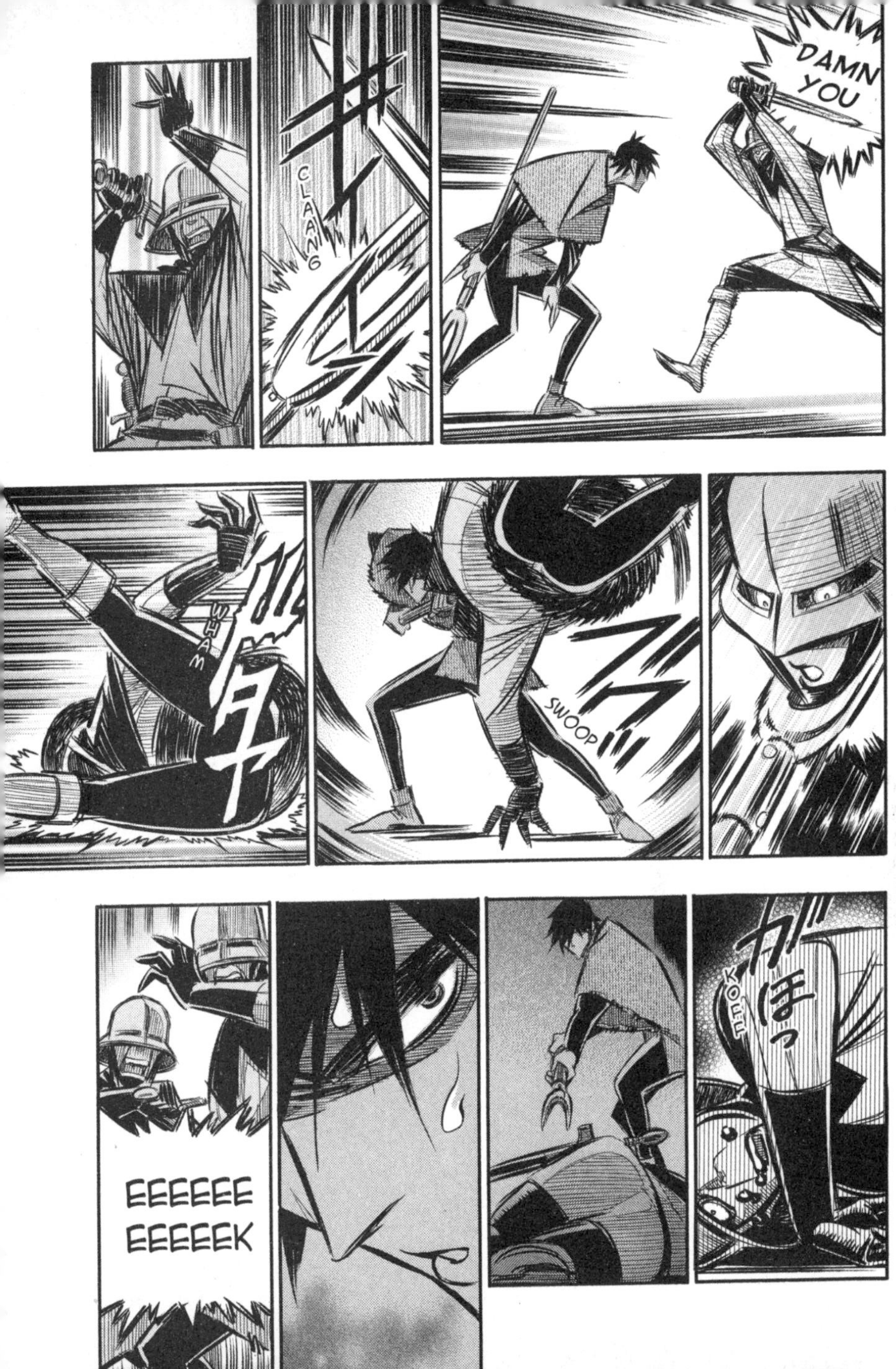
DAMN YOU
CLAANG
SWOOP
WHAM
KOFF
ガほっ
EEEEEEE EEEEEK

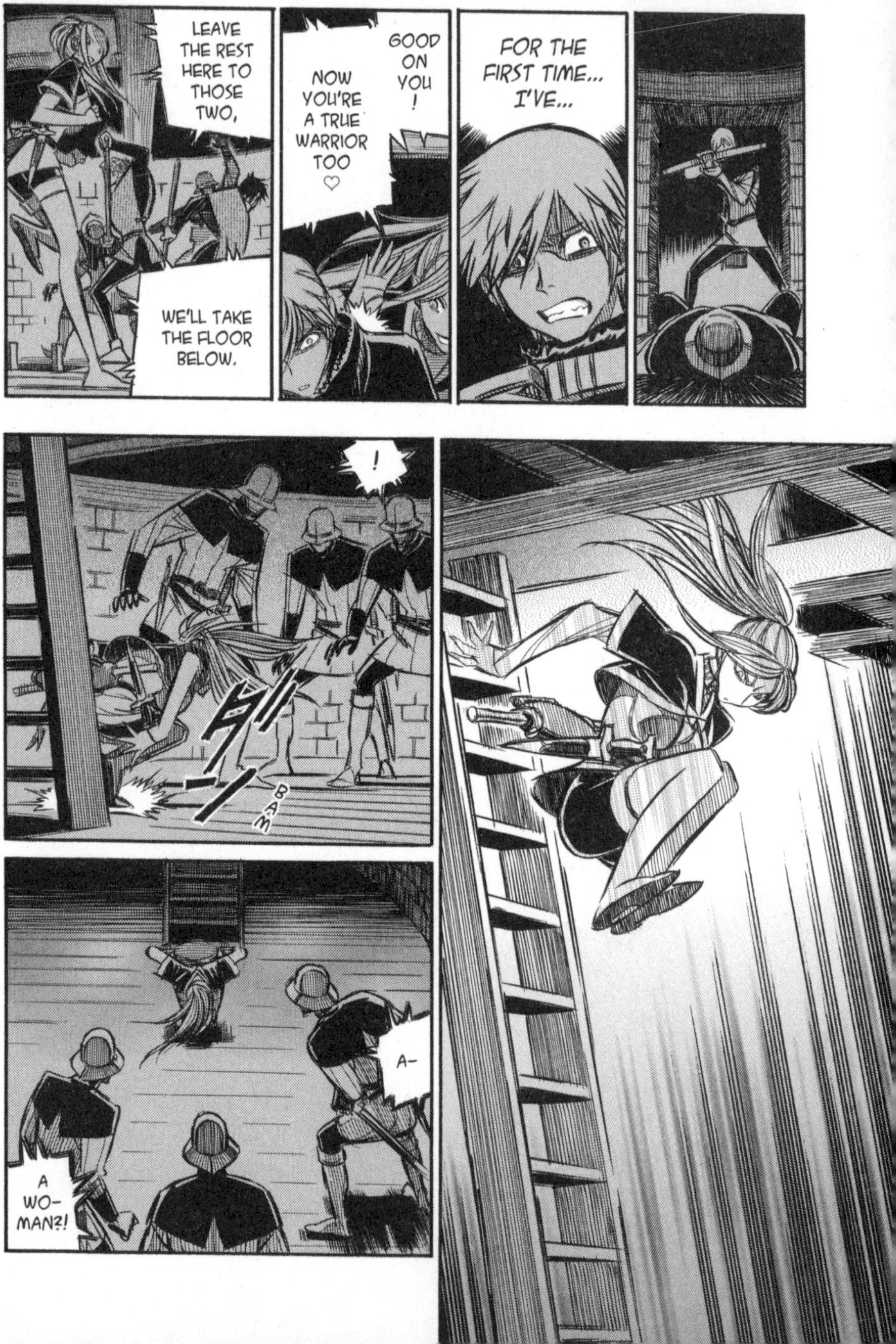

FOR THE FIRST TIME... I'VE...
GOOD ON YOU!
NOW YOU'RE A TRUE WARRIOR TOO ♡
LEAVE THE REST HERE TO THOSE TWO,
WE'LL TAKE THE FLOOR BELOW.
!
BAM
A-
A WO-MAN?!

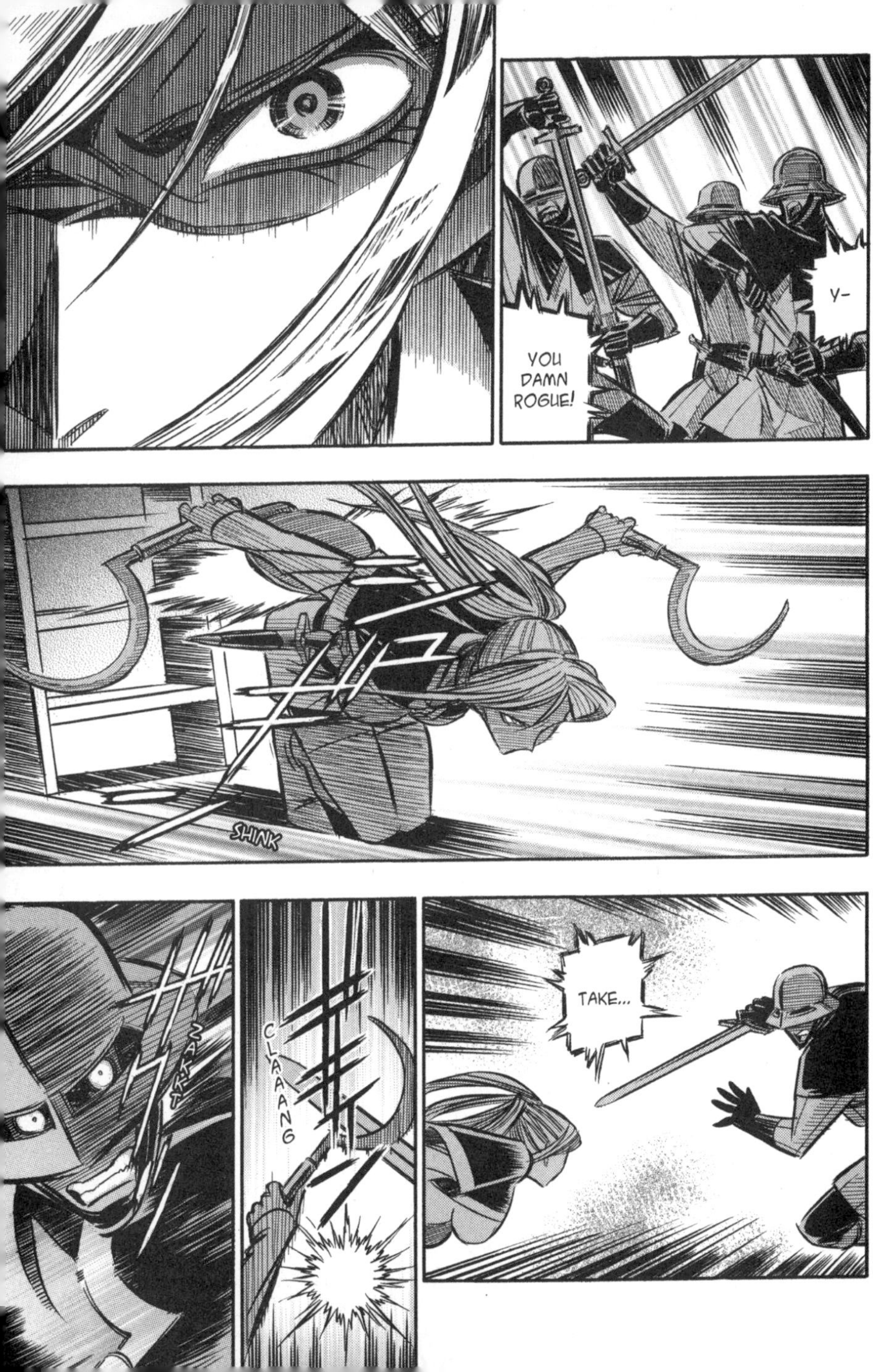
Y-
YOU DAMN ROGUE!
SHINK
TAKE...
CLAAAANG
ZAKKT

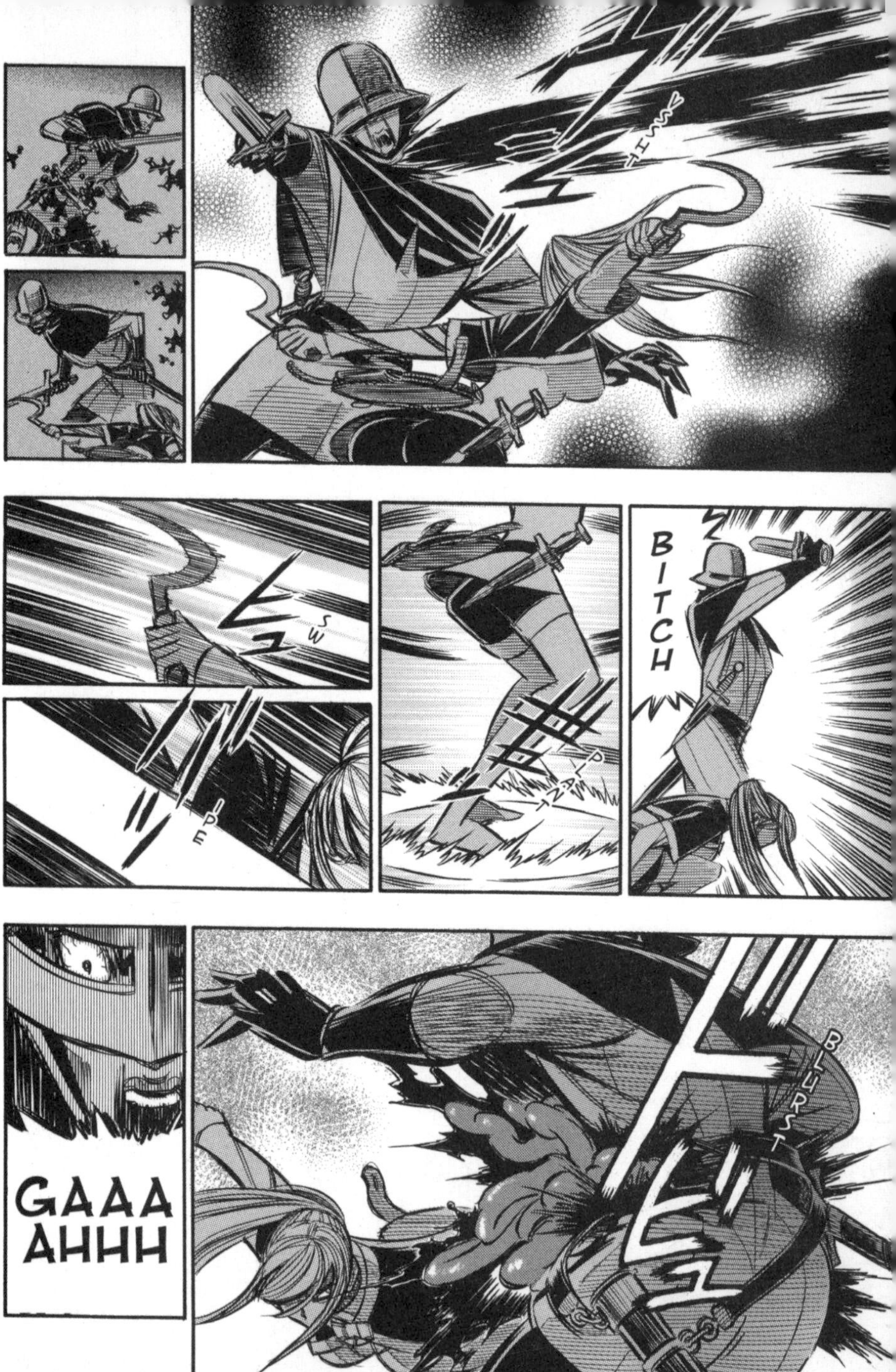
BITCH
PLANT
SW
IPE
BLURST
GAAA AHHH

STEP

STAMP

NWA
AAGH

RAA
AGH

JKKT

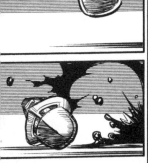

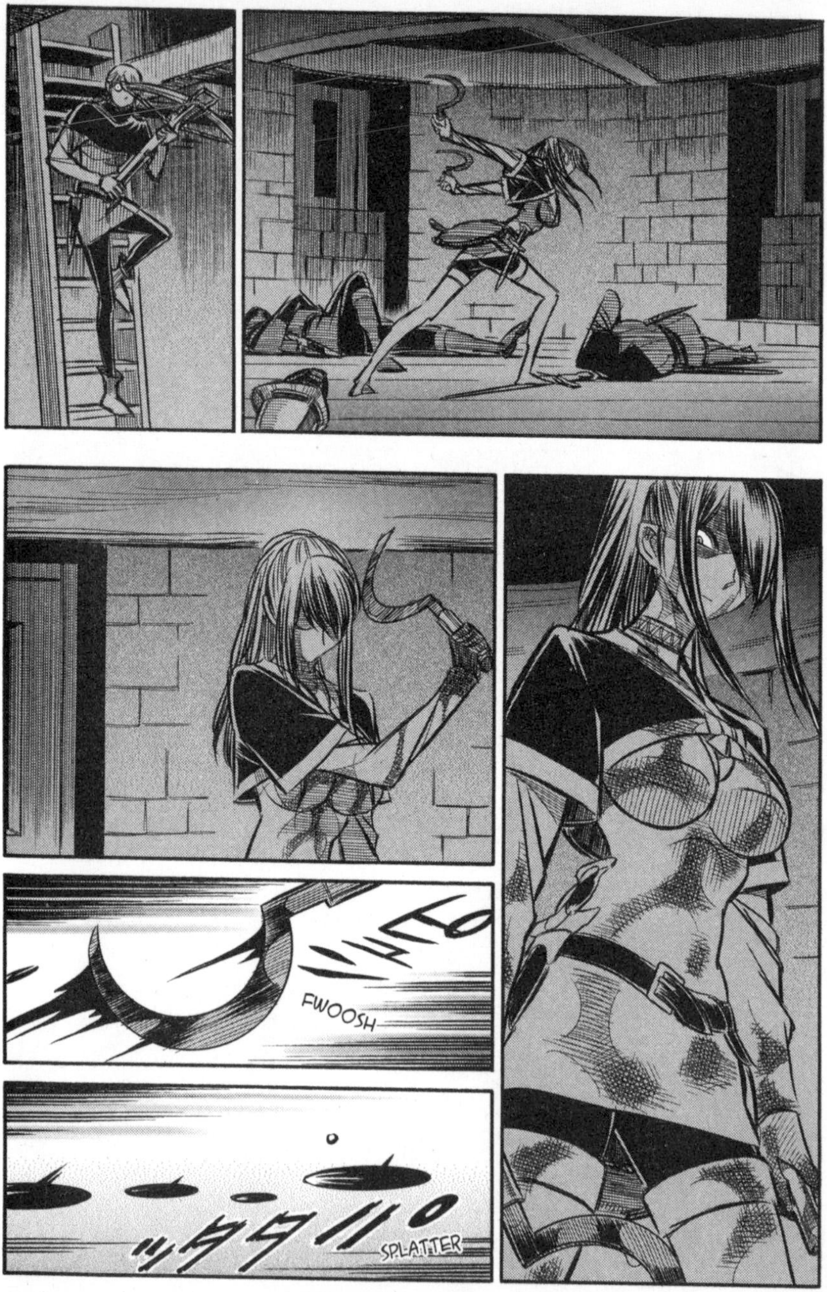
FWOOSH
SPLATTER

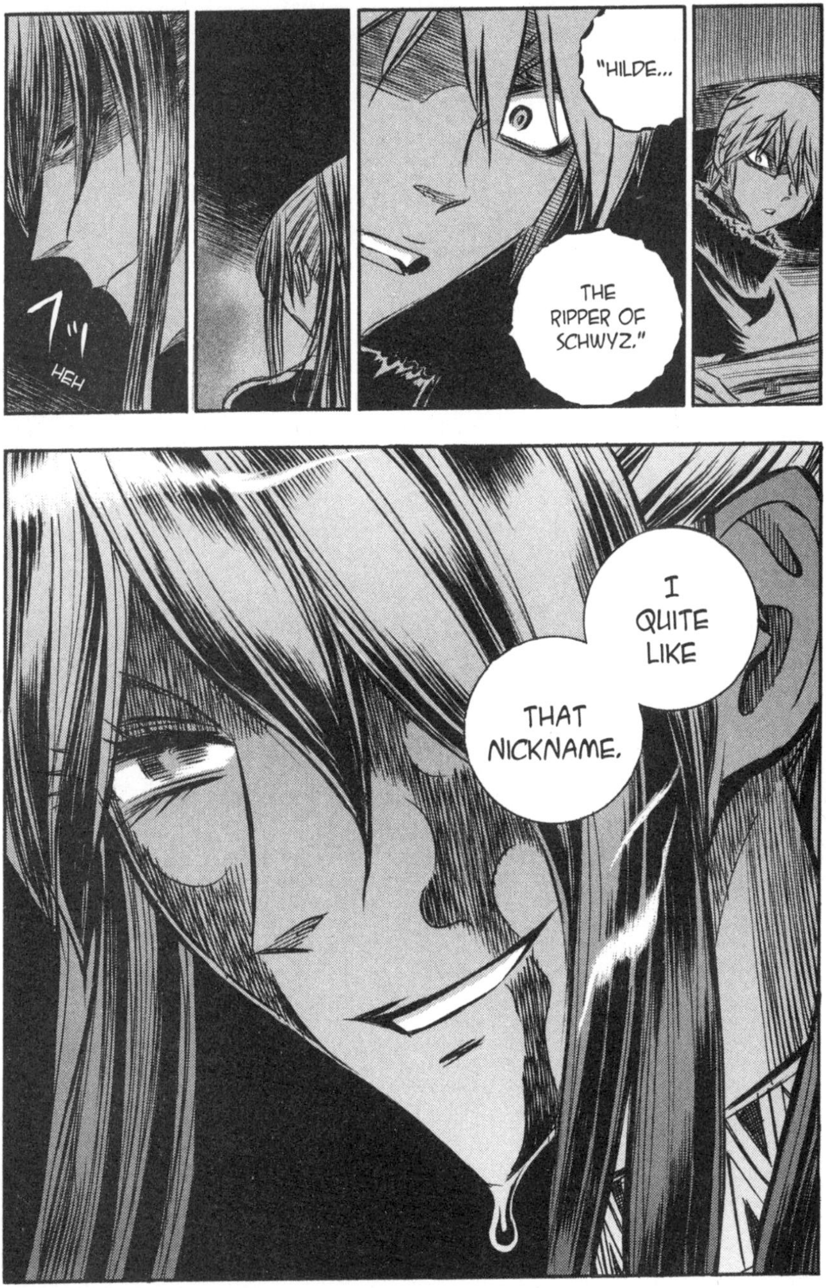
"HILDE...
THE RIPPER OF SCHWYZ."
フッ
HEH
I QUITE LIKE
THAT NICKNAME.

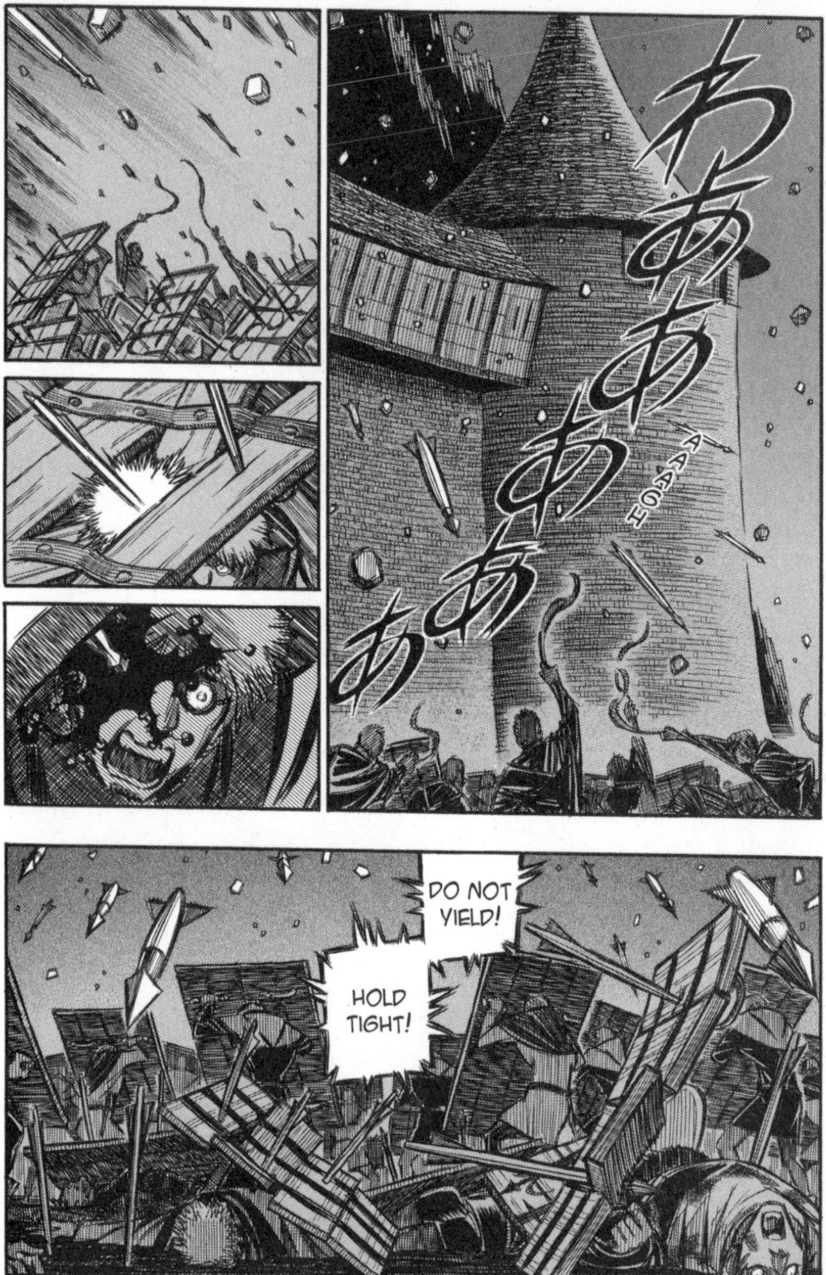
わあああああ
AAAAGH
DO NOT YIELD!
HOLD TIGHT!

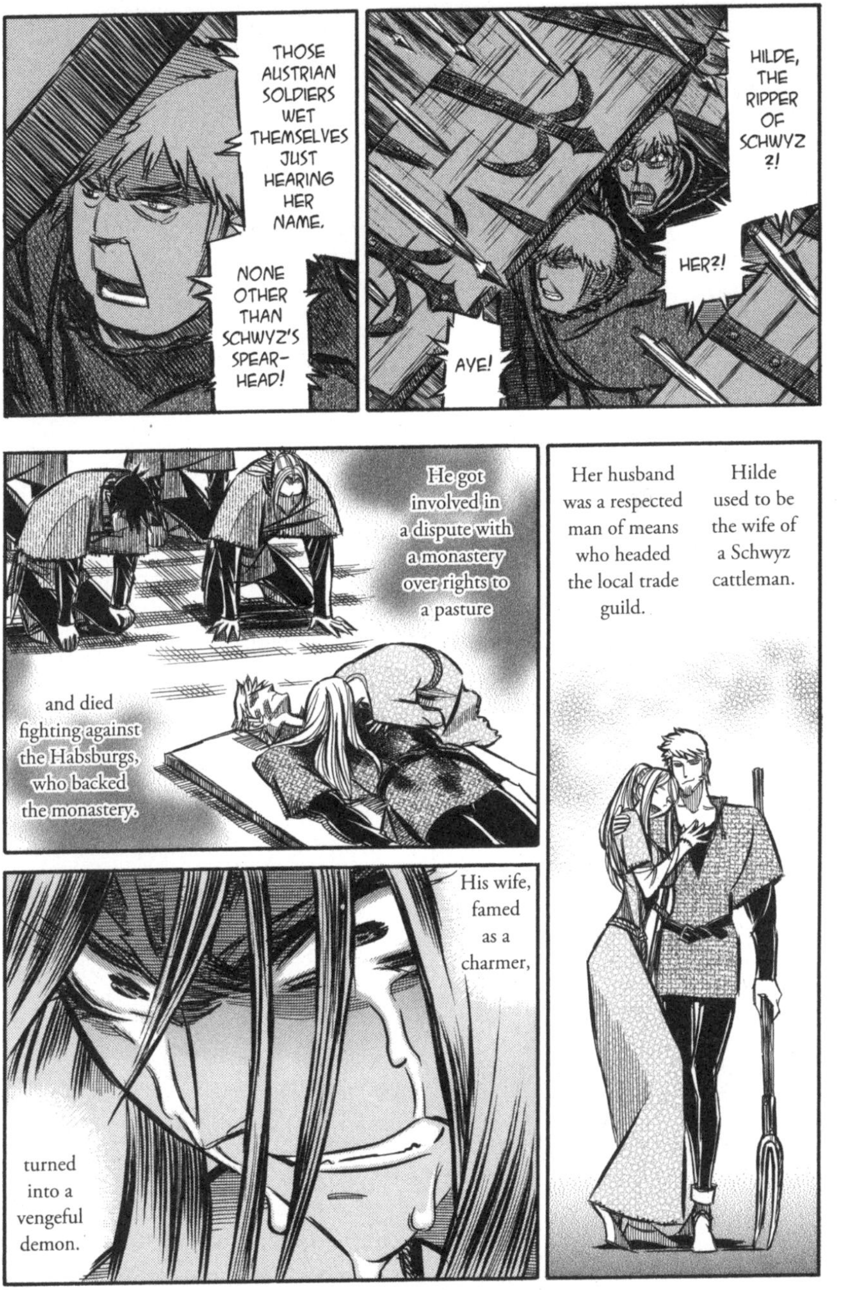
HILDE, THE RIPPER OF SCHWYZ?!
HER?!
AYE!
THOSE AUSTRIAN SOLDIERS WET THEMSELVES JUST HEARING HER NAME.
NONE OTHER THAN SCHWYZ'S SPEAR-HEAD!
Hilde used to be the wife of a Schwyz cattleman.
Her husband was a respected man of means who headed the local trade guild.
He got involved in a dispute with a monastery over rights to a pasture
and died fighting against the Habsburgs, who backed the monastery.
His wife, famed as a charmer,
turned into a vengeful demon.

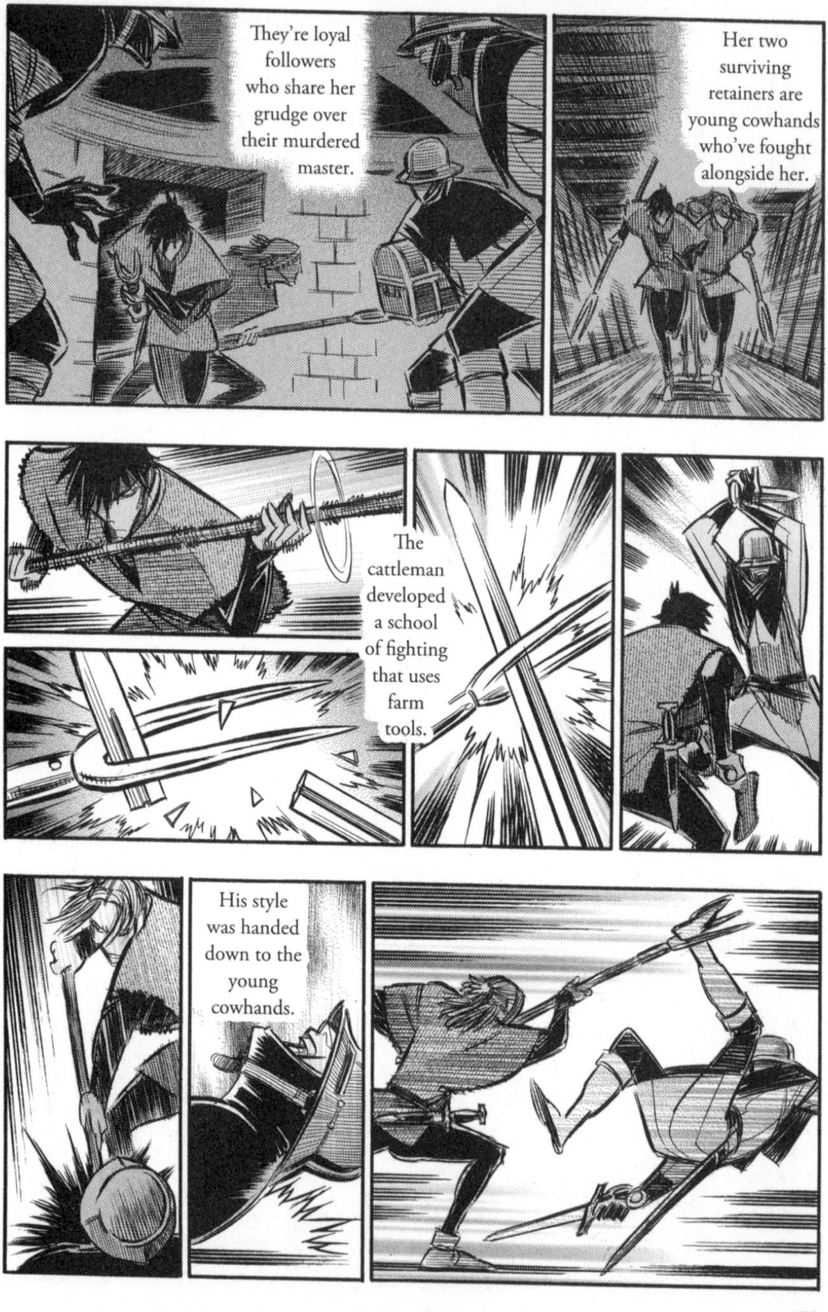
Her two surviving retainers are young cowhands who've fought alongside her.
They're loyal followers who share her grudge over their murdered master.
The cattleman developed a school of fighting that uses farm tools.
His style was handed down to the young cowhands.

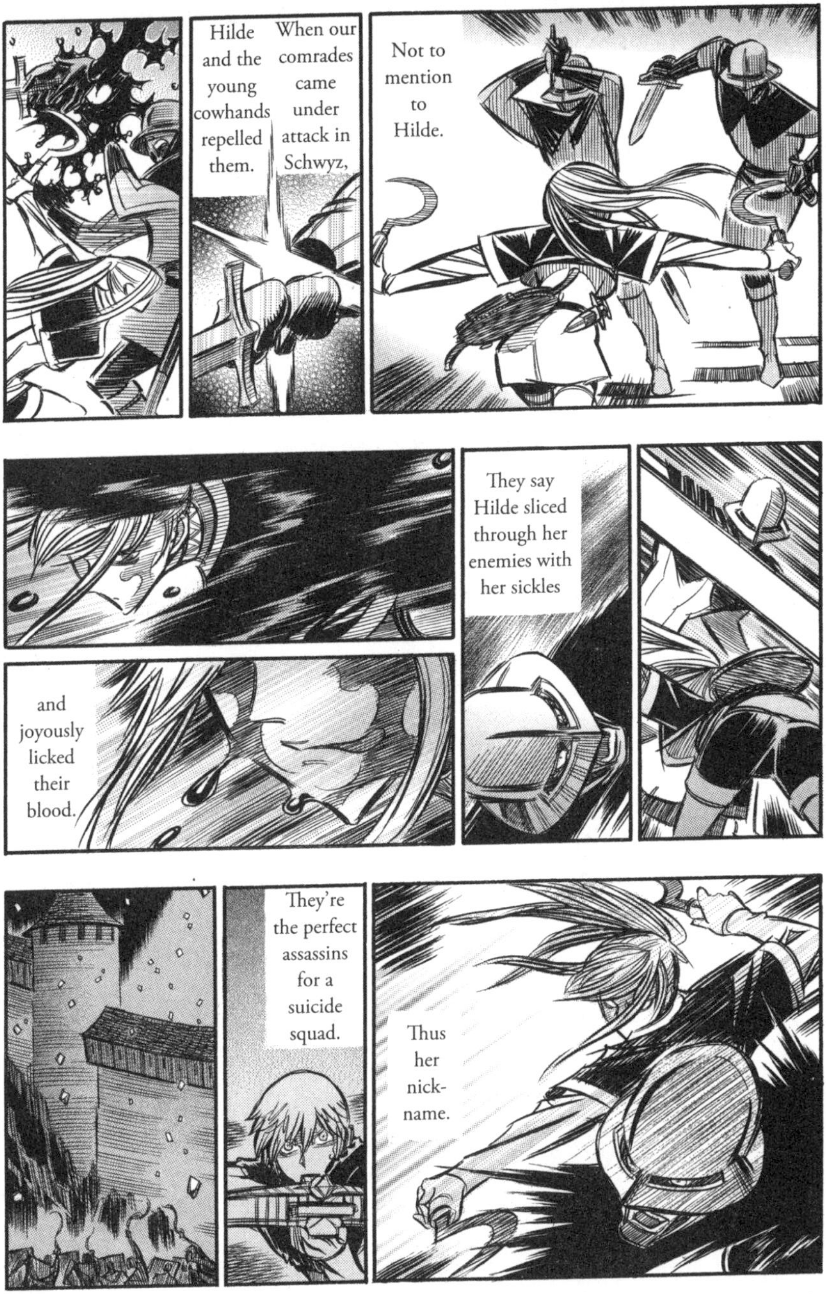
Not to mention to Hilde.
When our comrades came under attack in Schwyz,
Hilde and the young cowhands repelled them.
They say Hilde sliced through her enemies with her sickles
and joyously licked their blood.
Thus her nick-name.
They're the perfect assassins for a suicide squad.

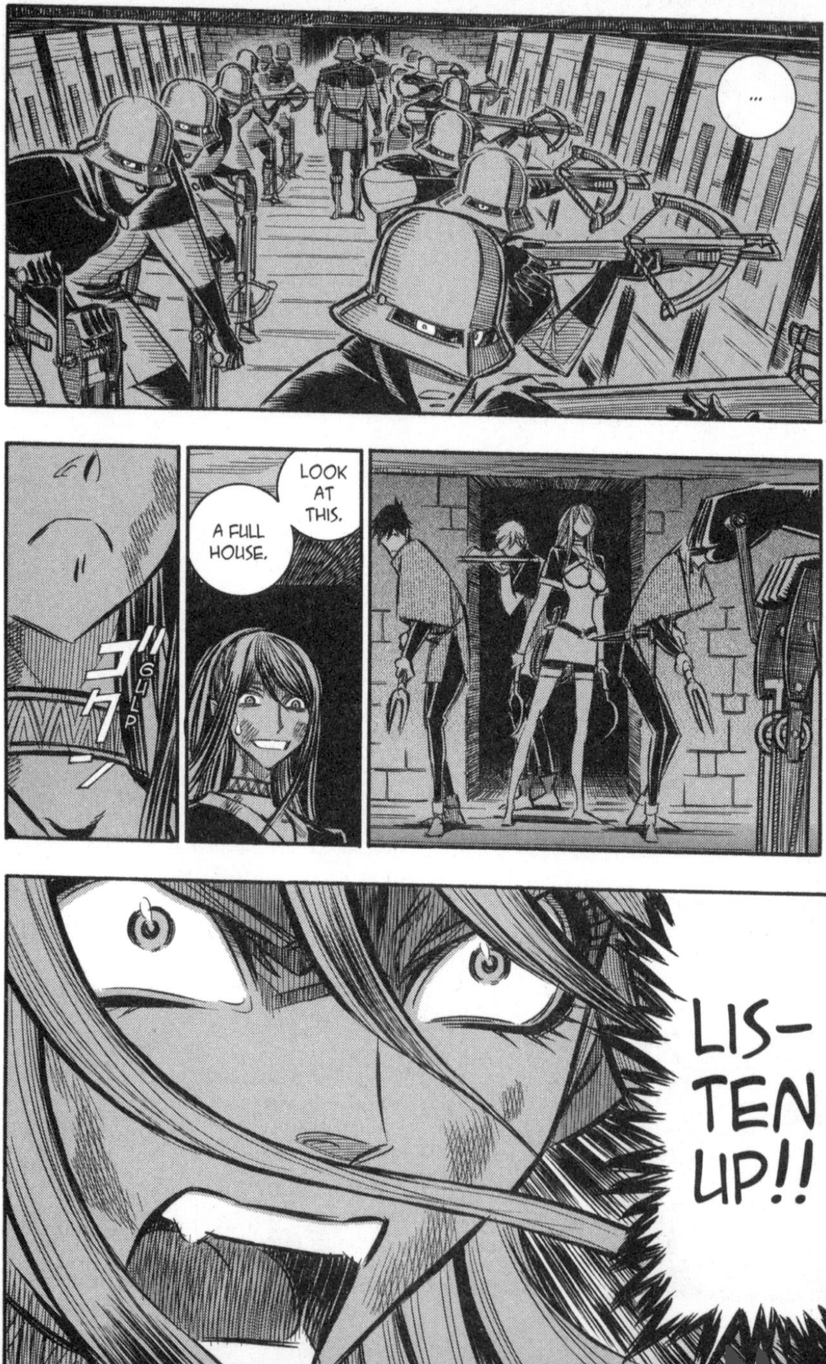
...
LOOK AT THIS.
A FULL HOUSE.
GULP
LIS-TEN UP!!

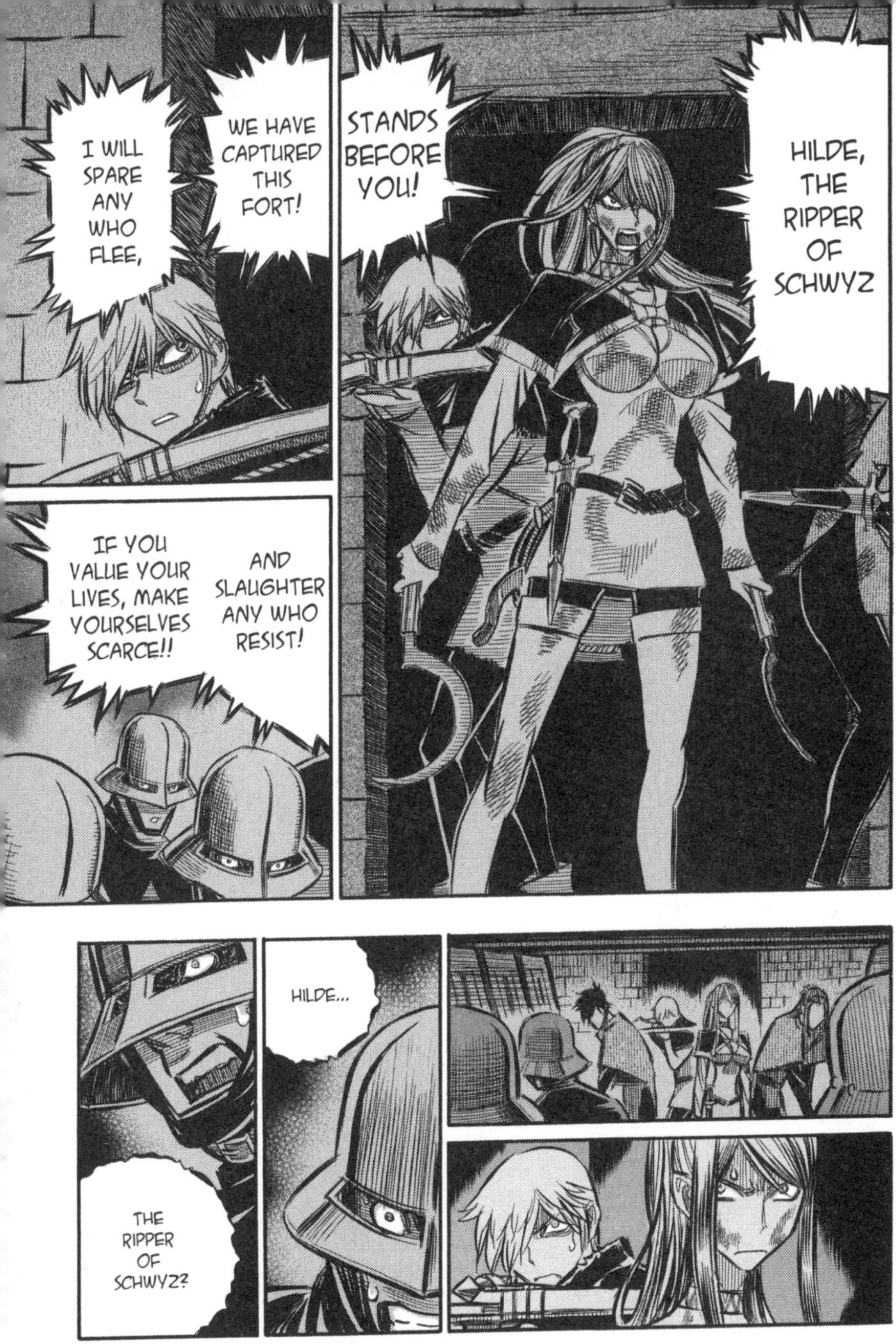
HILDE, THE RIPPER OF SCHWYZ
STANDS BEFORE YOU!
WE HAVE CAPTURED THIS FORT!
I WILL SPARE ANY WHO FLEE,
AND SLAUGHTER ANY WHO RESIST!
IF YOU VALUE YOUR LIVES, MAKE YOURSELVES SCARCE!!
HILDE...
THE RIPPER OF SCHWYZ?

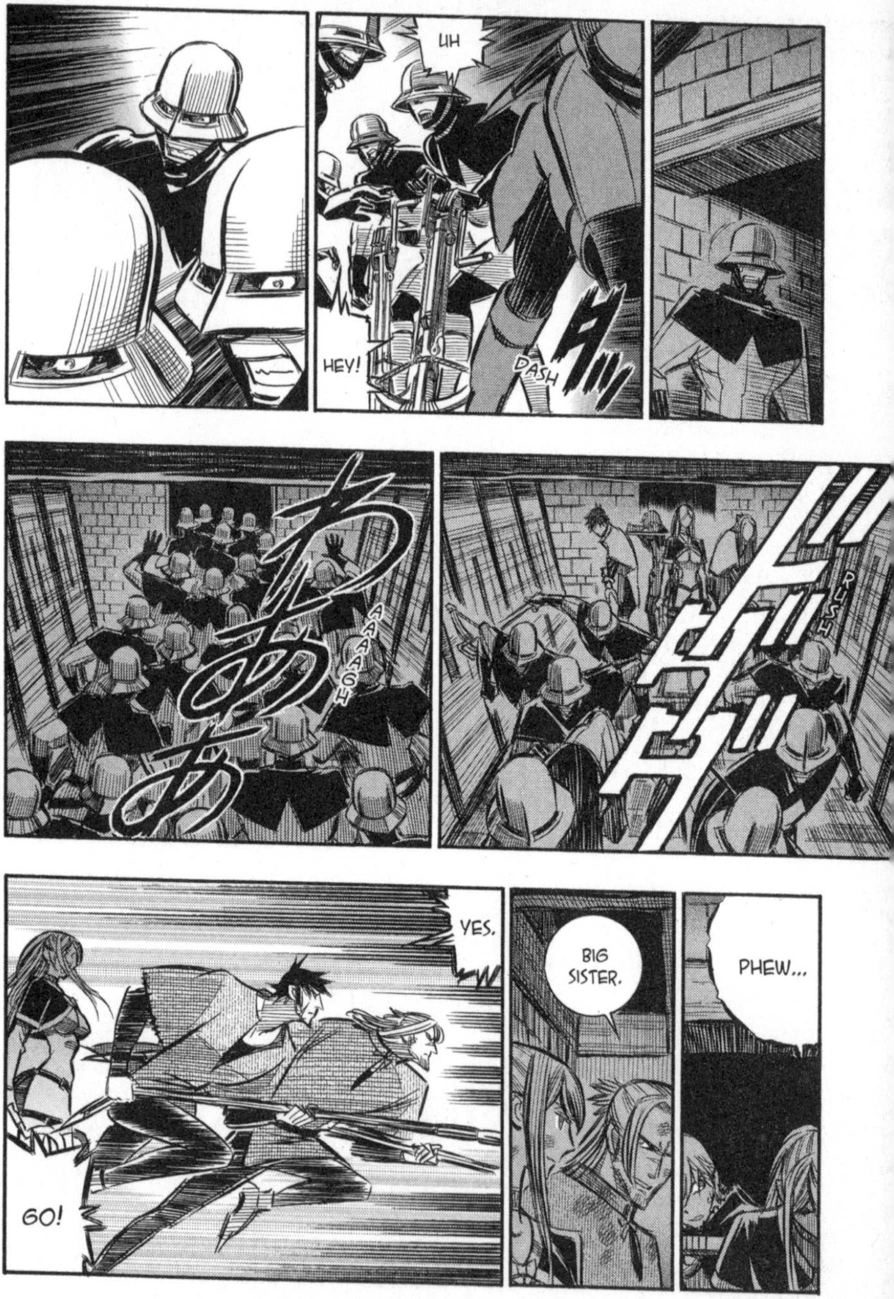
UH
HEY!
DASH
RUSH
AAAAAGH
PHEW...
BIG SISTER.
YES.
GO!

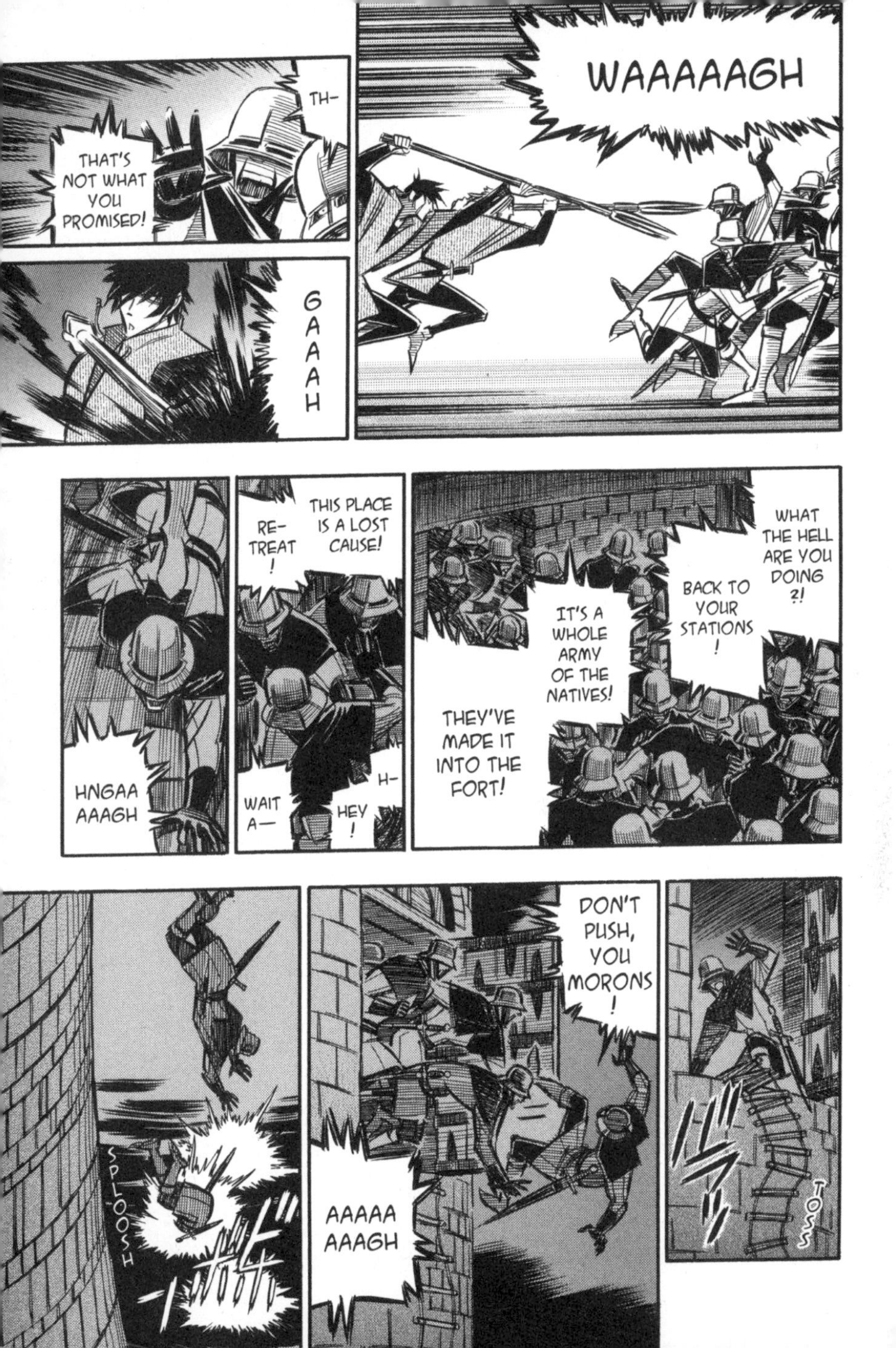
WAAAAAGH
TH- THAT'S NOT WHAT YOU PROMISED!
GAAAAH
WHAT THE HELL ARE YOU DOING?!
BACK TO YOUR STATIONS!
IT'S A WHOLE ARMY OF THE NATIVES!
THEY'VE MADE IT INTO THE FORT!
THIS PLACE IS A LOST CAUSE!
RE-TREAT!
H- HEY!
WAIT A—
HNGAA AAAGH
TOSS
DON'T PUSH, YOU MORONS!
AAAAA AAAGH
SPLOOSH

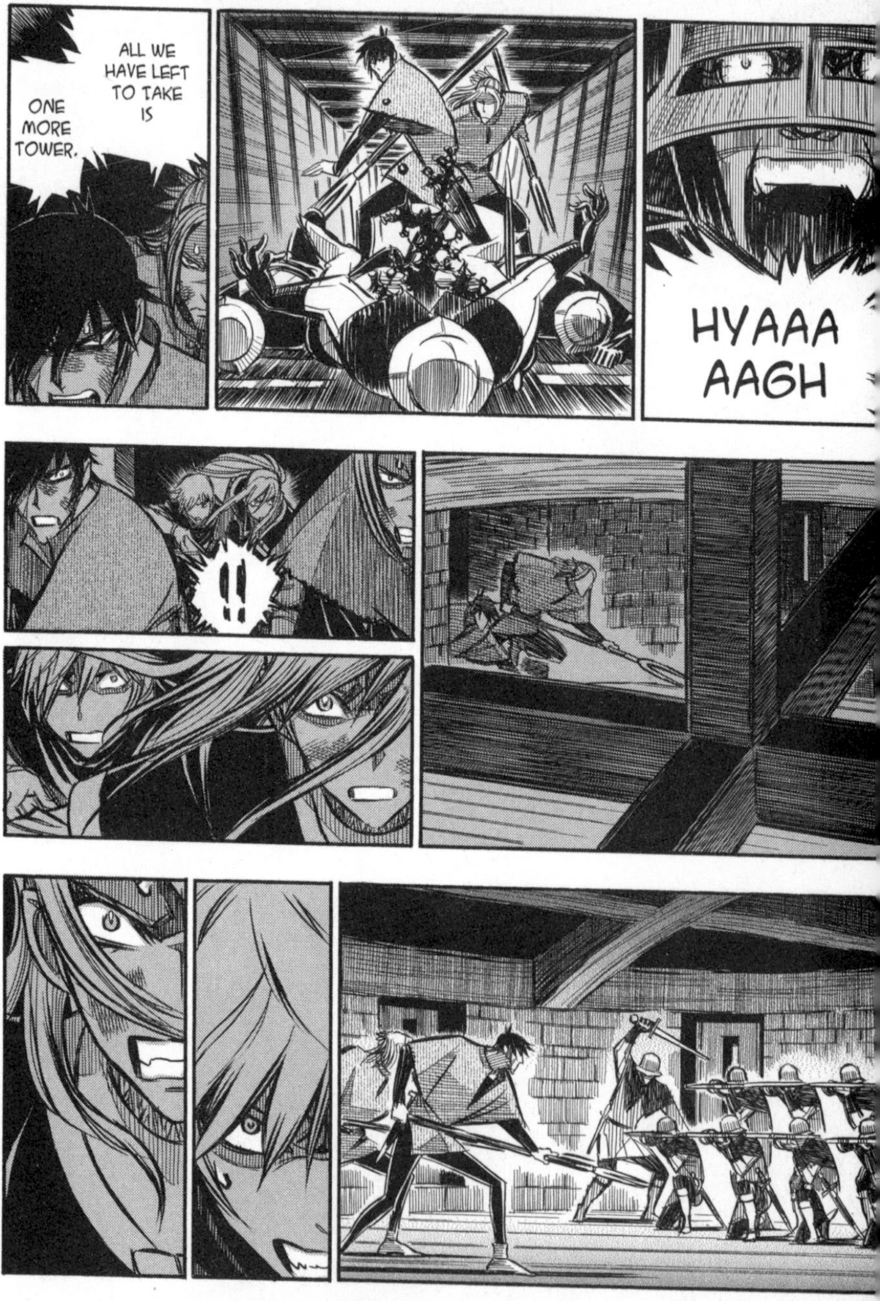
HYAAA AAGH
ALL WE HAVE LEFT TO TAKE IS
ONE MORE TOWER.
!!

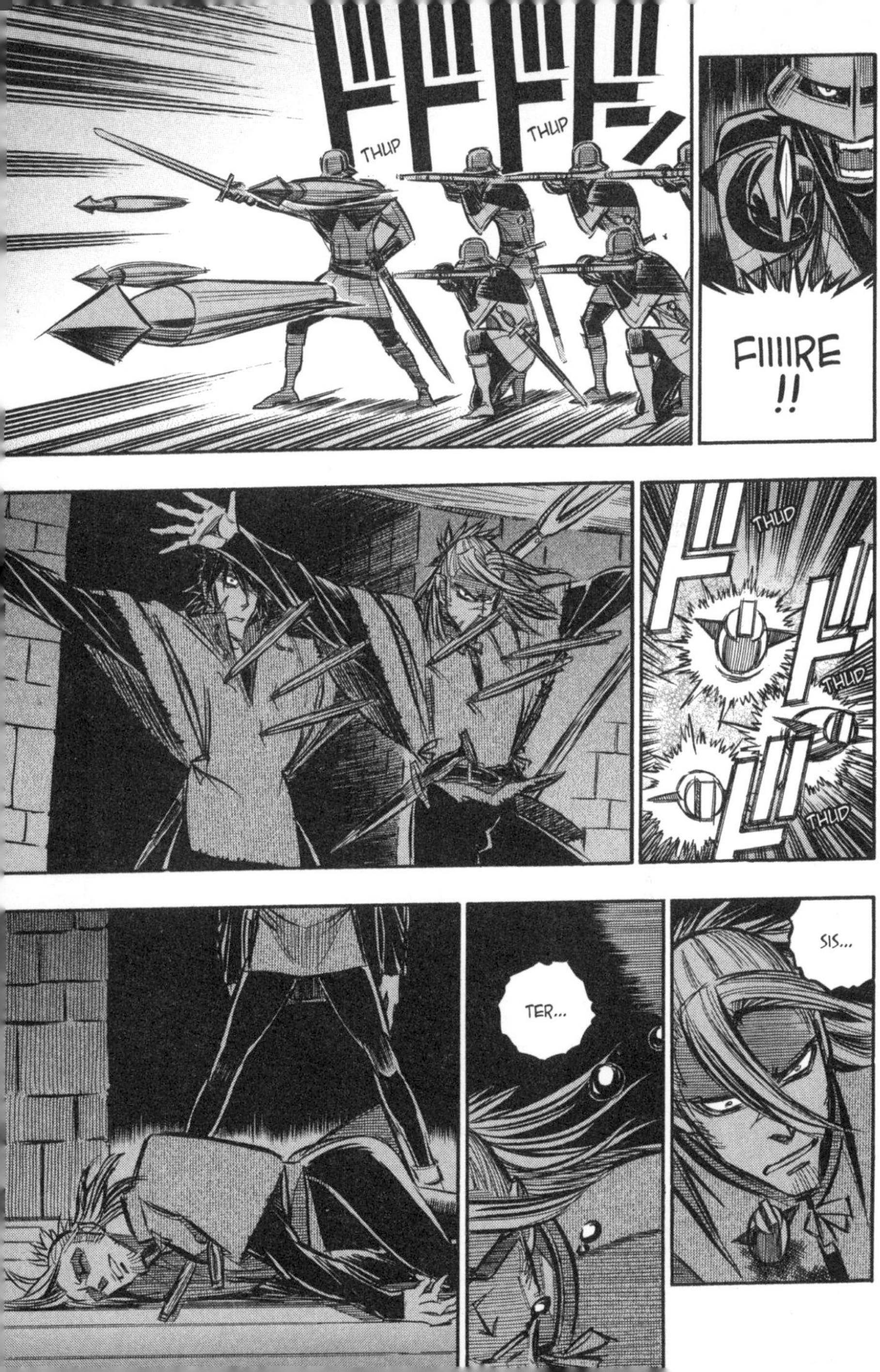
FIIIRE !!
THUP
THUP
THUD
THUD
THUD
SIS...
TER...

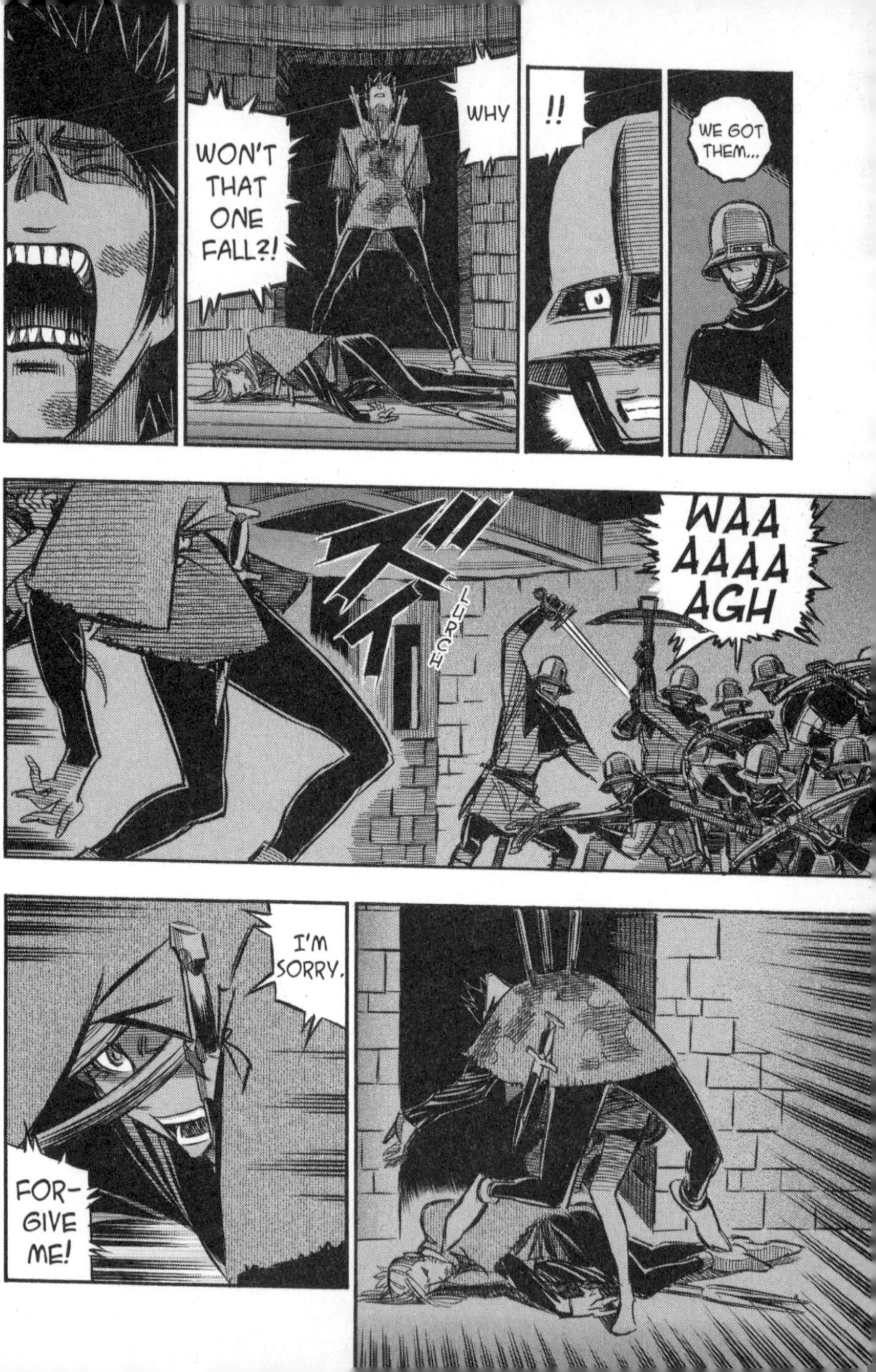
WE GOT THEM...
!!
WHY WON'T THAT ONE FALL?!
WAA AAAA AGH
LURCH
I'M SORRY.
FOR-GIVE ME!

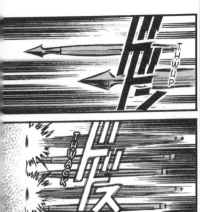

THWUP

THWACK

RE-
SERVES
!

FIRE
!!

NRAAAA
AAAHHH

HIIIIEEK

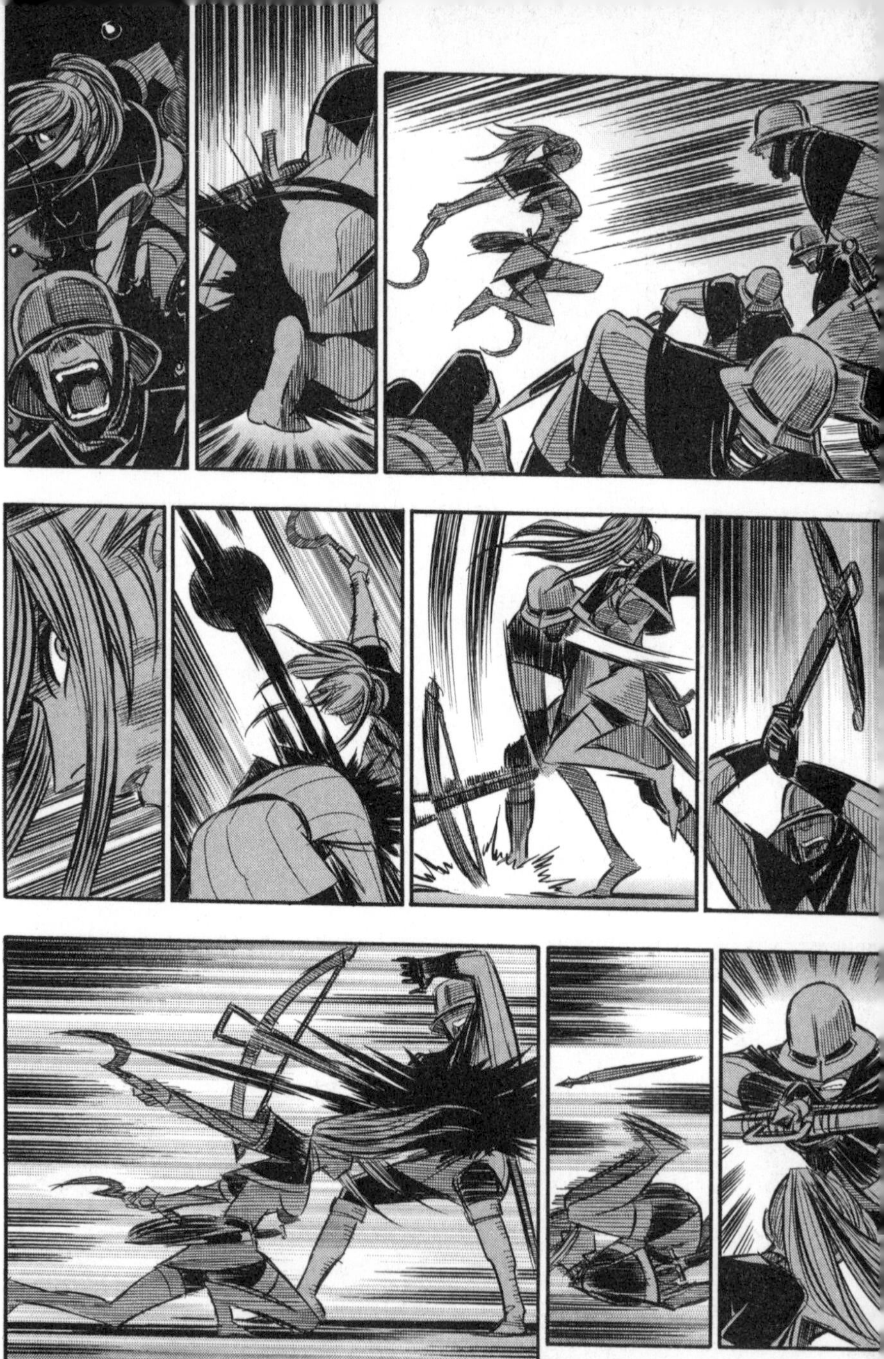

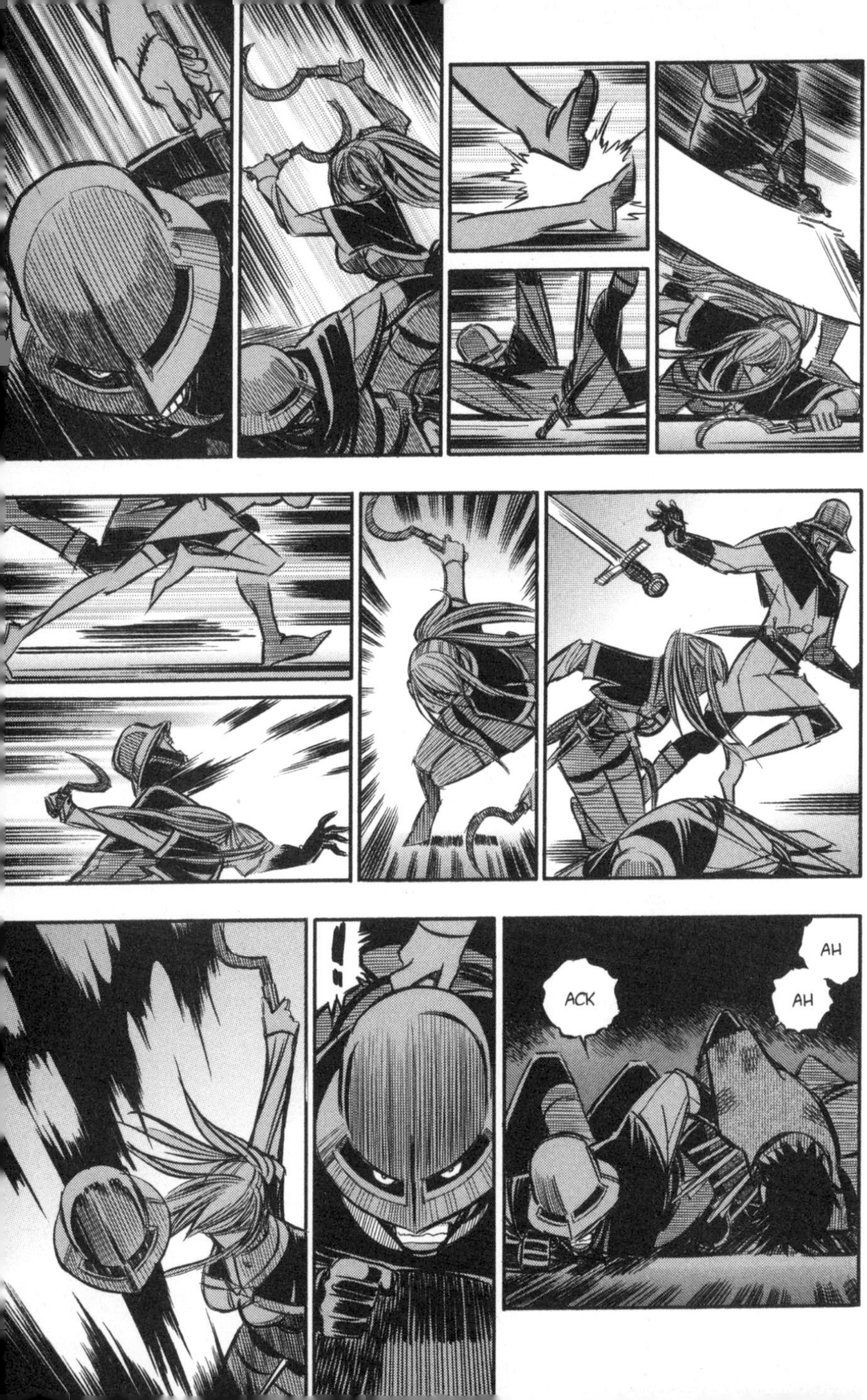
AH
AH
ACK
!!

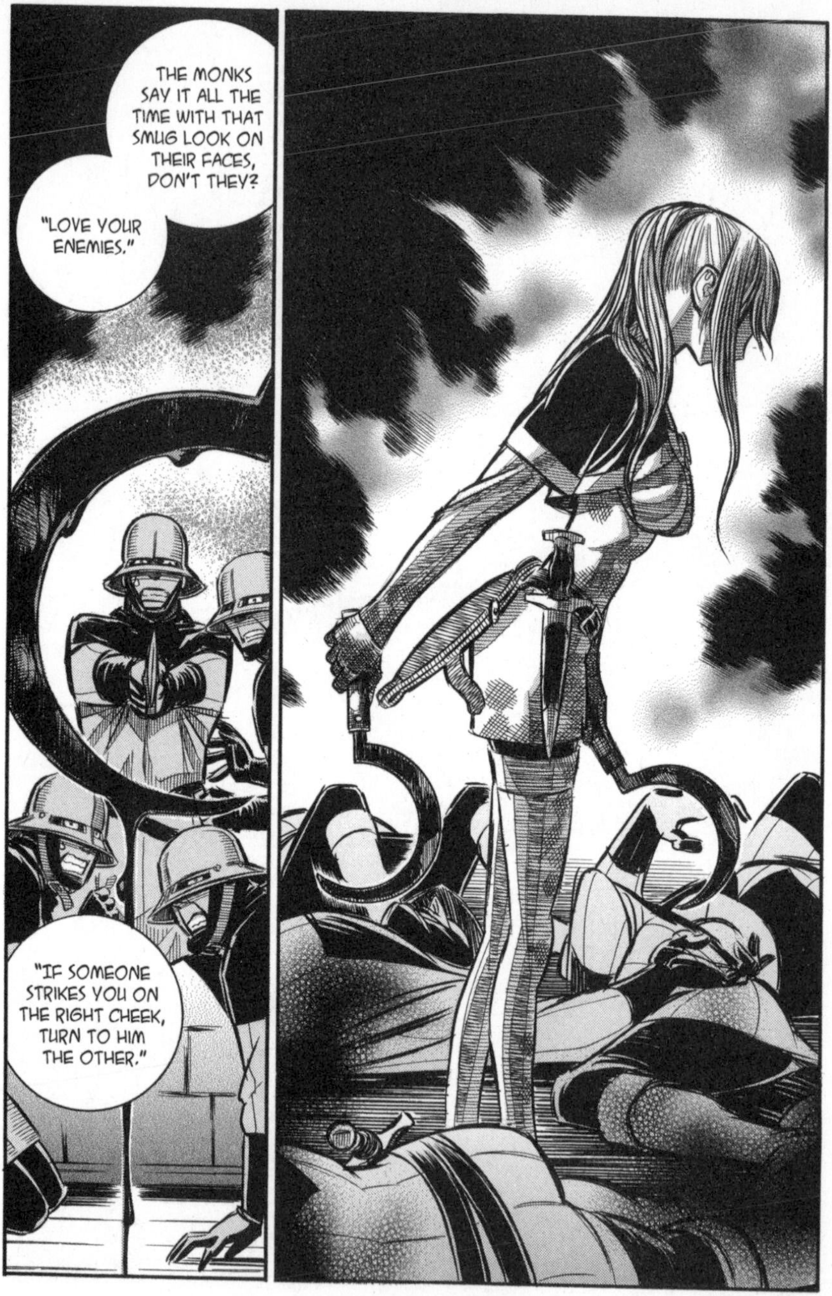
THE MONKS SAY IT ALL THE TIME WITH THAT SMUG LOOK ON THEIR FACES, DON'T THEY?
"LOVE YOUR ENEMIES."
"IF SOMEONE STRIKES YOU ON THE RIGHT CHEEK, TURN TO HIM THE OTHER."

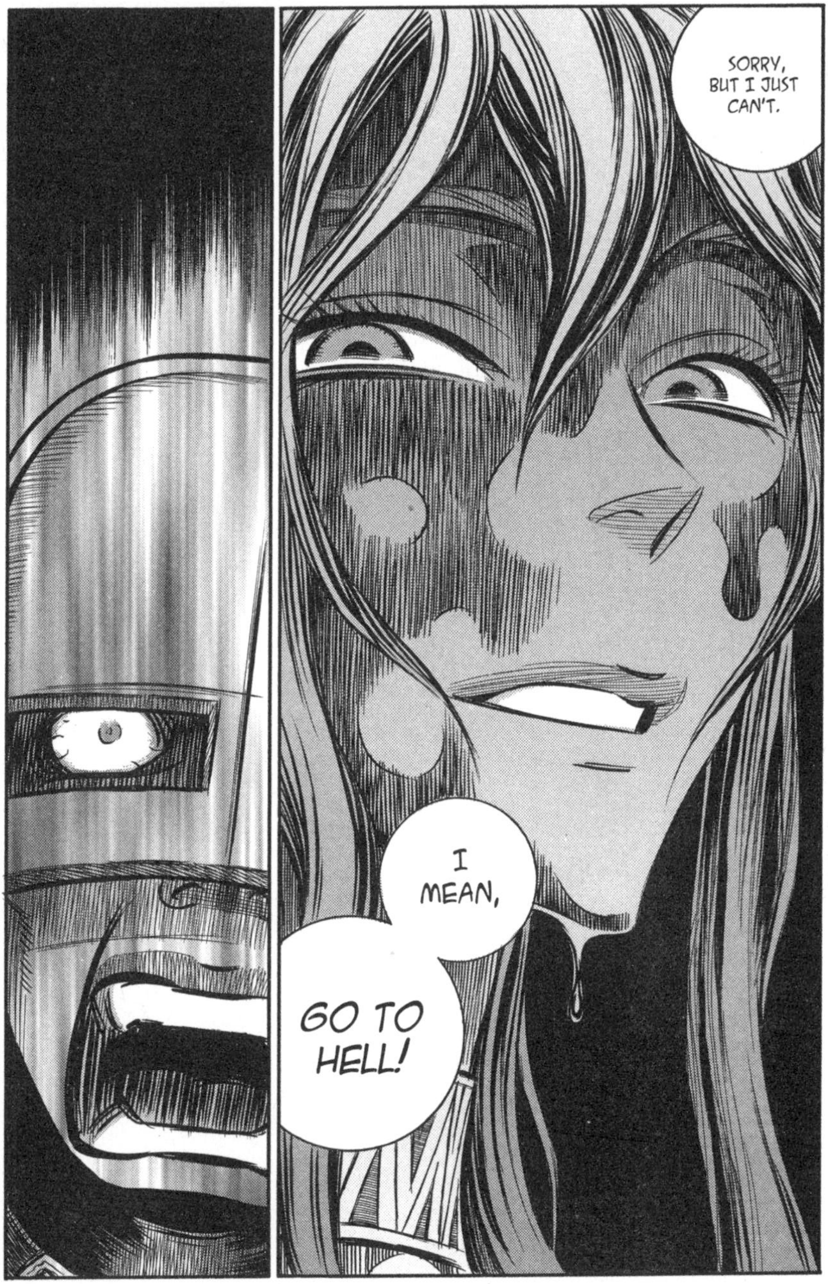
SORRY, BUT I JUST CAN'T.
I MEAN,
GO TO HELL!

HOW ODD.

THEY STOPPED FIRING.

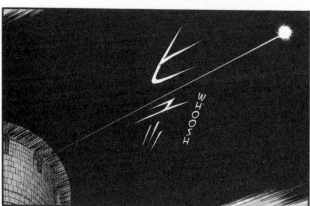

WHOOSH

POP

IT'S

FALLEN?

WE'VE TAKEN THIS FORT!

SUC-CESS!

THE SIGNAL!

192

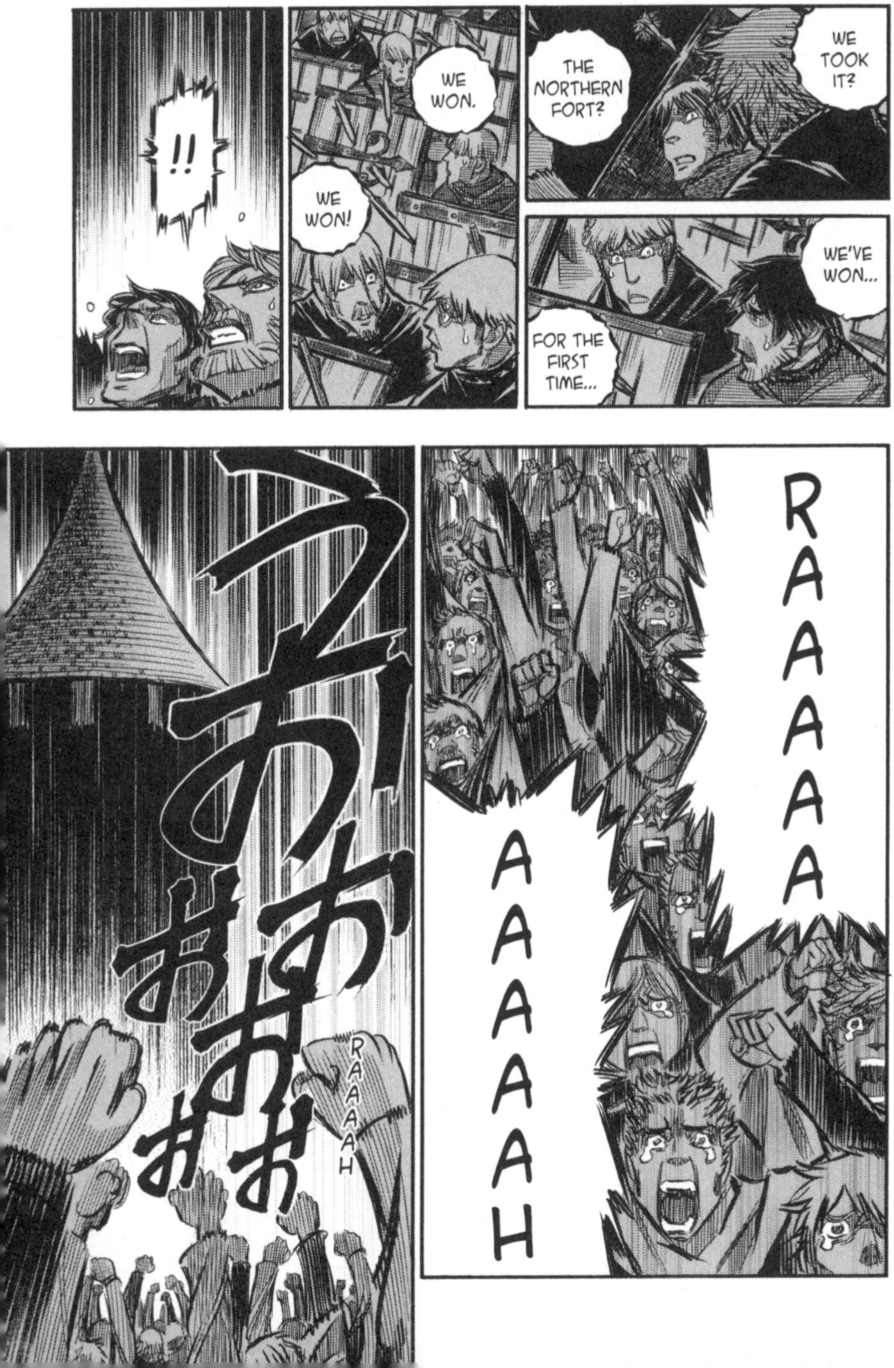
WE TOOK IT?
THE NORTHERN FORT?
WE'VE WON...
FOR THE FIRST TIME...
WE WON.
WE WON!
!!
RAAAAAAA
AAAAAAH
うおおおおおお
RAAAAAH

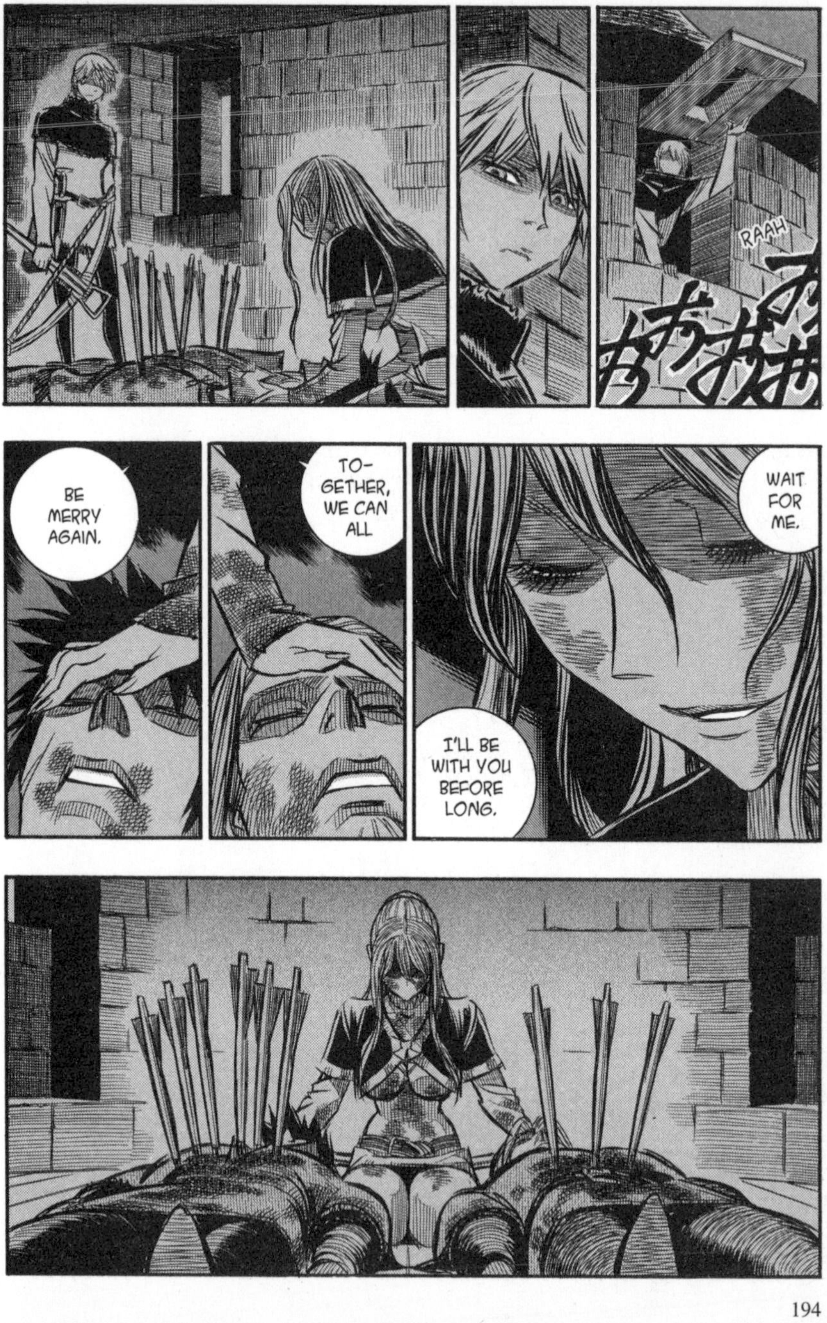
RAAH
WAIT FOR ME.
I'LL BE WITH YOU BEFORE LONG.
TO-GETHER, WE CAN ALL
BE MERRY AGAIN.

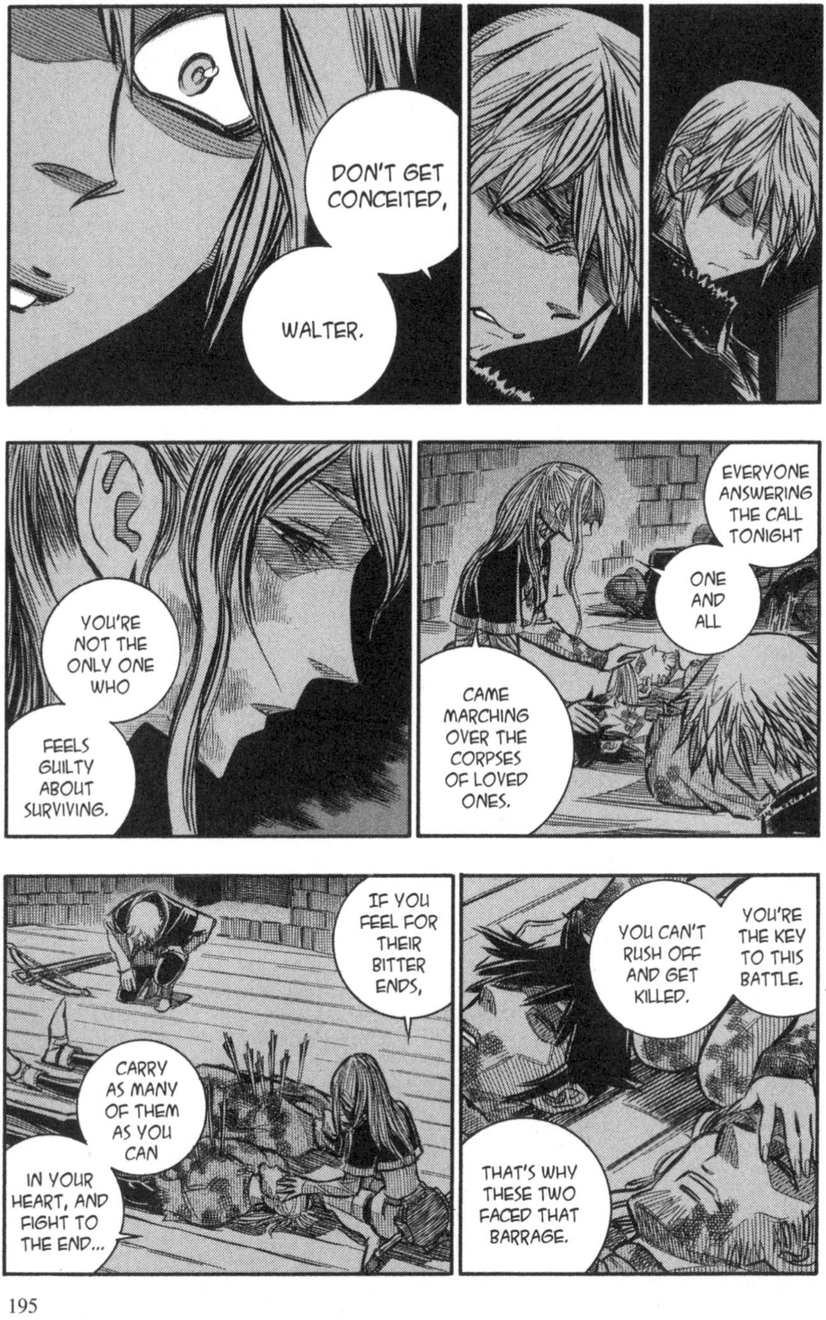
DON'T GET CONCEITED,
WALTER.
EVERYONE ANSWERING THE CALL TONIGHT
ONE AND ALL
CAME MARCHING OVER THE CORPSES OF LOVED ONES.
YOU'RE NOT THE ONLY ONE WHO
FEELS GUILTY ABOUT SURVIVING.
YOU'RE THE KEY TO THIS BATTLE.
YOU CAN'T RUSH OFF AND GET KILLED.
THAT'S WHY THESE TWO FACED THAT BARRAGE.
IF YOU FEEL FOR THEIR BITTER ENDS,
CARRY AS MANY OF THEM AS YOU CAN
IN YOUR HEART, AND FIGHT TO THE END...

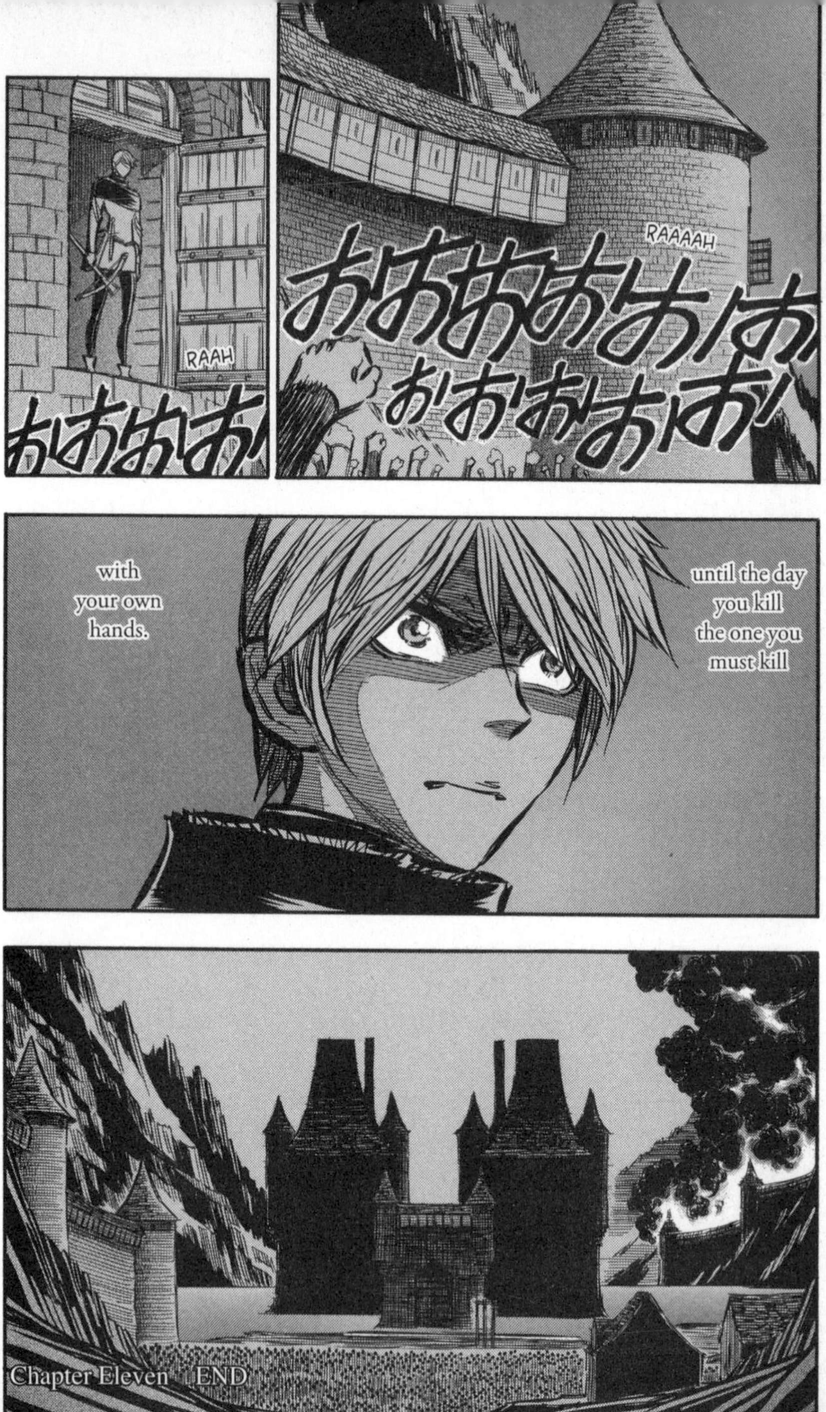
RAAAAH
おおあああお
おおおおお!
RAAH
おおおおお
until the day you kill the one you must kill
with your own hands.
Chapter Eleven END

Wolfsmund ③ Ende

olfsmund, volume 3

islation: Ko Ransom
luction: Risa Cho
              Nicole Dochych

published in Japan in 2011 by KADOKAWA CORPORATION ENTERBRAIN
ish translation rights arranged with KADOKAWA CORPORATION ENTERBRAIN
Vertical, Inc. through Tuttle-Mori Agency, Inc., Tokyo.

islation provided by Vertical, Inc., 2014
ished by Vertical, Inc., New York

ginally published in Japanese as *OOKAMI NO KUCHI: WOLFSMUND 3*
KADOKAWA CORPORATION ENTERBRAIN in 2011
serialized in *Fellows!*, 2009-

is a work of fiction.

N: 978-1-935654-96-4

nufactured in Canada

t Edition

ical, Inc.
Park Avenue South
Floor
York, NY 10016
w.vertical-inc.com